BERTOLT BRECHT
COLLECTED PLAYS

Volume 7

b.b.

BERTOLT

Bertolt Brecht: Plays, Poetry, & Prose

Edited by

Ralph Manheim and John Willett

Wolfgang Sauerlander, Associate Editor

BRECHT

COLLECTED PLAYS

VOLUME 7

The Visions of Simone Machard

Schweyk in the Second World War

The Caucasian Chalk Circle

The Duchess of Malfi

VINTAGE BOOKS, *A Division of Random House, New York*

FIRST VINTAGE BOOKS EDITION, JANUARY 1975

Library of Congress Cataloging in Publication Data

Brecht, Bertolt, 1898–1956.   Collected plays.

(His Plays, poetry, & prose)
CONTENTS: v. 1. Baal. Drums in the night. In the jungle of cities. The
life of Edward II of England. The wedding. The beggar, or the dead
dog. He drives out a devil. Lux in tenebris. The catch.—
v. 5. Life of Galileo. The trial of Lucullus. Mother Courage and her
children.—
v. 7. The visions of Simone Machard. Schweyk in the Second World
War. The Caucasian chalk circle. The Duchess of Malfi.
v. 9. Adaptations: The tutor. Coriolanus. The trial of Joan of Arc
at Rouen, 1431. Don Juan. Trumpets and drums.

I. Willett, John, ed. II. Manheim, Ralph, ed.
PT2603.R397A29 1971   832'.9'12   71-113718
ISBN 0-394-71670-1 (v. 1)
    0-394-71216-1 (v. 7)

Contents

Introduction

The American plays 1942–46

1

The plays in this volume are the ones which Brecht wrote during his six-year stay in the United States. He arrived on July 21, 1941, by ship from Vladivostok, after having set out from Helsinki two months earlier via Moscow and the Trans-Siberian railway. He left again by air on October 31, 1947, to return to Europe and in due course Berlin. Most of the time in between he spent living in the Los Angeles area where he had landed, though he also made prolonged visits to New York.

As in Munich nearly a quarter of a century earlier, his mentor in this new world was the now internationally successful novelist Lion Feuchtwanger, who persuaded him to remain on the West Coast where he would be close to Hollywood and its large German film colony, several of whom (like Fritz Lang and William Dieterle) were subscribing to the fund on which he and his family initially lived. Besides the three original plays which we print, therefore, and the *Duchess of Malfi* adaptation given in the appendix, his output in this period also embraced a number of rejected film outlines and synopses, including the story "Caesar and his Legionary," which was later taken into *Tales from the Calendar*, as well as an undetermined portion of the material for the film *Hangmen Also Die*, which Fritz Lang actually made. To this must be added the American version of *Galileo*, whose evolution is covered in volume 5, and a trickle of very fine but mostly rather short poems. His theoretical writing seems to have dried up almost entirely; major prose projects like the Caesar and "Tui" novels went into cold storage; and he gave up writing short stories. So it is mainly on the contents of the present volume that his American experience must be judged.

To start with, its impact on his work was disastrous. This was due above all to something that had happened on the journey: the death of his aide Margarete Steffin in Moscow from tuberculosis. Both the group of poems which he wrote "After the death of my collaborator M.S." (included in the selected *Poems*) and his own private notes and journal entries suggest that this was among the severest blows he ever suffered; a month later he could write commenting on it.

> for nearly a year i have been feeling deeply depressed as a result of the death of my comrade and collaborator steffin. up to now i have avoided thinking at all deeply about it. i'm not frightened so much of feeling pain as of being ashamed of the fact. but above all i have too few thoughts about it. i know that no pain can offset this loss, that all i can do is close my eyes to it. now and again i have even drunk a tot of whisky when her image rose before me. since i seldom do this even one tot affects me strongly. in my view such methods are just as acceptable as others that are better thought of. they are only external, but this is a problem which i don't see how to resolve internally. death is no good; all is not necessarily for the best. there is no inscrutable wisdom to be seen in this kind of thing. nothing can make up for it.

Very soon after arriving, too, he learned of the fate of another close friend, Walter Benjamin, who had killed himself on the French frontier in 1940 rather than risk being handed over to the Gestapo. At the same time, however, the atmosphere of southern California was hardly such as to relieve his depression. This was partly a matter of its utter remoteness from the war—"Tahiti in urban form" he called it soon after arriving—though Pearl Harbor that autumn brought reality closer; partly a deep-seated resentment of its artificiality and underlying commercial ethos. Thus a journal entry of March 1942 (one of many to the same effect):

> extraordinary in these parts how a universally demoralizing

cheap prettiness stops one from leading anything like a cultivated, i.e., dignified life.

On top of this came the often degrading experience of working for the films, which bore particularly painfully on him as he became drawn into the making of Fritz Lang's Czech resistance movie during the summer of 1942. Taking stock towards the end of April, he listed all the factors hampering him, from his loss of Steffin to his lack of money, and concluded that "for the first time in ten years I am not doing any proper work."

Yet even while he was battling over that film (for adequate representation of the Czech people, for his theme song, for a part for Helene Weigel and a scriptwriter's credit for himself: on all of which points he failed), his prospects in other ways were beginning to improve. Materially, he and his family no longer had to live on $120 a month, but were able to move into a bigger and very much pleasanter house in Santa Monica (1063 26th Street; it is still there, though the area has been much built up) on the strength of the $10,000 which Lang got for him. Once again he was working with the composer Hanns Eisler, who had arrived there in April and for whom he now wrote his "Hollywood Elegies," condensing much of what he felt about the civilization around him. He was also in touch with a young lecturer at UCLA called Eric Bentley, who differed from the rest of his friends in being neither central European nor involved in show business, and who seems immediately to have helped him to widen his English reading. From Feuchtwanger he heard that the Zurich Schauspielhaus wished to stage *The Good Person of Szechwan*, while Thornton Wilder had seen and been impressed by their production of *Mother Courage*. Still more changed for him when El Alamein was followed by Stalingrad (for it should never be forgotten how closely and continuously Brecht followed the war news). And during that October he and Feuchtwanger began collaborating on the war play, a modern Saint Joan story, which was to become *The Visions of Simone Machard*.

Like the other two original plays in this book, *Simone Machard* derived from a scheme which Brecht had brought in

his head with him from Europe. Already perhaps inspired by
the basic idea of Anna Seghers' radio play (which he was later
to adapt for the Berliner Ensemble, as described in volume 9),
he had conceived it in outline two years earlier, soon after the
collapse of France:

> a young frenchwoman in orléans, working at a filling sta-
> tion while her brother is away, dreams and daydreams of
> being joan of arc and undergoing her fate. for the germans
> are advancing on orléans. the voices joan hears are voices
> of the people—the things the blacksmith and the peasant
> are saying. she obeys these voices and saves france from
> the enemy outside, but is conquered by the enemy within.
> the court that sentences her is packed with pro-english
> clerics: victory of the fifth column.

Returning to it just before Christmas 1941, he sketched out a
play in nine scenes under the title *The Voices*, whose social
points should be (a) that vox dei is really vox populi, and (b)
that "owners and criminals stand shoulder to shoulder against
anyone who rejects the idea of property." Exactly at what
stage he first discussed this with Feuchtwanger is not clear,
but he now laid the plan aside in order to read *The Devil in
France*, the book in which the novelist described his own experiences in 1940, when he had been interned outside Aix-en-
Provence, then managed to escape across the Pyrenees at the
point where Benjamin was turned back. Other readings about
the French débâcle followed, though Feuchtwanger, who had
spent all the early part of his exile in that country, remained
in essential ways better informed about it than Brecht. Their
systematic collaboration began at the end of October, just before the shooting of *Hangmen Also Die*, which Brecht occasionally went to watch in the afternoons. They worked mostly
in Feuchtwanger's house, a quiet Spanish-style mansion on the
mountains overlooking Santa Monica and the sea, which has
now been made over to the University of Southern California.
The curfew imposed after Pearl Harbor, together with their
status as enemy aliens, prevented their meeting at night.

In one way the work went easily. The two men got on well
together, and despite their disagreement as to Simone's age
(for which see the Notes, pp. 246 and 271) the division of responsibility seems to have given no trouble. Brecht set up the

play's structure, which was then filled out in discussion between them—Feuchtwanger evidently doing his best to see
that the events were probable and the details authentic—after
which the actual writing of the scenes would be done by
Brecht and checked over at the next meeting. "He has a good
sense of structure," wrote Brecht approvingly,

> appreciates linguistic refinements, is also capable of making
> poetic and dramaturgical suggestions, knows a lot about
> literature, pays attention to arguments and is pleasant to
> deal with, a good friend.

At the same time, however,

> he wants to have nothing to do with the technical or social
> aspects (epic portrayal, A-effect, characters made up of so-
> cial rather than biological ingredients, class conflicts built
> into the story and so on), and tolerates all that merely as
> my personal style . . .

Perhaps because of the effect of the previous fifteen months of
largely pointless work ("that kind of thing can indeed be bad
for one's handwriting," noted Brecht of the role allotted by
Hollywood to its authors) he was less able than usual to resist
the pressure of convention, for aside from the dream element
(itself not particularly daring by local standards) the play is
quite Aristotelian in its observance of the unities. Moreover
the collaborators almost certainly had Hollywood's demands
in mind, both in the play and in the somewhat pot-boiling
novel which Feuchtwanger subsequently wrote on the same
theme (it appeared in 1944 and is briefly summarized on pp.
271–73). Before Brecht left for New York in February 1943,
leaving the ending of the play still not finally settled, an
agreement was drawn up between himself, Ruth Berlau (who
is neither named as a collaborator nor known to have had any
direct role in the work), and the Feuchtwangers, dividing the
stage and screen rights equally and giving Feuchtwanger all
rights to the proposed novel. Thereafter William Dieterle
took an interest, and arranged for a rough translation into English, which had been completed by April. On the strength of
this (so Feuchtwanger then wrote to Brecht) the agents
Curtis Brown were hoping to persuade either Ashley Dukes
or the Muirs to make a good English version. At Columbia

Pictures the story editor was favorably impressed. Not so Hanns Eisler, who had watched the development of the play throughout and made occasional suggestions, and was now embarking on the music. He told Brecht in May that he disliked Simone's instinctive patriotism and saw her as the poor victim of a patriotic upbringing. Brecht had failed to show that she was being exploited.

2

His visit to New York, which lasted from February to late May 1943, launched Brecht on the writing of *Schweyk in the Second World War* as well as on the first stage of *The Duchess of Malfi* adaptation. There is a long history to Brecht's fascination with Jaroslav Hašek's Good Soldier Švejk or Schweyk, arguably the outstanding fictional figure of our century; and his involvement in Erwin Piscator's dramatization of 1928 is discussed in our notes on the play. From then on he was repeatedly returning to the theme, first hoping that Piscator would film it in the USSR in the early 1930's, then expecting to be involved in the same director's scheme to film it elsewhere in 1937; "you really mustn't do it without me," he told Piscator that spring. Though these projects came to nothing, Piscator never abandoned his interest in this theme, and by 1943 was engaged in discussions with the Theater Guild in New York with a view to a new stage production. Brecht may well not have been informed about this, but the fact that *Hangmen Also Die* was a story of the Czech resistance (for Brecht and Lang were presumably unaware that Heydrich's— the hangman in question—assassins were for better or worse agents from Britain) almost certainly helped to turn his mind back to Hašek's anti-militarist epic, since it was during his work with Lang that he noted in his journal that

> once again i would like to do *Schweyk*, interspersed with scenes from [Karl Kraus's] *The Last Days of Mankind* so people can see the ruling forces up top with the private soldier down below surviving all their vast plans.

The man who actually got him to work on this project was Ernst-Josef Aufricht, the former Berlin impresario who had first staged *The Threepenny Opera* in 1928 and was now in New York after escaping from Unoccupied France. Partly involved in the Office of War Information German broadcasts, he was also on the lookout for a libretto to interest Kurt Weill, who had become well established on Broadway with *Lady in the Dark.* He helped to put on a mixed program at Hunter College (in New York) on April 3 in which Weill and Lotte Lenya performed some of the Brecht songs, including "Und was bekam des Soldaten Weib?" which Weill had recently set; this finished with a turn by the Czech clowns George Voskovec and Jan Werich entitled "Schweyk's spirit lives on." At some point he reintroduced the two former collaborators, and proposed that they should make a Schweyk musical, quickly raising the necessary $85,000 from émigrés who remembered their previous success.

According to Brecht's journal he then spent a week staying with the Weills at New City, where he outlined a version of *The Good Person of Szechwan* which the composer thought of producing; the Zurich première having taken place on February 4, just before Brecht came to New York. For a $500 advance (Hanns Eisler later recalled) he agreed to provide the Schweyk libretto, of which he wrote Weill an outline in May (it is printed on pp. 275–85). Having reread Hašek's novel in the train back to Los Angeles, he quickly settled down to work on the play and had finished the first three scenes by June 9 and the whole thing by the end of the month. Though it is quite untrue to say as Aufricht does (in his memoirs) that "Brecht had copied whole pages of dialogue from the Schweyk book" the work clearly flowed very much more easily than *Simone Machard*, without the awkward changes and compromises that mar that work. Brecht himself thought well enough of it to term it (again, in his journal),

a counterpart to *Mother Courage.* compared with the schweik which i wrote for piscator around 27 (a pure montage based on the novel) the present second world war version is a lot sharper, and corresponds to the shift from the hapsburgs' well-ensconced tyranny to the nazis' invasion.

He and Weill met again in Hollywood to discuss it. Then at the beginning of July he sent Weill the finished script, assuring him that it was not especially important that Schweyk himself should talk as he does in the German version of the novel, where he speaks a now-defunct kind of Prague German. Paul Selver's translation, he found, managed to be comic without this, and without attempting to find Anglo-Saxon equivalents for the social and political setting. He recommended getting the American poet Alfred Kreymborg to do a version of the play, saying that he was known to Ruth Berlau and "has the right sort of opinions (liberal)." It is not clear whether Weill agreed, though apparently he was already nervous that the script would prove too un-American for Broadway. Brecht, however, went ahead and commissioned Kreymborg, paying him out of a loan from his friend the actor Peter Lorre, who he hoped might play the name part. The translation was finished by September 4, all except for the "Moldau Song," which Brecht himself was still struggling to get right. The unavoidable effect was to infuriate Piscator, who not only regarded Schweyk almost as his own property—and indeed had spent much time in negotiations with the Hašek lawyer, who now gave the rights to Aufricht—but was expecting Kreymborg to translate the 1928 version for the Theater Guild.

However, the finished play never appealed to Weill, despite assurances that the publican's part had been written for Lotte Lenya and that he was welcome to get in an American lyric writer for the songs; there is no sign that he composed a note of music for it. Nor did he pursue the *Good Person of Szechwan* project, about which Brecht still hoped they might come to a formal agreement. By August it seems that Aufricht had lost interest, but Brecht none the less went carefully over Kreymborg's translation when it arrived and sent it back to New York for him and Ruth Berlau to revise. This had been done by the time of Brecht's return to New York in mid-November. Shortly afterwards Weill, now in California, wrote to Brecht to summarize his objections. He could only collaborate, he said, on three conditions:

1. if the play is written by a top-class American author in the Ben Hecht category and put on by a top-class American producer.
2. if Lenya plays the publican.
3. if the play is written as a "musical play," with more openings for music than the present version, as I do not under any circumstances wish to write incidental music.

As it stood, he thought that it

has no prospect of succeeding on the American stage without major alterations, unless there is some prominent American author (in the Ben Hecht category) who can find a way of rendering the humor of your script in American terms. Nor do I think the rights position clear enough to ensure the backing for a first-class Broadway production. But these are entirely private opinions, and I'm only telling you them because I don't want you to waste time and energy on a project which in my view hasn't much chance.

Similarly with *The Good Person of Szechwan*, where any agreement must be conditional on getting hold of an American writer. Their "collaboration on the present version of Szechwan" was now at an end.

3

Around October, when *Schweyk* was still uppermost in his mind, Brecht went to visit Luise Rainer, who was living in Westwood not far from his 26th Street house, and without any personal acquaintance with him had signed the affidavit allowing him to come to the United States. She was then at the height of her fame after her performance in the film of *The Good Earth,* and as they were walking on the beach Brecht asked her what, of all plays, she would most like to appear in. When she named the *Chalk Circle* he instantly responded, for once again this was a theme which (as the editorial note will show) he had been taking up intermittently for several years previously; indeed, he told her that he had suggested it in the first place to Klabund, whose adaptation had so successfully been performed by Elisabeth Bergner in Berlin in 1925. Miss Rainer in turn got in touch with a New York backer called Jules Leventhal, who was anxious to bring her to Broadway in a suitable work, and advised him that it would be worth commissioning Brecht and paying him a monthly salary till he had finished the play. This was formally arranged during Brecht's second New York visit, which lasted from mid-November to the middle of March. But he does not seem to have given Leventhal much information about his plans for the play, so that when the actress returned from performing to the troops in the Mediterranean she saw Brecht in New York to find out what was happening. According to her, he reacted so disagreeably as to make her call off her participation. None the less Brecht got down to the writing very soon after his return to Santa Monica, finishing the play in something close to its final version by June 5, when he sent it off to her (so he noted in his journal). She was then ill with the after-effects of jaundice and malaria from her Mediterranean tour, and can no longer even recollect its arrival. She was, however, aware that the play had developed an extra act since Brecht started on it, and that this was connected with his wish to give his friend Oscar Homolka a good part as Azdak, something that had not originally been bargained for.

In the meantime Brecht's financial circumstances, which nine months before had been very precarious, had changed as a result of the sale of the film rights of *Simone Machard* to MGM in February. This seems to have been due entirely to Feuchtwanger, who when Sam Goldwyn failed to understand the play got him to read the much more conventional *Simone* novel, buy the rights, and then buy those of the play as well. Brecht and Feuchtwanger had $50,000 to divide, in return for which there could be no stage production without Goldwyn's permission for the next three and a half years. Perhaps this is one reason why Brecht seemed so little discouraged by the collapse of the original *Chalk Circle* plan (which was not yet Caucasian when his journal first mentions it in March) as to carry his preoccupation with it right through the summer of

1944. Thus he reworked the character of Grusha, whose good-ness, like Simone's patriotism, had seemed too arbitrary, and tried to make her tougher; he rewrote the prologue; and he asked neighbor Christopher Isherwood (who refused) to make a translation. Then at some point James and Tanya Stern, who had first translated the play for Leventhal and Broadway, made a new version with W. H. Auden, who was sharing a house with them on Fire Island. (Part of this new version ap-peared in spring, 1946, in *The Kenyon Review*.) By Septem-ber 1944, Brecht seems to have more or less finished the fully revised script, which was to remain virtually unchanged for the next ten years. That month his child by Ruth Berlau, called Michel like the child in the play, was born and died in Los Angeles. Coincidentally or not, he laid the play aside and by the end of the year was deeply involved instead in the *Galileo* project with Charles Laughton, who had recently become very taken with Brecht's work.

4

Galileo apart—and it must be remembered that for all the effort Brecht put into it over the next two and a half years this was just a revision of a previous play—the only one of his "Ameri-can" works to reach the professional stage was *The Duchess of Malfi*, a play whose text has never formed part of the German collected works; it is printed for the first time as an appendix to the present volume. This interesting but largely frustrated adaptation was the result of Brecht's keenness to write some-thing for the most famous of all the exiled German actresses, Elisabeth Bergner, whom he had first met in his Munich days. Soon after his arrival in the United States he had shown her the script of *The Good Person of Szechwan*, which she found boring; the trouble (so he later noted in his journal) being that she could not conceive of the theater audience as a group of people who would change the world—

so that the basic climate of this kind of theater is alien to her: the beginner's enthusiasm for a new millennium, the spirit of inquiry, the urge to unshackle *everybody's* productivity. in her eyes it is all a new "style," a matter of fashion, something arbitrary.

None the less she and her producer-husband, Paul Czinner, shared the Brechts' first family Christmas in Santa Monica, entertained them in turn on New Year's Eve, and set Brecht to work on a film story, now lost, which according to him was successfully plagiarized by some other (unidentified) writer.

One of his projects for her was an adaptation of Heywood's *A Woman Killed with Kindness*, with which he apparently thought of asking Feuchtwanger to help him. Instead, however, they tackled *Simone Machard*, and by the time that was finished and Brecht had set off for New York, either he or Miss Bergner had decided that another Elizabethan work would suit her better, Webster's *The Duchess of Malfi*. Once in New York, Brecht got in touch with the poet H. R. Hays, a friend of Hanns Eisler's who had already translated *Mother Courage* and *Lucullus* (first two of his major plays to be published in the U.S.) and also provided immigration affidavits. It was arranged with the Czinners that Hays and Brecht should adapt the play together, Hays doing the actual writing while Brecht concentrated on story and structure. The work began in April 1943, and by June 26, when Brecht was back in Santa Monica finishing *Schweyk*, a first script had been completed and copyrighted in both collaborators' names. Though Brecht then showed it to Eisler and asked him to write the music nothing more seems to have been done till he returned to New York that winter, when he went back (in the words of his journal) to

work with hays and bergner on the *Duchess of Malfi*. not completely finished, since bergner is short of time.

Meanwhile he asked W. H. Auden to collaborate, seemingly without mentioning or consulting Hays. "I have been treating Webster's text with great care," he wrote on December 5,

but I had to add a few new scenes and verses. These are now available in English, but it seems advisable to improve

> them and I have told Miss Bergner that no one could do it
> as well as you.

When Czinner told Hays of this proposal he walked out,
leaving Auden to carry on as and when he could. The whole
project now seems to have simmered for some eighteen months
till in mid-summer of 1945 Brecht, who had come to New
York a third time to help stage *The Private Life of the Master
Race*, went to the Czinners' summer place near Woodstock,
Vermont, to finish it off "in the rough." There is no more
mention of it in his journal after that point, but a final Brecht-
Auden script was copyrighted in April 1946, and it was at
last decided to go ahead with its production. Spurred by the
production of the original play at the Haymarket Theater in
London a year earlier, with Peggy Ashcroft as the Duchess
and John Gielgud as Ferdinand, the Czinners engaged as director George Rylands, a friend of Auden's and an eminent
Cambridge Elizabethan scholar, but almost ludicrously out of
tune with Brecht's personality and ideas. The Duchess was of
course Miss Bergner; Bosola, the black actor Canada Lee playing with a whitened face; John Carradine and Robert Speaight
were also in the cast; the music was by Benjamin Britten,
"arranged" by Ignatz Strasfogel; Harry Bennett did the sets.
Brecht's reactions can be gauged from the ultimatum which
he sent Czinner after seeing the Boston production that September (see pp. 423–24). His criticisms were disregarded and
at the Broadway opening at the Ethel Barrymore Theater on
October 15 his contribution—which no critic could have de-
tected once Rylands had chosen mainly to return to Webster
—was no longer mentioned, credit being given to Auden alone.
It is not known whether he even attended, despite his strong
condemnatory note. The play got a bad press and ran only a
few days.

Such was the one tangible result of Brecht's four attempts
to write for Broadway. As for the others, the *Simone Machard*
film was never made, first because Teresa Wright, whom
MGM had cast for the part of the adolescent girl, was inap-
positely expecting a baby, and then because the liberation of
France in 1944 made the theme so much less topical. It re-

mained MGM's property, so Feuchtwanger told Brecht as late
as 1956, when the latter wanted to propose it to Cavalcanti,
director of the previous year's second-rate *Puntila* film.
Around the same time there were various inquiries about the
play—from Akimov in Leningrad, from Norman Lloyd in
New York, and from Jean-Marie Serreau and Benno Besson
for a mixed German-French tour—and these led Brecht to
stress that

> the most important thing for any production of Simone is
> that the title part must on no account be played by a young
> actress—not even one that looks like a child. It must be an
> eleven-year-old, and one that looks like a child.

This principle was followed in the eventual première of the
play at Frankfurt in March 1957, which Brecht of course
never saw. For there Simone was played by a child who had
been trained specially for the part by Ruth Berlau in Berlin.
Eisler, who had started writing the music in 1943, now finished
it off and the whole production was a great success. None the
less Eisler himself once again did not like it. "The play's too
heroic for me," he told Hans Bunge later. It was "a tribute
to heroism. And that's not right. I don't need to tell you how
utterly contrary to Brecht's whole way of looking at things
that is." Nor did the Berliner Ensemble ever stage it, though
there was an East German television version that included a
number of the Ensemble actors.

Schweyk remained a play, which Brecht never amended so
as to provide the greater musical opportunities which Weill
had asked for. None the less in the autumn of 1947, when
Wolfgang Langhoff at the Deutsches Theater in (East) Berlin
was planning to present it, it was to Weill that Brecht turned
for the incidental music. Once again Weill put him off, and
there is no further record of this plan. Eighteen months later,
however, when Brecht was setting up his Ensemble, he hoped
to get Peter Lorre to come to Berlin to create the part. Again,
it was not possible to organize a production before Brecht's
death in 1956, though in 1955 (if we are to believe Hanns
Eisler's slightly erratic recollections) he had asked Eisler to
start writing the music and to give it priority over that for

Simone Machard. "Interesting that you can be so amusing," he told Eisler when he brought him the result a few weeks before he died.

> He made me play it, and I still see him smiling at my weaknesses and his advantages.

In the event the play was first staged not in Germany at all but at the Polish army theater in Warsaw, where Ludwik René directed it in January 1957. This was nearly fourteen years after it had been written. The *Duchess of Malfi* adaptation has never been performed again.

The Caucasian Chalk Circle was put on in America by students at Northfield, Minnesota, under the direction of Henry Goodman (now of UCLA Drama Department) who had been bitten with Brecht on seeing the *Galileo* production of July 1947. This took place in May 1948 after Brecht had left the country, and used Eric and Maja Bentley's translation, which had apparently superseded that by the Sterns and Auden. Two and a half years later, when Brecht was back in Berlin, he saw the Austrian composer Gottfried von Einem in Munich and tentatively arranged for a German-language première at the Salzburg festival, to be directed by Berthold Viertel with Homolka as Azdak and Käthe Gold as Grusha. Though their plan never materialized, he managed to interest Carl Orff in the idea of writing the music: something that Hanns Eisler found uncongenial. This was partly because there was no real certainty of a production, but above all because in his view "Brecht was pursuing a chimera":

> Brecht said he wanted a kind of music to which lengthy epics can be narrated. After all, Homer was sung. He used to say, "Isn't it possible to write a setting or note down a cadence that would permit the delivery of a two-hour epic?"

By his own account Eisler made one or two sketches before deciding that this was beyond him. In 1953 therefore when Brecht determined to stage the play himself with the Ensemble he went instead to Paul Dessau, who had already in America been interested enough in "The Augsburg Chalk Circle" version of the story to draft out the framework of an oratorio. Following very much the requirements posed by Brecht in the note on pp. 297–98, Dessau provided him with the kind of orientally-derived music which he wanted for his recycling of a popular narrative tradition still observable in North Africa and the Far East. The production itself took about eight months to rehearse before its première in June 1954. Though it fell foul of the party critics in East Germany it made a great impression at the Paris International Theater Festival the following year; since then the play has been among the best-known of Brecht's works. After 1964 it was even one of those most performed in the USSR, though according to the critic Kats (reported by Henry Glade), the prologue (or first scene) is simply not playable before a Soviet audience, presumably because it gives too unreal a picture of conditions there.

5

Particularly among those who disapprove of his decision to settle finally in East Germany, it has become common to contrast Brecht's six years in America with his seven years in East Berlin. And certainly the latter were not productive so far as his actual writing went. But his American record is not all that impressive either, at least by the standards which he had set himself in Scandinavia and before that in pre-Nazi Berlin. Of course his initial difficulties did not last forever, and some of the poems which he wrote from 1942 on show new qualities of concentrated observation which were a genuine gain; nor were they any the less deeply political for being independent of day-to-day party tactics. Though he always remained in some measure dependent on the goodwill of his fellow exiles—it is difficult, for instance, to think of his involvement in *The Duchess of Malfi* as due to anything less than a wish to help on the Czinners' part—he did gradually make his mark among the non-Germans with whom he came in contact, and here his addiction to English literature, whether classical or criminal, must surely have helped. He worked hard and systematically, witness the "plan for the day" which he drew up on concluding *The Caucasian Chalk Circle* in Santa Monica in 1944:

> get up 7 A.M. newspaper, radio. make coffee in the little copper pot. morning: work. light lunch at twelve. rest with crime story. afternoon: work or pay visits. evening meal at 7 P.M. then visitors. night: half a page of shakespeare or waley's collection of chinese poems. radio. crime story.

But three of our four plays are to a greater or lesser extent flawed, and there was only one which he chose to stage himself when he had the chance. Thus *Simone Machard* not only reflects Brecht's uncertainties while writing it (as our editorial note attempts to show), but is in essential ways inconsistent with his own attitude, just as Eisler—a judge whom he always respected—pointed out. (Of course some audiences like it all the better for that.) *Schweyk*, despite its success in capturing Hašek's tone of voice, has none of the panoramic sweep of the novel, or even of the Piscator adaptation, while there is something deeply inappropriate about pitting the amiable Good Soldier—so perfect an instrument for undermining the whiskered Emperor Franz Josef—against political psychopaths and mass murderers. Both plays, moreover, take a romanticized view of the resistance movements, whose topical appeal they were in some measure surely designed to exploit. Since *The Duchess of Malfi* was so mangled that there is difficulty in reconstructing Brecht's conception of it—something that he never seems to have wished to do himself, to judge from the absence of any German version—the only one of the American plays to succeed in Brecht's own terms is *The Caucasian Chalk Circle*. Despite its awkward combination of two largely unrelated stories (though these had long been married up in the author's mind) and the uncharacteristic sweetness of the heroine, it is a truly epic work, embodying many of Brecht's special ideas, tastes, and talents. In many opinions it is a masterpiece.

It is significant that although this play was originally commissioned for a Broadway production Brecht himself could attribute its structure to "a revulsion against the commercialized dramaturgy of Broadway." For everything else that Brecht wrote in America, apart from his poems, was written for more or less commercial ends; and if he kicked against the commercial spirit it was surely because he knew that he was being conditioned by it. Most obviously this was so of his film stories, which were without exception what he termed "daily bread and butter work" even though he could hardly help imbuing them with some of his own qualities (whence, no doubt, their ill success). But *Simone Machard* too was written with one eye at least to the film industry; *Schweyk* was to be a Broadway musical, while not only the other two plays but also the adaptation of *Galileo* were written with Broadway productions in view. For the first time in the fourteen years since the success of *The Threepenny Opera*, Brecht was writing exclusively for the commercial stage in its most nakedly competitive form; nor was anything that he is known to have written in America (apart possibly from a short unpublished ballet libretto for Lotte Goslar) performed by the students, musicians, or left-wing amateurs who had helped to shape some of his most original works. He was never particularly good at working for the box office or respecting other people's conventions, while his natural cussedness made him spoil any chance he might have had of succeeding: witness his wanton (was it unconsciously deliberate?) antagonizing of Leventhal and Luise Rainer. One might almost say that it was his very failures that justify this group of plays.

Why then did he never make contact with any other form of theater (or cinema) in the United States during those years? Perhaps it was the result of his experiences over the New York production of *Mother* in 1935 that alienated him so from the American left-wing stage; certainly he seems to have had little use for the ideas of Odets or John Howard Lawson, while even so good a friend as Gorelik was largely in disagreement with him. Nor was university theater then anything like so active as it has since become. Perhaps too the identification of Hollywood and Broadway with the war effort was itself misleading, for Brecht was always primarily concerned to see the Nazis beaten. *Hangmen, Simone,* and *Schweyk* all deal with the same theme of European resistance to Hitler, while the revised prologue to *The Caucasian Chalk Circle* sets it too within the framework of the war, despite the remoteness of the legend. Oddly enough he never again took up those American themes which had fascinated him earlier, from *In the Jungle of Cities* to *Arturo Ui*, in other words from Munich days right up to his departure from Europe. As Professor James Lyon has pointed out, he did come to take a good deal of interest in the affairs of his half-adopted country and at one point considered basing a script on Edgar Lee Masters's *Spoon River Anthology;* but the only direct reflection of his surroundings is in his poems. Much must have been due to his lack of money and dependence on the German colony's esteem for him; much too to the lack of his two most-valued women collaborators, Margarete Steffin and Elisabeth Hauptmann (though the latter was then living elsewhere in the U.S.). One can only speculate what might have happened if he had come into contact with the student movement as it later developed, or chosen to associate himself with the blacks. As it was he did not.

He already seems to have decided to return to Germany well before his summons to appear before the House Un-American Activities Committee in 1947. 1946 is a mysteriously blank year in his life, when he wrote virtually no poems, worked on no plays other than *Galileo*, and made no entries in his journal (unless the relevant pages have somehow been lost). But by that winter he was already planning his return, to judge from his correspondence with Piscator and Caspar Neher, to whom he reported receiving offers "to be able to use the Theater am Schiffbauerdamm for certain purposes." His hearing by J. Parnell Thomas's committee the following autumn was in some measure a by-product of their investigation of the motion-picture industry, though his only real link with the so-called Hollywood Ten was his friendship with Donald Ogden Stewart and his wife. What clearly was of more interest to the investigators was his association with Hanns Eisler and through him with his brother Gerhart, the one genuinely important international Communist functionary whom they were able to unearth. This was in some measure due to the Eislers' sister Ruth Fischer, who had been one of the leaders of the German Communist Party in her youth, knew Brecht, and now coined the pleasant phrase for him "minstrel of the GPU." Hanns was effectively deported in February 1948; Gerhart (whose prosecution was called for by Richard Nixon in his maiden speech as a Representative) left the U.S. on a Polish liner and was lucky to escape arrest. Brecht stood up well under examination, made the committee laugh, and left for Europe under his own steam a day later. He never came back.

THE EDITORS

The Visions of
Simone Machard

Play

This play was written in collaboration with Lion Feuchtwanger

Translator: Ralph Manheim

CHARACTERS

PHILIPPE CHAVEZ, mayor of
  Saint-Martin (King
  Charles VII in the dreams)
HENRI SOUPEAU, owner of the
  hostelry (the constable)
MARIE SOUPEAU, his mother
  (Isabeau, the queen
  mother)
CAPTAIN HONORÉ FÉTAIN, a
  wealthy vineyard owner
  (the duke of Burgundy)
THE COLONEL (bishop of
  Beauvais)
A GERMAN CAPTAIN (an
  English general)

SIMONE MACHARD (the Maid
  of Orleans in the dreams)
MAURICE and ROBERT, truck
  drivers
GEORGES, PÈRE GUSTAVE,
  employees of the hostelry
MADAME MACHARD, MONSIEUR
  MACHARD, Simone's parents
A SERGEANT
REFUGEES
SUPPORTING CHARACTERS
  (soldiers and people in
  the dreams)
THE ANGEL

The scene represents the yard of the "Au Relais" hostelry. The background consists of the garage, a low building. To the right of the audience is the hostelry with its back door. To the left the storehouse, with rooms for the truck drivers. Between the storehouse and the garage a rather large gate, opening out on the street. The garage is conceived as a large one, since the hostelry also operates a trucking business.

The action takes place in June 1940, in Saint-Martin, a small town on one of the main roads from Paris to the south of France.

1

The Book

*Georges, a soldier, is sitting smoking. His right arm is ban-
daged. Beside him old Père Gustave is mending a tire. The
brothers Maurice and Robert, truck drivers employed by the
hostelry, are looking intently at the sky. Airplanes are heard.
It is the evening of June 14.*

ROBERT They must be ours.

MAURICE They're not ours.

ROBERT (*calling over to Georges*) Georges, are they ours or
are they Boches?

GEORGES (*gingerly moving his bandaged arm*) Now it's gone
numb above the elbow.

PÈRE GUSTAVE Don't move it; that's no good.
(*Simone Machard comes in. She is a young teenager; her
skirt is too long and her shoes are too big. She is carrying a
heavy basket full of washing*)

ROBERT Heavy?
(*Simone nods and carries the basket as far as the gas pump.
Smoking, the men watch her*)

GEORGES (*to Père Gustave*) Think it could be the bandage?
It's got stiffer since yesterday.

PÈRE GUSTAVE Simone, go get Monsieur Georges some cider
out of the storehouse.

SIMONE (*puting down her basket*) What if Monsieur Soupeau catches me again?

PÈRE GUSTAVE Do as you're told.
(*Simone goes out*)

ROBERT (*to Georges*)   Can't you answer a question? The guy
wears a uniform and he doesn't even look up when he hears
a plane! With soldiers like you they'll lose the war.

GEORGES   What do *you* think, Robert? Now it's numb above
the elbow too. Père Gustave thinks it's only the bandage.

ROBERT   I asked you about those planes.

GEORGES (*without looking up*)   Germans. Ours don't get off
the ground.

(*Simone has come back with a bottle of cider, from which
she pours a glass for Georges*)

SIMONE   Do you think we're going to lose the war, Monsieur
Georges?

GEORGES   Win or lose, I'm going to need two arms.

(*Monsieur Henri Soupeau, the owner of the hostelry, comes
in from the street. Simone quickly hides the cider. Monsieur
Soupeau stops in the gateway, looks to see who is in the
yard, and motions to someone in the street. A gentleman in
a long dust coat appears. Monsieur Soupeau escorts him
across the yard, carefully shielding him from the others, and
disappears with him into the hostelry*)

PÈRE GUSTAVE   Did you see that dust coat? That's an officer.
A colonel. One more who's beat it from the front. They
don't want to be seen. But they eat like a horse.

(*Simone has gone over to her basket and sat down on the
support of the gas pump; she starts reading a book that was
on top of her basket*)

GEORGES (*over his cider*)   Robert gives me a pain. He says
they'll lose the war with soldiers like me. But thanks to me,
they've won something else, you can't deny it. A gentleman
in Tours has made good money on my shoes and a gentleman in Bordeaux on my helmet. My jacket brought in a
castle on the Riviera, and my leggings seven race horses.
France was making a good thing out of me before the war
even started.

PÈRE GUSTAVE   And now it's being lost. By the dust coats.

GEORGES   Exactly. There are 200 hangars with 1000 fighter
planes, paid for, tested and manned, but in the hour of
France's peril they never get off the ground. The Maginot
Line cost 10 billion; steel and concrete, 700 miles long, seven

stories deep, in open country. And when the battle started, our colonel hopped into his car and drove to the rear, followed by two cars full of food and wine. Two million men waiting for orders, ready to die, but the war minister's mistress was on the outs with the prime minister's mistress, so no orders came. Our forts are dug in, they don't move; their forts are on wheels, they roll over us. Nothing is going to stop their tanks as long as they have gas, and they get gas from our gas stations. Tomorrow they'll be here at your station, Simone, drinking up your gas. Thanks for the cider.

ROBERT   Don't talk about tanks (*with a motion of his head in Simone's direction*) when she's around. Her brother's at the front.

GEORGES   She's busy with her book.

PÈRE GUSTAVE (*to Robert*)   How about a game of belote?

ROBERT   I've got a headache. All day we've been driving the captain's wine barrels through crowds of refugees. A regular migration.

PÈRE GUSTAVE   The captain's wine is the most important refugee of all. Can't you get that through your head?

GEORGES   Everybody knows the man's a fascist. His pals on the general staff must have told him that something's gone wrong again up front.

ROBERT   Maurice is fit to be tied. He says he's good and sick of driving those damn wine barrels through women and children. I'm hitting the hay. (*He goes out*)

PÈRE GUSTAVE   Those crowds of refugees are ruinous for warfare. Tanks can get through any swamp, but in a human swamp they bog down. The civilian population has turned out to be a terrible nuisance in wartime. When a war breaks out they ought to be moved to another planet, they're only in the way. One or the other has got to be abolished: the people or the war; you can't have both.

GEORGES (*has sat down beside Simone; reaching into the basket*)   You've taken the washing down dripping wet.

SIMONE (*still reading*)   The refugees keep stealing the table-cloths.

GEORGES   Probably for diapers or to wrap their feet in.

SIMONE (*still reading*)   Madame counts them just the same.

GEORGES (*pointing at the book*) Is it still the Maid of Orleans? (*Simone nods*) Who gave you this book?

SIMONE   Monsieur Soupeau. But I never get a chance to read.
I'm only up to page 72, where the Maid defeats the English
and crowns the king in Rheims. (*Goes on reading*)

GEORGES   Why do you read that old-fashioned stuff?

SIMONE   I want to know what happens next.—Monsieur
Georges, is it true that France is the fairest land on earth?

GEORGES   Is that what it says in the book? (*Simone nods*) I've
never seen the rest of the world. But they say the fairest
land is the one you live in.

SIMONE   What's the Gironde like, for instance?

GEORGES   I think they grow wine there too. They say France
is the biggest wine drinker in the world.

SIMONE   Are there a lot of barges on the Seine?

GEORGES   About a thousand.

SIMONE   And Saint-Denis, where you were working. What's
it like?

GEORGES   Nothing to write home about.

SIMONE   But all in all it's the fairest land.

GEORGES   It's good for bread, wine, and fish. I wouldn't say
anything against the cafés with their orange awnings. Or
the food markets with all the meat and fruit, especially in
the early morning. Never mind the bistros with their per-
nod. The country fairs and the brass bands at ship launch-
ings are all right. And who could object to the poplars we
play boules under? Have you got to take food parcels to
the schoolhouse again today?

SIMONE   If only the engineers get here before I have to go.

GEORGES   What engineers?

SIMONE   They're expecting engineer troops in the kitchen.
Their field kitchen got lost in the crowd of refugees.
They're from the 132nd.

GEORGES   Isn't that your brother's regiment?

SIMONE   Yes. They're moving up to the front.—It says in the
book that the angel commanded the Maid to slay all the
enemies of France, God wills it.

GEORGES   You'll be getting your nightmares again if you go
on reading that bloodthirsty stuff. Why do you think I
took the newspapers away from you?

SIMONE Do their tanks really plow through crowds of people, Monsieur Georges?

GEORGES Yes. And now you've done enough reading.

(*He tries to take the book away from her. Monsieur Soupeau steps into the door from the hostelry*)

MONSIEUR SOUPEAU Georges, you're not to let anyone into the breakfast room. (*To Simone*) You're reading at your work again, Simone. That's not what I gave you the book for.

SIMONE (*has begun to count the tablecloths eagerly*) I was only taking a quick look while I was counting the washing. I'm sorry, Monsieur Henri.

PÈRE GUSTAVE I wouldn't have given her that book if I were you, Monsieur Henri; it's getting her all upset.

MONSIEUR SOUPEAU Nonsense. In times like these it won't hurt her to learn something about the history of France. These youngsters don't even know what France is. (*Speaking over his shoulder back into the house*) Jean, take the hors d'oeuvres to the breakfast room. (*Again to those in the yard*) It wouldn't hurt you to read about the spirit they had in those days. God knows we could use a Maid of Orleans.

PÈRE GUSTAVE (*affecting interest*) Where would she come from?

MONSIEUR SOUPEAU Where would she come from! From anywhere. It could be anybody. You! Or Georges! (*Indicating Simone*) She could be the one. Any child could tell them what needs to be done, it's simple. Even she could tell the country.

PÈRE GUSTAVE (*looking Simone over*) Maybe kind of small for a Maid of Orleans.

MONSIEUR SOUPEAU Kind of small, kind of young, kind of big, kind of old: where the spirit is lacking there's always an alibi. (*Over his shoulder into the house*) Jean, did you serve the Portuguese sardines?

PÈRE GUSTAVE (*to Simone*) How about it? Would you like to change your job? I'm only afraid no angels would come along these days.

MONSIEUR SOUPEAU That will do, Père Gustave. I wish you'd keep your cynicism to yourself in front of the child. Let her read her book; she can do without your nasty remarks.

(*On his way into the hostelry*) But it doesn't have to be during work hours, Simone. (*Goes out*)

PÈRE GUSTAVE (*grinning*) Hey, Georges, can you beat that? Now he wants his kitchen maid to learn how to be the Maid of Orleans, on her own time of course. They cram kids full of patriotism. And they disguise themselves in dust coats. Or hide their hoarded gasoline in certain brickyards instead of handing it over to the army.

SIMONE Monsieur Soupeau isn't doing anything wrong.

PÈRE GUSTAVE No, he's a public benefactor. He gives you twenty francs a week, so your people "won't be left entirely high and dry."

SIMONE He keeps me on so my brother's job will be waiting for him.

PÈRE GUSTAVE And gets a gas station attendant, a waitress, and a dishwasher out of it.

SIMONE That's because there's a war on.

PÈRE GUSTAVE Which doesn't hurt him any, does it?

MONSIEUR SOUPEAU (*appears in the doorway of the hostelry*) Père Gustave, a half bottle of the '23 Chablis for the gentleman with the trout. (*Back into the hostelry*)

PÈRE GUSTAVE The gentleman in the dust coat, alias the colonel, desires a bottle of Chablis before the fall of France. (*Out into the storehouse. During the following, he takes the bottle of Chablis across the yard into the hostelry*)

A WOMAN'S VOICE (*from the second floor of the hostelry*) Simone, where are those tablecloths?
(*Simone picks up the basket and starts toward the hostelry. At this moment a sergeant and two soldiers come in from the street with a large stew pot*)

SERGEANT We've come to pick up rations. The people at the town hall said they'd phoned.

SIMONE (*beaming, eagerly*) It must be ready by now. Go right into the kitchen. (*To the sergeant, while the two soldiers go in*) Monsieur, my brother André Machard is with the 132nd. Do you know why we haven't heard from him?

SERGEANT Everything's in a muddle up front. We lost contact with the front line the day before yesterday.

SIMONE   Is the war lost, monsieur?

SERGEANT   Of course not, mademoiselle. A few enemy tanks have broken through, that's all. The monsters are bound to run out of gas pretty soon. Then they'll be stuck.

SIMONE   They say they'll never get as far as the Loire.

SERGEANT   No, nothing to worry about. It's a long way from the Seine to the Loire. The only trouble is the crowds of refugees. We can hardly move. And we've got to repair the bombed bridges, or the reserves won't get through. (*The two soldiers come back with the pot; the sergeant looks inside it*)

SERGEANT   Is that all? It's a disgrace. Take a look, mademoiselle. It's not even half full. This is the third restaurant we've been sent to. The first two gave us nothing at all. Here we get this.

SIMONE (*looks into the pot with consternation*)   There must be some mistake. We've got plenty, lots of lentils and smoked pork. I'll speak to Monsieur Soupeau myself. Your pot will be full. Just a minute. (*She rushes inside*)

GEORGES (*offering cigarettes*)   Her brother's only seventeen. He was the only one in Saint-Martin to volunteer. She's very fond of him.

SERGEANT   Damn this war. What kind of a war is it anyway? The army's treated like an enemy in its own country. And the premier says on the radio: "The army is the people."

PÈRE GUSTAVE (*who has come out of the house*) "The army is the people." And the people are the enemy.

SERGEANT (*hostile*)   What do you mean by that?

GEORGES (*looks into the half-empty pot*)   Why do you stand for it? Go get the mayor.

SERGEANT   We know mayors; they don't do a thing.

SIMONE (*comes out slowly; without looking at the sergeant*) Monsieur Soupeau says he can't give you any more on account of all the refugees.

PÈRE GUSTAVE   And we can't give them anything because the troops get it all.

SIMONE (*in despair*)   Monsieur Soupeau is angry because the mayor is always making demands.

SERGEANT (*wearily*)   It's the same all over.

MONSIEUR SOUPEAU (*comes into the doorway and gives Simone a folded check*)   Here's the check for the gentleman with the trout. Tell him we're giving him the strawberries at cost price, say your parents sold them to the hostelry. (*He shoves her into the house*) What's the matter? You're not satisfied? Would you kindly stop to think of the civilian population? We've been bled white, and every day they ask more of us. God knows that nobody feels for France more than I do, but . . . (*With a sweeping gesture of help-lessness*) I have to make big sacrifices to keep this business going. Look at the help I've got. (*With a gesture in the direction of Père Gustave and Georges*) An old man and a cripple. And a child. I employ them because they'd starve if I didn't. I can't feed the French army into the bargain.

SERGEANT   And I can't send my men out in the night on an empty stomach to work under fire for your benefit. Repair your own bridges. I'll wait for my field kitchen. If it takes seven years. (*Goes out with his men*)

MONSIEUR SOUPEAU   What can I do? You can't please every-body. (*Making up to the help*) Friends, thank your stars that you don't own a restaurant. You see how it is? Like fighting off wolves. After all the trouble we've had getting two stars in the guidebook. (*Since Père Gustave and Georges show little sympathy for his troubles, angrily*) Don't stand there like bumps on a log. (*Calls back into the house*) Monsieur, there's no one in the yard now.

COLONEL (*the gentleman in the dust coat—comes out of the hostelry. To Monsieur Soupeau who is escorting him across the yard to the road*)   Your prices are outrageous, mon-sieur. One hundred and sixty francs for a meal.

GEORGES (*goes in the meantime into the hostelry and drags out Simone, who is burying her face in her hands*)   They left long ago. You don't have to hide in the hallway any more. It's not *your* fault, Simone.

SIMONE (*drying her tears*)   It's only because they're from the 132nd, Monsieur Georges. The boys at the front are waiting for help, and the engineers have to repair the bridges first.

MONSIEUR SOUPEAU (*returns from the street*)   Foie gras,

trout, roast lamb, asparagus, Chablis, coffee, brandy, Martell '84. In times like these. And when the check comes, they make a face a mile long. But the service has to be double quick, because they can't wait to get out of the war zone. An officer! A colonel! Poor France! (*Sees Simone; with a guilty conscience*) And you, don't butt in. What goes on in the kitchen is none of your business! (*Out into the hostelry*)

GEORGES (*to Père Gustave, pointing at Simone*)   She's ashamed on account of the engineers.

SIMONE   What will they think of our hostelry, Monsieur Georges?

GEORGES (*to Simone*)   You have no reason to be ashamed. The hostelry will cheat people as sure as God made little red apples, and the boss will charge scandalous prices as sure as a dog farts. You're not the hostelry. When a guest praises the wine, you've got nothing to be pleased about; when the roof caves in, you've got nothing to cry about. It wasn't you that chose the bed linen. It wasn't you that refused them food. See?

SIMONE (*not convinced*)   Yes, Monsieur Georges.

GEORGES   André knows you took the job on his account. That's enough. And now go on over to the schoolhouse to see little François. But don't let his mother scare you with her talk about the stukas, or you'll dream half the night that you're on the battlefield. (*He pushes her gently into the hostelry; to Père Gustave*) Too much imagination.

PÈRE GUSTAVE (*mending his tire*)   She doesn't like going to the schoolhouse. They insult her because the food parcels are too expensive.

GEORGES (*with a sigh*)   As I know her, she probably sticks up for the boss. She's a loyal one.

MONSIEUR SOUPEAU (*comes out of the hostelry and calls out in the direction of the storehouse, clapping his hands*)   Maurice, Robert!

ROBERT'S VOICE (*from the storehouse, sleepily*)   Yes?

MONSIEUR SOUPEAU   Captain Fétain just called up. He wants you to take the rest of the wine barrels to Bordeaux right away.

ROBERT'S VOICE   Tonight? That's impossible, Monsieur Henri. We've been on the road for two days.

MONSIEUR SOUPEAU   I know. I know. But what can I do? The captain thinks we're being too slow about his shipments. Of course it's because of the clogged roads. I really hate to deprive you of your night's sleep, but . . . (*A gesture of helplessness*)

ROBERT'S VOICE   The roads are clogged at night too, and we have to drive with blackout lights.

MONSIEUR SOUPEAU   C'est la guerre. We can't antagonize our best customers. Mother insists. So get started. (*To Père Gustave*) Aren't you through with that tire yet? (*Monsieur Chavez, the mayor, has come in from the street, with a briefcase under his arm. He is very much excited*)

PÈRE GUSTAVE (*calling Monsieur Soupeau's attention to him*) Monsieur le maire.

MAYOR   Henri, it's about your trucks again. I'm sorry. You've got to let me have them for the refugees.

MONSIEUR SOUPEAU   But I've told you that I'm under contract to haul Captain Fétain's wine. I can't refuse him. He and mother are childhood friends.

MAYOR   "The captain's wine!" Henri, you know I don't like to interfere with anyone's business activities, but at a time like this I can't worry my head over your relations with that fascist Fétain.

(*Simone has come out of the hostelry. A tray full of large parcels is slung round her neck, and she is carrying two baskets full of parcels*)

MONSIEUR SOUPEAU (*menacingly*)   Philippe, watch your step about calling the captain a fascist.

MAYOR (*angrily*)   "Watch your step!" That's all you and your captain can think of, with the Germans on the Loire. France is going to the dogs!

MONSIEUR SOUPEAU   What! Where are the Germans?

MAYOR (*emphatically*)   On the Loire. And the Ninth Army can't get through to relieve our boys because Route 20 is clogged with refugees. Your trucks are confiscated along with every other truck in Saint-Martin; I want them ready tomorrow morning to evacuate the refugees in the school-house. That's official. (*He takes a small red poster out of his briefcase and starts fastening it to the garage door*)

SIMONE (*horrified, in a low voice to Georges*) The tanks are coming, Monsieur Georges.

GEORGES (*puts his arm over her shoulder*) Yes, Simone.

SIMONE They're on the Loire. They'll be coming to Tours.

GEORGES Yes, Simone.

SIMONE They'll come here too, won't they?

MONSIEUR SOUPEAU Now I see why the captain was in such a hurry. (*Shaken*) The Germans on the Loire, that's terrible. (*Goes over to the mayor who is still posting his notice*) Philippe, never mind about that. Come inside with me. I want to talk to you in private.

MAYOR (*angrily*) No, Henri, I'm through talking with you in private. I want your employees to know that your trucks are confiscated and your gas too. I've looked the other way long enough.

MONSIEUR SOUPEAU Are you out of your mind? Confiscating my trucks in this situation! Anyway, I haven't got any gas. Except for the few gallons I've got here.

MAYOR What about the black-market stuff you haven't declared?

MONSIEUR SOUPEAU What's that? Are you accusing me of illegally hoarding gas? (*Furious*) Père Gustave, have we any illegal gas?
(*Père Gustave pretends not to hear and starts rolling his tire into the garage*)

MONSIEUR SOUPEAU (*shouting*) Maurice! Robert! Come down here this minute! Père Gustave! (*Père Gustave stops*) Speak up! Have we any illegal gas around here?

PÈRE GUSTAVE I don't know anything about it. (*To Simone, who is staring at him*) Attend to your work and stop listening to other people's business.

MONSIEUR SOUPEAU Maurice! Robert! Where are you!

MAYOR If you have no extra gas, what do you truck the captain's wine with?

MONSIEUR SOUPEAU You can't catch me with that one, monsieur le maire. I truck the captain's wine with the captain's gas. Georges, did you ever hear of my having any illegal gas?

GEORGES (*with a look at his arm*) I've only been back from the front for four days.

MONSIEUR SOUPEAU That's right, you wouldn't know. But there's Maurice and Robert. (*Maurice and Robert have entered*) Maurice and Robert! Monsieur Chavez has been accusing us of hiding gasoline. I ask you in the presence of Monsieur Chavez: is that true?

(*The brothers hesitate*)

MAYOR Maurice and Robert. You know me. I'm not a policeman, I don't like to meddle in other people's business. But France needs gasoline. I'm asking you to testify that there is gasoline here. You're decent young fellows.

MONSIEUR SOUPEAU Well?

MAURICE (*sullenly*) We never heard of any gas.

MAYOR So that's your answer. (*To Simone*) Your brother's at the front, isn't he? But I presume you won't tell me either that there's gas hidden here?

(*Simone stands motionless, then starts to cry*)

MONSIEUR SOUPEAU Oh, now you're asking children to give evidence against me? Monsieur le maire, you have no right to undermine this child's respect for her employer. (*To Simone*) Run along, Simone.

MAYOR (*wearily*) Sending some of your fraudulent food parcels to the schoolhouse? Robbing the refugees again? You only filled the soldiers' pot half full. How can the refugees get anywhere if they're robbed of their last sou all along the line?

MONSIEUR SOUPEAU This is a restaurant, not a charitable institution.

MAYOR I see. Only a miracle can save France. It's rotten to the core. (*He goes out. Silence*)

MONSIEUR SOUPEAU All right, Simone. Get going!

(*Simone goes out slowly and hesitantly toward the gate, repeatedly looking back. The book which she has hidden in the tray falls to the ground. She picks it up on the sly and goes out through the gate with her tray and baskets*)

Simone Machard's First Dream

The night of June 14.

Music. The angel emerges from the darkness. He stands on the garage roof. His face is golden and expressionless. In his hand he holds a small drum. Three times he cries out in a loud voice: "Joan!" Then the stage lights up. Simone is standing in the deserted yard with her wash basket on her arm, looking up at the angel.

THE ANGEL
Daughter of France, Joan: something must be done
Or our great France will perish before two weeks have run.
The Lord our God has looked around for aid
And now His eyes have fallen on His little Maid.
Here is a drum. God sends it. Beat it mightily
To shake the people from their lethargy.
But to be heard, you must set this drum upon the ground
As though to make the soil of France itself resound.
Now drum, and wake this people from its trance
Till rich and poor take pity on their mother France.
For shipping call on the bargemen of the Seine
On the peasants of Gironde to feed our fighting men.
For tanks you will go to the metal workers of Saint-Denis
And to pull the bridges down before the enemy
Round up the carpenters of Lyons. Tell them all
That France, the mother they have scoffed at, sends this call
That France the great toiler and wine drinker is in need
And peril. Go now and seek them out. Godspeed!

SIMONE (*looks around to see if anyone else is there*)   Do I
have to, monsieur? Aren't I too little to be a Saint Joan?
THE ANGEL   No.
SIMONE   Then I'll do it.
THE ANGEL   It will be hard. Leftit cribble clump.
SIMONE (*timidly*)   Are you my brother André?
(*The angel is silent*)
SIMONE   How are you getting along?

(*The angel disappears. But Georges comes sauntering out of the garage, bringing Simone his helmet and bayonet*)

GEORGES   Helmet and sword. You'll need them. It's not the job for you, but the boss hasn't got anybody but a cripple and a kid. Forget about your work; listen, the tanks are breaking through like meat choppers: no wonder your brother's already an angel.

SIMONE (*takes the helmet and bayonet*)   Should I clean them for you, Monsieur Georges?

GEORGES   No, you'll be needing them now that you're the Maid of Orleans.

SIMONE (*puts on the helmet*)   You're right. I've got to go to the king in Orleans right away. It's twenty miles, the tanks do fifty an hour, and my shoes are full of holes, I won't get new ones until Easter. (*Turns to go*) Would you wave to me as I go down the road, Monsieur Georges? I'll be afraid if you don't, war is old-fashioned, bloodthirsty stuff.

(*Georges tries to wave with his bandaged arm, and disappears. Simone starts on her way to Orleans, marching in a small circle*)

SIMONE (*sings loudly*)

On my way to Saint-Nazaire
I had lost my breeches.
All the people shouted loud:
"Where'd you put your breeches?"
I said: hard by Saint-Nazaire
Look, the sky is azure
And the oats are much too high
And the sky too azure.

(*Suddenly the truck drivers Maurice and Robert start trotting behind her, in overalls but with medieval weapons*)

SIMONE   What are you doing here? Why are you following me?

ROBERT   We're following you because we're your bodyguard. But kindly stop singing that song, it's indecent. We're betrothed to you, Joan, so be dignified.

SIMONE   Am I betrothed to Maurice too?

MAURICE   Yes, secretly.

(Père Gustave comes toward them in primitive medieval armor. He looks away and begins to pass them by)

SIMONE   Père Gustave!

PÈRE GUSTAVE   You leave me out of this. Expecting me to man guns at my age. Ridiculous! Live on tips and die for France!

SIMONE *(softly)*   But France, your mother, is in *danger*.

PÈRE GUSTAVE   My mother was Madame Poirot, the washer-woman. She was coming down with pneumonia. But what could I do? I had no money for all the medicines.

SIMONE *(shouting)*   Then I command you, in the name of God and the angel, to come back and take charge of the guns. *(In a kindlier tone)* I'll clean them for you.

PÈRE GUSTAVE   All right. That's something else again. Here, carry my pike. *(He gives her his pike and trots along with the others)*

MAURICE   How much farther is it, Simone? It's all for the capitalists anyway. Workers gobbie girl, belie! *(Simone also answers in a dream language unintelligible to the audience. She speaks with great force of conviction)*

MAURICE *(who has understood her)*   That's God's truth. All right, we'll keep going.

ROBERT   You're limping, Simone. That hardware is too heavy for you.

SIMONE *(suddenly exhausted)*   I'm sorry. It's only because I didn't get much breakfast. *(Stops and dries her sweat)* I'll be all right in a minute. Robert, do you remember what I'm supposed to say to the king?

ROBERT *(says something unintelligible in the dream language; then)*   That's all.

SIMONE   Of course. Thanks. Look, there are the towers of Orleans.

(The colonel enters in armor with the dust coat over it. He sneaks across the yard)

PÈRE GUSTAVE   A fine beginning. The marshals are leaving town, they're clearing out.

SIMONE   Why are the streets so empty, Père Gustave?

PÈRE GUSTAVE   I suppose they're all having supper.

SIMONE   And Père Gustave, why aren't they ringing the bells if the enemy's coming?

PÈRE GUSTAVE I suppose Captain Fétain has sent the bells to Bordeaux.

(*Monsieur Soupeau is standing in the entrance to the hostelry. He is wearing a helmet with a red plume and around his chest something of glittering steel*)

MONSIEUR SOUPEAU Joan, you're to take the fraudulent parcels to the schoolhouse this minute.

SIMONE But Monsieur Henri, France, our mother, is in danger. The Germans are on the Loire and I must speak to the king.

MONSIEUR SOUPEAU This is an outrage. I'm doing all I can. Don't forget the respect you owe to your employer. (*A man in a purple garment appears in the garage*)

SIMONE (*proudly*) Look, Monsieur Henri, there's King Charles VII. (*The man in purple proves to be the mayor, who is wearing the royal cloak over his suit*)

MAYOR Good morning, Joan.

SIMONE (*astonished*) Are you the king?

MAYOR Yes. I'm here on official business. I hereby confiscate the trucks. We wish to speak to you in private, Joan. (*The drivers, Père Gustave, and Monsieur Soupeau disappear in the darkness. Simone and the mayor sit down on the stone support of the gasoline pump*)

MAYOR Joan, it's all over. The marshal has gone off without leaving his address. I've written to the constable for guns, but my letter with the royal seal has been returned unopened. The master of the horse says he's been wounded in the arm, though no one has ever seen the wound. They're all rotten to the core. (*He weeps*) I know, you've come here to scold me, to tell me I'm a weakling. And so I am. But what about you, Joan? First of all I want you to tell me where that illegal gas is.

SIMONE In the brickyard, of course.

MAYOR I know I've been looking the other way. But you're robbing the refugees of their last sou with your fraudulent parcels.

SIMONE I do it because I have to keep a job for an angel, King Charles.

MAYOR And is it to keep their jobs that the drivers have been trucking Captain Fétain's wine instead of refugees?

SIMONE   Yes. And because the boss has registered them as indispensable to keep them out of the army.

MAYOR   Ah yes, my bosses and nobles. They're the ones that have given me my gray hairs. The nobility is against the king. It says so in your book. But you've got the people behind you, especially Maurice. Couldn't we make a pact, Joan, you and I?

SIMONE   Why not, King Charles? (*Hesitantly*) Only you've got to interfere with people's business activity and make sure the stew pots are always full.

MAYOR   I'll see what I can do. I've got to watch my step, though, or they'll cut off my royal salary. You see, I'm the man who looks the other way, so naturally when I say something nobody listens. I'm expected to do all the dirty work. Take those engineers. Instead of taking their rations from the hostelry by force, they come to me: "Repair your own bridges. We'll wait for our field kitchen." Is it any wonder that the duke of Burgundy deserts me and goes over to the English?

MONSIEUR SOUPEAU (*stands in the doorway*)   King Charles, I hear you're dissatisfied? Would you kindly stop to think of your civilian population? We've been bled white. Nobody feels for France more than I do, but . . . (*Gesture of helplessness; goes out*)

MAYOR (*with resignation*)   Then how do you expect us to defeat the English?

SIMONE   I'll just have to beat my drum. (*She sits down on the ground and beats her invisible drum. Every stroke resounds as though it came out of the earth*) Come on, you bargemen of the Seine! Come on, you metal workers of Saint-Denis. You carpenters of Lyons, come on. The enemy is coming.

MAYOR   What do you see, Joan?

SIMONE   They're coming. Stand fast, men. First comes the drummer with the voice of a wolf, *his* drum is made out of a Jew's skin; he's got a vulture on his shoulder, with the face of Fauche, the Lyons banker. Right behind him comes Field Marshal Firebug. He's on foot, a fat clown in seven uniforms, and he doesn't look human in any of them. It's easy to recognize the two devils, because there's a canopy of newspapers over them. Behind them ride the executioners and marshals. A swastika is branded on their low foreheads, and behind them as far as the eye can see come tanks and guns and railroad trains, and cars with altars on them and torture chambers, all very fast, on wheels. The battle wagons in the lead and behind them the loot wagons. The people get mowed down, but the grain gets gathered. Wherever they go, cities collapse, and every place they leave is a naked desert. But now they're done for, because here stand King Charles and the Maid of God, that's me.

(*All the Frenchmen who have appeared or will appear in the play have arrived, all with medieval weapons and odd pieces of armor*)

SIMONE (*radiant*)   See, King Charles, they've all come.

MAYOR   Not all, Joan. I don't see my mother Isabeau, for instance. And the constable has gone away in anger.

SIMONE   Don't be afraid. Now I must crown you king, then the whole French people will be united. I've brought you a crown. See?

(*She takes a crown out of the basket*)

MAYOR   But who am I going to play rummy with if the constable doesn't come back?

SIMONE   Ockal grisht burlap. (*Simone sets the crown on the king's head. In the background the engineers appear, pounding their stew pot with ladles and making a loud noise*)

MAYOR   What's that sound?

SIMONE   It's the bells of Rheims cathedral.

MAYOR   Isn't it the engineer troops that I sent to the hostelry for food?

SIMONE   They didn't get any. That's why their pots are empty. The empty pots are your coronation bells, King Charles.

MAYOR   Clidder dunk frim. Klemp!

ALL   Long live the king and Joan, the Maid, who has crowned him.

MAYOR   Many thanks, Simone. You have saved France.

(*The stage darkens. The voice of a radio announcer mingles with the confused music*)

2

The Handshake

It is early morning. Maurice and Robert, Père Gustave, and Georges are eating breakfast. The radio is heard from the hostelry.

RADIO   We repeat the war ministry bulletin issued at three-thirty this morning. Due to an unexpected crossing of the Loire by German tank formations the strategically important highways of central France have been swamped by new waves of refugees. The civilian population is requested to stay put, so the roads can be open for reinforcements.

MAURICE   It's time to get out of here.

GEORGES   The waiter and the rest of them cleared out at five; they'd worked all night packing the china. The boss threatened to call the police. It didn't do him any good.

ROBERT (*to Georges*)   Why didn't you wake us up?
   (*Georges is silent*)

MAURICE   The boss told you not to, eh? (*Laughs*)

ROBERT   Aren't you clearing out, Georges?

GEORGES   No. I'll take off my uniform and stay. They feed me here. I've given up hope of my arm getting better.
   (*Monsieur Soupeau comes bustling out of the hostelry. He is carefully dressed. Simone comes trotting behind him, carrying his suitcases*)

MONSIEUR SOUPEAU (*clapping his hands*)   Maurice, Robert, Gustave, get moving. The china has to be loaded. Everything in the storehouse goes into the trucks. Pack the hams in salt. But load the vintage wines first. You can have your coffee later, there's a war on. We're going to Bordeaux.
   (*The help go on with their breakfast. Maurice laughs*)

MONSIEUR SOUPEAU   What's the matter? Didn't you hear me? The trucks have got to be loaded.

MAURICE (*negligently*)   The trucks have been requisitioned.

MONSIEUR SOUPEAU   Requisitioned? Nonsense. (*With a grand gesture*) That was yesterday. The German tanks are heading for Saint-Martin. That changes everything. Yesterday's arrangements don't apply any more.

PÈRE GUSTAVE (*in an undertone*)   Right.

MONSIEUR SOUPEAU   Stop drinking when I'm talking to you. (*Simone has put the suitcase down and crept back into the hostelry*)

MAURICE   Let's have another coffee, Robert.

ROBERT   Right, how do we know when we'll eat again?

MONSIEUR SOUPEAU (*repressing his anger*)   Be reasonable. Help your boss pack his belongings. There's a tip in it for you. (*When no one looks up*) Père Gustave, come on now. Get started on the china. Well?

PÈRE GUSTAVE (*stands up hesitantly*)   I haven't finished my breakfast yet. Don't look at me like that. It won't do you any good now. (*Angrily*) You can stick your china up your ass for all I care. (*He sits down again*)

MONSIEUR SOUPEAU   Are you crazy, too? At *your* age? (*He looks from one to the other, then at the motorcycle; angrily*) So that's it? You're waiting for the Germans? Your boss is through? Is that the affection and respect you owe your employer? (*To the drivers*) Three times I've signed statements that you were indispensable to my trucking business; if I hadn't, you'd be at the front, and this is how you thank me. This is my reward for treating my help as if we were all one happy family. (*Over his shoulder*) Simone, get me some brandy! I feel weak. (*When there is no answer*) Simone, where are you?—Now she's gone too. (*Simone comes out of the hostelry, wearing a jacket, dressed to go out; she tries to sneak past Monsieur Soupeau*)

MONSIEUR SOUPEAU   Simone! (*Simone keeps going*)

MONSIEUR SOUPEAU   What, you won't answer me? Are you crazy? (*Simone starts to run and goes out. Monsieur Soupeau shrugs his shoulders and points at his forehead*)

GEORGES   What's got into Simone?

MONSIEUR SOUPEAU (*turns back to the truck drivers*)   So you refuse to obey orders?

MAURICE   Not at all. As soon as we've finished our breakfast, off we go.

MONSIEUR SOUPEAU   And the china?

MAURICE   We'll take it. If you'll load it.

MONSIEUR SOUPEAU   Me?

MAURICE   Yes, you. It's yours, isn't it?

ROBERT   Of course we can't guarantee that we'll get to Bordeaux, can we, Maurice?

MAURICE   Who can guarantee anything these days?

MONSIEUR SOUPEAU   This is an outrage. Do you know what will happen to you if you disobey orders in the face of the enemy? I'll have you shot right here, up against this wall! (*Simone's parents come in from the street*)

MONSIEUR SOUPEAU   What do *you* want?

MADAME MACHARD   Monsieur Soupeau, we've come on account of our Simone. We hear the Germans will be here soon and that you're leaving. Simone is a little girl, and Monsieur Machard is worried about the twenty francs.

MONSIEUR SOUPEAU   She's run away, God knows where.

GEORGES   Didn't she go home, Madame Machard?

MADAME MACHARD   No, Monsieur Georges.

GEORGES   That's funny.

(*The mayor comes in with two policemen. Simone is hiding behind them*)

MONSIEUR SOUPEAU   You've come at the right time, Philippe. (*With a grand gesture*) Philippe, I'm faced with rebellion. Do something.

MAYOR   Henri, Mademoiselle Machard has informed me that you're planning to abscond with your trucks. That is illegal. I shall use every means at my disposal to prevent it. Including the police. (*Points at the policemen*)

MONSIEUR SOUPEAU   Simone, you had the gall . . . ? Gentlemen, I employed this creature out of kindness for her family!

MADAME MACHARD (*shakes Simone*)   Now look what you've done! (*Simone is silent*)

MAURICE   I sent her.

MONSIEUR SOUPEAU   I see. And you took orders from Maurice?

MADAME MACHARD   Simone, how could you!

SIMONE   I wanted to help monsieur le maire, mother. They need our trucks.

MONSIEUR SOUPEAU   *Our* trucks!

SIMONE   (*growing confused*)   André's roads are clogged. (*Unable to continue*)   Please, monsieur le maire, you explain.

MAYOR   Henri, try to keep your selfishness within bounds. The child was right in calling me. At a time like this everything we own belongs to France. My sons are at the front and so is her brother. In other words, even our own sons don't belong to us.

MONSIEUR SOUPEAU   (*beside himself*)   So order has ceased to exist. Property doesn't exist any more. Why don't you give my hostelry to the Machards? Maybe my truck drivers here would like to help themselves to the contents of my safe? This is anarchy! Permit me to remind you, Monsieur Chavez, that my mother went to school with the prefect's wife. And there's still such a thing as a telephone.

MAYOR   (*weakening*)   Henri, I'm only doing my duty.

MONSIEUR SOUPEAU   Philippe, be reasonable. You talk about the property of France. What about my supplies, my precious china, my silverware? Aren't they the property of France? Do you want them to fall into the hands of the Germans? Not one coffee cup must fall into enemy hands, not one ham, not one can of sardines. Wherever they go they must find a desert. Have you forgotten that? You're the mayor. You should have come to me and said: Henri, it's your duty to safeguard your possessions from the Germans. And my answer would have been: Philippe, in that case I need my trucks.

(*The sound of a crowd is heard from the street. A bell rings in the hostelry, and there is pounding on one of the doors*)

MONSIEUR SOUPEAU   What's going on? Georges, go see what's going on. (*Georges goes into the hostelry*)   And to my staff, who have forgotten their duty so far as to leave my possessions in the lurch, you must say (*to the drivers*): Gentlemen, I appeal to you as Frenchmen. Go pack the china.

GEORGES   (*coming back*)   It's a crowd of people from the schoolhouse, Monsieur Henri. They heard the trucks were being sent away. They're all excited, they want to speak to the mayor.

MONSIEUR SOUPEAU (*turning pale*)   There you have it, Philippe. It's all Simone's fault. Quick, Georges, shut the gate. (*Georges goes to close the gate*) Quick, quick! Run!—This is the result of the agitation about my food parcels. The mob. (*To the policemen*) Do something! This minute! Philippe, you've got to phone for reinforcements, you owe me that. They'll kill me, Philippe. Help me! Please, Philippe.

MAYOR (*to the policemen*)   Guard the gate. (*To Monsieur Soupeau*) Nonsense, they won't hurt you. You heard him, they only want to talk to me. (*Since there is pounding on the gate*) Admit a delegation, not more than three.

(*The policemen open the gate a crack and talk with the crowd. Then they admit three people, two men and a woman with a babe in arms*)

MAYOR   What is it?

ONE OF THE REFUGEES (*excitedly*)   Monsieur le maire, we demand the trucks!

MONSIEUR SOUPEAU   Haven't you heard that the roads have to be kept clear?

THE WOMAN   For you? What do you want us to do? Wait here for the German bombers?

MAYOR (*to the refugees*)   Madame, messieurs, don't panic. It's all settled about the trucks. Monsieur Soupeau merely wants to save a few valuable possessions from the threat of enemy action.

THE WOMAN (*indignantly*)   You see? There you have it! They want to evacuate crates instead of people.

(*The sound of planes is heard*)

VOICES (*from outside*)   Stukas!

MONSIEUR SOUPEAU   They're diving.

(*The noise grows deafening. The planes have dived. All throw themselves on the ground*)

MONSIEUR SOUPEAU (*when the planes have gone*)   That's dangerous. I've got to get out of here.

VOICES (*from outside*)   Give us the trucks!—Do they want us all to be killed?

MONSIEUR SOUPEAU   They're not loaded yet! Philippe!

SIMONE (*angrily*)   This is no time to think of your supplies!

MONSIEUR SOUPEAU (*flabbergasted*) How dare you, Simone!

SIMONE Why not give the food to the people?

THE REFUGEE Oh, it's food? It's food they want to load in the trucks?

MAURICE That's right.

THE WOMAN And we couldn't even get soup this morning.

MAURICE It's not the Germans he wants to save his supplies from. It's the French.

THE WOMAN (*runs back to the gate*) Open up! (*When the policemen hold her back, she shouts over the wall*) It's the hotel's food supplies that's going in the trucks!

MONSIEUR SOUPEAU Philippe! Don't let her broadcast that.

VOICES (*from outside*) They're evacuating the food supplies! —Break down the gate!—Aren't there any men here?— They're taking away the food and they're leaving us for the German tanks!

(*The refugees break through the gate. The mayor goes toward them*)

MAYOR Messieurs, mesdames, no violence! Everything will be straightened out.

(*While the mayor argues by the gate, a violent dispute arises in the yard. Two main groups form. On the one side Monsieur Soupeau, one of the male refugees, the woman refugee, and Simone's parents. On the other side, Simone, the two truck drivers, the second refugee, and Père Gustave. Georges does not take part, but goes on with his breakfast*)

(*Unnoticed, old Madame Soupeau has come out of the hostelry. She is very old, dressed all in black*)

THE WOMAN There's still at least eighty people without transportation.

MONSIEUR SOUPEAU You're taking your bundles, madame. Why should I leave everything behind? They're my trucks, aren't they?

MAYOR How much space

SIMONE You know the roads. You can go around the back way so's to leave Route 20 clear for the troops.

ROBERT What makes you think we're going to drive his supplies through the flood for him?

do you need, Monsieur Soupeau?

MONSIEUR SOUPEAU Enough for at least sixty crates. There'll be room for about thirty refugees in the other truck.

THE WOMAN So you want to leave fifty of us behind. Is that it?

MAYOR Let's say you'll manage with half a truck. Then at least there'll be room for the children and sick people.

THE WOMAN Do you want to break up families? You wicked man!

MONSIEUR SOUPEAU Eight or ten of them can sit on the crates. (*To Madame Machard*) Your daughter's to blame for all this.

THE WOMAN The child has more heart than the whole lot of you put together.

MADAME MACHARD You must forgive our Simone, Monsieur Henri. She got these ideas from her brother. It's dreadful.

SIMONE But you'll take the children and sick people?

ROBERT Refugees—that's something else again.

PÈRE GUSTAVE You keep out of this, Simone. That's my advice to you.

SIMONE But our fair France is in danger, Père Gustave.

PÈRE GUSTAVE She got that out of that damn book! "Is our fair France not in danger?"

ROBERT Here comes Madame Soupeau. She wants you.
(*Simone goes over to Madame Soupeau*)

THE WOMAN (*to the crowd in the doorway*) Why don't we take the trucks and the food too?

MADAME SOUPEAU Here's the key, Simone. Let the people take all the food they want. Père Gustave, Georges, give them a hand.

MAYOR (*in a loud voice*) Bravo, Madame Soupeau!

MONSIEUR SOUPEAU Mother, how can you? What are you doing down here anyway? You'll catch your death in this draft. There are vintage wines and 70,000 francs worth of supplies in the cellars.

MADAME SOUPEAU (*to the mayor*) The township is free to use them as it sees fit. (*To Monsieur Soupeau, coldly*) Would you rather have looting?

SIMONE (*to the woman with the baby*) There's going to be food for you.

MADAME SOUPEAU Simone! At your suggestion, my son has just made all the hostelry's food supplies available to the township. That leaves only the china and silverware, which won't take up much room. Will somebody load them for us?

THE WOMAN What about room for us in the trucks?

MADAME SOUPEAU Madame, we'll take as many of you as possible, and as for those who are left behind, the hostelry will be honored to feed them.

A REFUGEE (*calling out toward the gate*) Gaston! Would the old Creveux couple and the Meuniers stay behind if they're fed?

SHOUT FROM OUTSIDE Maybe they would, Jean!

THE WOMAN Hey, if they'll feed us, I'd like to stay myself.

MADAME SOUPEAU You'll be welcome.

MAYOR (*in the gateway*) Messieurs, mesdames, help yourselves. The hostelry's supplies are yours.

(*A few of the refugees go hesitantly into the storehouse*)

MADAME SOUPEAU And bring us a few bottles of brandy, Simone, the 1884 Martell.

SIMONE Yes, madame. (*She motions to the refugees and goes with them, Père Gustave, and Georges into the storehouse*)

MONSIEUR SOUPEAU Mother, this is going to be the death of me.

ONE OF THE REFUGEES (*drags out a crate with Georges; in high spirits parodies a market crier*) Fruit, ham, chocolate! Provisions for your trip! Absolutely free of charge!

MONSIEUR SOUPEAU (*looking indignantly at the cans that the refugees and Georges are carrying across the yard to the gate*) But those are delicacies! That's foie gras!

MADAME SOUPEAU (*under her breath*) Shut up! (*To the refugee, politely*) I hope you enjoy it, monsieur. (*With Père

Gustave's help the other refugee hauls baskets of food across the yard)

MONSIEUR SOUPEAU (*lamenting*) My Pommard 1915. And that's caviar. And this is . . .

MAYOR This is a time for making sacrifices, Henri. (*In a choked voice*) We must let our hearts speak.

MAURICE (*imitating Monsieur Soupeau's outcry*) "My Pommard!" (*Laughing uproariously, slaps Simone on the back*) Just for that I'll load your china for you, Simone.

MONSIEUR SOUPEAU (*offended*) I fail to see what's so funny. (*Pointing at the vanishing baskets*) This is looting.

ROBERT (*good-naturedly with a basket*) Don't let it get you down, Monsieur Henri. We'll load your china to make up for it.

MADAME SOUPEAU It's a deal. (*She picks up some cans and bottles of wine and takes them to Simone's parents*) Here. You have some too. And get glasses for your parents, Simone. (*Simone does so; then she gets a stool, puts it down by the wall and hands provisions from a basket to the refugees on the other side of the wall*)

MADAME SOUPEAU Maurice, Robert, Père Gustave, go get yourselves glasses. (*Pointing to the policemen*) I see that the law is already served. (*To the woman with the baby*) Won't you join us in a drink, madame? (*To all*) Mesdames, messieurs, I propose a toast to our fair France.

MONSIEUR SOUPEAU (*standing alone and excluded*) What about me? Are you going to drink a toast to France without me?

(*He pours himself a glass and joins the group*)

MAYOR (*to Madame Soupeau*) In the name of the township of Saint-Martin, I wish to thank the hostelry for its generosity. (*He raises his glass*) To France and to the future.

GEORGES But where's Simone?

(*Simone is still busy handing provisions over the wall to the refugees*)

MAYOR Simone!

(*Simone is flushed. She approaches hesitantly*)

MADAME SOUPEAU Go get a glass, Simone. All of use here owe you a debt of gratitude.

(*All drink*)

MONSIEUR SOUPEAU (*to the drivers*) Are we friends again?
Did you think I objected to transporting refugees in my
trucks? Maurice and Robert, I like to get my own way, but
I respect noble motives when I see them. I'm willing to admit a mistake. You do the same. Let's forget our little personal differences and stand together, shoulder to shoulder,
against the common enemy. Shake on it.

(*He begins with Robert, who gives him his hand with a
sheepish grin; next Georges gives him his left hand. Then
Monsieur Soupeau embraces the woman with the baby.
Grumbling, still angry, Père Gustave gives him his hand.
Finally, Monsieur Soupeau turns to Maurice, who, however,
makes no move to give him his hand*)

MONSIEUR SOUPEAU Oh la la. Are we Frenchmen, or aren't
we?

SIMONE (*reproachfully*) Maurice!

MAURICE (*hesitantly giving Monsieur Soupeau his hand; ironically*) Long live our new St. Joan, come to unite the
French people.

(*Monsieur Machard gives Simone a slap in the face*)

MADAME MACHARD (*explains*) That's for your obstinacy, for
disobeying your employer.

MONSIEUR SOUPEAU (*to Machard*) Don't, monsieur. (*He puts
his arms around Simone consolingly*) Simone is my pet, madame. I've got a weakness for her. (*To the drivers*) But
come on, boys, let's start loading. I'm sure Monsieur Machard will help us.

MAYOR (*to his policemen*) How about you fellows giving
monsieur a hand?

MONSIEUR SOUPEAU (*bows to the woman with the baby*)
Madame!

(*The group breaks up, the crowd outside also drifts away.
Only Monsieur Soupeau, the mayor, Madame Soupeau,
Simone, the two truck drivers, and Georges remain on the
stage*)

MONSIEUR SOUPEAU Friends, I wouldn't have missed that for
anything. Damn the caviar and the Pommard. I'm for unity.

MAURICE   What about the brickyard?

MAYOR (*cautiously*)   That's right, Henri. Something's got to be done about the brickyard.

MONSIEUR SOUPEAU (*distressed*)   What? What more do you want? All right, send any trucks that are out of gas to the brickyard. They can fill up. Now are you satisfied?

ROBERT   In Abbeville the German tanks got their gas from the filling stations. That's why they get ahead so fast.

GEORGES   Our 132nd had tanks on its tail before they had time to look around. They made mincemeat out of two regiments.

SIMONE (*frightened*)   But not the Seventh?

GEORGES   No, not the Seventh.

MAYOR   Gasoline stocks have to be destroyed, Henri.

MONSIEUR SOUPEAU   Aren't you in a bit too much of a hurry? We can't destroy everything just like that. Maybe we'll throw the enemy back. What do you say, Simone? Tell Monsieur Chavez that France isn't lost yet, not by a long shot. (*To Madame Soupeau*) And now good-bye, mother. I hate to leave you here. (*Kisses her*) But Simone will be a great help to you. Good-bye, Simone. I'm not ashamed to thank you. You're a real Frenchwoman. (*Kisses her*) As long as you're here, nothing will fall into the hands of the Germans, I can be sure of that. I want the whole place stripped bare, understand? I know you'll carry out my wishes. Good-bye, Philippe, old man. (*Embraces him, picks up his bags. Simone wants to help him, he waves her away*) Never mind. Have a talk with mother, decide what to do about our supplies.

(*Goes out in the direction of the street*)

SIMONE (*runs after the two truck drivers*)   Maurice, Robert. (*She kisses them both on their cheeks. Then finally Maurice and Robert go out too*)

VOICE OF THE RADIO ANNOUNCER   Attention! Attention! German tank formations have reached Tours. (*The announcement is repeated several times until the end of the scene*)

MAYOR (*pale, beside himself*)   Then we can expect them here by tonight.

MADAME SOUPEAU   Don't be such an old woman, Philippe.

SIMONE   Madame, I'll run over to the brickyard with Père Gustave and Georges. We'll destroy the gasoline.

MADAME SOUPEAU   You've heard your employer's orders. He told us not to be in too much of a hurry. You must leave certain decisions to us, my dear.

SIMONE   But madame, Maurice says the Germans go so fast.

MADAME SOUPEAU   That will do, Simone. (*Turns to go*) There's a nasty draft here. (*To the mayor*) Thank you, Philippe, for all you've done for the hostelry today. (*In the doorway*) Besides, Simone, now that they're all gone, I'll probably close the hostelry. Give me the key to the storehouse. (*Simone, stunned, gives her the key*) I think you'd better go home to your parents. I've been satisfied with you.

SIMONE (*does not understand*)   But can't I help when the people from the town hall come to get supplies?

(*Without a word Madame Soupeau goes into the hostelry*)

SIMONE (*after a silence, haltingly*)   Have I been fired, monsieur le maire?

MAYOR (*comfortingly*)   I'm afraid so. But you mustn't feel badly. You heard her say she was satisfied with you. Coming from her, that means a good deal, Simone.

SIMONE (*tonelessly*)   Yes, monsieur le maire.

(*The mayor goes out dejectedly*)
(*Simone looks after him*)

Simone Machard's Second Dream

The night of June 15.

Confused, festive music. A waiting group emerges from the darkness: the mayor in his royal cloak, Monsieur Soupeau and the colonel, both in armor and with marshal's batons; the colonel is wearing his dust coat over his armor.

COLONEL   Our Joan has now taken Orleans and Rheims after clearing Route 20 for our advancing troops. She must be suitably honored, that much is plain.

MAYOR   I, the king, will see to that, monsieur. The dignitaries and great families of France, who are to assemble here to-day, will bow down to the ground before her.

(*From now until the end of the scene the titles and names of France's dignitaries and leading families are called out backstage, as though they were assembling*)

MAYOR   By the way, I hear she's been fired? (*Discreetly*) At the behest of the queen mother, the proud Queen Isabeau, so I hear.

MONSIEUR SOUPEAU   I don't know anything about that, I wasn't there. If you ask me, it's not right. She's my pet. I say she stays.

(*The mayor says something unintelligible, apparently evasive, in the dream language*)

COLONEL   Here she comes.

(*Simone strides in with sword and helmet, preceded by her bodyguard, consisting of Maurice, Robert, and Georges. The three are in armor. From the darkness have emerged Simone's parents and the staff of the hostelry: "the people." The bodyguard pushes the people back with long pikes*)

ROBERT   Make way for the Maid.

MADAME MACHARD (*craning her neck*)   It's her. That helmet looks pretty good on her.

MAYOR (*steps forward*)   Dear Joan, what can we do for you? Tell me your wishes.

SIMONE (*with a bow*)   My first request, King Charles, is to go on feeding my beloved native town with the hostelry's supplies. You know I've been sent to help the poor and needy. Their taxes must be remitted.

MAYOR   That goes without saying. What else?

SIMONE   In the second place, Paris must be taken. The second campaign must begin at once, King Charles.

MONSIEUR SOUPEAU (*astonished*)   A second campaign?

COLONEL   What will old Madame Soupeau, the proud Queen Isabeau, say to that?

SIMONE   You must give me an army, King Charles, with which to defeat the enemy completely before the year is out.

MAYOR (*smiling*)   Dear Joan, we are very well satisfied with

you. Coming from us, that means a good deal. That will do.
You must leave certain decisions to us. I shall now close the
hostelry, and you will go home. But first of course you will
be ennobled. Give me your sword, I've mislaid mine, and I
shall dub you a lady of France.

SIMONE (*gives him the sword and kneels*) Here's the key.
(*Confused music, organ and chorus, indicates festive church
rites in the distance*)
(*The mayor solemnly touches Simone's shoulder with the
sword*)

BODYGUARD AND PEOPLE Long live the Maid! Long live the
great lady of France!

SIMONE (*when the mayor starts to leave*) Just a minute, King
Charles. Don't forget to give me back my sword. (*Urgently*) The English haven't been defeated yet, the Burgundians are raising a new army, more formidable than the first.
The hardest is yet to come.

MAYOR Many thanks for the offer. And many thanks for
everything else, Joan. (*Gives Simone's sword to Monsieur
Soupeau*) Take it to Bordeaux, Henri, there it will be safe.
We for our part must now have a confidential talk with
Madame Soupeau, the proud Queen Isabeau. Farewell, Joan,
it has been a pleasure! (*Goes out with Monsieur Soupeau
and the colonel*)

SIMONE (*in terror*) But the enemy's coming, don't you see!
(*The music sinks to a murmur, the light grows dim, the
people vanish in the darkness*)

SIMONE (*stands motionless. Then*) André! Help! Archangel,
come down! Speak to me! The English are raising an army,
the Burgundians have turned traitor, and our men are running away.

THE ANGEL (*appears on the garage roof; reproachfully*)
Where is your sword, Joan?

SIMONE (*confused, apologetically*) They dubbed me a noble
lady with it and they never gave it back. (*Softly, ashamed*)
I've been fired.

THE ANGEL I see. (*After a silence*) Maid of France, don't let

them send you away. Hold out. France wishes it. Don't go
back to your parents yet, they'd eat their hearts out about
your being fired. Besides, you promised to keep your
brother's job in the garage for him; because one day he'll
be coming back. Stay, Joan. How can you leave your post
when the enemy may burst in from one minute to the next?

SIMONE   Should we go on fighting if the enemy has already
won?

THE ANGEL   Is the night wind blowing?

SIMONE   Yes.

THE ANGEL   Isn't there a tree in the yard?

SIMONE   Yes, the poplar.

THE ANGEL   Do its leaves rustle when the wind blows?

SIMONE   Oh yes.

THE ANGEL   Then you should fight, even if the enemy has
won.

SIMONE   But how can I fight when I have no sword?

THE ANGEL

Hark:
When the conqueror comes to your town or village
Let there be nothing left for him to pillage.
Let no one give him a key
He's vermin, not company.
Let there be nothing for him to feed on
No chair to sit on and no bed to sleep on.
Hide what you cannot burn. Bury the bread and meat
Pour out the milk, let the dearth be complete.
Let him curse his fate, for Monster is his name
Let him eat earth and dwell in flame.
Let there be no court where he can plead
For mercy; let your city be gone, demolished, dead.
Let him find emptiness at every step. Let it be
As though there had never been a hostelry.
Go forth and destroy.
(*The stage grows dark. Confused music. Intermittently one
hears the angel's soft but insistent "Go forth and destroy"
and, very distinctly, the rumble of heavy tanks*)

3

The Fire

(a)

Old Madame Soupeau all in black, and behind her Thérèse the chambermaid and Père Gustave wearing his Sunday suit, are waiting in the gateway for the German captain. Georges, now in civilian clothes, is leaning against the garage wall. Simone is inside the garage hiding from Madame Soupeau and listening to him. The clanking of passing tanks is heard from outside.

SIMONE She's as white as a sheet. She's scared.

GEORGES She thinks they'll arrest her as a hostage and shoot her. She's been having fits all night. Thérèse heard her screaming: "The butchers will kill us all." But that didn't keep her from staying here, it's her greed, and now she's waiting for the German captain—I really don't understand why you don't want her to see you. Is anything wrong?

SIMONE (*lying*) No, no. Except she'd send me away if she saw me. For fear the Germans might hurt me.

GEORGES (*suspiciously*) Is that the only reason you don't want her to see you?

SIMONE (*changing the subject*) Do you think the Germans have caught up with Maurice and Robert?

GEORGES Maybe.—Say, why have you moved out of your room upstairs?

SIMONE (*lying*) There's room for me in the storehouse now that the drivers have gone away.—Do you think André will be coming back soon?

GEORGES Probably.—She hasn't fired you, Simone?

SIMONE (*lying*) No.

GEORGES Here come the Germans.

(*The German captain comes in from the street, accompanied*

by Captain Fétain. In the gateway Madame Soupeau ex-
changes polite greetings with the two officers. Their conver-
sation cannot be heard)

GEORGES   The captain and secret fascist has the honor of introducing the enemy to madame. All too polite for words.
They're sniffing, they don't seem to dislike each other's
smell. The enemy is a gentleman. Madame seems enormously
relieved. (*Whispers*) They're coming.

(Simone steps back. Madame Soupeau leads the two officers
across the yard to the hostelry; Thérèse the chambermaid
follows)

PÈRE GUSTAVE   (*to whom Madame Soupeau has whispered*
something, goes over to Georges and Simone)   Madame
doesn't want the mob from the schoolhouse in the hostelry
any more. The German officers might not like it. But it
looks as if the boss could just as well have stayed.

GEORGES   The first thing they announced over the radio was:
"No one who observes law and order has anything to fear."

PÈRE GUSTAVE   The one in there says "please" when he wants
something. "Please show my orderly my rooms."

SIMONE   He's the enemy all the same.

(Père Gustave goes out into the storehouse)

GEORGES   Has your cousin had another dream?

SIMONE   Yes, last night.

GEORGES   About the Maid again?

SIMONE   (*nods*)   They dubbed her a lady.

GEORGES   That must have been a big thing for her.

SIMONE   Her native place has had its taxes remitted, the same
as in the book.

GEORGES   (*rather harshly*)   But actually the hostelry's supplies
are not being distributed to the people, as promised.

SIMONE   (*flustered*)   My cousin didn't say anything about that.

GEORGES   Oh.

SIMONE   Monsieur Georges. If in a dream like my cousin has
now and then a certain person appears as an angel—does it
mean the person must be dead?

GEORGES   I don't think so. It probably just means that the
dreamer is afraid this person might be dead.—Tell me, what
more is your cousin expected to do?

SIMONE   Lots of things.

GEORGES   Did something bad happen in the dream?

SIMONE   Why?

GEORGES   Because you're telling me so little.

SIMONE (*slowly*)   No, nothing bad.

GEORGES   I'm asking, Simone, because it seems to me now and then that another person might take these dreams seriously and forget that we're living in broad daylight and not in a dream.

SIMONE (*violently*)   Then I won't talk about my cousin's dreams with you any more, Monsieur Georges.
(*The woman with the baby and another refugee from the schoolhouse come into the yard*)

SIMONE   They're coming for food. Tell them nicely, Monsieur Georges. (*She hides and looks on*)

GEORGES (*steps forward*)   Madame.

THE WOMAN   The tanks are here.

THE MAN   There are three of them outside the town hall.

THE WOMAN   Big ones. Twenty feet long.

THE MAN (*indicating the German sentry*)   Watch out!

MADAME SOUPEAU (*steps into the doorway of the hostelry*)   Georges! Père Gustave. Take the hors d'oeuvres to the breakfast room for the Herr Hauptmann.—What have you come for?

THE WOMAN   We've come to see about the food, madame. There are twenty-one people left in the schoolhouse.

MADAME SOUPEAU   Georges, didn't I tell you to keep beggars out of the hostelry?

THE MAN   What do you mean, beggars?

MADAME SOUPEAU   Why haven't you told these people that from now on they'll be dealing with the German commandant and not with us? Those happy days are over.

THE WOMAN   You want us to tell that to the people in the schoolhouse after we advised them all to stay here so you could send your china away?

MADAME SOUPEAU   Madame, I wouldn't start denouncing people if I were you.

THE WOMAN   Madame, don't hide behind the Germans.

MADAME SOUPEAU (*calls over her shoulder*)   Honoré!

THE WOMAN   Me and my baby could have been in Bordeaux with my sister by now. You promised to feed us, madame.

MADAME SOUPEAU   I was blackmailed into it, madame.

CAPTAIN FÉTAIN (*coming up behind her*)   The place was being looted, neither more nor less! But now, my friends, there's going to be order and discipline around here. (*Motioning toward the German sentries*) Do you want me to have you driven out of here with bayonets? Don't get worked up, Marie; remember your heart.

THE WOMAN   You bastards!

THE MAN (*holds her back and leads her away*)   Madame, this won't last forever.

MADAME SOUPEAU   It's beginning to stink of sewage around here. The gutters of the northern cities are pouring their rats into our peaceful villages. We're getting the riffraff from their cheap wine rooms. They'll have to pay for this, in blood. Père Gustave, breakfast for four.

CAPTAIN FÉTAIN (*to Georges*)   Hey you! The mayor will be coming here. Tell him I want to speak to him before he sees the Herr Hauptmann. (*He leads Madame Soupeau back into the hostelry*)

(*When the two are gone, Simone runs after the refugees*)

GEORGES   Père Gustave! The hors d'oeuvres for the Herr Hauptmann.

PÈRE GUSTAVE'S VOICE (*from the storehouse*)   I heard you. Nothing's too good for the Herr Hauptmann.

(*Simone comes back out of breath*)

GEORGES   What did you say to them?

SIMONE   To tell the people in the schoolhouse that they'll get their food. I'll take it to them tonight.

GEORGES   Yes, you've still got the key.

SIMONE   It was promised to them.

GEORGES   Just be very careful. That's theft.

SIMONE   Didn't the boss say: "As long as you're here, Simone, nothing will fall into the hands of the Germans, I can be sure of that"?

GEORGES   But now his mother's singing a different tune.

SIMONE   Maybe they're forcing her.

(*The mayor appears in the gateway*)

SIMONE (*rushes up to him; in a whisper*) Monsieur le maire, what's going to happen now?

MAYOR What do you think, Simone? I have good news for you: at my suggestion your father's being taken on as bailiff. You've deserved it, Simone. Now it won't matter that you lost your job.

SIMONE (*in a whisper*) Monsieur le maire, is it true that there are three tanks outside the town hall? (*Still more softly*) The gas is still there.

MAYOR (*absently*) Yes, that's bad. (*Suddenly*) But Simone, why are you still here?

SIMONE Something has to be done about the gas, monsieur le maire. Can't you do something? They're sure to ask Madame Soupeau for it.

MAYOR I don't think we have to worry about Madame Soupeau, Simone.

SIMONE I could do something. I know my way around the brickyard.

MAYOR (*vaguely*) I hope you're not thinking of doing anything foolish, Simone. I've got a great responsibility for the town of Saint-Martin. Do you understand?

SIMONE Yes, monsieur le maire.

MAYOR I don't know why I'm talking to you like this. You're still a child, Simone. But I think each one of us has to do his best. Don't you?

SIMONE Oh yes, monsieur le maire. If the brickyard were to burn down . . .

MAYOR Good God! You mustn't even think of such things. But now I have to go in. This is the hardest thing I've done in all my life. (*He starts to go in*)
(*Captain Fétain comes out*)

CAPTAIN FÉTAIN Monsieur Chavez. You're just in time for breakfast.

MAYOR I've had my breakfast.

CAPTAIN FÉTAIN That's unfortunate. You don't quite seem to understand. A good many unpleasant things happened here yesterday, with the connivance of the authorities. It is regrettable that no immediate measures were taken to stop the shameless attempts of certain elements to exploit the downfall of France for their own advantage. The least our German guests can expect is a polite gesture from us. The German commandant, for instance, has already been informed about certain supplies that are stored in a brickyard. Maybe you ought to take that into account, Chavez. Maybe that will improve your appetite? After you, monsieur le maire.

MAYOR (*very unsure of himself*) After you, mon capitaine.
(*The two go into the hostelry. Père Gustave comes out of the storehouse and follows them*)

PÈRE GUSTAVE (*going in with the hors d'oeuvres*) Fair weather and happy journey! Rich birds flock together, eh, Georges? They're selling France the same as they sell their wine and hors d'oeuvres! (*Goes out*)
(*Simone has followed the last exchange. She has sat down*)

GEORGES Simone! What's the matter with you? Simone!
(*Simone does not answer. Georges stands rigidly, preserving the gesture with which he has tried to shake her into consciousness. During Simone's daydream, Père Gustave's "Rich birds flock together" is repeated mechanically and more faintly*)

Simone Machard's Daydream

On June 20.

Confused martial music. The back wall of the hostelry becomes transparent. Before an enormous tapestry the mayor as King Charles, Captain Fétain as the duke of Burgundy, the German captain with his sword across his knees as the English general, and Madame Soupeau as Queen Isabeau are seated playing belote on a marble table.

MADAME SOUPEAU I wish to see the mob no more, my lord.
GERMAN CAPTAIN Hide behind us, Queen Isabeau. I'll have them all cleared out of the yard. Then we'll have order. My trick.
MAYOR Hark! Do I hear the sound of drums?
(*Joan's drum is heard in the distance*)

CAPTAIN FÉTAIN   I hear nothing. Play your ace of clubs.
   (*The drumming stops*)

MAYOR (*doubtfully*)   No? Duke of Burgundy, I'm afraid my
   Joan is in trouble and needs help.

CAPTAIN FÉTAIN   Ten of hearts. I need peace, so I can sell my
   wines.

GERMAN CAPTAIN   What is the price of your hors d'oeuvres,
   madame?

MADAME SOUPEAU   Whose deal? Ten thousand pieces of silver,
   my lord.

MAYOR   This time I'm sure. She must be in danger, mortal
   danger. I must hasten to her help and destroy everything.
   (*He stands up with his cards in hand*)

CAPTAIN FÉTAIN   I should be careful if I were you. If you go
   now, it's the last time. You don't understand. How can we
   play if we're disturbed all the time? Jack of clubs.

MAYOR (*sits down again*)   Very well.

MADAME SOUPEAU (*slaps him in the face*)   That's for being so
   independent.

GERMAN CAPTAIN   By your leave, Queen Isabeau. (*He lays
   coins down on the table*) One, two, three . . .

   (*Georges shakes Simone out of her daydream, while the
   German captain goes on counting*)

GEORGES   Simone! Now you're dreaming with your eyes open.

SIMONE   Will you come, Monsieur Georges?

GEORGES (*stares at his bandaged arm; joyfully*)   Simone, I
   can move it again.

SIMONE   That's good. But we have to go to the brickyard,
   Monsieur Georges. We haven't got much time. Père Gustave, you come too. Quick.

PÈRE GUSTAVE (*coming back out of the hostelry*)   Me?
   They've put up a notice: Anyone destroying essential war
   material will be shot. They mean business.

SIMONE   The mayor wants us to.

PÈRE GUSTAVE   The mayor's an asshole.

SIMONE   But you'll come, Monsieur Georges? It's for André.

I wouldn't know how to destroy all that gas. Will we have to set fire to the whole brickyard?

GEORGES   Don't you understand? I can move it again.

SIMONE (*looks at him*)   So you won't come?

PÈRE GUSTAVE   Here comes another one.

(*A German soldier comes into the yard, hauling baggage. As soon as she sees him, Simone runs away in a fright*)

THE GERMAN SOLDIER (*throws down the baggage; he is in a sweat. He lifts his steel helmet and, taking a friendly attitude, tries to communicate with gestures*)   Hauptmann? Inside?

GEORGES (*with gestures*)   In there. In the hostelry. Cigarette?

THE GERMAN SOLDIER (*takes the cigarette and grins*)   War— merde. (*Gesture of shooting, disparaging wave of the hand*)

GEORGES (*laughing*)   Boom boom. (*Farts with his lips, both laugh*)

THE GERMAN SOLDIER   Hauptmann—asshole.

GEORGES   What's that?

THE GERMAN SOLDIER   (*mimes the German captain with the monocle*)   Merde.

GEORGES (*understands. Happily mimes Captain Fétain and Madame Soupeau*)   All merde.

(*They laugh again, then the German soldier takes the baggage and goes in*)

GEORGES (*to Père Gustave*)   Oh la la, wouldn't it be easy for us to understand each other?

PÈRE GUSTAVE   Better watch your step.

GEORGES   Don't worry. Now that my arm is mending.

(*The German captain, Captain Fétain, the mayor, and Madame Soupeau come out of the hostelry*)

CAPTAIN FÉTAIN   Herr Hauptmann, I am glad to see that we understand each other so well.

GERMAN CAPTAIN   Madame, I wish to thank you for voluntarily offering us your gasoline. Not that the Wehrmacht needs it. But we accept your offer, because it demonstrates your good will and desire to cooperate.

MADAME SOUPEAU   It's not far to the brickyard.

GERMAN CAPTAIN   I'll send the tanks.

(*The sky has turned red. The group freezes into immobility.*

Explosions in the distance)

GERMAN CAPTAIN   What's that?

CAPTAIN FÉTAIN (*in a hoarse voice*)   The brickyard.

(b)

It is night. Pounding on the gate. Georges comes out of his room and opens for Monsieur Soupeau and the two drivers.

MONSIEUR SOUPEAU   How's it going, Georges? Is mother all right? Looks like the place is still standing. I feel like after the Flood. Hello, Simone.
(*Simone enters scantily dressed from the drivers' room. Robert hugs her. Père Gustave has also appeared*)

ROBERT   Have you been making yourself at home in our room? (*He dances around with her, singing in an undertone*)
Jo the strangler came back home
Rosa was still there
Mama had a green chartreuse
And Papa had a beer.

MONSIEUR SOUPEAU   What's been going on?

GEORGES   We've got a German captain here. Madame Soupeau's kind of tired from the investigation about the brickyard. The German captain . . .

MONSIEUR SOUPEAU   What investigation?

SIMONE   Monsieur Henri, everything has been done the way you wanted it. And last night I managed to take some food to the schoolhouse.

MONSIEUR SOUPEAU   I asked about the brickyard.

GEORGES (*hesitantly*)   It's burned down, Monsieur Henri.

MONSIEUR SOUPEAU   Burned down?—The Germans? (*Georges shakes his head*) An accident? (*He looks from one to the other. No answer*) Orders from town hall?

GEORGES   No.

MONSIEUR SOUPEAU   The scum from the schoolhouse?

GEORGES   No, Monsieur Henri.

MONSIEUR SOUPEAU Then it was arson. (*Bellowing as if his foot had been cut off*) Who did it? (*No one answers*) Aha, you're all in it together. (*In cold rage*) So now you've started committing crimes? Isn't that nice? I might have expected it after the proofs of gratitude you gave me on my last day here. "You can stick your china up your ass" —remember, Père Gustave? All right, I'll take up the challenge. We'll see.

GEORGES It was on account of the Germans, Monsieur Henri.

MONSIEUR SOUPEAU (*sarcastically*) I see. It so happens it was my brickyard, but you set it on fire to spite the Germans. In other words, you were so blinded by hate, so intent on destruction, that you slaughtered the cow that gave you milk. (*abruptly*) Simone!

SIMONE Yes, monsieur.

MONSIEUR SOUPEAU Tell me this instant who did it.

SIMONE Me, monsieur.

MONSIEUR SOUPEAU What? You dared . . . ? (*Clutches her arm*) Who told you? Who was behind it?

SIMONE Nobody, monsieur.

MONSIEUR SOUPEAU Don't lie! I won't stand for . . .

GEORGES Please, Monsieur Henri, leave her alone. She's not lying.

MONSIEUR SOUPEAU Who told you to do it?

SIMONE I did it for my brother, monsieur.

MONSIEUR SOUPEAU Ah, André! So he incited you against your employer? "We underdogs," is that it? I always knew he was a Red. Who helped you?

SIMONE Nobody, monsieur.

MONSIEUR SOUPEAU But why did you do it?

SIMONE On account of the gasoline, sir.

MONSIEUR SOUPEAU And for that you had to set fire to the whole brickyard? Why didn't you just open the taps?

SIMONE I didn't know, Monsieur Henri.

GEORGES She's a child, Monsieur Henri.

MONSIEUR SOUPEAU Firebugs? The whole lot of you! Criminals! Get off my place, Père Gustave! Georges, you're fired! You're worse than Germans.

GEORGES Very well, Monsieur Henri. (*He goes to stand beside Simone*)

MONSIEUR SOUPEAU   Weren't you saying something about an investigation? What kind of investigation?

GEORGES   The Germans are investigating.

MONSIEUR SOUPEAU   You mean it happened after the Germans got here?

GEORGES   Yes.

MONSIEUR SOUPEAU (*has to sit down; in despair*)   That's all I needed. The hostelry will be ruined! (*Props his head in his hands*)

PÈRE GUSTAVE   Monsieur Henri, yesterday afternoon all Saint-Martin was saying nice things about the hostelry. "Right under the Germans' noses!" they were saying.

MONSIEUR SOUPEAU   I'll be court-martialed. That's what you've done to me. (*in despair*) I'll be shot.

SIMONE (*steps forward*)   You won't be shot, monsieur, because I did it. Come to the German captain with me, and I'll take it all on myself.

MAURICE   That's out of the question.

MONSIEUR SOUPEAU   Why is it out of the question? She's a child. They won't touch her.

MAURICE   You can tell the Germans she did it, but we're going to take her away. Get dressed, Simone.

MONSIEUR SOUPEAU   That would make us accomplices.

SIMONE   Maurice, I've got to stay. I'm sure André wants me to.

MONSIEUR SOUPEAU   It all depends on whether she did it after the Germans got here or before. Before they came, we were at war, then they can't do anything to her.

PÈRE GUSTAVE (*fawningly*)   They put up a notice right away, Monsieur Henri, saying that anyone committing a hostile act would be shot.

MONSIEUR SOUPEAU   Did you see that notice, Simone?

SIMONE   Yes, Monsieur Henri.

MONSIEUR SOUPEAU   What did it look like?

SIMONE   It was on red paper.

MONSIEUR SOUPEAU   Is that right? (*Père Gustave nods*) Now comes the question the Germans will ask you, Simone. Did you read it after you set the fire? In that case it wasn't sabotage, Simone, and they can't do anything to you.

SIMONE I saw it first, monsieur.

MONSIEUR SOUPEAU You don't understand. If you didn't see it until afterwards, the Germans will probably just hand you over to the mayor, because then it's a matter that concerns only the French. And then you'll be all right, Simone. Do you understand?

SIMONE Yes, monsieur. But I saw it before.

MONSIEUR SOUPEAU She's confused. Père Gustave, you were in the yard at the time. When did Simone leave?

PÈRE GUSTAVE Before, Monsieur Henri. Of course. Before the notice was put up.

MONSIEUR SOUPEAU See?

SIMONE You're wrong, Père Gustave. You told me yourself before I went that the notice said it was forbidden.

PÈRE GUSTAVE I told you nothing of the kind.

MONSIEUR SOUPEAU Of course not.

MAURICE Monsieur Henri, can't you see that the child wants no part in your tricks? She's not ashamed of what she did.

SIMONE Monsieur Soupeau is only trying to help me, Maurice.

MONSIEUR SOUPEAU That's right. Then you trust me, Simone? Now listen carefully. It's the enemy we'll be speaking to now, Simone. That makes a big difference, you can see that. They'll ask a lot of questions, but you'll only say what's good for Saint-Martin and France. Isn't that simple enough?

SIMONE Yes, monsieur. But I don't want to say anything that's not right.

MONSIEUR SOUPEAU I understand. You don't want to tell an untruth. Not even to the enemy. Very well. I give in. I'll only ask one thing of you: don't say anything, leave it to us. Leave it to me. (*Almost in tears*) I'll stand behind you to the last, you know that. We're all behind you. We're Frenchmen.

SIMONE Yes, monsieur.

(*Monsieur Soupeau takes Simone by the hand and goes into the hostelry with her*)

MAURICE She didn't read her book right.

4

The Trial

(a)

Simone Machard's Fourth Dream

The night of June 21.

Confused music. In the yard stand the German captain in armor and Simone as the Maid of Orleans, surrounded by soldiers in black mail with red swastikas; one, recognizable as the German captain's orderly, is holding a swastika banner.

GERMAN CAPTAIN   We've got you now, Joan of Orleans. You will be handed over to a high court which will decide why you will be condemned to death at the stake.
   (*All go out with the exception of Simone and the standard bearer*)
SIMONE   What kind of court is it?
THE STANDARD BEARER   Not an ordinary one. An ecclesiastical court.
SIMONE   I'll confess nothing.
THE STANDARD BEARER   That's all very well, but the trial seems to be over already.
SIMONE   You mean I've been sentenced before they've even tried me?
THE STANDARD BEARER   Yes. Of course.
   (*A number of people who have apparently attended the trial come out of the hostelry and cross the yard to the street*)
PÈRE GUSTAVE   (*while crossing the yard, to Thérèse*)   To death! At her age!

THÉRÈSE My, who'd have expected such a thing only two days ago!

SIMONE (*plucks at her sleeve*) Is Hitler himself here?

(*Thérèse does not seem to notice her; she goes out with Père Gustave*)

(*Simone's parents cross the yard, the father in uniform, the mother in black*)

MADAME MACHARD (*sobbing*) Even as a little girl she was so obstinate. Just like her brother. It's a terrible blow to Monsieur Machard. And in his position as bailiff! The disgrace! (*Both go out*)

(*The brothers Maurice and Robert cross the yard*)

ROBERT She looked pretty good.

MAURICE Especially in the blue one with the ruffles.

SIMONE (*plucks Robert's sleeve*) Did you see the trial?

ROBERT (*nonchalantly*) Yes, of course.

SIMONE Will I see it too?

ROBERT Certainly. The judges will be coming out to break the staff over you. (*Both go out*)

A LOUD VOICE Quiet! Make way! The Maid will now be sentenced. By the ecclesiastical court of the high bishops and cardinals of Rouen. First the staff will be broken over the Maid.

(*A judge in resplendent cardinal's robes steps out of the hostelry. He holds a breviary in front of his face, so that he is not recognizable. He crosses the yard, stops behind a bronze tripod with a kettle on it, turns his back, claps the breviary shut, takes a small staff out of his sleeve, solemnly breaks it, and throws the pieces into the kettle*)

THE LOUD VOICE His Eminence, the bishop of Beauvais. For liberating the city of Orleans: death.

(*Before going further, he looks back indifferently over his shoulder. It is the colonel*)

SIMONE Monsieur le colonel!

(*A second judge steps out of the hostelry and repeats the ceremony*)

THE LOUD VOICE For liberating the city of Orleans and feeding the rats of the city of Orleans—with stolen goods: death.

(*The second judge likewise shows his face. It is Captain Fétain*)

SIMONE   Monsieur le capitaine!
(*A third judge steps out of the hostelry and repeats the ceremony*)

THE LOUD VOICE   For attacking the city of Paris and the black-market gasoline: death.
(*The third judge is Monsieur Soupeau*)

SIMONE   But Monsieur Henri, it's me you're condemning!
(*Monsieur Soupeau makes his gesture of helplessness; a fourth judge steps out of the hostelry and repeats the ceremony*)

THE LOUD VOICE   For uniting the whole French people: death.
(*The fourth judge is holding his breviary so convulsively that he drops it. He hurriedly bends down to pick it up and is recognized; it is the mayor*)

SIMONE   Heavens, the mayor. Oh, Monsieur Chavez!

THE LOUD VOICE   Your high judges have spoken, Joan.

SIMONE   But they're all Frenchmen. (*To the standard bearer*) It's a mistake!

THE STANDARD BEARER   No, mademoiselle, the high court is French. (*The four judges have stopped in the gateway*)

MAYOR   You must know that from your book. Naturally, the Maid is condemned by French judges, that's as it should be, because she's French.

SIMONE (*confused*)   That's true. I know from the book that I'm condemned to death. But I'd like to know why. I've never really understood that part of it.

MAYOR (*to the judges*)   She demands a trial.

CAPTAIN FÉTAIN   What's the point of a trial when the sentence has already been read?

MAYOR   Well, then at least the defendant will have been examined, questioned, and weighed in the balance.

COLONEL   And found wanting. (*Shrugging his shoulders*) But very well, if you insist.

MONSIEUR SOUPEAU   But we're not prepared.
(*They put their heads together and deliberate in whispers. Père Gustave brings out a table and puts dishes and candles on it. The judges sit down at the table*)

PÈRE GUSTAVE   The refugees from the schoolhouse are outside. They wish to be admitted to the trial.

MONSIEUR SOUPEAU   Impossible. I'm expecting mother. She

says they stink.

CAPTAIN FÉTAIN (*in the direction of the gate*)   The trial will take place behind closed doors. In the interests of the state.

MONSIEUR SOUPEAU   Where are the records? Probably gone down the drain, like everything else in this country.

MAYOR   Where is the complainant?

(*The judges look at each other*)

MAYOR   It can't be official without a complainant.

MONSIEUR SOUPEAU   Père Gustave, get a complainant out of the storehouse.

PÈRE GUSTAVE (*stands in the gateway and calls out toward the street*)   The high court of Rouen calls on each one of you to put forward his complaint against the Maid.—Nobody? (*He repeats the summons; then to the judges*)   The complainant: Isabeau, the queen mother, partisan of the renegade duke of Burgundy and of the mortal enemy.

MADAME SOUPEAU (*in armor, comes out of the hostelry and greets the judges, who bow low. With the practiced affability of a high-class hotelkeeper*)   Good evening, Herr Hauptmann. No, don't get up. (*Over her shoulder toward the hostelry*)   One Alsace-Lorraine for the Herr Hauptmann, well done. How would you like your peasants, constable? Are you satisfied with the service, colonel? (*Pointing to Simone*)   Everything would have been saved if this Maid of Orleans hadn't upset the negotiations. Everything: France and the brickyard as well. You're too weak, gentlemen. Who makes the decisions around here, the church or one of the hostelry's kitchen maids? (*Begins to scream furiously*)   I demand that this person be executed at once for heresy, disobedience, and obstinacy. Heads must roll. Blood must flow. She must be bloodily exterminated. A bloody example must be set. (*Exhausted*)   My drops.

CAPTAIN FÉTAIN   A chair for the queen mother.

(*Père Gustave brings a chair*)

MONSIEUR SOUPEAU   Isn't that armor too tight for you, mother? Why are you in armor anyway?

MADAME SOUPEAU   I'm making war too.

MONSIEUR SOUPEAU   What kind of a war is that?

MADAME SOUPEAU   My war. Against the seditious Maid, who incited those people in the schoolhouse.

CAPTAIN FÉTAIN (*sharply*) Shh! (*To Simone*) Maid, by what right did you incite the French people to make war?

SIMONE An angel told me to, venerable bishop of Beauvais. (*The judges exchange looks*)

MONSIEUR SOUPEAU Oh. An angel? What kind of an angel?

SIMONE The one in the church. On the left side of the altar.

CAPTAIN FÉTAIN Never seen him.

MAYOR (*friendly*) What did this angel look like, Simone? Describe him.

SIMONE He was very young and he had a lovely voice, your worships. He said I should . . .

COLONEL (*interrupting*) What he said is of no interest. What sort of dialect did he speak? Like an educated person? Or some other way?

SIMONE I don't know. The way people speak.

CAPTAIN FÉTAIN Aha.

MONSIEUR SOUPEAU How was this angel dressed?

SIMONE He was beautifully dressed. He was dressed in a kind of material you'd pay twenty or thirty francs a yard for in Tours.

CAPTAIN FÉTAIN Have I understood you correctly, Simone, I mean Joan? This angel was not one of the magnificent angels whose clothes cost maybe two or three hundred francs a yard?

SIMONE I don't know.

COLONEL In what condition was the robe? Rather worn?

SIMONE The angel was just a little crumbled away, in the sleeve.

COLONEL Aha. Crumbled away in the sleeve. As if he'd had to wear his robe at work, eh? Would you say torn?

SIMONE No, not torn.

CAPTAIN FÉTAIN But crumbled. Couldn't the sleeve in the crumbled part have been torn, from work? Maybe you couldn't see it, because the paint had crumbled away. But wouldn't you say that was possible?
(*Simone is silent*)

COLONEL Did the angel say anything that a person of rank could have said? Think before you answer.

SIMONE Plain, simple things.

MAYOR Did the angel look like anybody you know?

SIMONE (*softly*) My brother André.

COLONEL Private André Machard! Gentlemen, now we know. A very peculiar angel, to say the least.

MADAME SOUPEAU A barroom angel, a gutter Gabriel! Now at least we know what to think of those "voices." They come from the cheap wine rooms and manure pits.

SIMONE You oughtn't to say bad things about the angel, venerable bishops and cardinals.

MONSIEUR SOUPEAU On page 124 of your book you will find that we are the ecclesiastical court, the highest authority on earth, so to speak.

COLONEL Don't you think that we, the high cardinals of France, know better what God wants than some low-class angel?

CAPTAIN FÉTAIN Where is God, Joan? Down below or up above? And where did your so-called angel come from? From down below. So who sent him? God? Or could it have been the evil one?

MADAME SOUPEAU The devil! Joan of Orleans, the voices you heard came from the devil!

SIMONE (*in a loud voice*) No! No! Not from the devil!

CAPTAIN FÉTAIN Why don't you call your angel? Maybe he will defend the great Maid of Orleans. Usher, do your duty.

PÈRE GUSTAVE (*cries out*) The high ecclesiastical court of Rouen hereby summons the angel, name unknown, who allegedly appeared to the Maid on various nights, to testify in her behalf.

(*Simone looks up toward the roof of the garage. It remains empty. Père Gustave repeats his summons. In great distress Simone looks at the smiling judges. Then she crouches down and in her confusion begins to beat the ground. But no sound is heard and the garage roof remains empty*)

SIMONE It doesn't sound here. What has happened? It doesn't sound. The French earth doesn't sound any more! It doesn't sound here!

MADAME SOUPEAU (*steps up to her*) Have you any idea who France is?

(b)

The morning of June 22. Over the gate a French flag at half-mast, hung with crape. Georges, Robert, and Père Gustave are listening to Maurice, who is reading from a newspaper edged with black.

MAURICE   The marshal says the armistice conditions leave the honor of France intact.

PÈRE GUSTAVE   That makes me feel better.

MAURICE   It would. The marshal goes on to say that the French people must rally round him as round a father. A new order and discipline are needed.

PÈRE GUSTAVE   That's right. André has stopped fighting, they have laid down his arms. What he needs now is strict discipline.

GEORGES   It's good Simone has got away.

(The German captain, without his hat and sword-belt, comes out of the hostelry, smoking his after-breakfast cigar. He casts an indifferent glance at those present and saunters toward the gate. He looks out for a moment, turns around, and now walking more quickly, goes back into the hostelry)

PÈRE GUSTAVE   It always bothered him that she's only a child.

GEORGES   I can't get over her running away. She always said she'd stay no matter what. Something must have scared her. She just crawled through the window of the laundry room.

(Monsieur Soupeau comes out of the hostelry, rubbing his hands)

MONSIEUR SOUPEAU   Maurice, Robert. Unload the china and silverware! *(In an undertone, after looking around him)* I'm not going to ask you whether any of my staff helped a certain person to escape last night. What's done is done. I'll even go so far as to say that maybe it wasn't such a bad solution. Not that there was any real danger. The Germans aren't cannibals, and your boss knows how to handle them. Only this morning at breakfast I was saying to the German captain: "A farce! Before the notice, after the

notice, what's the sense in all that? A child! What do they
expect? Maybe a little soft in the head, psychopathic!
Tanks! Stop them! Destroy everything! And naturally the
fascination of matches. A political act? Nonsense! Pure
childishness!"

GEORGES (*looking at the others*) Childishness, Monsieur
Henri? Childishness?

MONSIEUR SOUPEAU I told mother the same thing: a child!

GEORGES That child was the only one of us here at the hostelry to do her duty; nobody else lifted a finger. And the
people of Saint-Martin won't forget it, Monsieur Henri.

MONSIEUR SOUPEAU (*disgruntled*) You just do *your* duty.
Unload those crates. I'm only glad the matter is settled. I'm
sure the captain won't waste much time looking for Simone.
And now to work! That's what our poor France needs
now! (*Goes out*)

GEORGES Relief all along the line: she's gone!

MAURICE And it had nothing to do with patriotism or anything like that. That would have been unpleasant. "The
Germans aren't cannibals." We were just getting ready to
make a noble gesture, to give the Germans the gasoline
we'd been withholding from our own army, when the rabble steps in and gets patriotic.

(*The mayor comes in through the gate. He is pale and does
not answer their greetings. Goes toward the hostelry*)

MAYOR (*turning around*) Are there sentries in the corridor
outside Madame Soupeau's room?

PÈRE GUSTAVE No, Monsieur Chavez.

(*The mayor goes out*)

PÈRE GUSTAVE He's probably come because the Germans
want the schoolhouse evacuated. Unless it's Madame Soupeau that wants it.

ROBERT The new order and discipline!

PÈRE GUSTAVE About Simone, Maurice: it had to be common
arson, because in that case the insurance company has to
pay up. They don't overlook things like that. (*Simone
comes in through the gate between two German soldiers
with fixed bayonets*)

GEORGES Simone! What's happened?

SIMONE (*stops, very pale*) I was in the schoolhouse.

ROBERT   Don't be afraid. The Germans won't hurt you.

SIMONE   When they questioned me last night they said I'd
be handed over to the French authorities.

GEORGES   Then why did you run away?

(*Simone does not answer. The soldiers push her into the
hostelry*)

MAURICE   So the Germans haven't washed their hands of it.
Monsieur Henri was mistaken.

(*Monsieur and Madame Machard come in through the gate,
the former in his bailiff's uniform*)

MADAME MACHARD   Have they already brought her here?
That's terrible. Monsieur Machard is beside himself. It's not
just because the rent is due; it's the disgrace that's killing
him. I always knew it would end like this; it's reading all
those books that drove her mad. At seven o'clock this morning there's a knocking at the door and the Germans are
outside. "Messieurs," I say, "if our daughter can't be found,
she's done something to herself. Fire or not, she'd never have
left the hostelry otherwise. If only for her brother's sake
she'd have stayed."

(*Monsieur Soupeau comes out of the hostelry*)

MONSIEUR SOUPEAU   It's too much, Madame Machard! She's
cost me 100,000 francs. Not to mention the wear and tear on
my nerves.

(*Madame Soupeau comes out of the hostelry. She has a
powerful hold on Simone's arm and drags her, despite her
resistance, to the storehouse. Behind them the mayor and
Captain Fétain. All go into the storehouse. Those present
in the yard look on in amazement*)

MAYOR (*at the storehouse door*)   Machard, run over to the
schoolhouse and get them to evacuate quietly. Tell them the
Germans need the premises. (*Out into the storehouse*)

MADAME MACHARD   Yes, monsieur le maire.

(*The two Machards go out with dignity*)

ROBERT   What do they want of her in the storehouse? What
are they doing to her, Monsieur Henri?

MONSIEUR SOUPEAU   Don't ask questions. We have an enormous responsibility. One false step and the hostelry is
ruined.

MADAME SOUPEAU (*comes out of the storehouse with Simone, followed by the mayor and Captain Fétain*) Monsieur le maire, I believe I have convinced you, you've seen it with your own eyes, that she left the cellars, with supplies including vintage wines valued at 50,000 francs, unlocked. How many cases of other goods have been lost I can only surmise. To deceive me, she handed me the key in your presence. (*Turns to Simone*) Simone, I hear that you yourself took whole baskets full of food to the schoolhouse. What did they pay you for it? Where is the money?

SIMONE I didn't take money, madame.

MADAME SOUPEAU Don't lie. And that's not all. The morning Monsieur Henri left, the mob threatened him because someone had spread a rumor that we were about to move our trucks. Did you spread that rumor?

SIMONE I told monsieur le maire, madame.

MADAME SOUPEAU Who was in the mayor's office at the time? Refugees?

SIMONE Yes, I think so.

MADAME SOUPEAU Oh, you think so. Then when the mob came here, what did you advise them to do about the supplies belonging to the hostelry where you were employed? (*Simone does not understand*) Did you or did you not advise them to take what they wanted?

SIMONE I don't remember, madame.

MADAME SOUPEAU So . . .

MAYOR What are you driving at, madame?

MADAME SOUPEAU Simone, who were the first to help themselves? Exactly, your parents. They took plenty.

ROBERT This is too much. (*To Madame Soupeau*) You yourself forced the stuff on the Machards.

GEORGES (*at the same time*) You told monsieur le maire to dispose of your supplies as he saw fit.

MAYOR That's right, madame.

MADAME SOUPEAU (*ignoring the last remarks, to Simone*) You were insolent, disloyal, and obstinate. For that reason I discharged you. Did you leave the hostelry when I ordered you to?

SIMONE No, madame.

MADAME SOUPEAU   No, you just hung around, and then to get
    even with me for discharging you, you set fire to the brick-
    yard. Out of pure vindictiveness. Is that right?
SIMONE *(excitedly)*   I did it because of the Germans.
ROBERT   Everybody in Saint-Martin knows that.
MADAME SOUPEAU   Oh, because of the Germans? Who told
    you the Germans would ever find out about the gasoline?
SIMONE   I heard monsieur le capitaine telling monsieur le
    maire.
MADAME SOUPEAU   Ah, you heard that we were going to de-
    clare the gasoline?
SIMONE   Monsieur le capitaine wanted you to.
MADAME SOUPEAU   So you burned the gasoline to keep us
    from handing it over. That's exactly what I wanted to
    know.
SIMONE *(in despair)*   I did it because of the enemy! There
    were three tanks on the square outside the town hall.
MADAME SOUPEAU   And they were the enemy? Or could it
    have been someone else?
    *(Two nuns appear in the gate, accompanied by a police-
    man)*
MAYOR   What brings you here, Jules?
THE POLICEMAN   The ladies are from the Sisters of St. Ursula.
CAPTAIN FÉTAIN   I phoned St. Ursula's in your name, Chavez.
    (To the nuns) Mes soeurs, this is the Machard girl.
MAYOR   How dare you . . . ?
CAPTAIN FÉTAIN   Monsieur Chavez, you can't be thinking of
    letting this girl run around loose? *(Sharply)* The least our
    guests can expect is that we clean up the dangerous elements
    in Saint-Martin. You don't seem to have studied the mar-
    shal's address. France is facing a period fraught with peril.
    Insubordination is contagious, and it is our duty to nip it in
    the bud. One such fire in Saint-Martin is enough, Chavez.
MAURICE   Oh, now we're expected to do the Germans' dirty
    work for them. And it looks like we're only too glad to.
MADAME SOUPEAU *(coldly)*   Obviously the girl must be for-
    mally committed. I shall apply to the public prosecutor in
    Tours. For sordid personal motives she set fire to *our* brick-
    yard.

GEORGES   How could Simone have personal motives?

MAYOR (*shaken*)   Do you want to destroy the child?

ROBERT (*menacingly*)   Who's being vindictive now?

MONSIEUR SOUPEAU   Don't start in again, Robert. She's a minor. She's being entrusted to the sisters' care. That's all there is to it.

MAURICE (*horrified*)   But they beat the inmates.

SIMONE (*screaming*)   No!

MAYOR   You can't send Simone to a home for the feeble-minded. It's a house of mental torture! A hell! Do you realize you're condemning her to madness?

MAURICE (*pointing at the brutish nuns*)   Just look at those ladies.

(*The nuns' faces remain masklike and unmoved*)

GEORGES   You'd have done better to let the Germans execute her.

SIMONE (*imploring help*)   That's where people's heads swell up and the spit runs out of their mouths, monsieur le maire. They tie you up!

MAYOR (*energetically*)   Madame Soupeau, I will testify before the board in Tours and tell them what the child's actual motives were. Don't worry, Simone, everyone knows your motives were patriotic.

MADAME SOUPEAU (*in an outburst*)   You want to make a national saint out of this little pétroleuse. Is that it? France is saved by fire. On one side the German tanks, on the other Simone Machard, the daughter of a common laborer.

CAPTAIN FÉTAIN   In view of your past, Monsieur Chavez, the judges of the new France are not likely to attach much importance to your testimony. Besides, the road to Tours has become rather unsafe for people of your stamp.

MAURICE (*angrily*)   Now I get it: you're clearing Saint-Martin of any suspicion that it has Frenchmen in it.

MADAME SOUPEAU   Frenchmen? (*Seizes Simone and shakes her*)   Do you think you can teach us what patriotism is? The Soupeaus have owned the hostelry for two hundred years. (*To all*)   Do you want to see a patriot? (*Pointing to Captain Fétain*)   Here he is. We're quite capable of telling you when war is necessary, and we can also tell you when peace

is better. You want to do something for France? Fine. We
are France. Understand?

CAPTAIN FÉTAIN   You're working yourself up, Marie.—Monsieur le maire, will you or will you not let them take the girl
away?

MAYOR   Me? *You* seem to have taken over the power here.
(*Turns to go*)

SIMONE (*frightened*)   Don't go away, monsieur le maire!

MAYOR (*helplessly*)   Chin up, Simone! (*Broken, he staggers
off*)

MADAME SOUPEAU (*breaking the silence, to Captain Fétain*)
Honoré, get this scandalous business over with!

CAPTAIN FÉTAIN (*to the policeman*)   On my responsibility.
(*The policeman seizes Simone*)

SIMONE (*terrified, softly*)   Not to St. Ursula's!

ROBERT   Swine! (*Wants to strike the policeman*)

MAURICE (*holds him back*)   Don't be a fool, Robert. There's
nothing we can do to help her. They've got their police
and they've got the Germans. Poor Simone, too many
enemies.

MADAME SOUPEAU   Simone, get your things.
(*Simone looks around. Her friends stand silent, with down-
cast eyes. Bewildered, she goes into the storehouse*)

MADAME SOUPEAU (*half to the personnel, calmly, explaining*)
The child is insubordinate, incapable of accepting authority.
It is our painful duty to teach her order and discipline.
(*Simone comes back carrying a tiny suitcase, with her
apron over her arm. She hands the apron to Madame Sou-
peau*)

MADAME SOUPEAU   And now open your suitcase. We want
to see what you're taking with you.

MONSIEUR SOUPEAU   Is that necessary, mother?
(*One of the nuns has already opened the suitcase. She takes
out Simone's book*)

SIMONE   Not the book!
(*The nun hands Madame Soupeau the book*)

MADAME SOUPEAU   This is the property of the hostelry.

MONSIEUR SOUPEAU   I gave it to her.

MADAME SOUPEAU   It wasn't much good to her. (*To Simone*)
Say good-bye to the staff.

SIMONE   Good-bye, Monsieur Georges.

GEORGES   Will you be brave, Simone?

SIMONE   Oh yes, Monsieur Georges.

MAURICE   Stay well.

SIMONE   Yes, Maurice.

GEORGES   I won't forget your cousin.

(*Simone smiles at him. She looks up at the garage roof. The light dims. Music announces the apparition of the angel. Simone looks up at the garage roof and sees the angel*)

THE ANGEL

Daughter of France, don't be afraid
None will endure who fight the Maid.
The Lord will blast the arm
That does you harm.
Where they take you it matters not
France is wherever you set foot.
The day will soon be coming when
Glorious France will rise again.

(*The angel vanishes. Full light. The nuns take Simone by the arms. Simone kisses Maurice and Robert and is led off. All look on in silence*)

SIMONE (*in the gateway, struggling desperately*) No, no! I won't go! Help me! Not to St. Ursula's! André! André! (*She is dragged away*)

MADAME SOUPEAU   Henri, my drops!

MONSIEUR SOUPEAU (*frowning*) Maurice, Robert, Georges, Père Gustave! Back to work! Don't forget, we're at peace now!

(*Monsieur Soupeau and Captain Fétain lead Madame Soupeau into the hostelry. Maurice and Robert go out through the gate. Père Gustave rolls a tire out into the yard to mend it. Georges examines his bad arm. The sky begins to turn red. Père Gustave points this out to Georges. Monsieur Soupeau comes rushing out of the hostelry*)

MONSIEUR SOUPEAU   Maurice, Robert! Find out what's burning. (*Goes out*)

PÈRE GUSTAVE   It must be the schoolhouse. The refugees! It looks like they've learned something.

GEORGES   The car can't have reached St. Ursula's yet. Simone must be able to see the fire from the car.

Schweyk in the
Second World War

Play

Translators: Max Knight and Joseph Fabry

CHARACTERS

SCHWEYK, dog hustler in
    Prague
BALOUN, photographer, his
    friend
ANNA KOPECKA, owner of
    the "Flagon"
YOUNG PROCHAZKA, a butcher's
    son, her admirer
ANNA, a maidservant
KATI, her girl friend

BRETTSCHNEIDER, Gestapo
    agent

BULLINGER, SS platoon leader
SS MAN MÜLLER 2
THE ARMY CHAPLAIN

HITLER
HIMMLER
GÖRING
GOEBBELS
VON BOCK

SUPPORTING CHARACTERS

Prelude in the Higher Regions

Martial music. Hitler, Göring, Goebbels, and Himmler around a globe. All are larger than life-size except Goebbels who is smaller than life-size.

HITLER

    Gentlemen, dear party members. Now that with iron hand
    I have subjugated our own German land
    I am fixing to conquer the whole world plus population
    In my opinion, a mere problem of tanks, stukas, and con-
        centration.
    But now, before I forget in my great eagerness
    Tell me, dear chief of police and SS
    The Little Man—what does he think of me
    Not only in Germany
    Also in Czechovakia or whatever name
    Those little countries used to be called (they're all the
        same)?
    Is he for me? Or does he—love me?
    Will he stand by me? Or will he—come to my help in an
        emergency?
    Does he revere me, grand master of all art, strategist most
        noted?
    In short, what is his attitude?

HIMMLER

                    Devoted.

HITLER

    Will he make sacrifices? Will he make concessions
    I mean, of his possessions

Which I need to make my war, for though a shining ge-
    nius, I
Still am only a man.

HIMMLER

That I deny.

HITLER

Thanks. I should hope so. But as I've said
When this damn insomnia agitates my head
Then I wonder: Where does the humble Little Man in
    Europe stand?

HIMMLER

My Führer, he worships you on one hand
As he would worship God. Meanwhile
On the other, he loves you just as dearly as the Germans
    do.

GÖRING, GOEBBELS, HIMMLER

Heil!

1

*Schweyk and Baloun are drinking their morning beer at the
"Flagon." Mrs. Anna Kopecka, the owner, is serving a drunken
SS man. At the bar sits young Prochazka.*

MRS. KOPECKA   You've had five Pilsners, and I'd rather not
give you a sixth because you're not used to it.

SS MAN   Give me one more. That's an order. You know what
that means. If you're sensible and carry it out, I'll let you
in on a secret. You won't regret it.

MRS. KOPECKA   I don't want to hear it. That's why I'm not
giving you any more beer. If you start blabbing your
secrets, I'll be in trouble.

SS MAN   That's very smart of you, take it from me. Anybody
who knows this secret will be shot. They tried to kill

Adolf in Munich. A hair's breadth and he'd have been a goner.

MRS. KOPECKA   You just keep quiet. You're drunk.

SCHWEYK (*amiably from the next table*)   Which Adolf was that? I know two Adolfs. One was a salesman in Prusha's drugstore, he's in a concentration camp because he wouldn't sell concentrated hydrochloric acid to anybody but Czechs, the other is Adolf Kokoschka, that collects dog shit and he's in a concentration camp too for saying—so I'm told—that the shit of the English bulldog is best. No great loss, either of them.

SS MAN (*rises and salutes*)   Heil Hitler!

SCHWEYK (*also rises and salutes*)   Heil Hitler!

SS MAN (*threateningly*)   You don't like it?

SCHWEYK   Beg to report, sir, I like it fine.

MRS. KOPECKA (*arrives with beer*)   Here's your Pilsner, it makes no difference now. But sit down and don't spill your Führer's secrets that nobody wants to know. No politics around here. (*She points to a sign saying: "Drink your slivovitz, drink your beer/but don't talk politics in here"*) I'm a businesswoman. If somebody orders a beer, I draw it for him, but that's all.

YOUNG PROCHAZKA (*when she returns to the bar*)   Mrs. Anna, why can't you let your customers have a little fun?

MRS. KOPECKA   Because the Nazis will shut the place down on me, Mr. Prochazka.

SCHWEYK (*who is again seated*)   If it was Hitler they tried to kill, that would be a good one.

MRS. KOPECKA   You keep still, too, Mr. Schweyk. It's none of your business.

SCHWEYK   If it happened, maybe it's because we're running short of potatoes. People don't go for that. The trouble is we've got so much order, everything has its place, every bunch of soup greens is a coupon in the ration book, that's order. I'm told that Hitler brought us more order than anybody ever thought possible. When there's plenty, there's no order. For instance, when I've sold a dachshund, my money is all mixed up in my pocket, bills and five and ten heller pieces, but when I'm broke all I've got is one little bill and one five-heller piece: how can you have disorder in that? In Italy when Mussolini came along the trains started running on schedule. They've tried to bump him off seven or eight times.

MRS. KOPECKA   Stop shooting your mouth off and drink your beer. If something's happened, we'll all catch it.

SCHWEYK   What I don't understand, Baloun, is why you're so down at the mouth about the news. I'll bet there aren't many like you in Prague.

BALOUN   It's all very well to say that food is short in wartime. But with all these ration books and half a pound of meat a week, I haven't had a square meal since Corpus Christi last year. (*Pointing to the SS man*) It's all right for those fellows, look how well fed they are. Got to ask him a few questions. (*He walks over to the SS man*) What did you have for lunch, neighbor, that made you so thirsty, if I may ask? I bet it was something good and spicy—goulash maybe?

SS MAN   That's none of your business, it's a military secret. Meat loaf.

BALOUN   With gravy. And fresh vegetables? I don't want you to give away a secret, but if it was cabbage, was it well chopped? That makes all the difference. Dear me, one time in Przlov, before Hitler—begging your pardon—I had a meat loaf at the "Swan," I tell you, it was better than at "Plattner's."

MRS. KOPECKA   (*to Schweyk*) Can't you get Baloun away from that SS man? Yesterday he kept asking Herr Brett-schneider of the Gestapo—funny he hasn't shown up yet—about the helpings in the German army; they almost arrested him as a spy.

SCHWEYK   You can't stop him. Food is his vice.

BALOUN   (*to the SS man*) Do you happen to know if the Germans in Prague are taking on volunteers for the Russian campaign, and if the helpings are as big as in the German army, or is it a false rumor?

MRS. KOPECKA   Mr. Baloun, don't bother the gentleman, he's here as a private citizen and you as a Czech ought to be ashamed of yourself asking such questions.

BALOUN   (*guiltily*) I don't mean any harm, or I wouldn't be asking questions so innocently; I know your opinions, Mrs. Kopecka.

MRS. KOPECKA   I haven't any opinions, I have a tavern. All I ask of my customers is common decency. And I have a terrible time with you, Mr. Baloun.

SS MAN   You want to volunteer?

BALOUN   I'm only asking.

SS MAN   If you're interested, I'll take you to the recruiting office. The food is excellent, if you want to know. The Ukraine is going to be the granary of the Third Reich. When we were in Holland, I sent so many packages home there was even enough for my aunt that I can't stand. (*Rises*) Heitler.

BALOUN (*also rises*) Heil Hitler.

SCHWEYK (*joining them*)   Don't say "Heil Hitler," say "Heit-ler" like this gentleman, who must know: that shows you're used to it and even say it at home in your sleep.

MRS. KOPECKA (*puts a schnapps down in front of the SS man*) Here, one for the road.

SS MAN (*embracing Baloun*)   So you want to volunteer against the Bolsheviks, that is good to hear; you're a lousy Czech but a smart one. I'll take you to the recruiting office.

MRS. KOPECKA (*pushes him back into his chair*)   Drink your slivovitz, that will calm you down. (*To Baloun*) I have a good mind to throw you out on your ear. You have no dignity, that comes from your unnatural passion for food. You know the song they're singing? I'll sing it for you, you've only had two beers, you must have some sense left in you. (*She sings* "The Song of the Nazi Soldier's Wife")

And what did the mail bring the soldier's wife
From the ancient city of Prague?
From Prague it brought her some high-heeled shoes
A letter with news and high-heeled shoes—
That's what she got from the town of Prague.

And what did the mail bring the soldier's wife
From Warsaw, the town on the plains
From Warsaw it brought her a nice linen blouse

It was all on the house, that nice Polish blouse
That's what she got from the Polish plains.

And what did the mail bring the soldier's wife
From Oslo, across the sound?
From Oslo it brought her an elegant fur
Just the thing for her, that elegant fur
That's what she got from over the sound.

And what did the mail bring the soldier's wife
From opulent Rotterdam?
From Rotterdam it brought her a hat
How nice to look at, that little Dutch hat
That's what she got from Rotterdam.

And what did the mail bring the soldier's wife
From Brussels, the city of sprouts?
From Brussels it brought her some delicate lace.
Oh, it flattered her face, that delicate lace
That's what she got from the city of sprouts.

And what did the mail bring the soldier's wife
From Paris, city of light?
From Paris it brought her a silken dress
She loved to impress with that silken dress—
Sent from Paris, the city of light.

And what did the mail bring the soldier's wife
From Libyan Tripoli?
From Tripoli it brought her a charm
To shield her from harm, a copper-chained charm—
That's what she got from Tripoli.

And what did the mail bring the soldier's wife
From the land of Russia?
From Russia it brought her a widow's weeds
That's all she needs, a widow's weeds
That's what she got from Russia.

(*The SS man triumphantly nods at the end of each stanza,*

but before the last one his head drops onto the table because he is now completely drunk)

SCHWEYK   A very nice song. (*To Baloun*) It shows that you'd better think twice before doing anything rash. Don't take it into your head to march to Russia with Hitler on account of the big helpings, you'll only freeze to death, you damn fool.

BALOUN *(shaken by the song, puts his head on his elbow and starts crying)* Holy Jesus and Mary, what's going to become of me and my appetite? You've got to do something for me or I'll crack up. How can I be a good Czech on an empty stomach?

SCHWEYK   If you'd swear by the Virgin Mary that you'll never volunteer, you'd keep your oath. (*To Mrs. Kopecka*) He's religious. But would you swear? No.

BALOUN   I can't swear just like that, it's no joke.

MRS. KOPECKA   Terrible. You're a grown-up man.

BALOUN   But a weak one.

SCHWEYK   If somebody put a dish of roast pork in front of your nose and said: "There, eat, you hopeless degenerate, but swear you'll always be a good Czech," you'd swear, as I know you. You'd swear if they kept a good hold on the dish and snatched it away if you didn't swear. With you that would work.

BALOUN   I guess it would, but they'd have to hold on tight.

SCHWEYK   And you'd only keep your oath if you'd gone down on your knees and sworn on the Bible in front of a lot of people? Am I right?

(Baloun nods)

MRS. KOPECKA   I'm almost tempted to try it. (*She goes back to young Prochazka*)

YOUNG PROCHAZKA   Just hearing you sing, I can hardly breathe.

MRS. KOPECKA *(absently)*   Why?

YOUNG PROCHAZKA   Love.

MRS. KOPECKA   How can you tell it's love and not just a passing fancy?

YOUNG PROCHAZKA   I can tell, Mrs. Anna. Yesterday I wrapped up a customer's purse instead of a schnitzel because I was thinking of you, and my father didn't like that at all. And every morning I have a headache. It's love.

MRS. KOPECKA   The question is: how much love?

YOUNG PROCHAZKA   What do you mean by that, Mrs. Anna?

MRS. KOPECKA   I mean, how far would your love go? Maybe only as far as blowing your nose; that's been known to happen.

YOUNG PROCHAZKA   Mrs. Anna, don't crush my heart with cold suspicions. My love would go to the ends of the earth if it were only requited. But it isn't.

MRS. KOPECKA   I wonder, for instance, if it would go as far as two pounds of smoked butt.

YOUNG PROCHAZKA   Mrs. Anna! How can you be so materialistic at a time like this?

MRS. KOPECKA   (*turning away to count bottles*)   See? Any favor is too much.

YOUNG PROCHAZKA   (*shaking his head*)   I don't understand you, Mrs. Anna. Ships that pass in the night.

BALOUN   (*hopelessly*)   It didn't start with this war, it's an old weakness, this craving for food. To cure it, my sister and her kids, where I was living then, went to the Klokota church fair. But even Klokota was no good. My sister and the kids come home from the fair and right away she counts the chickens. One or two were missing. But I just can't help myself. I knew she needed them for eggs, but I go outside and it's like I'm in love. Suddenly, so help me, I feel a bottomless pit in my stomach and an hour later I'm all right again and the chicken is gone. I'm probably hopeless.

YOUNG PROCHAZKA   Were you serious?

MRS. KOPECKA   Very serious.

YOUNG PROCHAZKA   Mrs. Anna, when do you want the smoked butt? Tomorrow?

MRS. KOPECKA   Aren't you being a little rash? You'll have to take it from your father's shop, without permission and without meat coupons. That's called black-marketing nowadays. You'll get shot if they find out.

YOUNG PROCHAZKA   Do you really think I'd mind being shot if I knew you'd love me for it?

(*Schweyk and Baloun have followed the conversation*)

SCHWEYK (*appreciatively*) That's the way a man in love should behave. In Pilsen a young man hanged himself from a rafter for a widow who wasn't even so young any more, because she remarked one day that he'd never done anything for her. And at the "Bear" a man slashed his wrist in the toilet because the waitress poured more beer in another customer's glass—a family man at that. A few days later two men jumped into the Moldau off Charles Bridge because of a woman, but that was on account of her money. Seems she was rich.

MRS. KOPECKA I must admit, Mr. Prochazka, that a woman doesn't get to hear such things very often.

YOUNG PROCHAZKA That's God's truth. I'll bring it tomorrow noon. Will that be soon enough?

MRS. KOPECKA I don't like you to take the risk but it's for a good cause, it's not for me. You heard what Mr. Baloun said: he needs a square meal with meat in it, or he gets terrible ideas.

YOUNG PROCHAZKA So you don't like me to take risks? That slipped out of you, didn't it? You do care if I get shot. You've made me happy, so don't take it back, Mrs. Anna. It's all settled—you can count on the smoked butt even if they blow my brains out for it.

MRS. KOPECKA Be here for lunch tomorrow, Mr. Baloun. I won't promise, but it looks like you'll get a meal.

BALOUN If I get just one more meal, I'll forget all my terrible ideas. But I won't start drooling before I see it. I've suffered too much.

SCHWEYK (*referring to the SS man*) I don't think he'll remember a thing when he wakes up; he's drunk. (*He shouts into the SS man's ear*) Hurrah for Beneš! (*When the man does not move*) That's the most reliable sign that he's out cold, or he'd make hash out of me because that's what they're scared of.

(*The Gestapo agent Brettschneider has entered*)

BRETTSCHNEIDER Who's scared?

SCHWEYK (*firmly*) The SS men. Sit down with us, Herr Brettschneider. A Pilsner for the gentleman, Mrs. Kopecka. It's hot today.

BRETTSCHNEIDER   And what are they scared of, in your opinion?

SCHWEYK   Of not being careful enough and letting a seditious remark slip by or some such thing. But maybe you want to read your newspaper in peace and I'm bothering you?

BRETTSCHNEIDER (*sits down with the paper*)   Nobody bothers me if he's got something interesting to say. Mrs. Kopecka, you're looking like a spring blossom again today.

MRS. KOPECKA (*putting a mug of beer down in front of him*)   Better say a summer bloom.

YOUNG PROCHAZKA (*when she returns to the bar*)   If I were you, I wouldn't let him get so fresh.

BRETTSCHNEIDER (*opening his paper*)   This is a special edition. There's been an attempt to assassinate the Führer, with a bomb, in a Munich beerhall. What do you think of that?

SCHWEYK   Did he suffer long?

BRETTSCHNEIDER   He wasn't hurt, the bomb exploded too late.

SCHWEYK   Probably a cheap bomb. Nowadays they do everything with mass production methods, and then people are surprised that the workmanship is no good. Those things just aren't made with the same loving care as in the old days when they made them by hand, am I right? But imagine not picking a better bomb for a job like that? I call that negligence. I remember one time in Česky Krumlov, a butcher . . .

BRETTSCHNEIDER (*interrupting*)   You call it negligence when the Führer almost loses his life?

SCHWEYK   A word like "almost" can be tricky, Herr Brettschneider. In '38 when they sold us out at Munich, we almost went to war, but then we almost lost everything because we didn't. In the First World War, Austria almost conquered Serbia, and Germany almost conquered France. You can't rely on "almost."

BRETTSCHNEIDER   Keep on talking, it's interesting. You have interesting customers, Mrs. Kopecka. So well informed about politics.

MRS. KOPECKA   One customer is like another. For a businesswoman like me there's no such thing as politics. And see here, Herr Brettschneider, I'll thank you not to needle my customers into making political statements so you can arrest them afterwards. And you, Mr. Schweyk, as long as you pay for your beer, you're free to sit down and shoot off your mouth as much as you like. But right now, Mr. Schweyk, you've shot it off enough for two glasses of beer.

BRETTSCHNEIDER I have the impression that you wouldn't consider it a great loss for the Protectorate if the Führer were dead.

SCHWEYK It would be a loss all right, you can't deny it. A terrible loss. You couldn't replace Hitler with any old idiot. A lot of people gripe about Hitler. It doesn't surprise me.

BRETTSCHNEIDER (*hopefully*) What do you mean by that?

SCHWEYK (*with animation*) As the editor of *Field and Garden* once wrote, great men are always unpopular with the common people. The masses don't understand them, they think all those things are unnecessary, even heroism. The little man doesn't give a shit about a great era. All he wants is to drop into the bar now and then and eat goulash for supper. Naturally a statesman gets riled at bums like that, when it's his job to get his people into the schoolbooks, the poor bastard. To a great man the common people are a ball and chain. It's like offering Baloun here, with his appetite, a small Hungarian sausage for supper, what good is that? I wouldn't want to listen in when the big shots get together and start griping about us.

BRETTSCHNEIDER Are you, by any chance, of the opinion that the German people grumble, that they're not behind the Führer?

MRS. KOPECKA Please, gentlemen, talk about something else. There's no point in it, the times are too serious.

SCHWEYK (*takes a big swig of beer*) The German people are behind the Führer, Herr Brettschneider, nobody can deny it. As Reich Marshal Göring said one time: "People don't always understand the Führer at first, he's too great." Göring must know. (*Confidentially*) It's amazing, the way even the big shots cross Hitler up every time he gets one of his ideas. Last fall, I'm told, he wanted to put up a building that would reach all the way from Leipzig to Dresden—a memorial temple to Germany after it collapsed according to his great plan that he'd worked out in every detail, but they shook their heads at the ministry. They said it was "too great," because they've got no appreciation for the incomprehensible things that a genius thinks up when he's got nothing else to do. He managed to get them into this war, but only by telling them that all he wanted was the city of Danzig, not an inch more. And, mind you, that's the higher-ups and the educated people, the generals and the directors of I. G. Farben who shouldn't give a damn, because, hell, do *they* pay for it? The common man is a lot worse. If they ask him to die for a great cause, he says it louses up his plans, he gripes and bellyaches, and pokes his spoon around in his tripe as if he didn't like the taste of it, and no wonder the Führer gets fed up, when he's gone out of his way to think up something really new for them, conquering the world for instance. What more is there to conquer? The world is limited like everything else. It's just as well.

BRETTSCHNEIDER   Then you maintain that the Führer wants to conquer the world? That his aim is not just to defend Germany against its Jewish enemies and the plutocrats?

SCHWEYK   Don't take it that way; he doesn't mean any harm. Conquering the world is nothing special for him, it's like drinking beer for you, he gets a kick out of it, so he thinks he'll give it a try. Woe to perfidious Albion, I won't say a word more.

BRETTSCHNEIDER (*rises*)   You don't need to say any more. Just come with me to Gestapo headquarters at the Petschek Bank, we'll have something to say to you.

MRS. KOPECKA   But Herr Brettschneider, Mr. Schweyk only made a few innocent remarks. Don't get him in trouble.

SCHWEYK   I'm so innocent that I get arrested. I had two beers and a slivovitz. (*He pays, then says to Brettschneider amiably*) I beg your pardon for going out ahead of you, it's to help you keep an eye on me and guard me.

(*Brettschneider and Schweyk leave*)

BALOUN   Maybe they'll shoot him.

MRS. KOPECKA   Better have a slivovitz, Mr. Prochazka. It's given you a bad shock, too, hasn't it?

YOUNG PROCHAZKA   They're very quick about arresting people.

2

Gestapo headquarters at the Petschek Bank. Schweyk and Gestapo agent Brettschneider are facing Platoon Leader Ludwig Bullinger. In the background an SS man.

BULLINGER   This "Flagon" seems to be a regular hotbed of subversive characters.

BRETTSCHNEIDER (*quickly*)   Not at all, Herr Platoon Leader. Frau Kopecka, who owns the place, is a very respectable woman who keeps her nose out of politics; Schweyk is a dangerous exception among her customers. I've had my eye on him for quite some time.

(*The telephone on Bullinger's desk rings. He lifts the receiver. The caller's voice can be heard*)

TELEPHONE VOICE   Motorized squad. Banker Krusha denies making any remarks about the attempted assassination. Says he couldn't have read the news because he was arrested before it happened.

BULLINGER   Is he the Commercial Bank? In that case, give him ten on the ass. (*To Schweyk*) So you're one of those bastards, are you? First, let me ask you a question. If you don't know the answer, you swine, Müller 2 (*pointing at the SS man*) will take you down to the cellar and educate you, understand? The question is: Do you shit thin or do you shit thick?

SCHWEYK   Beg to report, Herr Platoon Leader, I shit the way you want me to.

BULLINGER   Answer correct. But you made remarks endangering the security of the German Reich, referred to the Führer's defensive war as a war of conquest, criticized the rationing system, and so on and so on. What have you to say for yourself?

SCHWEYK   That's a good deal. You can have too much of a good thing.

BULLINGER (*with heavy irony*)   I'm glad you're aware of that.

SCHWEYK I'm aware of a lot of things. There's got to be discipline. Without discipline nobody would get nowhere, like our sergeant told us in the 91st: "If somebody doesn't chew you out, you'll throw your pants away and start climbing trees." That's what I said to myself last night when they were manhandling me.

BULLINGER So you were manhandled—you don't say.

SCHWEYK In the cell. A gentleman from the SS came in and hit me over the head with a leather strap, and when I groaned he shined his flashlight in my face and said, "It's a mistake, it's not him." And he was so mad about making a mistake that he hit me again in the back. That's human nature: a man makes mistakes till his dying day.

BULLINGER I see. And you confess that you made the remarks recorded here? (*Pointing at Brettschneider's report*)

SCHWEYK If you want me to confess, Your Excellency, I'll confess, it can't hurt me. But if you say, "Schweyk, don't confess," I'll talk myself out of it till they tear me to pieces.

BULLINGER (*shouting*) Shut up! Take him away!

SCHWEYK (*when Brettschneider has taken him to the door, raising his right hand, loudly*) Hurrah for our Führer Adolf Hitler. We're going to win this war!

BULLINGER (*startled*) Are you feebleminded?

SCHWEYK Beg to report, Herr Platoon Leader, I can't help it, I was discharged from the army for idiocy. A military commission officially declared me an idiot.

BULLINGER Brettschneider! Didn't you notice that this man is an idiot?

BRETTSCHNEIDER (*hurt*) Herr Platoon Leader, the way Schweyk talked at the "Flagon" he sounded like an idiot who puts his seditious remarks in such a way that you can't prove anything.

BULLINGER And it's your opinion that we've been listening to the remarks of a man who knows what he's talking about?

BRETTSCHNEIDER Herr Bullinger, that is still my opinion. But if for any reason you don't want him, I'll take him back. It's just that at Investigation we haven't got much time to waste either, you know.

BULLINGER And my opinion, Brettschneider, is that you're a shitass.

BRETTSCHNEIDER   Herr Platoon Leader, I don't have to take that from you.

BULLINGER   And I want you to confess it. It's not much, and it would make you feel better. Admit that you're a shitass.

BRETTSCHNEIDER   I don't know what makes you feel that way about me, Herr Bullinger. I do my duty down to the slightest detail, I . . .

TELEPHONE VOICE   Motorized squad. Krusha is willing to take in your brother as a partner in the Commercial Bank but definitely denies that he made those remarks.

BULLINGER   Ten more on the ass, I need the remarks. (*To Brettschneider, almost pleading*) Look, don't you see how little I'm asking of you? If you admit it, it won't hurt your reputation, it's just between you and me. You are a shitass, why not admit it? If I practically get down on my knees? (*To Schweyk*) You persuade him.

SCHWEYK   Beg to report, sir, I wouldn't want to come between you gentlemen, but I know what you mean, Herr Platoon Leader. On the other hand it's hard on Herr Brettschneider because he's such a good bloodhound, and he doesn't really deserve it.

BULLINGER   (*sadly*)   So you're betraying me, too, you swine. "And the cock crew a third time," as it says in the Jew Bible. I'll squeeze it out of you yet, Brettschneider, but right now I haven't any time for private affairs, I've got ninety-seven more cases to take care of. Throw out this idiot and try to bring me something better next time.

SCHWEYK   (*steps up to him and kisses his hand*)   A thousand thanks, the Lord bless you. If you ever need a nice little pooch, let me know. Dogs are my business.

BULLINGER   Concentration camp. (*Brettschneider is about to take Schweyk away*) Stop! Leave me alone with this man. (*Brettschneider leaves angrily. The SS man leaves too*)

TELEPHONE VOICE   Motorized squad. Krusha has confessed to the remarks, but only that the attempted assassination was all one to him. Not that he was happy about it, or that the Führer's a clown, but only that he's human like everybody else.

BULLINGER   Five more until he's happy and the Führer's a stinking clown. (*To Schweyk, who smiles at him amiably*)

You realize, I hope, that in the concentration camp we tear you limb from limb if you try playing any jokes on us, you bastard!

SCHWEYK   I know all about that. They shoot you before you can count to four.

BULLINGER   So you're a dog hustler. In the park the other day I saw a purebred spitz that appealed to me, with a white spot on one ear.

SCHWEYK (*interrupts*)   Beg to report, sir, I am professionally acquainted with the animal. A lot of people have asked for him. He's got a whitish spot on his left ear, right? He belongs to Undersecretary Voyta. That dog is the apple of his eye, he won't eat unless you beg him on bended knee, and it has to be breast of veal. That proves he's a purebred. Mongrels are smarter, but purebreds are racially superior and favored by dog thieves. Usually they're so dumb they need two or three maids to tell them it's time to shit or open their mouths to eat. High-class people are the same way.

BULLINGER   That's enough about racial superiority, you bastard. I want the spitz, and that's that.

SCHWEYK   You can't have him; Voyta won't sell. How about a police dog? The kind that sniffs out everything you want to know and leads you straight to the scene of the crime. A butcher in Vrshovitz has one, and it pulls his cart for him. That dog missed his calling, so to speak.

BULLINGER   I told you I wanted the spitz.

SCHWEYK   If Undersecretary Voyta were only Jewish, you could simply take the dog, and no questions asked. But he's an Aryan, with a blond beard, kind of moth-eaten.

BULLINGER (*interested*)   Is he a genuine Czech?

SCHWEYK   It's not the way you think, he doesn't commit sabotage and curse Hitler, that would be simple. Off to the concentration camp, just like with me when I was misunderstood. But he's a collaborationist, they even call him a Quisling, which is a headache as far as the spitz is concerned.

BULLINGER (*takes a gun from his drawer and cleans it ostentatiously*)   I see, you don't want to get me the spitz, you saboteur.

SCHWEYK   Beg to report, sir, I do want to get you the dog.

(*Lecturing*) There are several systems, Herr Platoon Leader. The way to steal a lap dog or a toy terrier is to cut its leash in a crowd. You can get a mean German spotted mastiff by using a bitch in heat for bait. A fried horse-meat sausage is almost as good. But some dogs are as spoiled and pampered as an archbishop. I remember a salt-and-pepper pinscher I needed for the dog kennel up over the Klamovka —he wouldn't take any sausage. Three days I tried, until I couldn't stand it any more and I went up to the woman who walked the dog and asked her what in the world he ate that made him so pretty. The woman was flattered and said he liked chops best. So I bought a schnitzel, that was even better, I thought. But do you know, that damn dog didn't even give it a second look because it was veal. He was used to pork. So I had to buy a pork chop. I let the dog sniff at it, then I ran, and the dog ran after me. And the woman shouted, "Puntik! Puntik!" But hell, her dear Puntik ran around the corner after the chop, I snapped a chain around his neck, and the next day he was in the Klamovka kennel. —But suppose people start asking you where you got your dog when they see the spot on his ear?

BULLINGER   I don't believe anybody will ask me where I got my dog. (*He rings the bell*)

SCHWEYK   Maybe not. It wouldn't get them very far.

BULLINGER   In my opinion you were spoofing when you claimed to be a certified idiot; but I'll give you a break, in the first place because Brettschneider is a shitass, and in the second place if you'll get me the dog for my wife, you criminal.

SCHWEYK   Herr Platoon Leader, if you'll allow me, it's true about my certificate, but I was spoofing a little too. As the innkeeper said in Budweis, "I'm an epileptic but I've also got cancer," which was only his way of not letting on that he was bankrupt. Or, as the saying goes, "An athlete's foot seldom comes singly."

TELEPHONE VOICE   Motorized squad 4. Mrs. Moudra, the grocer, denies overstepping the ordinance that shops must not be opened before nine A.M. She claims she opened at ten.

BULLINGER   Lock her up for a couple of months, the lazy

bitch, for *under*-stepping the ordinance. (*To the SS man who has entered, pointing at Schweyk*) Released until further notice!

SCHWEYK   Before I leave for good, I'd like to put in a word for a gentleman who is waiting outside. He was brought in with the rest of us, but he'd rather not sit on the same bench because he's afraid of being mistaken for a political offender. He's only here for attempting to rob and murder a peasant in Holitz.

BULLINGER (*shouting*)   Get out!

SCHWEYK (*at attention*)   Yes, sir. I'll bring the spitz as soon as I get him. Good morning, everybody.

(*Leaves with the SS man*)

Interlude in the Nether Regions

Schweyk and SS man Müller 2 talking on their way from the Petschek Bank to the "Flagon."

SCHWEYK   If I ask Mrs. Kopecka, she'll do it for you. I'm glad to hear you say the Führer doesn't chase skirts but saves his strength for important matters of state, and never touches liquor. What he's done, he's done with a cool head, which is more than a lot of people I know could say. And not eating anything but a little vegetables and cake is a good idea too, there isn't too much to go around what with the war and all, that makes one less mouth to feed. I knew a peasant in Moravia, he had a kink in the gut which spoiled his appetite, his hired hands were all as thin as a rail. The people in the village started gossiping, but the peasant went around saying, "At my place the hired hands eat the same as I do." Drinking is a vice, I'll admit that, Budova the leather dealer wanted to cheat his brother, and then when he was full of booze he signed over the inheritance to him, instead of the other way round. There are two sides to everything, and as far as I'm concerned, Hitler doesn't have to go without women. I wouldn't ask that of anybody.

3

At the "Flagon" Baloun is waiting for his meal. Two other guests are playing checkers, a fat lady shopkeeper is drinking a small slivovitz, and Mrs. Kopecka is embroidering.

BALOUN   It's ten after twelve, and no Prochazka. I knew it.

MRS. KOPECKA   Give him time. Haste makes waste, you've got to have the right mixture of hurrying and taking it easy. You know "The Song of the Gentle Breeze"?
(*She sings*)

> Haste to me, love, my dearest guest
> No one dearer do I know.
> But when within your arms I rest
> Then rather take it slow.
>> Learn from the plums in autumn
>> Ripe to be plucked with ease.
>> They fear the mighty tempest
>> They love the gentle breeze.
>> Ah, you hardly feel the little breeze
>> It gently rocks you round.
>> The plums want anyway to fall
>> And lie upon the ground.
>
> O reaper stop, you've done enough.
> Let one stalk stand, just one!
> Don't drink your wine in one swift draft
> Don't kiss me on the run.
>> Learn from the plums in autumn
>> Ripe to be plucked with ease.
>> They fear the mighty tempest
>> They love the gentle breeze.
>> Ah, you hardly feel the breeze
>> It gently rocks you round.

The plums want anyway to fall
And lie upon the ground.

BALOUN (*walks nervously over to the checker players*) You're
doing fine. Would you gentlemen be interested in postcards? I work for a photographer. We've got a hot series.
"German cities," we call it.

FIRST CUSTOMER I'm not interested in German cities.

BALOUN Then you'll like this series. (*He shows the postcards
furtively as if they were pornographic*) This is Cologne.

FIRST CUSTOMER It looks terrible. I'll take them. Nothing but
bomb craters.

BALOUN Fifty hellers. But be careful about showing them
around. People have been stopped by the police patrol for
showing them to each other, they think they're dirty pictures, the kind they like to confiscate.

FIRST CUSTOMER Here's a funny caption. "Hitler is one of the
greatest architects of all time." And it shows a heap of
wreckage that used to be Bremen.

BALOUN I sold two dozen to a German sergeant. He smiled
when he looked at them; I liked that. I told him to meet me
in the park in front of Havliček. I kept my knife open in
my pocket, in case he was a stool pigeon. But he was on the
level.

THE FAT WOMAN Them that live by the sword, die by the
sword.

MRS. KOPECKA Careful!

(*Schweyk enters with the huge SS man Müller 2 who has
escorted him from Bullinger's office*)

SCHWEYK Hello, everybody. This gentleman is off duty. Give
us a glass of beer.

BALOUN I didn't expect you back for a couple of years, but
a man can make mistakes. Herr Brettschneider is usually so
efficient. Last week when you weren't here, he left with the
upholsterer from around the corner, and *he* never came
back.

SCHWEYK Probably a sap that didn't knuckle under. Herr
Brettschneider will think twice before he misunderstands
me again. I've got influence.

THE FAT WOMAN Are you the man they took away yesterday?

SCHWEYK (*proudly*) The same. In times like these you have to knuckle under. It's a matter of practice. I licked his hand. In the old days, they sprinkled salt on the prisoners' faces. They were tied, and then big German shepherds were sicked on them, and the dogs licked their whole faces off. Nowadays people aren't so cruel any more except when they get mad. But I forgot: this gentleman (*referring to the SS man*) would like to know what joys the future holds in store for him, Mrs. Kopecka. And two beers. I told him you were a fortune-teller and it gave me the creeps. I advised him against it.

MRS. KOPECKA You know I don't like to do it, Mr. Schweyk.

SS MAN Why don't you like to do it, young woman?

MRS. KOPECKA A gift like that is a responsibility. How do I know how a customer is going to take it, and will he always have the strength to bear it? Because sometimes a look at the future gives people the holy horrors, and they blame me. Like Czaka the brewer when I had to tell him his wife was going to be unfaithful, and right away he smashes my valuable wall mirror.

SCHWEYK She made a fool of him all right. We predicted the same thing to Blaukopf the schoolteacher, and it happened again. When she predicts things like that they always happen. It's uncanny if you ask me. The time you told Councilman Czerlek that his wife . . . remember, Mrs. Kopecka? It came true.

SS MAN Then you have a rare gift, it shouldn't go to waste.

SCHWEYK I told her to tell the whole city council the same thing. I wouldn't be surprised if it came true.

MRS. KOPECKA Mr. Schweyk, don't joke about things we know nothing about except that they happen. They're supernatural.

SCHWEYK The time you told engineer Bulova right to his face that he'd be torn to pieces in a train wreck? His wife is already remarried. Women stand up better to predictions. They have more strength of character, I'm told. Mrs. Laslaczek on Hus Street had so much strength of character that her husband declared right out in public, "Anything is better than living with her," and went to work in Germany. But the SS can also stand a good deal, I'm told, they have to, what with concentration camps and interrogations where they need nerves of steel. Am I right? (*The SS man nods*) That's why you needn't have any qualms about foretelling this gentleman's future, Mrs. Kopecka.

MRS. KOPECKA   If he promises to take it as a harmless bit of fun, and not to worry about it, I might take a look at his palm.

SS MAN (*suddenly hesitating*)   I don't want to force you. You say you don't like to.

MRS. KOPECKA (*brings him his beer*)   That's a fact. Forget it and drink your beer.

THE FAT WOMAN (*in a low voice to the checker players*)   If you suffer from cold feet, try cotton.

SCHWEYK (*sitting down with Baloun*)   I've got a little business to discuss with you. I'm doing some work with the Germans in connection with a dog, and I need you.

BALOUN   I'm not in the mood for anything.

SCHWEYK   There'll be something in it for you. When you get the dough, you can take your appetite to the black market and get something in no time.

BALOUN   Young Prochazka isn't coming. Nothing but soggy potatoes again. Another disappointment like this will be the end of me.

SCHWEYK   It seems to me we could set up a little club, six or eight men. All of them would agree to pool their eighth of a pound of meat, and you'd have a meal.

BALOUN   But how would we find them?

SCHWEYK   You're right, it won't work. They'll say, for a stinker like you, a Czech without any willpower, they wouldn't think of giving up a meal.

BALOUN   That's true, they wouldn't give a shit about me.

SCHWEYK   Can't you pull yourself together and think of the honor of your country when temptation raises its head and all you can see in the world is a leg of veal or a roasted tenderloin with a little red cabbage, or maybe a few pickles? (*Baloun groans*) Think what a disgrace it would be if you weakened!

BALOUN   Can't help it. (*Silence*) Anyway I'd rather have cabbage than pickles.

(*Young Prochazka enters with a briefcase*)

SCHWEYK   Here he is. You've been too pessimistic, Baloun.
Good afternoon, Mr. Prochazka, how's business?

MRS. KOPECKA (*with a glance at the SS man*)   Sit down with
the gentlemen, I've got something to attend to. (*To the SS
man*) You know, I think your palm might interest me, may
I take a look? (*Takes his hand*) I thought so: your palm is
very very interesting. I mean, it's the kind of palm that's
almost irresistible for us astrologists and chiropracticians,
really interesting. How many other men are there in your
squad?

SS MAN (*painfully, as if having a tooth pulled*)   In the storm
squad? Twenty. Why?

MRS. KOPECKA   I thought so. It's written in your palm. You're
tied up for life and death with twenty men.

SS MAN   Can you really see that in my palm?

SCHWEYK (*has joined them, cheerfully*)   You'll be surprised
at all the things she can see. But she's cautious, she only
says things that are absolutely sure.

MRS. KOPECKA   There's something electrifying about your
palm, you're lucky with women, the well-developed mount
of Venus shows that. They throw themselves at you, kind
of, but then they get a pleasant surprise and they wouldn't
have missed it for the world. You're a serious man, you've
got a way of talking that's almost severe. Your success line
is tremendous.

SS MAN   What does that mean?

MRS. KOPECKA   Nothing to do with money, much more than
that. You see this H, these three lines here? That's an act
of heroism, something you're going to do very soon.

SS MAN   Where? Can you see where?

MRS. KOPECKA   Not around here. Or in your own country
either. Far away. Here's a strange thing that I don't quite
understand. There's something mysterious about this act of
heroism, as if only you and the men with you would know
about it. Nobody else, not even afterwards, never.

SS MAN   How can that be?

MRS. KOPECKA (*sighs*)   I don't know, maybe it'll be on the battlefield, in an advanced position or something. (*As if in confusion*) But that's enough now, isn't it? I've got to get back to my work, it's only in fun anyway, you promised not to take it seriously.

SS MAN   But you can't stop now. I want to know more about the secret, Mrs. Kopecka.

SCHWEYK   He's right, Mrs. Kopecka. You oughtn't to leave him up in the air like that. (*Mrs. Kopecka winks at him in such a way that the SS man can see it*) But, then, maybe you've told him enough at that. It's better not to know about some things. Varczek the schoolteacher once looked in the dictionary to find out what schizziphonia was, and after a while they had to put him in the insane asylum in Ilmenau.

SS MAN   You saw more in my palm.

MRS. KOPECKA   No, no, that's all. Leave me be.

SS MAN   You won't tell me what you saw. And you winked at this gentleman here, I saw you, to make him stop pushing you, because you didn't want to say any more. But you won't get away with it.

SCHWEYK   That's a fact, Mrs. Kopecka, the SS won't let you get away with it. When I was at the Gestapo, I had to speak up, like it or not. Right away I confessed that I wished the Führer a long life.

MRS. KOPECKA   Nobody can force me to tell a customer disagreeable things, so he'll never come back.

SS MAN   You see, you know something and won't tell me, you've given yourself away.

MRS. KOPECKA   But the second H is very faint, ninety-nine people out of a hundred wouldn't even have noticed it.

SS MAN   What's this about a second H?

SCHWEYK   Another beer, Mrs. Kopecka. This is so exciting, it makes me thirsty.

MRS. KOPECKA   It's always the same, it only gets you in trouble to give in and examine a palm to the best of your knowledge and ability. (*Brings Schweyk a beer*) I didn't expect the second H, but if it's there what can I do? If I tell you, it'll make you miserable, you can't do anything about it anyway.

SS MAN About what?

SCHWEYK (*amiably*) It must be something terrible. As long as I've known Mrs. Kopecka, I've never seen her like this— and she's read a lot of things in palms. Are you sure you can take it, do you feel strong?

SS MAN (*hoarsely*) What is it?

MRS. KOPECKA Suppose I have to tell you that the second H means a hero's death, that's what it usually means, and suppose it upsets you? You see, now you feel miserable. I knew it. Three beers—that will be two crowns.

SS MAN (*pays, crushed*) Palm reading is all a lot of nonsense. There's nothing in it.

SCHWEYK You're perfectly right. Don't give it a second thought.

SS MAN (*leaving*) Heil Hitler!

MRS. KOPECKA (*calling after him*) Promise me at least that you won't tell the other gentlemen.

SS MAN (*stops*) What other gentlemen?

SCHWEYK The ones on your squad! You know, the twenty.

SS MAN What business is it of theirs?

MRS. KOPECKA Oh, only because they're tied up with you for life and death. No use getting them all worried over nothing!

(*SS man leaves, cursing*)

MRS. KOPECKA Come again!

THE FAT WOMAN (*laughing*) You're all right, Mrs. Kopecka. Keep it up.

SCHWEYK We knocked out the whole platoon. Open your briefcase, Mr. Prochazka, Baloun can't stand it another minute.

MRS. KOPECKA Yes, Rudolf, hand it over, nice of you to bring it.

YOUNG PROCHAZKA (*weakly*) I haven't got it. When I saw them taking Schweyk away, it shook me up. I saw the scene all night. Good afternoon, Mr. Schweyk, I see you're back. I didn't have the nerve, I admit it. I feel terrible on account of you, Mrs. Kopecka, giving you a black eye in front of all these people, but I couldn't help it. (*Desperate*) Please, say something, anything is better than saying nothing.

BALOUN Nothing.

MRS. KOPECKA Well, so you haven't got it. But when you came in and I motioned that I had to get rid of the SS man first, you nodded as if you had it.

YOUNG PROCHAZKA I didn't have the nerve . . .

MRS. KOPECKA That's enough. I know your kind. You flunked your test as a man and a Czech. Get out, you coward, and never set foot here again.

YOUNG PROCHAZKA I don't deserve to be treated any better. (*Slinks away*)

SCHWEYK (*after a moment's silence*) Talking about palm reading: Krish, the barber from Mnishek—you know Mnishek?—did a little palm reading at the parish fair and got drunk on the money he made, and a young peasant took him home with him, so he could tell him his future when he came to. Before falling asleep, Krish asked the peasant: "What's your name? Take my notebook out of my pocket. So your name is Kunert. Come back in fifteen minutes and you'll find the name of your future wife on a slip of paper." Then he started snoring, but woke up again and scribbled something in his notebook. He tore out the page, threw it on the floor, and put his finger on his lips and said, "Not yet, in another fifteen minutes. It's best if you look for the slip of paper blindfolded!" And do you know what he'd written on the slip of paper? "Your future wife's name will be Mrs. Kunert."

BALOUN That Prochazka is a criminal.

MRS. KOPECKA (*angrily*) Don't be a fool. The criminals are the Nazis who threaten and torture people until they go against their better nature. (*Looking out the window*) That fellow coming now is a criminal, Rudolf Prochazka is only a weakling.

THE FAT WOMAN We're guilty too, I tell you. Seems to me we could do more than drink slivovitz and crack jokes.

SCHWEYK Don't ask too much of yourself. It's quite a job just to be around nowadays. Keeps you so busy just staying alive, you haven't much time for anything else.

(*Brettschneider enters with yesterday's SS man*)

SCHWEYK (*cheerfully*) I wish you a good afternoon, Herr

Brettschneider. Will you have a beer? I'm working with the SS now, it can't hurt me.

BALOUN (*spitefully*) Out!

BRETTSCHNEIDER What do you mean by that?

SCHWEYK We were talking about food, and Mr. Baloun thought of the chorus from a popular song we were trying to remember. They mostly sing this song at church fairs, it's about the way they fix radish around Mnishek. They grow those big black ones, you must have heard about them, they're famous. Why don't you sing the song for Herr Brettschneider, Baloun? It'll cheer you up. He's got a good voice, he even sings in the church choir.

BALOUN (*sullenly*) I'll sing it. It's about radishes.

(*Baloun sings "The Song of How to Fix a Black Radish." During the entire song Brettschneider, at whom everyone is looking, is trying to make up his mind whether to take action. Several times he gets up and sits down again*)

BALOUN (*sings*)

You'd better take a black one, a big full one
And tell him gaily: "Brother, get on out!"
Don't leave your hands bare when you pull one
By the snout.
    Better put gloves on, this black radish lives in rot.
    Not a doubt! Must be got
    Out!

And you can also buy one (at low prices)
And don't forget, first wash his dirty skin.
When you have cut him up in little slices
Put salt in.
    And rub it in the wound, no matter how he frets.
    Salt him down till he sweats.
    Put salt in.

Interlude in the Higher Regions

Hitler and Reich Marshal Göring in front of a tank model. Both are larger than life-size. Martial music.

HITLER
> My dearest Göring, we're now in the fourth year
> And victory is ours, at least pretty near.
> But my war keeps spreading to more and more vast new
>   regions.
> I therefore now need more tanks, bombers, and new legions.
> Which means the people have just got to stop lying around
>   and snoring
> They've got to labor for my war until sweat and blood are
>   pouring.
> So tell me now if you can:
> How do things stand in Europe with the Little Man?
> Will he work hard and long when no one's paying?

GÖRING
> My Führer, that in times like these goes without saying.
> The Little Man in Europe will work for your great war as
>   cheerfully
> As the Little Man does in Germany.
> Labor Service will see to that.

HITLER
> Good. To such an organization I gladly take off my hat.

4

*On a bench in a park along the Moldau. Evening. Two lovers
enter, stop for a moment, stand closely embraced, gaze at the
Moldau in the background, and go on. Schweyk and his friend
Baloun come in. They look back.*

SCHWEYK   That Voyta is mean to his servants. This is his
third maid since Candlemas, and I hear she wants to quit,
the neighbors are mean to her because she works for a
quisling. It'll be all the same to her if she comes home without the dog as long as it's not her fault. You'd better sit

down before she gets here, she doesn't like to sit down on a
bench with nobody on it.

BALOUN   Don't you want me to hold the sausage?

SCHWEYK   And have you gobble it up on me? Go on, sit
down.

(*Baloun sits down on the bench. Two maidservants enter,
Anna and Kati, the first with a spitz on the leash*)

SCHWEYK   Excuse me, miss, how do I get to Palacky Street
from here?

KATI   (*suspiciously*)   You cross Havliček Square. Come on,
Anna.

SCHWEYK   Pardon me if I ask where the square is. I'm a
stranger here.

ANNA   I'm a stranger here myself. Go on, Kati, tell him.

SCHWEYK   So you're a stranger, too, miss? That's a good one.
I'd never have known you weren't from the city, and such
a nice little dog. Where are you from?

ANNA   I'm from Protivin.

SCHWEYK   Then we're practically neighbors. I'm from Budweis.

KATI   (*tries to pull her away*)   Come along, Anna.

ANNA   Just a second. Then you must know Pejchara the
butcher, on the main street, in Budweis?

SCHWEYK   Of course I know him! He's my brother. Everybody likes him, he's honest and helpful, he has fresh meat,
and he throws in an extra bone for soup.

ANNA   Yes.

(*Silence, Kati waits mockingly*)

SCHWEYK   What a coincidence running into each other like
this, so far from home! Have you got a moment? We've
got to talk about Budweis, here's a bench with a nice view.
That's the Moldau.

KATI   Really? (*Ironically*) That's news to me.

ANNA   Somebody's sitting there.

SCHWEYK   A gentleman enjoying the view. You better keep a
close watch on your dog.

ANNA   Why?

SCHWEYK   Don't quote me, but the Germans are crazy about
dogs, it's amazing, especially the SS. A dog like that is gone

before you can look twice, they send them home. I was talking to a platoon leader myself the other day, name of Bullinger, he wanted a spitz for his missus in Cologne.

KATI So you run around with platoon leaders and people like that? Come along, Anna, that's enough now.

SCHWEYK I talked to him when I was under arrest for remarks endangering the security of the Third Reich.

KATI Really? Then I take it back. We still have a little time, Anna.

(*She walks ahead to the bench. All three sit down next to Baloun*)

KATI What kind of remarks did you make?

SCHWEYK (*indicates that he cannot talk about it in the presence of the stranger, and speaks with pointed innocence*) Do you like it in Prague?

ANNA Oh yes. But you can't trust the men around here.

SCHWEYK That's only too true. I'm glad you realize that. People in the country are more honest, am I right? (*To Baloun*) A fine view, isn't it, neighbor?

BALOUN Not bad.

SCHWEYK Something for a photographer.

BALOUN As a background.

SCHWEYK A photographer could do something with it.

BALOUN I am a photographer. In the studio where I work we painted the Moldau on a screen, but a little more picturesque. We use it for the Germans, mostly the SS men who pose in front of it for a souvenir when they have to leave and can't come here any more. Only it's not the Moldau, it's just some lousy river.

(*The girls laugh approvingly*)

SCHWEYK That's very interesting. Couldn't you snap a picture of the ladies, in bust, excuse me, that's what they call it.

BALOUN I could.

ANNA That would be nice. But not in front of your Moldau, eh?

(*They laugh abundantly at the joke, then silence*)

SCHWEYK You know this one? A Czech on the Charles Bridge hears somebody shouting for help in German from the Moldau. He leans over the rail and calls down: "Shut up,

you should have learned swimming instead of German!"
(*The girls laugh*)

SCHWEYK Yes, that's the Moldau. A lot of immorality goes on along its banks in wartime.

KATI In peacetime too.

BALOUN And at spring fairs.

SCHWEYK Out in the open until after All Saints' Day.

KATI And I suppose nothing happens indoors?

BALOUN Oh yes, plenty.

ANNA And at the movies.
(*Again they all laugh*)

SCHWEYK Ah yes, the Moldau. Do you know the song, "Henry Slept beside his Newly-wedded"? They sing it a lot in Moravia.

ANNA You mean the one that goes on "Heiress to a castle on the Rhine?"

SCHWEYK That's it. (*To Baloun*) Got something in your eye? Don't rub. Could you take care of the gentleman, miss? Use the corner of your handkerchief, that's the best way.

ANNA (*to Schweyk*) Would you mind holding the dog? You've got to be careful in Prague. The air is full of soot.

SCHWEYK (*ties the dog loosely to the lamppost beside the bench*) Excuse me, I've got to be going now, to Palacky Street, on business. I'd like to hear you sing, but I can't. Good afternoon. (*Leaves*)

KATI (*while Anna tries to fish something out of Baloun's eye with a handkerchief*) He's really in a hurry.

ANNA I can't find anything.

BALOUN I feel better already. What's that song about?

ANNA Would you like us to sing it for you? Before we go? Oh, keep quiet, Lux. I'll sure be glad to see the last of you and your master. (*To Baloun*) He's too fond of the Germans. I'll start. (*The two girls sing the ballad "Henry Slept beside his Newly-wedded"* with much feeling. Meanwhile Schweyk, behind a bush, uses a tiny sausage to lure the dog to him, and leaves with the animal*)

BALOUN (*after the song*) You sang that beautifully.

KATI We have to go now. Jesus, where's the dog?

---

* [The text of this ballad is given at the end of the play.]

ANNA Holy Virgin, he's gone. He never runs away. What will Mr. Voyta say?

BALOUN He'll call up his German friends, that's all. Don't worry, it's not your fault. I guess that gentleman didn't tie him very well, it seems to me I saw a shadow while you were singing.

KATI Quick, we'll go to the lost-and-found.

BALOUN Drop in some Saturday night at the "Flagon," 7 Hus Street. (*They nod to Baloun and leave quickly. Baloun looks at the view again. The lovers come back, but no longer holding each other tight. Then Schweyk enters with the spitz on the leash*)

SCHWEYK He's a typical quisling's dog—bites the second you look away. Been giving me a terrible time on the way. When I was crossing the railroad tracks, he lay down and wouldn't budge. Maybe he wanted to be run over, the scoundrel. Come along, now.

BALOUN Did he go for the horse sausage? I thought you only ate veal?

SCHWEYK War is no bed of roses. Not even for purebred dogs. I won't give him to Bullinger unless he puts the cash on the line, or he'll swindle me. They can't have collaboration for nothing.

(*A tall, sinister-looking man has appeared in the background and has been watching the two. Now he approaches them*)

THE INDIVIDUAL Taking a walk, gentlemen?

SCHWEYK That's right. What business is it of yours?

THE INDIVIDUAL Would you please identify yourselves? (*He shows them an official badge*)

SCHWEYK I've got nothing on me. Have you?

BALOUN (*shakes his head*) We haven't done anything.

THE INDIVIDUAL I haven't stopped you for doing anything but because it seems to me that you're not doing anything. I'm from the Voluntary Labor Service.

SCHWEYK Are you one of those gentlemen who stroll around in beer gardens and outside movie houses, picking up people to work in the factories?

THE INDIVIDUAL What is your occupation?

SCHWEYK I'm in the dog business.

THE INDIVIDUAL   Have you a certificate that your enterprise
is essential for the war effort?

SCHWEYK   No, Your Excellency. But it is essential for the war
effort. Same in war as in peace, a dog is a friend in need,
what do you say, spitz? People are much calmer during an
air raid if a dog looks at them as if to say, "Is this really
necessary?" And this gentleman is a photographer, maybe
that's even more essential for the war effort. He photographs
soldiers, so the folks at home at least have pictures of their
loved ones, which is better than nothing, you've got to admit.

THE INDIVIDUAL   I think I'd better take you to headquarters.
I wouldn't advise you to give them any of your applesauce.

BALOUN   But we caught the dog on orders from higher up.
Tell him.

SCHWEYK   It's no use. The gentleman has orders from higher
up too.

(*They go with him*)

SCHWEYK   So your job is catching people?

5

*Noon break at the freight station in Prague. On the rails sit
Schweyk and Baloun, now railroad workers in Hitler's service,
guarded by a German soldier armed to the teeth.*

BALOUN   I wonder where Mrs. Kopecka is with the grub. I
hope nothing's happened to her.

A TRANSPORTATION CORPS LIEUTENANT (*passing by, to the soldier*)   Guard! If anybody asks you which of these freight
cars goes to Lower Bavaria, remember it's this one, number
4268.

SOLDIER (*at attention*)   Yes, sir.

SCHWEYK   With the Germans, organization is everything.

The world has never seen anything like the organization
they have now. If Hitler pushes a button, it's the end of
China, for instance. They've got the pope in Rome in their
files, with everything he ever said about them, he's a dead
duck. Even an underling, an SS leader for instance, has his
buttons to push, and the next thing you know your ashes
are delivered to your widow. It's lucky for us that we're
here with a heavily armed guard watching us to keep us
from committing sabotage and getting shot.

(*Mrs. Kopecka hurriedly enters with enamel dishes. The
soldier absentmindedly studies her pass*)

BALOUN   What is it?

MRS. KOPECKA   Carrot cutlet and potato sausage. (*While the
two men eat, dishes on knees, softly*) The dog has got to
go. He's getting political. Don't stuff yourself like that, Mr.
Baloun, you'll get ulcers.

BALOUN   Not from potatoes. Maybe from a capon.

MRS. KOPECKA   The morning paper had a story that the disappearance of Undersecretary Voyta's dog was an act of
vengeance by the population against a civil servant friendly
to the Germans. They're looking for him, they want to
smoke out the nest of subversive elements. He can't stay
at the "Flagon" another day.

SCHWEYK (*eating*)   It's a little inconvenient now. Yesterday
I wrote a special-delivery letter to Platoon Leader Bullinger
telling him that my price is two hundred crowns, and I
won't deliver till I get them.

MRS. KOPECKA   Mr. Schweyk, you're taking your life in your
hands writing a letter like that.

SCHWEYK   I don't think so, Mrs. Kopecka. Herr Bullinger
is a fat pig but he'll say it's perfectly natural, business is
business, or where would we be; the story is that he needs
the spitz for his missus in Cologne. Collaborationists don't
work for nothing. The fact is they're making more than
ever, because their countrymen despise them. I've got to be
paid for this thing or there's no point in it.

MRS. KOPECKA   But you can't do business while you're locked
up.

SCHWEYK (*amiably*)   I won't grow moss around here. I've

already cost them a carload of soap. It's easy. One time in Austria, when they made a law against strikes, the railroad workers tied everything up for eight hours just by observing all the safety regulations.

MRS. KOPECKA (*firmly*)   That dog can't stay at the "Flagon," Mr. Schweyk, and that's that. I can count on a certain amount of protection from Herr Brettschneider, he's still hoping to get somewhere with me, but it doesn't amount to much.

(*Schweyk listens to her only with half an ear because two German soldiers have passed by carrying a large, steaming cauldron and have ladled out some goulash soup into the soldier's mess tin. Baloun, who has finished his meal long since, stands up and takes a few steps as in trance, sniffing the soup*)

SCHWEYK   I'll pick him up. Say, take a look at that!

GERMAN SOLDIER (*calling sharply after Baloun*)   Halt!

MRS. KOPECKA (*to Baloun who returns disgruntled and agitated*)   Pull yourself together, Mr. Baloun.

SCHWEYK   There was a doctor in Budweis with such a bad case of diabetes that all they let him eat was a sip of rice soup—and he was built like an ox. He couldn't stand it, he kept sneaking into the pantry to stuff himself on leftovers, and he knew what he was doing. Then he got good and sick of it all and he told his housekeeper to bring him a seven-course meal, with pastry and all, she was blubbering so bad she could hardly serve him, and he made her play a funeral march on the gramophone, and it really did him in. It'll be the same with you, Baloun. You'll end up under a Russian tank.

BALOUN (*still trembling all over*)   They're dishing out goulash.

MRS. KOPECKA   I've got to go. (*She takes the dishes and leaves*)

BALOUN   I just want to take a look. (*To the eating soldier*) Are the helpings always that big in the army, Herr Soldier? That's a pretty big one you've got. But maybe only for guards to keep you awake, or maybe we'd run away, wouldn't we? Couldn't I take just one sniff?

(The soldier sits there eating, but moves his lips between bites)

SCHWEYK   Don't ask him questions. Can't you see he's got to learn the number by heart, or the wrong freight car will go to Lower Bavaria on him, you dope. *(To the soldier)* You're right to keep thinking about it, all sorts of things can happen. They've stopped painting the destination on freight cars because the saboteurs wipe it off and put wrong addresses on instead. What number is it? 4268, isn't it? Well, you don't have to sit here for half an hour counting with your lips. I'll tell you how to do it, I got it from a clerk in the license bureau: this is the way he explained it to a peddler who couldn't keep his number in his head. I'll show you with your own number and you'll see how easy it is. 4268. The first number is a four, the second a two. So remember 42, that's two times 2, I mean from front to back 4, divided by 2, and that gives you 4 and 2 next to each other again. Don't panic! How much is two times 4? 8, isn't it? So keep well in mind that the 8 in number 4268 is the last in the row, all you've got to remember is that the first number is a 4, the second a 2, and the fourth an 8. Now you've only got to find a good way to remember the 6 that comes before the 8. It's easy. The first number is a 4, the second a 2, 4 plus 2 is 6. So now you're sure as shooting that the second from the end is a 6. As the gentleman from the license bureau would have said, the order of those numbers will never fade from your memory. There's an even simpler way of getting the same result. He explained that one to the peddler, too. I'll show you with your own number.

(The soldier has listened with wide-open eyes. His lips have stopped moving)

SCHWEYK   8 take away 2 is 6. That gives him the 6 already. Six take away 2 is 4, so he knows the 4 too. 8 and the 2 in between makes it 4-2-6-8. There's still another easy way, with multiplication and division. This is how it works: just remember, I'm quoting the clerk again, that two times 42 is 84. The year has 12 months. So you take away 12 from 84, and you get 72, and another 12 months, that's 60. That

definitely gives us 6, we cross out the zero. So we know
42-6-84. When we cross out the zero, we also cross out the
4 in back. And again our number is complete. It works with
division too, and I'll show you the way it goes. Now, what
was our number?

VOICE (*from behind*) Guard, what's the number of that
freight car that's supposed to go to Lower Bavaria?

SOLDIER What is it?

SCHWEYK Just a second, I'll try the method with the months.
There are 12 of them, aren't there? We agree on that.

SOLDIER (*desperately*) Tell me the number.

VOICE Guard! Are you asleep?

SOLDIER (*calling*) Forgot. I for-got! (*To Schweyk*) Damn
your hide!

VOICE (*gruffly*) That car's got to leave for Passau with the
12:50.

SECOND, MORE DISTANT VOICE Take this one. This is the one, I
think.

BALOUN (*satisfied, referring to the soldier who looks back in a
fright*) He wouldn't even let me sniff at his goulash.

SCHWEYK Maybe now they'll be sending a carload of machine guns to Bavaria. (*Philosophically*) But maybe by that
time they'll need harvesting machines in Stalingrad and
machine guns in Bavaria. Why not?

6

*Saturday night at the "Flagon." Among the customers are
Baloun, Anna, Kati, young Prochazka and off to one side, two
SS men. Dancing to the music of the electric piano.*

KATI (*to Baloun*) When Herr Brettschneider questioned me,
I told him I'd heard the SS was after the spitz. I didn't mention you, only your friend, Mr. Schweyk. And I didn't say
anything about Mr. Schweyk pretending not to know you

so he could start up a conversation with us. Was that all right?

BALOUN Anything is all right with me. You won't see me very long around here. Man, won't they be surprised to see me!

ANNA You mustn't talk so glum, Mr. Baloun, it doesn't help. And that SS man over there will ask me to dance if I'm just sitting here. You'd better ask me.

(*Baloun is about to get up when Mrs. Kopecka steps forward and claps her hands*)

MRS. KOPECKA Ladies and gentlemen, it's almost half past eight, which is time for the beseda (*half to the SS men*), the folk dance we dance among ourselves. Some people don't like it, but we do. The music is on the house.

(*Mrs. Kopecka puts a coin into the piano and those present dance the beseda, stamping very loudly. Baloun and Anna dance, too. The purpose of the dance is to drive the SS men away, bumping into their table, etc.*)

BALOUN (*sings*)

Strikes the midnight hour, smack
Jumps the barley from the sack.
Yuppidiyah, yuppidoh.
Every girl lets go.

THE OTHERS (*joining in*)

Lets the fellows tweak her cheeks,
Almost all have got four cheeks.
Yuppidiyah, yuppidoh.
Every girl lets go.

(*The SS men get up, cursing, and make their way to the door. After the dance Mrs. Kopecka comes back from the adjoining room and continues washing her glasses. Kati brings the First Customer from scene 3 with her to the table*)

THE FIRST CUSTOMER Folk dancing is something new at the "Flagon" and very popular because the regular customers know that while it's going on Mrs. Kopecka tunes in on Radio Moscow.

BALOUN There won't be any more dancing for me. Where I'm going they don't dance the beseda.

ANNA   They tell me we should have thought twice before going to the park. It's dangerous on account of the German deserters that attack you.

THE FIRST CUSTOMER   They only attack men. Deserters need civilian clothes. Every morning these days you can find German uniforms in Stromovka Park.

KATI   If you lose a suit it's not easy to get another. They say the clothing control office made a rule against paper suits and hats. On account of the paper shortage.

THE FIRST CUSTOMER   The Germans are crazy about those kind of offices. They pop up like mushrooms. They make jobs for themselves to keep them out of the war. They'd rather pester the Czechs with milk control, food control, paper control, and so on. Keeps them out of the draft.

BALOUN   They'll be too much for me. I can see my future. It's inevitable.

ANNA   I don't know what you're talking about.

BALOUN   You'll know soon enough, Miss Anna. I'm sure you know the song, "Countless Gates and Hallways," about the painter who died young. Sing it for me, will you. I'm just in the mood for it.

ANNA (*sings*)
Countless gates and hallways he was painting always
Meanwhile giving kisses to the little misses.
Now his painting's over, he is pushing clover.

Is that it?

BALOUN   That's it.

ANNA   Goodness, you're not going to do something to yourself?

BALOUN   What I'm going to do to myself will give you the cold shivers, miss. I won't lay a hand on myself, I'm going to do something worse.

(*Schweyk enters with a package under his arm*)

SCHWEYK (*to Baloun*)   Here I am with the goulash meat. Don't thank me, I'm swapping it for the cot you've put up in the kitchen.

BALOUN   Let's see, is it beef?

SCHWEYK (*firmly*)   Hands off. We're not going to unpack

it here. Good evening, ladies, you here too?

ANNA   Good evening, we know the whole story.

SCHWEYK (*draws Baloun into a corner*)   What did you blab to them this time?

BALOUN   Only that we knew each other and pretending not to was a trick. I didn't know what to tell them. My cot is yours. You're saving a friend from the abyss, just let me sniff at it, through the paper. Mrs. Mahler across the street offered me twenty crowns for it, I wouldn't even consider it. How did you get it?

SCHWEYK   It's from the black-market, from a midwife that got it from the country. Around 1930 she delivered a baby at a peasant's house. The baby had a little bone in his mouth, she started crying and said, "It means we'll all be starving." She said that before the Germans came; and every year the peasant woman has been sending her a little package to keep her from starving, but this year the midwife needed the money for taxes.

BALOUN   If only Mrs. Kopecka has some real paprika!

MRS. KOPECKA (*joining them*)   Go back to your table, in half an hour I'll call you into the kitchen. Meanwhile act as if nothing had happened. (*To Schweyk, after Baloun has returned to his table*) What kind of meat is it?

SCHWEYK (*reproachfully*)   Mrs. Kopecka, I'm surprised at you.
    (*Mrs. Kopecka takes the package from him and cautiously peeks in*)

SCHWEYK (*seeing that Baloun is talking to the girls with big, excited gestures*)   Baloun is getting too excited to suit me. Put in a lot of paprika to make it taste like beef. It's horse-meat. (*She looks at him sharply*) All right, it's Mr. Voyta's spitz. I had to do it, because the "Flagon" would be disgraced if starvation made one of your steady customers join the Germans.

A CUSTOMER AT THE BAR   Service!
    (*Mrs. Kopecka hands Schweyk the package to hold so that she can quickly serve her customer. At that moment the sound of a large car is heard. SS men enter, led by Platoon Leader Bullinger*)

BULLINGER (*to Schweyk*) Your housekeeper was right that you'd be at the tavern. (*To the SS men*) Clear the floor! (*To Schweyk while the SS men push the other guests back*) What have you done with the dog, you stinker?

SCHWEYK Beg to report, Herr Platoon Leader, the papers said he was stolen. Haven't you read about it?

BULLINGER Is this more of your impudence?

SCHWEYK Beg to report, Herr Platoon Leader, I only wish to say that if you don't keep up with the daily papers, you might miss something and then you won't be able to take vigorous action.

BULLINGER I don't know why I bother with you, there must be something wrong with me. I probably want to see how far a character like you can go before he dies.

SCHWEYK Yes, sir, Herr Platoon Leader, and because you want the dog.

BULLINGER You admit you wrote me a letter asking me to pay two hundred crowns for that dog?

SCHWEYK Herr Platoon Leader, I admit that I wanted the two hundred crowns because I'd have had expenses if the dog hadn't been stolen.

BULLINGER We'll talk about that at the Petschek Bank. (*To the SS men*) Search tavern for spitz! (*One SS man leaves*) (*The sound of furniture being overturned, objects smashed, and so on, comes from the adjoining room. Schweyk waits in stoic calm, his package under his arm*)

SCHWEYK (*suddenly*) We've also got good slivovitz here. (*An SS man jostles a little man in passing. While drawing back, the latter steps on a woman's foot and says, "Pardon me," whereupon the SS man turns, knocks him down with a club, and, at a nod from Bullinger, carries him out with the help of another SS man. An SS man comes in with Mrs. Kopecka*)

SS MAN Tavern searched, dog not present.

BULLINGER (*to Mrs. Kopecka*) This innocent tavern of yours is a hornet's nest of subversive activity. But I'll smoke you out.

SCHWEYK Yes, sir, Herr Platoon Leader, Heil Hitler. If you don't, we might get fresh and snap our fingers at the regula-

tions. Mrs. Kopecka, you've got to run your tavern so
everything's as clear as fresh spring water, like Chaplain
Vyvoda said when he . . .

BULLINGER   Shut up, you bastard. I have a good mind to pull
you in and shut your place down, Mrs. Kosheppa.

BRETTSCHNEIDER (*who has appeared at the door*)   Herr Platoon Leader Bullinger, may I have a word with you in
private?

BULLINGER   I can't see anything to talk to you about. You
know what I think of you.

BRETTSCHNEIDER   The Gestapo has received new information
concerning the whereabouts of Voyta's missing dog. I
thought it might be of interest to you, Herr Platoon Leader
Bullinger.

(*The two men go to a corner and begin to gesticulate
wildly. Brettschneider seems to be intimating that Bullinger
has the dog, Bullinger seems to be saying "Me?" and to
grow angry, etc.*)

(*Mrs. Kopecka has calmly resumed washing glasses.
Schweyk stands there unconcerned and amiable. Unfortunately Baloun now embarks on a maneuver to get hold of
his package and succeeds. At a sign from him a customer
takes it from Schweyk and passes it on. It reaches Baloun
and he fingers it, having lost all self-control.*)

(*An SS man has watched the wandering package with
interest*)

SS MAN   Hey, what's going on here? (*With a few steps he is
at Baloun's side, and takes away the package*)

SS MAN (*handing the package to Bullinger*)   Herr Platoon
Leader, this package has been smuggled to one of the
customers, that man over there.

BULLINGER (*opens the package*)   Meat! Owner, step forward!

SS MAN (*to Baloun*)   You there, you opened the package.

BALOUN (*bewildered*)   It was handed to me. It doesn't belong
to me.

BULLINGER   Oh, it doesn't belong to you? Ownerless meat,
huh? (*Suddenly shouting*) Why did you open it then?

SCHWEYK (*when Baloun doesn't know how to answer*)   Beg

to report, Herr Platoon Leader, this dumbbell must be innocent because he wouldn't have peeked if it was his; he'd have known what was in it.

BULLINGER (*to Baloun*)   Who did you get it from?

SS MAN (*when Baloun again fails to answer*)   The first thing I noticed was this man (*pointing at the customer who took the package from Schweyk*) passing the package.

BULLINGER   Where did you get it from?

THE CUSTOMER (*unhappily*)   It was handed to me, I don't know by whom.

BULLINGER   This tavern seems to be a branch of the blackmarket. (*To Brettschneider*) And if I'm not mistaken, Herr Brettschneider, you vouched just a minute ago for the woman who owns it?

MRS. KOPECKA (*stepping forward*)   Gentlemen, the "Flagon" is not a black-market.

BULLINGER   No? (*Slaps her face*) I'll show you, you Czech swine!

BRETTSCHNEIDER (*excitedly*)   Mrs. Kopecka is known to me as an unpolitical person. I'll have to ask you not to pass judgment on her without a hearing.

MRS. KOPECKA (*very pale*)   Don't you dare strike me!

BULLINGER   What's this? Backtalk? (*Slaps her again*) Take her away!

(*As Mrs. Kopecka prepares to haul off at Bullinger, the SS man hits her on the head. She falls*)

BRETTSCHNEIDER (*bending over her*)   You'll have to answer for this, Bullinger. You're only trying to distract attention from Voyta's dog, but you won't get away with it.

SCHWEYK (*steps forward*)   Beg to report, sir, I can explain everything. The package doesn't belong to anybody here. I know because I laid it down myself.

BULLINGER   So it's you.

SCHWEYK   A gentleman gave it to me to hold, then he said he was going to the toilet. Man of medium height with a blond beard.

BULLINGER (*amazed at the explanation*)   Say, are you feebleminded?

SCHWEYK (*looking him earnestly in the eye*)   Yes, sir, as I've already told you. I was officially certified an idiot by a commission. I was fired from the Voluntary Labor Service for the same reason.

BULLINGER   But you're intelligent enough for the blackmarket, huh? Maybe when we get you to Gestapo headquarters you'll begin to realize that it won't do you a damn bit of good, even if you can show a hundred certificates.

SCHWEYK   (*softly*)   Beg to report, Herr Platoon Leader, I realize it won't do me a damn bit of good, because ever since I was a kid I've always gotten into a mess when I had the best of intentions and only wanted to help people. Like in Lubova one time, when I tried to help this school caretaker's wife to hang out her washing. If you'll step out in the hall with me, I'll tell you what happened. I got into this black-market business same as Pontius Pilate got into the Creed.

BULLINGER   (*staring at him*)   I don't know why I listen to you, and this isn't the first time. You've probably got me hypnotized, because I never saw such a villain before.

SCHWEYK   It must be like you suddenly saw a lion on Karlova Street where it's unusual, or like in Chotebor when a postman caught his wife with the janitor and stabbed her one two three. He went straight to the police station to give himself up, and when they asked him what he did after the crime, he said that the minute he stepped out of the house he'd seen a naked man turning the corner, so they decided he was mentally deranged and let him go. But two months later they found out that a lunatic really had escaped from the asylum stark naked. The postman had told the truth, but they hadn't believed him.

BULLINGER   (*amazed*)   I'm still listening. I can't tear myself away. I know what you're thinking. You think the Third Reich is good for a year, or maybe ten years, but I'm here to tell you that ten thousand years is probably more like it. Makes your eyes pop out, doesn't it?

SCHWEYK   That's a long time, like the sexton said when the lady that runs the "Swan" married him and dropped her teeth into the water glass for the night.

BULLINGER   Do you piss yellow or do you piss green?

SCHWEYK (*amiably*) Beg to report, Herr Platoon Leader, I piss yellowish-green.

BULLINGER But now you're coming with me even if certain people (*referring to Brettschneider*) vouch for you till they're blue in the face.

SCHWEYK Yes, sir, Herr Platoon Leader. There's got to be order. Black-marketing is an evil and it won't stop until there's nothing left. Then we'll have order right away, am I right?

BULLINGER And we'll find the dog too.

(*He leaves with the package under his arm. The SS men seize Schweyk and take him along*)

SCHWEYK (*while leaving, good-naturedly*) I only hope you won't be disappointed. Some customers are so keen on a dog they move heaven and earth to get him, and once they have him, they don't like him any more.

BRETTSCHNEIDER (*to Mrs. Kopecka who has recovered consciousness*) Mrs. Kopecka, you have been the victim of certain conflicts between certain sections of the Gestapo and the SS. I say no more. However, you are under my protection, I'll be back to talk this over with you in private. (*Leaves*)

MRS. KOPECKA (*staggering back to the bar where she ties a dish towel around her bleeding forehead*) Does anybody want some beer?

KATI (*looking at Schweyk's hat still hanging over the table*) They didn't even let him take his hat.

THE CUSTOMER He'll never come off alive.

(*Young Prochazka enters shyly. He is horrified at the sight of Mrs. Kopecka's blood-soaked bandage*)

YOUNG PROCHAZKA What's happened to you, Mrs. Kopecka? I saw the SS driving away—did the SS do it?

CUSTOMERS They clubbed her on the head because they said the "Flagon" was a black-market.—Even Herr Brettschneider of the Gestapo stood up for her, or they'd have pulled her in.—They took one man away.

MRS. KOPECKA Mr. Prochazka, you have no business here at the "Flagon." This is a place for real Czechs.

YOUNG PROCHAZKA Believe me, Mrs. Anna, I've been miserable and I've learned my lesson. Can't I hope to make it up to you?

(*Mrs. Kopecka's icy look makes him shudder and he sneaks guiltily away*)

KATI   They're nervous at the SS, too, because yesterday they fished another SS man out of the Moldau, with a hole in his left side.

ANNA   They throw in plenty of Czechs.

CUSTOMER   That's only because things are going badly for them in the East.

THE FIRST CUSTOMER (*to Baloun*)   Wasn't it your friend they took away?

BALOUN (*bursts into tears*)   It's all my fault. That's what I get for my gluttony. I've prayed and prayed to the Virgin Mary to give me strength and somehow shrink my stomach, but it's no use. I dragged my best friend into this and maybe they'll shoot him tonight, or if he's lucky tomorrow morning.

MRS. KOPECKA (*puts down a slivovitz in front of him*)   Drink that. Bawling won't help.

BALOUN   God bless you. You broke with your admirer on account of me, you won't find a better one, he's only weak, same as me. If I'd taken that oath you asked me to, things wouldn't look so desperate. If I could take it now—but can I? On an empty stomach? Good God, what's going to happen now?

MRS. KOPECKA (*goes back to the bar and starts washing glasses*)   Somebody put a nickel into the piano. I'll tell you what's going to happen.

(*A customer puts a coin into the electric piano. A light goes on inside, a transparency shows the moon over the majestically flowing Moldau. Washing her glasses, Mrs. Kopecka sings "The Song of the Moldau"*)

The stones on the Moldau's bottom go shifting
In Prague three emperors molder away.
The top won't stay top, for the bottom is lifting
The night has twelve hours and is followed by day.

The times will be changing. The intricate plotting
Of people in power must finally fail.
Like bloodthirsty cocks though today they are strutting
The times will be changing, force cannot prevail.

The stones on the Moldau's bottom go shifting
In Prague three emperors molder away.
The top won't stay top, for the bottom is lifting
The night has twelve hours and is followed by day.

Interlude in the Higher Regions

*Hitler and General von Bock, known as "The Killer," facing
a map of the Soviet Union. Both men are larger than life-size.
Military music.*

VON BOCK

Respected Herr Hitler, your expedition
In Russia's costing a lot of bombers, guns, tanks, and ammunition
To say nothing of men. "The Killer" is what they now call me.
To be thought a spoil-sport would appall me
But if you think you will get to Stalingrad, you're very much mistaken.

HITLER

Herr General von Bock, Stalingrad will be taken
I've given the German people my promise.

VON BOCK

Herr Hitler, the winter is nearly on us
And when it starts to snow out here in the east you know it's snowing.
If we're stuck when the north winds start blowing . . .

HITLER

Herr von Bock, I will throw the peoples of Europe into the disaster
And the Little Man will extricate his master.
Herr von Bock, don't let me down, you would not dare.

VON BOCK
As for replacements . . .

HITLER
That's my care.

7

Cell in a military prison with Czech prisoners waiting to be drafted into military service, among them Schweyk. They are waiting, stripped to the waist, and are simulating the most pitiful ailments. One of them, for instance, is lying on the floor as if he were dying.

A STOOPED MAN   I talked to my lawyer, he was very encouraging. They can't put us in the army if we're not willing. It's illegal.

A MAN WITH CRUTCHES   Then why do you double up like that, if you don't expect to be taken?

THE STOOPED MAN   Just in case.

(*The man with crutches laughs scornfully*)

THE DYING MAN (*on the floor*)   They wouldn't dare, we're all invalids. They're unpopular enough already.

A NEARSIGHTED MAN (*triumphantly*)   One night in Amsterdam a German officer was crossing what they call the Gracht, it was almost eleven and he was beginning to feel nervous. He asked a Dutchman for the time. The Dutchman gives him a solemn look and all he says is: "My watch has stopped." The officer walks on, feeling pretty glum, and stops a second man. Before he can even ask the question, the man says he left his watch home. They say the officer shot himself.

THE DYING MAN   He couldn't take it. All that contempt.

SCHWEYK   They're more likely to shoot other people than themselves. In Vralava a tavern keeper's wife was carrying on with his brother. He punished them with contempt. He found a pair of her panties in his brother's wagon and put them on the bedside table, he thought that would make her feel ashamed. They went to the district court and had him declared legally incompetent, then they sold the tavern out from under him and went away together. But in a way he was right, because his wife admitted to her girl friend that she was almost ashamed to take his lined winter coat.

THE STOOPED MAN   What are you here for?

SCHWEYK   Black-marketing. They could have shot me but the Gestapo needed me as a witness against the SS. The big shots are at loggerheads and I benefited. They told me I was lucky about my name, because it's Schweyk with a "y". If I wrote it with a plain "i", I'd be of German descent and then I could be drafted.

THE MAN WITH CRUTCHES   They're even drafting them out of jail these days.

THE STOOPED MAN   Only if they're of German descent.

THE MAN WITH CRUTCHES   Or if they volunteer to be of German descent like him over there.

THE STOOPED MAN   The only hope is to be a cripple.

THE NEARSIGHTED MAN   I'm nearsighted, I could never recognize an officer and salute.

SCHWEYK   They can put you at a listening post reporting enemy planes. In that line of work blindness is an advantage, the blind develop extra-special hearing. A peasant in Socz, for instance, cut out his dog's eyes to improve his hearing. In other words you're fit for service.

THE NEARSIGHTED MAN (*in despair*)   I know a chimney sweep in Brevnov who can give you such a fever for ten crowns that you'll jump out of the window.

THE STOOPED MAN   That's nothing. There's a midwife in Vrshovitz who can dislocate your leg so good for twenty crowns that you'll be a cripple the rest of your life.

THE MAN WITH CRUTCHES   I got my leg dislocated for five crowns.

THE DYING MAN   I didn't have to pay anything. I've got a genuine strangulated hernia.

THE MAN WITH CRUTCHES   Then they'll operate on you in Pankratz hospital, and then what will you do?

SCHWEYK (*cheerfully*) Listening to you people, somebody
could get the idea that you're trying to keep out of this war
that's got to be fought to defend civilization against Bolshevism.

(*A soldier enters and busies himself with the pail*)

SOLDIER You got crap all over the bucket again, you pigs.
You haven't even learned how to shit.

SCHWEYK We're discussing Bolshevism. Do you fellows know
what Bolshevism is? It's the sworn ally of Wall Street which
has planned our destruction under the leadership of the Jew
Rosenfeld in the White House. (*The soldier keeps busy
with the pail in order to listen, and Schweyk continues pa-
tiently*) But they don't know us. Do you know the song
about the cannoneer from Przemysl in the First World War,
which was fought against the tsar? (*He sings*)

Standing behind the gun
He loads from sun to sun.
Standing behind the gun
He loads from sun to sun.
Then a bullet comes on swiftly
Carries both his hands off deftly.
But he stands by his gun
Loading from sun to sun.
Stands steady at his gun
Loading from sun to sun.

The Russians fight because they have to. They got no
agriculture, because they wiped out the big land-owners,
and their industry is ruined because they want everybody to
be equal and that's depressing and because the thoughtful
workers are bitter about the big salaries of the bureaucrats.
You see, there's nothing there, and once we get there, the
Americans will be too late. Am I right?

SOLDIER Shut up. Conversation is prohibited.

(*He leaves angrily with the pail*)

THE DYING MAN Seems to me you're a stoolpigeon.

SCHWEYK (*cheerfully*) I'm not a stoolpigeon. I only listen
regularly to the German radio. You ought to listen, once in
a while. It's a scream.

THE DYING MAN   It is not. It's a disgrace.

SCHWEYK (*firmly*)   It's a scream.

THE NEARSIGHTED MAN   There's no reason to crawl up their asses.

SCHWEYK (*lecturing*)   Don't say that. It's an art. A lot of small animals would be glad if they could squeeze into a tiger. That way he couldn't get at them and they'd feel relatively safe; only it's hard to get in.

THE STOOPED MAN   Don't be vulgar. It's not pretty to see the Czechs putting up with everything.

SCHWEYK   Like this Jaroslav Vaniek said to the consumptive peddler. The owner of the "Swan" in Budweis, a big tall fellow, filled the peddler's glass only half full, and when the little runt didn't say anything, Vaniek gave him hell: "How can you take it lying down?—that makes you a partner in the offense." The peddler socked Vaniek, and that was the end of it. And now I'm going to ring the bell and make them hurry up with their war, I've got no time to waste. (*He stands up*)

A SHORT, FAT MAN (*who has been sitting apart from the others*)   You will not ring the bell.

SCHWEYK   Why not?

THE FAT MAN (*with authority*)   Because things are going fast enough to suit us.

THE DYING MAN   That's right. What did they pick you up for?

THE FAT MAN   Because somebody stole my dog.

SCHWEYK (*interested*)   Was it a spitz?

THE FAT MAN   What do you know about it?

SCHWEYK   I bet your name is Voyta. I'm glad to meet you. (*He proffers his hand which the fat man overlooks*) My name is Schweyk. Maybe that doesn't mean anything to you, but you can shake hands with me. I bet you're not a German-lover any more since they brought you here.

THE FAT MAN   On the strength of what my maid told me, I accused the SS of kidnaping my dog. Is that enough for you?

SCHWEYK   Plenty. At home in Budweis we had this teacher who was accused by a student he'd been picking on of having the newspaper on his music rack while he was play-

ing the organ in church. The teacher was a religious man,
and he made his wife miserable by not letting her wear
short skirts. But by the time they were through pestering
him with questions, he said he didn't even believe in the
Marriage at Cannae anymore. So you'll march to the Cau-
casus and shit on Hitler—only, like the owner of the "Swan"
said, it all depends where you shit on what.

THE FAT MAN   If your name is Schweyk, when they were
leading me through the gate, a young fellow sidled up to
me. He only had a chance to whisper, "Ask for Mr.
Schweyk," then they opened the gate. He must still be
down there.

SCHWEYK   I'll have a look right away. I always thought
there'd be a crowd down there in the morning, the owner
of the "Flagon," who wouldn't want to miss the chance, and
maybe a big fat fellow, waiting for Schweyk, but in vain.
Give me a hand, one of you gentlemen!

(*He goes to the little cell window and climbs onto the back
of the man with the crutches, to look out*)

SCHWEYK   It's young Prochazka. I doubt if he can see me.
Give me your crutches.

(*He gets them and waves them. Young Prochazka seems
to have noticed him, and Schweyk communicates with him
with sweeping gestures. He indicates a tall man with a
beard—Baloun—and makes the gestures of stuffing food into
his mouth and of carrying something under his arm. Then
he climbs down off the back of the man with crutches*)

SCHWEYK   You're probably wondering what I was doing up
there. We made a gentleman's agreement, that's why he
came here. I always knew he was a decent sort. I was only
repeating his gestures, so he'd know I caught on. He probably didn't want me marching off to Russia with a weight
on my mind.

(*Orders are heard from outside, and marching steps; a band
begins to play the "Horst Wessel" march*)

THE DYING MAN   What's going on? Did you see anything?

SCHWEYK   A lot of people at the gate. Probably a battalion,
marching off.

THE STOOPED MAN   That music is terrible.

SCHWEYK   I think it's pretty because it's sad and rousing.

THE MAN WITH CRUTCHES   We'll soon be hearing it more often. They play the "Horst Wessel" march every time they get a chance. It was written by a pimp. I wish I knew what the words mean.

THE FAT MAN   I can oblige you with a translation. The flag raised high/ and tightly closed the columns/ Storm troops march on with firm and steady tread./ The comrades who have shed their heroes' blood before us/ March on with us in spirit straight ahead.

SCHWEYK   I know another version we used to sing at the "Flagon."

(*He sings accompanied by the military band. He sings the chorus to the tune, the preceding stanzas to the drums*)

After the drummer come
Sheep in great masses.
The skin for the drumhead
Comes from their asses.
  The butcher calls. With eyelids tightly shuttered
  The sheep march on with firm and steady tread.
  And those who at the yard have shed their blood before
    them
  March on with them in spirit straight ahead.

They lift up their hands to show
What rough work they do
Already stained with blood
And empty too.
  The butcher calls. With eyelids tightly shuttered
  The sheep march on with firm and steady tread.
  And those who at the yard have shed their blood before
    them
  March on with them in spirit straight ahead.

They carry a blood-red flag
Which has a cross on it.
A cross with a hook to hang
Poor people upon it.
  The butcher calls. With eyelids tightly shuttered

The sheep march on with firm and steady tread.
And those who at the yard have shed their blood before
   them
March on with them in spirit straight ahead.

(*The other prisoners have joined in the chorus from the
second stanza on. At the end the door opens and a German
army doctor appears*)

THE ARMY DOCTOR   It's nice to hear you all singing so happily.
   You'll be glad to know that I consider you well enough
   to join the army. You're accepted. Everybody up. Put your
   shirts on. Be ready to march in ten minutes. (*He leaves*)
   (*The prisoners, crushed, put on their shirts*)

THE STOOPED MAN   Without a medical examination, that's absolutely illegal.

THE DYING MAN   I have a stomach ulcer, I can prove it.

SCHWEYK (*to the fat man*)   I hear they'll put us in different
   outfits to keep us from being together and making trouble.
   Good-bye, Mr. Voyta, I was glad to meet you, I'll see you
   at the "Flagon" at six o'clock, after the war.
   (*Overcome with emotion, he shakes hands all around as the
   cell door opens. Schweyk marches out first with military
   bearing*)

SCHWEYK   Heitler! On to Moscow!

8

*Weeks later. Deep inside the wintry steppes of Russia the good
Hitler soldier Schweyk is marching to join his company near
Stalingrad. Because of the cold he is wrapped in many layers
of miscellaneous garments.*

SCHWEYK (*sings*)
   Onward to Jaromersh hoofing
   Probably you think I'm spoofing

We arrived there just about
Almost dinner time.

(*A German patrol stops him*)

FIRST SOLDIER   Halt. Password!

SCHWEYK   Victory! Can you tell me the way to Stalingrad?
Something went wrong, I got separated from my company,
and I've been hiking all day.

(*The first soldier examines his papers*)

SECOND SOLDIER (*hands him his canteen*)   Where are you
from?

SCHWEYK   Budweis.

SECOND SOLDIER   Then you're a Czech.

SCHWEYK (*nods*)   I hear things aren't going so well up front.

(*The two soldiers who have been exchanging looks give an
ugly laugh*)

FIRST SOLDIER   What's a Czech like you looking for at the
front?

SCHWEYK   I'm not looking for anything. I only want to help
defend civilization against Bolshevism, same as you, if we
don't, it's a bullet in the chest, am I right?

FIRST SOLDIER   You could be a deserter.

SCHWEYK   Oh no, you'd shoot me right away for breaking
my soldier's oath and not dying for the Führer, Heil Hitler.

SECOND SOLDIER   What? You still believe that stuff? (*Takes
back his canteen*)

SCHWEYK   I believe as much as Tonda Novotny in Vysočan
who went to the parish house to apply for a job as a sexton.
He didn't know if the church was Protestant or Catholic,
but the minister was in suspenders and there was a woman
in the room, so he said he was Protestant, and guess what:
he was wrong.

FIRST SOLDIER   Why does it have to be Stalingrad, you fishy
ally?

SCHWEYK   Because that's where my regimental headquarters
is, comrades, and I need a stamp to show that I reported
for duty, or my papers won't be any good and I won't be
able to show my face in Prague. Heil Hitler!

FIRST SOLDIER   And suppose we said "Shit on Hitler," we're deserting to the Russians and want to take you with us because you understand Russian because it's supposed to be like Czech.

SCHWEYK   Czech is very similar. But I advise you against it. I don't know my way around here, gentlemen, I'd rather you told me how to get to Stalingrad.

FIRST SOLDIER   Maybe you don't trust us. Is that it?

SCHWEYK (*amiably*)   In my opinion you're good soldiers because, if you were deserters, you'd have something for the Russians, a machine gun or maybe a good field glass, something they could use, and you'd hold it up in the air so they wouldn't start shooting right away. That's the way it's done, I'm told.

FIRST SOLDIER (*laughs*)   You mean they'd catch on, even if it wasn't Russian? I see, you're the cautious kind. So you think it's better to ask the way to your grave in Stalingrad. Go in that direction. (*He shows him*)

SECOND SOLDIER   And if anybody asks you: we're an army patrol and we gave you a good grilling. Just in case.

FIRST SOLDIER (*leaving*)   And your advice isn't bad, brother.

SCHWEYK (*waves after them*)   Glad to help, and good-bye!

(*The soldiers leave quickly. Schweyk starts in the direction indicated but is seen to deviate from it. He disappears into the twilight. When he emerges on the other side, he stops for a moment in front of a signpost and reads, "Stalingrad —30 miles." He shakes his head and marches on. The drifting clouds in the sky are now reddish from a distant conflagration. He watches them with interest while marching*)

SCHWEYK (*sings*)
    Thought that in the service
    We would have a ball
    Thought the war would last a week or two or three weeks
    But that would be all.

(*Smoking his pipe, he keeps on marching. The clouds pale, and Schweyk's table at the "Flagon" emerges in a pink light.*

*His friend Baloun is kneeling on the floor. Beside him stands
Mrs. Kopecka with her embroidery. At a table, behind a
glass of beer, sits Anna, the maidservant)*

BALOUN *(in the tone of a litany)* I swear without hesitation
and on an empty stomach, because all efforts by various
people to get me some meat have failed; without a square
meal under my belt, I swear to the Virgin Mary and all the
saints that I'll never volunteer for the Nazi army, so help
me God Almighty. I swear in memory of my friend
Schweyk who is now marching over the icy steppes of
Russia in faithful fulfillment of his duty, because there's no
help for it. He was a good man.

MRS. KOPECKA All right, you can get up now.

ANNA *(takes a sip from the glass of beer, stands up, and hugs
him)* And the wedding can take place as soon as the papers
from Protivin get here. *(After kissing him, to Mrs. Kopecka)* Too bad there's no happy ending for you.

*(Young Prochazka stands in the door, a package under his
arm)*

MRS. KOPECKA Mr. Prochazka, I forbade you ever to darken
my door again. It's all over between us. Now that I know
your grand passion isn't even good for two pounds of
smoked butt.

YOUNG PROCHAZKA But suppose I've brought it? *(Shows it)*
Two pounds of smoked butt.

MRS. KOPECKA What, you've got it? In spite of the heavy
penalties?

ANNA But we don't really need it any more. Mr. Baloun took
the oath without.

MRS. KOPECKA But you've to admit that it shows true love.
Rudolf!

(She embraces him passionately)

ANNA That would make Mr. Schweyk happy, if he only
knew, the good soul! *(She looks tenderly at Schweyk's
bowler hanging over his table)* Take good care of that hat,
Mrs. Kopecka, I'm sure Mr. Schweyk will come and get it
after the war.

BALOUN *(sniffing at the package)* It would be good with
lentils.

(*The "Flagon" disappears. A drunken man, wearing two heavy sheepskins and a steel helmet, staggers from the background. Schweyk meets him*)

THE DRUNK   Halt! Who are you? I see you're one of ours and not a gorilla, thank God. I'm Chaplain Ignaz Bullinger from Metz. Would you happen to have some kirsch?

SCHWEYK   Beg to report, sir, I haven't.

CHAPLAIN   That's hard to believe. I don't need it to drink, as you may have thought, you stinker. Admit it, that's what you think of your priest. I need it for my car back there, the portable altar's in it; I've run out of gas. In Rostov they're trying to save gas on God, that'll cost them plenty when they step up to God's throne and he asks them in a thundering voice: "You motorized my altar, but where was the gas?"

SCHWEYK   I don't know, Your Reverence. Can you tell me the way to Stalingrad?

CHAPLAIN   God only knows. Do you know the one about the bishop who asks the captain during a storm, "Will we get through?" And the captain answers, "We're in the hands of God, bishop." And the bishop only says, "Is it as bad as all that?" and bursts into tears! (*He sits down in the snow*)

SCHWEYK   Is Platoon Leader Bullinger your brother?

CHAPLAIN   Yes, God help us, then you know him? You haven't any kirsch or vodka?

SCHWEYK   No, and you'll catch cold if you sit in the snow.

CHAPLAIN   It doesn't matter what happens to me. They want to save on gas, do they, let them see how long they can fight a war without God and God's word. On land, in the air, and on the sea, etcetera. I joined their stupid Nazi League for German Christians, but with a very troubled conscience. To suit them, I stopped saying that our Lord Jesus was a Jew, in my sermons I make him a thumping one hundred percent Christian, with blue eyes. I throw in Wotan for good measure, and I tell them the world has got to be German, even if the price is an ocean of blood, because I'm a renegade swine who's betrayed his faith for wages, and they don't give me enough gas, and now see where it's got me.

SCHWEYK To the Russian steppes, Your Reverence. You'd better go back to Stalingrad with me and sleep it off. (*He pulls him up and drags him along a few feet*) But you'll have to use your own legs too, or I'll drop you right here. I've got to get back to my company. Hitler needs me.

CHAPLAIN I can't leave my altar here, it'll be captured by the Bolsheviks, and then what? They're heathen. I passed a hut back there, there was smoke coming out of the chimney, I wonder if they've got any vodka. Just hit them over the head with your rifle butt, that'll do it. Are you a German Christian?

SCHWEYK No, the plain kind. Don't puke all over yourself, it freezes on you.

CHAPLAIN Yes, I'm frozen stiff. I'll make it hot for them at Stalingrad.

SCHWEYK First you've got to get there.

CHAPLAIN I'm not very optimistic. (*Calmly, almost soberly*) Do you realize—what's your name anyway?—that they laugh in my face, me a priest of God, when I threaten them with hell? The only way I can explain it is that they think they're there already. Religion is going to the dogs, it's all Hitler's fault, don't tell anybody I said so.

SCHWEYK Hitler's a fart, I can tell you because you're drunk. And who's to blame for Hitler? The people who handed him Czechoslovakia in Munich, in the name of "peace in our lifetime," which turned out to be a blitz peace. But the war turned out to be a long one, and for quite a lot of people a lifetime. That's the kind of mistakes people make.

CHAPLAIN Then you're against this war that it's our duty to fight against the godless Bolsheviks, you stinker. Do you know that I'm going to have you shot when we get to Stalingrad?

SCHWEYK If you don't pull yourself together and walk like a human being, you'll never make it to Stalingrad. And I'm not against the war, I'm not marching to Stalingrad for the fun of it, but because, "Where the bullets fly, the grub stands by," as Naczek the cook said in the First World War.

CHAPLAIN Don't tell me fairy tales. Deep down, you say to yourself, "Fuck your war," I can tell from the look on your

face. (*Grabs him*) How can you claim to be for the war,
what's in it for you—admit it, you don't give a shit for this
war.

SCHWEYK (*rudely*) I'm marching to Stalingrad, and so are
you, because those are our orders, and because two lone
stragglers would starve around here. I've said that before.
(*They march on*)

CHAPLAIN On foot, war is depressing. (*Stops*) There, I see
the hut, let's go in. Got your rifle off safety?
(*A hut appears, they walk toward it*)

SCHWEYK But don't make a stink. They're people too, and
you've had enough to drink.

CHAPLAIN Keep your rifle at the ready. They're heathen, and
no backtalk!
(*From the hut step an old peasant woman and a young
woman with a small child*)

CHAPLAIN Look, they're going to run away. We've got to
prevent them. Ask them where they've buried their vodka.
And look at that shawl she's wearing, I'll take it, I'm frozen
stiff.

SCHWEYK You're freezing because you're drunk, you've got
two fur coats on already. (*To the young woman who stands
motionless*) Good morning, which way to Stalingrad?
(*The young woman points as in a trance*)

CHAPLAIN Does she admit they have vodka?

SCHWEYK You sit down, I'll do the talking, and then we'll
move on, I don't want any trouble. (*To the woman, amiably*) Why are you standing here outside your house?
Were you leaving? (*The woman nods*) Your shawl is so
thin. Haven't you anything else to keep you warm? It's not
really enough.

CHAPLAIN (*sitting on the ground*) Use your rifle butt.
They're all gorillas, heathen.

SCHWEYK (*rudely*) You shut up. (*To the woman*) Vodka?
The man is sick.
(*Schweyk has accompanied all his questions with illustra-
tive gestures. The woman shakes her head*)

CHAPLAIN (*viciously*) Shaking your head, huh? I'll show you.
I'm freezing and you shake your head. (*He struggles to his

feet and staggers toward the woman with raised fist. She withdraws into the hut, closing the door behind her. The chaplain kicks the door in and enters the hut) I'll finish you off.

SCHWEYK *(trying in vain to hold him back)* You stay out here. It's not your house. *(He follows him in. The old woman also goes in. Then the woman's scream is heard, and sounds of struggle. Schweyk, from inside)* You better put your knife away, lady. Hold still, you bastard, or I'll break your arm. Get going, quick.

(From the hut steps the woman with the child. She is wearing one of the chaplain's coats. Behind her the old woman)

SCHWEYK *(coming out of the hut behind them)* He'll sleep it off. You'd better clear out.

THE OLD WOMAN *(bows low before Schweyk in the traditional manner)* God bless you, soldier, you're a good man. If we had some bread left, I'd give you a chunk. You could use it. Where are you going?

SCHWEYK To Stalingrad, babushka, to the battle. Can you tell me the way?

THE OLD WOMAN You're a Slav, you talk like us, you didn't come here to murder people, you're not with the Hitlers. God bless you. *(She blesses him with sweeping gestures)*

SCHWEYK *(without embarrassment)* No hard feelings, babushka. I'm a Slav all right, but don't waste your blessing on me, because I'm a satellite.

THE OLD WOMAN God protect you, son, your heart is pure, you've come to help us, you'll help us beat the Hitlers.

SCHWEYK *(firmly)* No offense but I've got to be moving on, it wasn't my idea. Say, babushka, I'm beginning to think you're deaf.

THE OLD WOMAN *(although her daughter keeps tugging at her sleeve)* You'll help us get rid of the robbers. Hurry, soldier, and God bless you.

(The young woman pulls the old woman away; they leave. Schweyk marches on, shaking his head. Night has come and the stars appear in the sky. Schweyk stops again at a road sign and shines his blacked-out flashlight on it. Surprised, he reads "Stalingrad—30 miles" and marches on.

Suddenly shots ring out. Schweyk immediately raises his rifle in surrender. But nobody appears and the shots stop. Schweyk keeps marching faster. When he appears again in his circular course, he is out of breath and sits down on a snowdrift)

SCHWEYK (*sings*)

When we came marching to Kovno
It was pretty stinking.
For a slug of booze those dogs
Took our shoes and left us limping.

(His pipe drops from his mouth, he falls asleep and dreams. Schweyk's table at the "Flagon" appears in a golden light. Around the table sit Mrs. Kopecka in her wedding dress, young Prochazka in his Sunday suit, Kati, Anna, and Baloun with a full plate in front of him)

MRS. KOPECKA   And for the wedding banquet you're getting your smoked butt, Mr. Baloun. You took the oath without it, that does you honor, but to help you keep your oath, a little piece of meat once in a while can't do any harm.

BALOUN (*eating*)   I just love eating. God bless our food. God created everything, from the sun to caraway seeds. (*Pointing at the plate*) Can this be sin? The pigeons fly, the chickens pick seeds off the ground. The landlord of the "Hus" knew seventeen ways of cooking a chicken, five sweet, six sour, and four with stuffing. Wine grows from the earth for me, and so does bread, said the pastor in Budweis, that couldn't eat because of diabetes, and they're forbidden me. In Pilsen, in 1932, I ate a hare at the "Schlossbräu"—the cook has died in the meantime, so don't bother to go there any more—I tell you, I never tasted such a hare in all my life. It was served with gravy and dumplings. That's not unusual, but there was something in that gravy that made the dumplings go crazy like they didn't know themselves, like something got into those dumplings. It was really good, I've never seen the like of it since. The cook took the recipe with him to the grave. It's lost to mankind.

ANNA   Don't complain. What would dear Mr. Schweyk say—

he probably doesn't even know what fried potatoes look
like any more.

BALOUN That's true. There's always a way. In Pudonitz,
when my sister was married, they did it with quantity:
Thirty people at the Pudonitz tavern, men and women, and
old people, too—they never weakened: soup, veal, pork,
chicken, two calves and two fat pigs, from head to tail, plus
dumplings and sauerkraut in kegs, and beer to start with,
then schnapps. I only remember that my plate was never
empty, and after every mouthful a bucket of beer and a
waterglass of schnapps as a chaser. Once there was silence
like in church when they brought in the pork. They were
all good people when they sat there together, stuffing
themselves. I'd have gone through fire for every one of
them. And there were all sorts of characters, a judge from
the district court in Pilsen, in private life he hounded thieves
and workers. Eating takes the sting out of people.

MRS. KOPECKA In honor of Mr. Baloun I will now sing the
"Song of the Flagon."
(*She sings*)

Come, dear guest, and have a seat
Share with us our dishes
Have some soup and cabbage meat
Or some Moldau fishes.

What you need is salt and bread
And a roof above your head.
As a man, these you deserve
And we honor whom we serve
For just eighty hellers.

No credentials, rank, and place
Ever need be cited.
If your face includes a nose
You will be invited.

Just a little friendliness
Wit and bragging count for less.
Eat your cheese and drink your beer

> And you will be welcome here—
> You and eighty hellers.

One day, looking out to see
If the sky is clearing
We will find the earth to be
Friendly, warm, and cheering.

> Everyone a man will be
> Overlooked by nobody.
> When it's cold we'll all keep warm
> Have a roof 'gainst snow and storm.
> With but eighty hellers!

(All have joined in the chorus)

BALOUN   When my grandfather who was auditor at the water department went to Pankratz hospital and they told him he'd have to cut down on his food or he'd lose his eyesight, he said, "I've seen enough, but I haven't eaten enough yet." *(Suddenly stops eating)* Christ, if only Schweyk doesn't freeze to death in the terrible cold out there!

ANNA   He mustn't lie down. It's when they feel warm and cozy, I hear, that they're closest to freezing to death.

(The "Flagon" vanishes. It is daytime again. Driving snow. Schweyk stirs under a blanket of snow. The clanking of tank treads is heard)

SCHWEYK *(sitting up)*   I almost fell asleep. But let's go now, on to Stalingrad!

(He pulls himself up and starts marching again. A large armored car appears out of the driving snow, carrying German soldiers with chalky white or bluish faces under steel helmets, wrapped in all sorts of clothes, skins, even women's skirts)

THE SOLDIERS   *(sing "The German Miserere")*

One fine day our generals handed down the order
To overrun Danzig by crossing the border.
With tanks and bomber squadrons Poland we invaded
And after two weeks' blitzing we had made it.
God have mercy and lead us back home again.

One fine day our generals handed down the order

To cross the Norwegian and then the French border.
With tanks and bombers France and Norway we invaded
And after five weeks' blitzing we had made it.
God have mercy and lead us back home again.

One fine day our generals handed down the order
To make war on Russia and trample its border.
With tanks and bomber squadrons Russia we invaded
And after two years we still haven't made it.
God have mercy and lead us back home again.

One fine day the order will come down from our dictator
To conquer the ocean's depths and the moon's deepest
    crater
But it is bad enough in Russia's landscape
Strong is the enemy, cold the winter, and there is no escape.
God have mercy and lead us back home again.

(*The armored car disappears in the driving snow. Schweyk
keeps on marching*)
(*A road sign appears, pointing at right angles. Schweyk
ignores it. But suddenly he stops and listens. Then he bends
down, whistles softly and snaps his fingers. From under the
snow-covered underbrush crawls a starving dog*)

SCHWEYK Ha! I knew you were hiding in the brush, wondering whether to come out. You're a cross between a schnau-
zer and a German shepherd, with a little bulldog thrown in,
and I'll call you Ajax. Don't cringe, and stop that trembling,
I can't stand it. (*He marches on, followed by the dog*)
We're going to Stalingrad. You'll meet other dogs, it's a
busy place. If you want to survive in a war, stick to the
crowd and the regular routine, don't do anything original,
and keep quiet until you get a chance to bite. War doesn't
last forever, neither does peace, and when it's all over, I'll
take you back to the "Flagon." But we've got to watch
Baloun or he'll gobble you up, Ajax. People will be wanting
dogs again, and pedigrees will be faked because they want
purebreds, it's crazy, but that's what they want. Don't get
tangled up in my feet, or I'll give you a licking. On to
Stalingrad!
(*The snowstorm becomes more dense and hides them*)

Epilogue

The good Hitler-soldier Schweyk marches untiringly toward the ever-distant Stalingrad. Out of the driving snow wild music flares up and a larger-than-life-sized shape emerges: Adolf Hitler. The historic meeting between Schweyk and Hitler takes place.

HITLER
  Halt. Friend or foe?

SCHWEYK (*with a routine salute*)
  Heitler!

HITLER   (*outshouting the storm*)
  What? I can't hear what you say.

SCHWEYK   (*louder*)
  I said Heitler. Can you hear me now?

HITLER
  Yes.

SCHWEYK
  The wind carries everything away.

HITLER
  True enough. Not to mention all this snow.
  Do you know who you're speaking to?

SCHWEYK
  Sorry, no.

HITLER
  I am the Führer.
  (*Schweyk, who has been standing with one arm upraised, is now frightened. He drops his rifle and raises the other arm as in surrender*)

SCHWEYK
  Holy Saint Joseph!

HITLER
  At ease. Who are you?

SCHWEYK
  I'm Schweyk from Budweis at the bend of the Moldau. I've hurried here to help you at Stalingrad. Just tell me how to get there.

HITLER

How in all the devil's creation
Do I know that, with the rotten Bolshevik transportation!
From Rostov to Stalingrad, on the map
Seemed about the length of my little finger
Now it turns out to be a good deal longer.
What's more, the winter this year most unfairly
Started on the third of November instead of the fifth.
This is the second time it's started early.
This winter is a typically underhanded Bolshevik stunt
As a result I can't tell back from front.
I started on the assumption that the stronger side would
    prevail.

SCHWEYK

And so it has done.
(*Schweyk is very cold. He has been stamping his feet and
now beats his sides with his arms*)

HITLER

Herr Schweyk, if the Third Reich should fail
Nature will have played us a very dirty trick.

SCHWEYK

From all I hear, it's nature plus the Bolshevik.

HITLER   (*getting ready for a long explanation*)

Eastward or westward. That's the question, so history shows.
Let me start with Herman the Cheruscan . . .

SCHWEYK

We'd better keep moving while you talk, or we'll be froze.

HITLER

Very well. Move on.

SCHWEYK

But where do you want me to go?

HITLER

Let's try the north.
(*They push on a few steps toward the north*)

SCHWEYK

But this way we're up to our necks in the snow.

HITLER

Then the south.
(*They push a few steps toward the south*)

SCHWEYK
  This way there are mountains of dead men.
HITLER
  Then I'll push east.
  (*They push a few steps toward the east*)
SCHWEYK   (*stops, whistling him back*)
  That way there are armies of Red men.
HITLER
  True enough.
SCHWEYK
  Let's go home. Here we are nowhere.
HITLER
  There stand my German people. I cannot go there.
  (*Hitler starts in all directions one after the other. Schweyk
  whistles him back each time*)
HITLER
  To the east. To the west. To the north. To the south.
SCHWEYK
  You can't stay here and you can't get out.
  (*Hitler's movements in all directions are getting faster*)
SCHWEYK   (*starts to sing*)

  Yes, you cannot go back and you cannot move on
  You're all rotten on top and your bottom's gone
  And the east wind's too cold and the Reds are too red
  So I simply don't know whether to pump you with lead
  Or take down my pants and shit on your head.
  (*Hitler's desperate thrusts have become a wild dance*)
CHORUS OF ALL PLAYERS
  (*who take off their masks and step forward to the edge
  of the stage*)

  The times will be changing. The intricate plotting
  Of people in power must finally fail.
  Like bloodthirsty cocks though today they are strutting
  The times will be changing, force cannot prevail.

  The stones on the Moldau's bottom go shifting
  In Prague three emperors molder away.

The top won't stay top, for the bottom is lifting
The night has twelve hours and is followed by day.

HENRY SLEPT BESIDE HIS NEWLY-WEDDED*

Henry slept beside his newly wedded,
Heiress to a castle on the Rhine.
Snake bites, which tormented the false lover,
Would not let him peacefully recline.

At the stroke of twelve the curtain parted.
On the sill a pale cold hand appeared.
In a shroud he saw his Wilhelmina
And her mournful, ghostly voice he heard.

Do not tremble, said his Wilhelmina;
Faithless lover, do not be afraid.
I have not come here in hate or anger,
I've not come to curse your marriage bed.

Bitter grief my poor young life has shortened,
I have died because I loved you well,
But the Lord has fortified my spirit
Saved me from the headlong plunge to hell.

Why did I believe your protestations
That your love would always be the same,
Never dreaming that for you to vanquish
Maiden's heart was but a paltry game?

Do not weep. This world does not deserve it,
'Tis not worth a single tear or moan.
Live serene and happy with Eliza
Now that you have got her for your own.

Henry, you have treasure, ah, uncounted,
Use it now to give my soul repose.
Give your Wilhelmine the peace of spirit
You denied her living, heaven knows.

Sacrifice! cried Henry in his fever;

* [This street ballad is sung by Kati and Anna in scene 4—Translated
by Ralph Manheim.]

That's what you have come to ask, he cried.
Whereupon the poor spurned woman vanished
And the churl committed suicide.

God had mercy on her, but the faithless
Lover was condemned beyond repair.
Still he lives, an evil spooky monster
Wand'ring in the dreary midnight air.

The Caucasian
Chalk Circle

Play

Collaborator: R. Berlau

Translator: Ralph Manheim

CHARACTERS

DELEGATES OF THE "GALINSK"
GOAT-BREEDING KOLKHOZ:
an old peasant, a peasant
woman, a young peasant,
a very young worker
MEMBERS OF THE "ROSA LUX-
EMBURG" FRUIT-GROWING
KOLKHOZ: an old peasant, a
peasant woman, the
woman agronomist, the
girl tractor driver, the
wounded soldier, and
other peasants and peasant
women
THE EXPERT FROM THE CAPITAL
ARKADI CHEIDZE, the singer
HIS MUSICIANS
GEORGI ABASHVILI, the governor
HIS WIFE NATELLA
THEIR SON MICHAEL
SHALVA, the aide-de-camp
ARSEN KAZBEKI, the fat prince
THE RIDER FROM THE CAPITAL
NIKO MIKADZE and MIKHA
LOLADZE, doctors
SIMON CHACHAVA, a soldier
GRUSHA VACHNADZE, a kitchen
maid
THREE ARCHITECTS
BROTHER ANASTASIUS, a monk

FOUR CHAMBERMAIDS: Assya,
Masha, Zulika, Fat Nina
THE NURSE
THE WOMAN COOK
THE MAN COOK
THE STABLE HAND
SERVANTS IN THE GOVERNOR'S
PALACE
IRONSHIRTS AND SOLDIERS OF
THE GOVERNOR AND THE FAT
PRINCE
BEGGARS AND PETITIONERS
THE OLD DAIRY MAN
TWO UPPER-CLASS LADIES
THE LANDLORD
THE HOUSE SERVANT
THE CORPORAL
BLOCKHEAD, a soldier
A PEASANT WOMAN AND HER
HUSBAND
THREE PEDDLERS
LAVRENTI VACHNADZE, Grusha's
brother
HIS WIFE ANIKO
THEIR HIRED HAND
THE PEASANT WOMAN, for a
time Grusha's mother-in-
law
HER SON YUSSUP
THE BLACKMAILER

WEDDING GUESTS
CHILDREN
AZDAK, the village scribe
SHAUVA, a policeman
A FUGITIVE, the grand duke
THE NEPHEW OF THE FAT
     PRINCE
THE DOCTOR
THE INVALID
THE LAME MAN

LUDOVIKA, the landlord's
     daughter-in-law
A POOR OLD PEASANT WOMAN
HER BROTHER-IN-LAW IRAKLI,
     a bandit
THREE KULAKS
ILLO SHUBOLADZE and SANDRO
     OBOLADZE, lawyers
THE VERY OLD COUPLE

The Dispute over the Valley

Amid the ruins of a war-torn Caucasian village the members of two kolkhoz villages, for the most part women and old men, but also a few soldiers, are sitting in a circle, smoking and drinking wine. With them is an expert from the state reconstruction commission in the capital.

A PEASANT WOMAN, LEFT (*pointing*) Over there in the hills we stopped three Nazi tanks, but by that time the apple orchard was ruined.

AN OLD PEASANT, RIGHT Our beautiful dairy farm: nothing but rubble!

A GIRL TRACTOR DRIVER, LEFT I set that fire, comrade.

(*Pause*)

THE EXPERT Now listen to the minutes: Delegates of the Galinsk goat-breeding kolkhoz have come to Nukha. At the approach of Hitler's armies, the kolkhoz, by order of the authorities, drove its goats eastward. Its members are now contemplating a return to this valley. Their delegates have inspected the village and surroundings and found much destruction. (*The delegates, right, nod*) The adjoining Rosa Luxemburg kolkhoz grows fruit. (*Turning to those on the right*) Within the framework of the reconstruction program they have put in a petition that the former territory of the Galinsk kolkhoz, a valley where the grazing is poor, should be converted to orchards and vineyards. As expert for the reconstruction commission, I call on the two kolkhoz villages to decide between them whether the Galinsk kolkhoz should return here or not.

THE OLD PEASANT, RIGHT First I wish to protest again against the restriction of discussion time. It has taken us delegates of the Galinsk kolkhoz three days and three nights to get here, and now we're told that only half a day has been set aside for discussion.

A WOUNDED SOLDIER, LEFT Comrade, we haven't as many villages or as much manpower or as much time as we used to.

THE GIRL TRACTOR DRIVER All pleasures have to be rationed. Tobacco and wine are rationed, and that goes for discussion too.

THE OLD PEASANT, RIGHT (*with a sigh*) Death to the Fascists! Very well, I'll come straight to the point and explain why we want our valley back. There are many reasons, but I'll begin with the simplest. Makinä Abakidze, bring out the goat cheese.

(*A peasant woman, right, takes an enormous cheese wrapped in a cloth from a basket. Applause and laughter*)

THE OLD PEASANT, RIGHT Help yourselves, comrades. Take some.

AN OLD PEASANT, LEFT (*distrustfully*) Are you trying to influence us?

THE OLD PEASANT, RIGHT (*amid laughter*) How can I expect to influence you, Surab, you valley-thief! Everybody knows you'll take the cheese and the valley too. (*Laughter*) All I want from you is an honest answer: do you like the taste of this cheese?

THE OLD PEASANT, LEFT The answer is yes.

THE OLD PEASANT, RIGHT You do, do you? (*Bitterly*) I ought to have known you wouldn't know anything about cheese.

THE OLD PEASANT, LEFT Why not? I've told you I liked it.

THE OLD PEASANT, RIGHT Because you can't like it. Because it's not the same as in the old days. And why isn't it the same? Because our goats don't like the new grass the way they liked the old grass. Cheese isn't cheese because grass isn't grass, that's the trouble. Kindly put that in your minutes.

THE OLD PEASANT, LEFT But your cheese is perfect.

THE OLD PEASANT, RIGHT   It is not perfect, it's barely middling. The new pasture is no good, whatever the young folks may say. I say we can't live there. It doesn't even smell like morning in the morning.

(*Several laugh*)

THE EXPERT   Let them laugh, they know what you mean. Comrades, why does a man love his home country? Because the bread tastes better, the sky is higher, the air is spicier, voices ring out more clearly, the ground is softer to walk on. Am I right?

THE OLD PEASANT, RIGHT   The valley has always belonged to us.

THE SOLDIER   What do you mean "always"? Nothing has always belonged to anybody. When you were young, you didn't even belong to yourself, you belonged to the princes Kazbeki.

THE OLD PEASANT, RIGHT   The valley belongs to us by law.

THE GIRL TRACTOR DRIVER   The laws will have to be reexamined in any case to see if they still apply.

THE OLD PEASANT, RIGHT   Of course. I suppose it doesn't make any difference what kind of tree grows outside the house where you were born? Or who you've got for a neighbor? Doesn't that make any difference? Why, one of our reasons for wanting to come back is to have you near our kolkhoz, you valley-thieves. Now you can laugh again.

THE OLD PEASANT, LEFT (*laughs*)   Then why don't you listen quietly to what your "neighbor," Kato Vachtang our agronomist, has to say about your valley?

A PEASANT WOMAN, RIGHT   We haven't said half of what we've got to say about our valley. The houses aren't all gone, the foundations of the dairy are still intact.

THE EXPERT   You have a right to government aid in either place—you know that.

THE PEASANT WOMAN, RIGHT   Comrade expert, this isn't a matter for bargaining. I can't take your cap and give you another and say "this one is better." Maybe the other is better, but you like your own best.

THE GIRL TRACTOR DRIVER   It's not the same with a piece of land as with a cap. Not in our country, comrade.

THE EXPERT   Don't get excited. It's true we must regard a

piece of land largely as an implement for producing something useful, but it's equally true that we must recognize people's love for a particular piece of land. Before proceeding with the discussion, I propose that you tell the comrades from the Galinsk kolkhoz what you are planning to do with the disputed valley.

THE OLD PEASANT, RIGHT   Agreed.

THE OLD PEASANT, LEFT   Right, give Kato the floor.

THE EXPERT   Comrade agronomist!

THE AGRONOMIST, LEFT (*stands up, she is in army uniform*) Comrades, last winter, when we were partisans fighting in these hills, we talked about the possibility of vastly increasing our fruit production once the Germans were driven out. I drew up an irrigation project. By damming our mountain lake we can irrigate three hundred acres of barren ground. That will enable our kolkhoz not only to plant more fruit trees, but to put in vineyards as well. However, the project will only be worthwhile if we can include the disputed valley, now belonging to the Galinsk kolkhoz. Here are my calculations. (*She hands the expert a portfolio*)

THE OLD PEASANT, RIGHT   Put it down in the minutes that our kolkhoz is planning to start breeding horses.

THE GIRL TRACTOR DRIVER   Comrades, the project was worked out in the days and nights when we were hiding in the mountains, half the time without cartridges for the few rifles we had. Even a pencil was hard to get.

(*Applause on both sides*)

THE OLD PEASANT, RIGHT   Our thanks to the comrades of the Rosa Luxemburg kolkhoz and to all those who fought for our country!

(*They shake hands all around and embrace*)

THE PEASANT WOMAN, LEFT   Our idea was that our soldiers, our men and yours, should come home to a still more fertile country.

THE GIRL TRACTOR DRIVER   As the poet Mayakovski said, "The home of the Soviet people shall also be the home of reason!"

(*The delegates right, except for the old peasant, have stood up and are studying the agronomist's sketches with the expert. Exclamations such as "Why a twenty-three-yard*

*fall?"—"The rock here will be blasted."—"All they really
need is concrete and dynamite!"—"They'll make the water
come down here; mighty clever!"*)

A VERY YOUNG WORKER, RIGHT (*to the old peasant, right*)
They're going to irrigate all the fields between the hills.
Look at that, Alleko.

THE OLD PEASANT, RIGHT   I won't look. I knew their project
would be good. I refuse to be forced at gunpoint.

THE SOLDIER, LEFT   But they're only trying to force you at
pencil point.

(*Laughter*)

THE OLD PEASANT, RIGHT (*stands up gloomily and goes to look
at the drawings*)   The trouble is these valley-thieves know
perfectly well that nobody in this country can resist machines and projects.

THE PEASANT WOMAN, RIGHT   Alleko Bereshvili, you're the
worst sucker of all for new projects, everybody knows that.

THE EXPERT   How about my minutes? Can I say that you'll
go back to your kolkhoz and recommend that they re-
linquish their old valley in the interest of this project?

THE PEASANT WOMAN, RIGHT   I'll recommend it. How about
you, Alleko?

THE OLD PEASANT, RIGHT (*over the drawings*)   I request copies
of the plans to take back with us.

THE PEASANT WOMAN, RIGHT   In that case we can sit down
to eat. Once he has the plans and a chance to discuss them,
the matter is settled. I know him. And the rest of our
people are the same.

(*The delegates embrace each other again, laughing*)

THE OLD PEASANT, LEFT   Three cheers for the Galinsk kolkhoz
and good luck with your horses!

THE PEASANT WOMAN, LEFT   Comrades, in honor of the delegates from the Galinsk kolkhoz and of the expert, we have
arranged to put on a play related to our problem. Arkadi
Cheidze, the singer, will take part.

(*Applause. The girl tractor driver has run off to get the
singer*)

THE PEASANT WOMAN, RIGHT   Comrades, your play had better
be good, we're paying a valley for it.

THE PEASANT WOMAN, LEFT Arkadi Cheidze knows 21,000 lines by heart.

THE OLD PEASANT, LEFT We've worked up the play under his direction. He's a hard man to get. You people from the planning commission should arrange to have him come north more often, comrade.

THE EXPERT Economics is more in our line.

THE OLD PEASANT, LEFT (*smiling*) You organize the redistribution of vineyards and tractors, why not of songs?

(*Led by the girl tractor operator, Arkadi Cheidze, the singer, enters the circle. He is a powerfully built man of simple ways. He is accompanied by musicians with their instruments. The artists are greeted with applause*)

THE GIRL TRACTOR DRIVER Arkadi, this is the comrade expert.

(*The singer greets those around him*)

THE PEASANT WOMAN, RIGHT I am greatly honored to make your acquaintance. I heard about your songs when I was a little girl in school.

THE SINGER This time it will be a play with songs, and almost everyone in the whole kolkhoz will take part.

THE OLD PEASANT, RIGHT Will it be one of the old legends?

THE SINGER A very old one. It is called *The Chalk Circle* and comes from the Chinese. We play it in different form, though. Shura, show them the masks. Comrades, it is an honor for us to entertain you after a difficult debate. We hope you will find that the old poet's voice still rings true, even in the shadow of the Soviet tractors. It may be wrong to mix different wines, but old and new wisdom make an excellent mixture. Well, I hope we shall all get something to eat before the play begins. That helps.

VOICES Of course.—Everybody to the club house.

(*All go gaily to dinner. As they are leaving, the expert turns to the singer*)

THE EXPERT How long will this story take, Arkadi? I've got to go back to Tiflis tonight.

THE SINGER (*offhand*) Actually there are two stories. A couple of hours.

THE EXPERT (*confidentially*) Can't you make it shorter?

THE SINGER No.

2

The Noble Child

(*The singer is sitting on the ground in front of his musicians. A black sheepskin cloak over his shoulders, he leafs through a worn-out copybook with slips of paper inserted*)

In olden times, in bloody times
There ruled in this city, known as "the accursed city"
A governor by the name of Georgi Abashvili.
He was as rich as Croesus.
He had a beautiful wife.
He had a thriving child.
No other governor in Gruzinia had
So many horses in his stable
And so many beggars at his door
So many soldiers in his service
And so many petitioners in his courtyard.
How shall I tell you the kind of man Georgi Abashvili was?
He enjoyed his life.
One Easter Sunday morning
The governor and his family went
To church.

(*From the archway of a palace pour beggars and petitioners, holding up emaciated children, crutches and petitions. Behind them two Ironshirts, then, splendidly attired, the governor and his family*)

THE BEGGARS AND PETITIONERS Mercy, your grace, the taxes are too high.—I lost my leg in the Persian War, where can I get . . .—My brother is innocent, your grace, a misunderstanding.—He's starving on me.—He's our last remaining son—please release him from military service.—Please, your grace, the water inspector has been bribed.

(*A servant collects the petitions, another hands out coins*) *from a pouch. The soldiers push back the crowd, striking at them with heavy leather whips*)

A SOLDIER   Back! Clear the church door.

(*Behind the governor, his wife, and an aide-de-camp, the governor's child is rolled out through the archway in a magnificent baby carriage. The crowd presses forward again to see him*)

THE SINGER (*while the crowd is whipped back*)

That Easter the people saw the governor's heir for the first time.

Two doctors never stirred from the side of the Noble Child Apple of the governor's eye.

(*Cries from the crowd: "The child!"—"I can't see him, don't push so." "God bless you, your grace."*)

THE SINGER

Even the powerful Prince Kazbeki

Paid his respects to him at the church door.

(*A fat prince steps forward and greets the family*)

THE FAT PRINCE   Happy Easter, Natella Abashvili.

(*A command is heard. A dust-covered rider dashes in and holds out a roll of papers to the governor. At a sign from the governor the aide-de-camp, a handsome young man, goes to the rider and holds him back. A brief pause while the fat prince looks distrustfully at the rider*)

THE FAT PRINCE   What a beautiful day! When it rained last night, I thought to myself: gloomy holidays. But this morning, the sky was clear. I love clear skies, Natella Abashvili, and a simple heart. And little Michael, every inch a governor. Ti-ti-ti-ti. (*He tickles the child*) Happy Easter, little Michael, ti-ti-ti-ti.

THE GOVERNOR'S WIFE   What do you think, Arsen, Georgi has finally decided to start building the new east wing. The whole neighborhood with its wretched shacks is being torn down to make room for the garden.

THE FAT PRINCE   That is good news after so much bad news. What do you hear about the war, brother Georgi? (*The governor makes a gesture meaning that he doesn't wish to speak of it*) A strategic withdrawal, I hear? Oh well, there are always these little setbacks. Good days and bad days. The fortunes of war. Not very important, is it?

THE GOVERNOR'S WIFE He's coughing! Georgi, did you hear?
(*Sharply to the two dignified doctors standing right behind
the baby carriage*) He's coughing!

FIRST DOCTOR (*to the second*) Permit me to remind you,
Niko Mikadze, that I was opposed to that lukewarm bath.
A slight error in the temperature of the bath water, your
grace.

SECOND DOCTOR (*also very polite*) I am unable to agree with
you, Mikha Loladze. The temperature of the bath water
was that prescribed by our great and beloved Mishiko
Oboladze. More likely a draft during the night, your grace.

THE GOVERNOR'S WIFE But do something for him! He looks
feverish, Georgi.

FIRST DOCTOR (*over the child*) No cause for alarm, your
grace. We shall make his bath water a little warmer and
it won't happen again.

SECOND DOCTOR (*with a venomous look at him*) I won't
forget that, my dear Mikha Loladze. No cause for concern,
your grace.

THE FAT PRINCE Ai, ai, ai, ai. I always say: If my liver pains
me, give the doctor fifty strokes across the soles of his feet.
And that's only because the times have gone soft; in the
old days it was simply: Off with his head!

THE GOVERNOR'S WIFE Let's go inside, it's probably because of
the draft out here.

(*The procession consisting of the family and their servants
turns into the church door. The fat prince follows. The
aide-de-camp steps out of the procession and indicates the
rider*)

THE GOVERNOR Not *before* mass, Shalva.

THE AIDE-DE-CAMP (*to the rider*) The governor does not
wish to be molested with reports before mass, especially if,
as I presume, they are depressing. Go to the kitchen, my
friend, and tell them to give you something to eat.

(*The aide-de-camp joins the procession while the rider with
a curse enters the palace gate. A soldier comes out of the
palace and stops in the archway*)

THE SINGER

The city is silent.

Pigeons are strutting on the square.

A soldier of the palace guard
Is joking with a kitchen maid
Who is coming up from the river with a bundle.
(*A kitchen maid with a bundle wrapped in large green leaves tries to enter the archway*)

THE SOLDIER   What's this? Not in church? Playing hooky from services, young lady?

GRUSHA   I was all dressed, but then they were missing a goose for Easter dinner and they asked me to get one, because I know about geese.

THE SOLDIER   A goose? (*With affected suspicion*) I'd like to see that goose.

(*Grusha does not understand*)

THE SOLDIER   You've got to watch your step with women. "I've only been getting a goose." That's what they say, when actually it's something entirely different.

GRUSHA (*goes resolutely up to him and shows him the goose*) Here it is. And if it isn't a good fifteen-pound goose crammed full of corn, I'll eat the feathers.

THE SOLDIER   A queen of a goose. The governor himself will eat it. So you've been down by the river again?

GRUSHA   Yes, at the poultry farm.

THE SOLDIER   Oh, at the poultry farm down by the river? Not upstream in those willows?

GRUSHA   I only go to the willows when I wash clothes.

THE SOLDIER (*pointedly*)   Exactly.

GRUSHA   Exactly what?

THE SOLDIER (*winking*)   Exactly what I meant.

GRUSHA   Why shouldn't I wash clothes by the willows?

THE SOLDIER (*with exaggerated laughter*)   "Why shouldn't I wash clothes by the willows?" That's good, really good.

GRUSHA   I don't understand you, soldier. What's good?

THE SOLDIER (*slyly*)   If someone finds out what I know, hot and cold she's sure to grow.

GRUSHA   I fail to see what anybody can know about those willows.

THE SOLDIER   Even if there were bushes nearby, where someone can sit and see everything? Everything that goes on when a certain person "washes clothes"!

GRUSHA   What goes on, soldier? Can't you just say what you mean and be done with it?

THE SOLDIER   Something that someone can see.

GRUSHA   Why, soldier, you wouldn't mean that on a hot day I sometimes put my toes in the water, because that's all there is to it.

THE SOLDIER   There's more. Your toes and something more.

GRUSHA   What more? Well, maybe my foot.

THE SOLDIER   Your foot and a little more. (*He laughs loudly*)

GRUSHA   (*angrily*) Simon Chachava, you ought to be ashamed. Sitting in the bushes on a hot day, waiting for someone to put her leg in the water. And probably with some other soldier at that! (*She runs away*)

THE SOLDIER   (*calls after her*)   Not with another soldier!

(*As the singer resumes his story, the soldier runs after Grusha*)

THE SINGER

The city lies silent, but why these men in arms?
The governor's palace is at peace.
Why then is it a fortress?

(*The fat prince comes quickly out of the church door, left. He stops and looks around. Two Ironshirts are waiting outside the archway to the right. The prince sees them and passes them slowly, making a sign to them; then he goes out quickly. One Ironshirt goes through the archway into the palace; the other stays behind on guard. Muffled cries are heard from various directions in the background. "Ready!" The palace is surrounded. Church bells are heard in the distance. Out of the church door comes the governor's family and the rest of the procession*)

THE SINGER

Then the governor returned to his palace
And the palace was a trap.
The goose was plucked and roasted
But the goose was not eaten
Noon was no longer a time for eating
Noon was a time for dying.

THE GOVERNOR'S WIFE   (*passing by*)   It's really impossible to live in this hovel, but of course Georgi builds only for his

little Michael, not for me. Michael is everything, everything for Michael!

THE GOVERNOR Did you hear that? Brother Kazbeki wishing
us a happy Easter! That's all very well, but as far as I
know it didn't rain in Nukha last night. Where brother
Kazbeki was, it rained. Where was brother Kazbeki?

THE AIDE-DE-CAMP We must investigate.

THE GOVERNOR Yes, immediately. Tomorrow.

(*The procession turns into the archway. The rider who
has meanwhile come out of the palace steps up to the
governor*)

THE AIDE-DE-CAMP Excellency, won't you listen to the rider
from the capital? He arrived this morning with confidential
papers.

THE GOVERNOR (*continuing on his way*) Not before dinner,
Shalva!

THE AIDE-DE-CAMP (*while the procession disappears into the
palace and only two soldiers of the palace guard remain at
the gate; to the rider*) The governor does not wish to be
molested with military reports before dinner, and his excellency is devoting the afternoon to a conference with
eminent architects who have also been invited to dinner.
Here they come. (*Three gentlemen have entered. While the
rider goes off, the aide-de-camp welcomes the architects*)
Gentlemen, his excellency is expecting you for dinner. He
will devote the whole afternoon to you. And your great
new plans! Come quickly!

ONE OF THE ARCHITECTS We are filled with admiration that
his excellency should think of building despite the alarming
reports about the Persian war.

THE AIDE-DE-CAMP "Because of them" would be more accurate. It's nothing. Persia is far away! The garrison here
would let themselves be hacked to pieces for the governor.
(*Noise from the palace. A woman's shrill scream. Cries
of command. Aghast, the aide-de-camp goes toward the
archway. An Ironshirt steps out and stops him with his pike*)

THE AIDE-DE-CAMP What's going on? Put down that pike,
you dog! (*Furiously to the palace guard*) Disarm this man!
Don't you see this is a plot against the governor's life?

(The soldiers of the guard do not obey. They look coldly and indifferently at the aide-de-camp and watch the following scene without interest. The aide-de-camp fights his way into the palace)

ONE OF THE ARCHITECTS   The princes! The princes met in the capital last night. They are opposed to the grand duke and his governors. Gentlemen, we'd better clear out.

(They go off quickly)

THE SINGER

O blindness of the great! They live like gods on high
Great over bended backs, trusting
In hired fists, confident
Of their power that has already endured so long.
But long is not forever.
O passage of time, o hope of the poor.

(Out through the archway comes the governor, in chains, between two soldiers armed to the teeth. His face is gray)

Forever good-bye, great lord. Deign to walk with head erect.

From your palace windows hostile eyes look down upon you.

You will need no more architects. A plain carpenter is all you'll need.

You will not be moving to a new palace, but to a small hole in the ground.

Look round you one last time, blind man.

(The arrested man looks around)

Are you pleased with what you had? Between Easter mass and Easter meal

You will go to the place whence no one returns.

(He is led away. The palace guard falls in behind. A horn sounds the alarm. Noise behind the archway)

When the house of the great man collapses
Many small folk will be crushed under the ruins.
Those who never shared the fortune of the mighty
Will often share their downfall. The
Swift-plunging wagon
Drags the sweating draft horses
Down to the abyss.

(*Panic-stricken servants come rushing out of the archway*)

THE SERVANTS (*all at once*)   The baskets! All into the third courtyard! Provisions for five days.—The mistress has fainted.—Carry her downstairs, somebody, she can't stay here.—What about us?—They'll slaughter us like chickens. They always do.—Mother of God, what's going to happen? —They say there's been bloodshed in the city.—Nonsense, the governor has only been politely requested to attend a meeting of the princes. Everything will be settled peaceably, I have it from a reliable source.

(*The two doctors rush into the courtyard*)

FIRST DOCTOR (*trying to hold back the other*)   Niko Mikadze, it is your duty as a physician to stay with Natella Abashvili.

SECOND DOCTOR   My duty? Yours!

FIRST DOCTOR   Whose turn is it with the child today, Niko Mikadze, yours or mine?

SECOND DOCTOR   Mikha Loladze, do you really suppose I'm going to spend another minute in a plague-ridden house on account of that brat?

(*They start to fight. All that can be heard is: "You're neglecting your duty!" and "Duty be damned!" Then the second doctor strikes the first one down*)

SECOND DOCTOR   Oh, go to hell! (*Out*)

THE SERVANTS   Nothing to worry about until tonight, the soldiers won't be drunk before then.—Doesn't anybody know if they've mutinied?—The palace guard has ridden away.—Doesn't anybody know what's happened?

GRUSHA   Meliva the fisherman says a comet with a red tail was seen over the capital; that means calamity.

THE SERVANTS   They say news reached the capital yesterday that the Persian war has been completely lost.—The princes have all risen up. They say the grand duke has fled. All his governors are going to be executed.—They won't hurt the little people. I've got a brother in the Ironshirts. (*The soldier Simon Chachava appears, looking for Grusha in the crowd*)

THE AIDE-DE-CAMP (*appears in the archway*)   Into the third courtyard, all of you! Everybody help with the packing! (*He drives the servants off*)

(*Simon finally finds Grusha*)

SIMON There you are, Grusha. What are you going to do?

GRUSHA Nothing. If the worst comes to the worst, I have a brother with a farm in the mountains. But what about you?

SIMON Me? Nothing. (*Again with formality*) Grusha Vachnadze, your question about my plans gives me pleasure. I have received orders to escort Lady Natella Abashvili.

GRUSHA But hasn't the palace guard mutinied?

SIMON (*gravely*) It has.

GRUSHA Isn't it dangerous to escort her?

SIMON In Tiflis they say: Is stabbing dangerous for the knife?

GRUSHA You're not a knife, Simon Chachava, you're only a man. What's the lady to you?

SIMON The lady is nothing to me, but I've got orders and I'm going.

GRUSHA Then you're just stubborn, soldier, running into danger for no reason at all. (*Someone calls her from the palace*) They want me in the third courtyard, I'm in a hurry.

SIMON If you're in a hurry, let's not argue. A good argument takes time. May I ask whether the young lady still has her parents?

GRUSHA No. Only my brother.

SIMON Since the time is short, my second question is: Is the young lady as healthy as a fish in water?

GRUSHA Maybe a stitch in my right shoulder now and then, but otherwise strong enough for every kind of work. No one has ever complained.

SIMON That is common knowledge. When it's Easter Sunday and someone has to go for the goose nevertheless, she's the one. Third question: Is the young lady impatient? Does she want cherries in the winter?

GRUSHA Not impatient, but when people go off to war for no reason and there's no news, it's bad.

SIMON There will be news. (*Again Grusha is called from the palace*) And now the main question . . . .

GRUSHA Simon Chachava, I have to go to the third courtyard and I'm in a big hurry, so the answer is "Yes."

SIMON (*very much embarrassed*) They say that haste is the wind that blows the scaffolding down. But they also say that the rich are never in a hurry. I'm from . . .

GRUSHA Kutsk . . .

SIMON So the young lady has made inquiries? I'm healthy, I have no one to look out for, I get ten piasters a month, it'll be twenty when I'm paymaster, and with all my heart I ask for your hand.

GRUSHA Simon Chachava, it's all right with me.

SIMON (*takes from his neck a thin chain with a little cross on it*) The cross belonged to my mother, Grusha Vachnadze, the chain is silver; please wear it.

GRUSHA Many thanks, Simon.

(*He puts it around her neck*)

SIMON I've got to harness the horses, the young lady must understand that. The young lady had better go to the third courtyard now, or there will be trouble.

GRUSHA Yes, Simon.

(*They stand undecided*)

SIMON I'm only taking her to the troops who are still loyal. When the war is over, I'll be back. Two or three weeks. I hope the time won't hang heavy on my betrothed until I return.

GRUSHA

Simon Chachava, I will be waiting for you.

Never fear. Go off to war, soldier
The grim, bloody war, the hard bitter war
From which not every man returns.
But when you return I'll be there.
I will be waiting for you under the green elm tree
I will be waiting for you under the bare elm tree
I will be waiting till the last has come home again
And even more.
When you come back from the war
No boots will be standing at the door.
You will find no one in bed but me

And my mouth will be unkissed.
When you come back home
You'll be able to say everything's just the same.

SIMON   I thank you, Grusha Vachnadze. And good-bye!
(*He bows low to her. She bows just as low to him. Then she runs away quickly without looking back. The aide-de-camp steps out of the archway*)

THE AIDE-DE-CAMP   Harness the horses to the big carriage, don't stand around, you stinker!
(*Simon Chachava comes to attention and goes off. Out the archway creep two servants, bowed under the weight of enormous trunks. Behind them stumbles Natella Abashvili supported by her waiting-women. Following her, a woman carrying the child*)

THE GOVERNOR'S WIFE   Nobody attends to anything. I'm at my wits' end. Where is Michael? Don't hold him so clumsily. Load the trunks on the carriage. Is there any news of the governor, Shalva?

THE AIDE-DE-CAMP (*shakes his head*)   You must leave at once.

THE GOVERNOR'S WIFE   Any word from the city?

THE AIDE-DE-CAMP   No. It's been quiet so far, but there's no time to be lost. There's no room in the carriage for the trunks. Take out what you need. (*The aide-de-camp goes out quickly*)

THE GOVERNOR'S WIFE   Just the barest necessities! Quick! Open the trunks, I'll tell you what's needed.
(*The trunks are put down and opened*)

THE GOVERNOR'S WIFE (*pointing to some brocade dresses*) The green one and of course the one with the fur trimming! Where are the doctors? That terrible migraine is coming on again, it always starts at the temples. The one with the pearl buttons . . .
(*Enter Grusha*)

THE GOVERNOR'S WIFE   Taking your time, aren't you? Get the hot water bottles.
(*Grusha runs out, comes back in a moment with the hot water bottles, and is silently ordered about by the governor's wife*)

THE GOVERNOR'S WIFE (*watching a young chambermaid*) Don't tear the sleeve!

THE YOUNG WOMAN But gracious lady, nothing has happened to the dress.

THE GOVERNOR'S WIFE Because I caught you. I've been watching you for a long time. All you're good for is making eyes at the aide-de-camp! I'll kill you, you bitch! (*Strikes her*)

THE AIDE-DE-CAMP (*comes back*) You must hurry, Natella Abashvili. There's fighting in the city. (*Off again*)

THE GOVERNOR'S WIFE (*lets the young woman go*) Good God! Do you think they'll dare lay hands on me? Why should they? (*All are silent. She begins to rummage in the trunks*) Find my brocade jacket! Help her! What's Michael doing? Is he asleep?

THE NURSE Yes, gracious lady.

THE GOVERNOR'S WIFE Then put him down a minute and bring me my red boots from the bedroom, I need them for my green dress. (*The nurse puts the child down and runs. To the young woman*) Don't stand around, you! (*The young woman runs away*) Stay right here or I'll have you whipped. (*Pause*) Look how these things have been packed! Without love, without understanding. If I'm not there standing over them . . . In times like these you see what kind of servants you've got. Masha! (*With an imperious gesture*) You know how to fill your bellies, but you never heard of gratitude. I'll remember this.

THE AIDE-DE-CAMP (*in great agitation*) Natella, you must come at once. The carpet weavers have revolted, they've just hanged Judge Orbeliani of the superior court.

THE GOVERNOR'S WIFE Why? I must take the silver one, it cost a thousand piasters. And this one and all the furs, and where's my wine-red dress?

THE AIDE-DE-CAMP (*trying to pull her away*) Riots have broken out in the slums. We've got to be going. (*A servant runs off*) Where is the child?

THE GOVERNOR'S WIFE (*calling the nurse*) Maro! Get the child ready! Where are you?

THE AIDE-DE-CAMP (*on his way out*) We may have to forget about the carriage and go on horseback.

(*The governor's wife rummages among the dresses, throws some on a pile that is to go along, then takes them off again. Sounds are heard. Drums. A red glow appears in the sky*)

THE GOVERNOR'S WIFE (*rummaging desperately*) My wine-red dress, I can't find it. (*Shrugging her shoulders, to the second woman*) Take the whole pile to the carriage. Why hasn't Maro come back? Have you all gone crazy? I knew it would be on the bottom.

THE AIDE-DE-CAMP (*returning*) Quick! Quick!

THE GOVERNOR'S WIFE (*to the second woman*) Run! Just throw them in the carriage!

THE AIDE-DE-CAMP We're not taking the carriage. Come now, or I'll go without you.

THE GOVERNOR'S WIFE Maro! Bring the child! (*to the second woman*) Look for her, Masha! No, first take the dresses to the carriage. Nonsense, I wouldn't dream of going on horseback! (*Turning around, sees the fiery glow and freezes with fright*) Fire! (*She rushes off; the aide-de-camp follows her. Shaking her head, the second woman follows her with the bundle of dresses*)

(*Servants come out from the archway*)

THE WOMAN COOK The east gate must be on fire.

THE MAN COOK They've gone. They've left the carriage and all the provisions. How are we going to get out of here?

A STABLE HAND Yes, this house won't be healthy for a while. (*To the third woman*) Zulika, I'll get a couple of blankets and we'll clear out.

THE NURSE (*coming out of the archway with a pair of boots*) Gracious lady!

A FAT WOMAN She's gone.

THE NURSE What about the child? (*She runs to the child and picks him up*) The beasts, they've left him. (*She hands the child to Grusha*) Hold him a second. (*Lying transparently*) I'm going to see about the carriage. (*She runs off after the governor's wife*)

GRUSHA What have they done to our master?

THE STABLE HAND (*drawing his finger across his throat*) Fft!

THE FAT WOMAN (*growing hysterical at his gesture*) Merciful heavens above! Georgi Abashvili, our master! Hale and hearty at morning mass, and now . . . take me away. We're lost! We'll die in sin. Like Georgi Abashvili our master.

THE THIRD WOMAN (*trying to soothe her*) Calm down, Nina. You're not in danger. You've never hurt anybody.

THE FAT WOMAN (*while she is being led away*) Merciful heavens above, we must all get away before they come, before they come.

THE THIRD WOMAN Nina takes it more to heart than his wife. These people can't even do their own mourning! (*She catches sight of the child that Grusha is still holding*) The child! What are you doing with the child!

GRUSHA They left it behind.

THE THIRD WOMAN She left him? Michael, who was sheltered from every draft!

(*The servants gather around the child*)

GRUSHA He's waking up.

THE STABLE HAND Better put him down! I don't like to think what would happen to anybody they find with that child. I'll get our stuff; wait here, all of you. (*Goes off into the palace*)

THE WOMAN COOK He's right, once they start fighting each other, they wipe out whole families. I'm getting my things. (*All have gone out except for two maids and Grusha with the child in her arms*)

THE THIRD WOMAN Didn't you hear? Put him down.

GRUSHA His nurse gave him to me to hold for a second.

THE WOMAN COOK You simple soul, she won't be back.

THE THIRD WOMAN Keep away from him.

THE WOMAN COOK They'll be hunting him more than his mother. He's the governor's heir. Grusha, you're a good soul, but you're not very bright. Take it from me, if he had leprosy it couldn't be worse. Just save your skin.

(*The stable hand has come back with bundles which he distributes among the women. All except Grusha prepare to leave*)

GRUSHA (*obstinately*) He hasn't got leprosy. He's looking at me. He's somebody.

THE WOMAN COOK Then stop looking at him. You're the

boneheaded kind that falls for anything. Go get the lettuce, they say, you have the longest legs; and you run. We're taking the oxcart, you can come with us if you hurry. Lord, the whole district must be on fire!

THE THIRD WOMAN Haven't you packed anything? There isn't much time, the Ironshirts will be here any minute.

(*The two women and the stable hand go off*)

GRUSHA I'm coming.

(*Grusha lays the child down, looks at it for a few moments, takes pieces of clothing from the trunks that are standing around, and covers the sleeping child. Then she runs into the palace to get her things. Hoofbeats and women's screams are heard. Enter the fat prince with some drunken Ironshirts. One is carrying the governor's head on a pike*)

THE FAT PRINCE Here in the center! (*One of the soldiers climbs on the back of another, takes the head and holds it tentatively over the archway*) That's not the center, further to the right, that's it. When I give orders, I see to it that they're carried out properly. (*While the soldier, with hammer and a nail, fastens the head to the wall by the hair*) This morning at the church door I said to Georgi Abashvili: "I love clear skies," but to tell the truth I prefer the lightning that strikes out of a clear sky. Yes, indeed. The only trouble is they've taken the brat away. I need him badly. Search all Gruzinia for him. A thousand piasters.

(*While Grusha, looking cautiously around, comes to the portal, the fat prince goes off with the Ironshirts. Again the sound of hoofbeats is heard. Carrying a bundle, Grusha goes toward the archway. When she has almost reached it, she turns around to see if the child is still there. The singer starts singing. She stands motionless*)

THE SINGER

As she stood there between door and archway, she heard
Or thought she heard a faint cry: the child
Called out to her, he didn't whimper, but said quite reasonably
Or so at least it seemed to her.
"Woman," he said, "help me."

And he went on, not whimpering, but saying quite reason-
     ably
"Consider, woman, that one who does not hear a cry for
     help
But passes by with distracted ear will never
Hear again the hushed call of her lover nor
The blackbird in the dawn nor the contented
Sighs of the tired grape pickers at angelus."
Hearing this
(*Grusha takes a few steps toward the child and bends over
him*)
                    she went back for one last look
At the child. Just to stay with him
For a few moments until someone should come—
His mother perhaps or someone else—
(*She sits down, leaning against a trunk and facing the child*)
Until she should have to go, for the danger was too great,
     the city was full
Of flames and lamentation.
(*The light dims as though evening were turning to night.
Grusha has gone into the palace and come back with a lamp
and some milk which she gives the child to drink*)

THE SINGER   (*in a loud voice*)
Terrible is the temptation to do good!

(*All through the night, Grusha sits watching the child.
Once she lights the little lamp to look at the child, once she
throws a brocade mantle over him. From time to time she
listens and looks around to make sure no one is coming*)

THE SINGER
Long she sat with the child
Till evening came, till night came
Till the dawn came. Too long she sat
Too long she saw
The quiet breathing, the little fists
Until toward morning the temptation grew too great
And she stood up, bent down and with a sigh picked up the
     child
And carried him away.
(*She does as the singer says*)

Like something stolen she took him
Like a thief she crept away.

3

The Flight to the Northern Mountains

THE SINGER
When Grusha Vachnadze left the city
On the Gruzinian military highway
On the way to the northern mountains
She sang a song, she bought milk.

THE MUSICIANS
How can she, so human, hope
To escape the bloodhounds, the setters of snares?
To the deserted mountains she plodded
Along the Gruzinian military highway she plodded
She sang a song, she bought milk.
(*Grusha Vachnadze plodding along, carying the child in a sack on her back, in one hand a bundle, in the other a large stick*)

GRUSHA (*sings*)
Four old commanders
Set out for Iran.
The first commander never fought
The second's fighting came to naught
The third one found the weather not right
The fourth one found his soldiers would not fight.
Four old commanders
Away they ran.
Sosso Robakidze
Marched off to Iran.
The war he fought was hard and tough
He won the battle soon enough
The weather was all right for him

His soldiers hacked away with vim.
Sosso Robakidze
Is our man.

(*A peasant hut appears*)

GRUSHA (*to the child*)   Noon, time to eat. So we'll sit in the grass and wait impatiently while good old Grusha buys a cup of milk. (*She sets the child on the ground and knocks at the door of the hut; an old peasant opens*) Could you give me a cup of milk, grandfather, and a millet cake perhaps?

THE OLD MAN   Milk? We haven't got any milk. The high and mighty soldiers from the city have taken our goats. Go to the high and mighty soldiers if you want milk.

GRUSHA   But you must have a cup of milk left for a child, grandfather?

THE OLD MAN   For a "God-reward-you," I suppose?

GRUSHA   Who said anything about God rewarding you? (*Takes out her purse*) We pay like princes. Our heads in the clouds, our behinds in the water! (*Grumbling, the peasant brings milk*) And what is the price of this cup of milk?

THE OLD MAN   Three piasters. Milk has gone up.

GRUSHA   Three piasters? For a thimbleful? (*Without a word the old man slams the door in her face*) Michael, did you hear that? Three piasters! We can't afford it. (*She goes back and sits down and gives the child her breast*) We'll just have to try it again this way. Suck hard, think of those three piasters! There's nothing there, but you think you're drinking, and that's something. (*She sees that the child has stopped sucking, and shakes her head. She stands up, goes back to the door and knocks again*) Grandfather, open up, we'll pay! (*In an undertone*) I hope you drop dead. (*When the old man opens the door again*) I expected to pay half a piaster, but the child needs it. How about one piaster?

THE OLD MAN   Two.

GRUSHA   Don't close the door again. (*She rummages a long while in her purse*) Here are two piasters. But this milk had better be filling, we have a long way to go. It's highway robbery and a sin.

THE OLD MAN   Kill the soldiers if you want milk.

GRUSHA (*giving the child milk to drink*) It's an expensive treat. Drink, Michael, it's half a week's wages. The people around here think we've made our money sitting on our asses. Michael, Michael, I've certainly let myself in for something. (*Looking at the brocade mantle in which the child is wrapped*) A brocade mantle worth a thousand piasters, and not one piaster for milk. (*She looks back*) Now there's a carriage full of rich refugees. Let's try and get a ride.

(*Outside a caravanserai*)
(*Grusha, wearing the brocade mantle, is seen approaching two fine ladies. She is holding the child in her arms*)

GRUSHA   Oh, do the ladies wish to spend the night here too? It's so dreadfully crowded everywhere, and not a carriage to be had! My coachman simply took it into his head to go back. I've come at least half a mile on foot. Barefoot! My Persian shoes—you know those heels. But why doesn't somebody come?

OLDER LADY   The landlord is taking his time. Ever since the events in the capital, the whole country has lost its manners. (*Out comes the landlord, a very dignified old man with a long beard, followed by his house servant*)

THE LANDLORD   Forgive an old man for making you wait, my ladies. My little grandson was showing me a peach tree in blossom, over there on the slope, beyond the corn fields. We have a few fruit trees over there, a few cherry trees. Further west (*he points*) the ground is stonier, the peasants drive their sheep there to graze. You ought to see the peach blossoms, such an exquisite pink.

OLDER LADY   You have a fertile region here.

THE LANDLORD   God has blessed it. How are the fruit blossoms coming along further south, my ladies? You're from the south, aren't you?

YOUNGER LADY   I must admit I didn't pay much attention to the landscape.

THE LANDLORD (*politely*) I understand. The dust. On our

highway it's best to proceed at a moderate pace, provided one isn't in too much of a hurry.

OLDER LADY   Put your veil around your neck, dearest. The evening breezes here seem rather cool.

THE LANDLORD   They come from the Yanga-Tau glaciers, my ladies.

GRUSHA   Oh, I'm so afraid my son will catch cold.

OLDER LADY   It's a good-sized caravanserai. Shall we go in?

THE LANDLORD   Oh, the ladies desire rooms? But my caravanserai is overcrowded and the servants have run away. I'm dreadfuly sorry but I can't accommodate any more people, not even with references . . .

YOUNGER LADY   But we can't spend the night on the road.

OLDER LADY (*dryly*)   How much is it?

THE LANDLORD   My ladies, surely you must understand that a landlord must be extremely careful in times like these with so many refugees looking for a place to stay. Perfectly respectable persons of course, but frowned on by the authorities. And so . . .

OLDER LADY   My dear man, we are not refugees. We are on our way to our summer residence in the mountains, and that's all there is to it. It would never occur to us to ask your hospitality if we . . . if we needed it *that* badly.

THE LANDLORD (*nodding agreement*)   Of course not. Still, I doubt whether the one tiny room I have available would suit the ladies. I am obliged to charge sixty piasters per person. Are the ladies together?

GRUSHA   In a way. I, too, am in need of lodging.

YOUNGER LADY   Sixty piasters! The man's a cutthroat!

THE LANDLORD (*coldly*)   My ladies, I have no desire to cut anyone's throat, and so . . . (*Turns to go*)

OLDER LADY   Must we talk about throats? Come along. (*Goes in, followed by the house servant*)

YOUNGER LADY (*in despair*)   A hundred and eighty piasters for one room. (*Looking around at Grusha*) But not with a child! That's impossible! Suppose it cries!

THE LANDLORD   The price of the room is a hundred and eighty piasters, for two persons or for three.

YOUNGER LADY (*changed on hearing this, to Grusha*)   On the

other hand, my dear, I couldn't bear to think of you out
on the road. Do come in.

(*They go into the caravanserai. On the other side of the
stage the house servant enters from the rear with baggage.
Behind him the elderly lady, then the second lady and
Grusha with the child*)

YOUNGER LADY   A hundred and eighty piasters! I haven't been
so upset since they brought poor Igor home.

OLDER LADY   Must you talk about Igor?

YOUNGER LADY   Actually there are four of us, the child is a
person, isn't it? (*To Grusha*) Couldn't you pay at least half?

GRUSHA   That is impossible. You see, I had to leave in a great
hurry and the aide-de-camp forgot to give me enough
money.

OLDER LADY   Maybe you haven't even got the sixty?

GRUSHA   I will pay that.

YOUNGER LADY   Where are the beds?

THE HOUSE SERVANT   No beds. There are blankets and sacks.
You'll just have to make do. Be glad you're not being
lowered into the ground, like plenty of others. (*Goes out*)

YOUNGER LADY   Did you hear that? I'm going straight to the
landlord. The man must be flogged.

OLDER LADY   Like your husband?

YOUNGER LADY   You're so cruel. (*She bursts into tears*)

OLDER LADY   How will we ever make anything resembling
beds out of this?

GRUSHA   Leave it to me. (*She puts the child down*) It's always
easier when there's more than one. And there's still your
carriage. (*Sweeping the floor*) I was taken utterly by
surprise! "My dear Anastasia Katarinovska," my husband
said to me before dinner, "lie down a while, you know
how those migraine headaches will come over you." (*She
drags sacks into place, makes up beds; the ladies watch her
at work and exchange glances*) "Georgi," I said to the
governor, "with sixty guests for dinner I can't lie down,
the servants aren't to be trusted, and Michael Georgivitch
won't eat without me." (*To Michael*) You see, Michael,
everything's going to be all right, didn't I tell you? (*She
suddenly notices that the ladies are looking at her strangely*

and whispering) There. At least we won't be lying on the bare ground. I've folded the blankets double.

OLDER LADY (*in a tone of command*)   You're very clever at bedmaking, my dear. Show me your hands!

GRUSHA (*frightened*)   What do you mean?

YOUNGER LADY   You've been told to show your hands.
(*Grusha shows the ladies her hands*)

YOUNGER LADY (*triumphantly*)   Cracks! A domestic!

OLDER LADY (*goes to the door, calls out*)   Servants!

YOUNGER LADY   We've caught you, you hussy. What have you been up to? Confess.

GRUSHA (*confused*)   I haven't been up to anything. I thought maybe you'd take us with you in your carriage, just a little way. Please don't make a fuss. I'll go of my own accord.

YOUNGER LADY (*while the older lady continues to call for servants*)   You'll go all right, but with the police. In the meantime stay here. Don't move!

GRUSHA   But I was even going to pay the sixty piasters. Here. (*shows her purse*) See for yourself, I've got them. Four tens and a five, no it's a ten, that makes sixty. I only wanted the child to ride in the carriage, that's the truth.

YOUNGER LADY   Oh, you wanted to ride in the carriage! Now it comes out.

GRUSHA   Gracious lady, I confess, I'm of lowly descent, please don't call the police. The child is of high station, look at his linen, he's a refugee like yourselves.

YOUNGER LADY   Of high station, we've heard that one. His father's a prince, isn't he?

GRUSHA (*wildly to the elderly lady*)   Stop screaming! Haven't you any heart?

YOUNGER LADY (*to the elderly lady*)   Be careful, she's going to attack you. She's dangerous! Help! Murder!

THE HOUSE SERVANT (*entering*)   What's wrong?

ELDERLY LADY   This person has wormed her way in here by playing the lady. Probably a thief.

YOUNGER LADY   And dangerous too. She wanted to kill us. Call the police. I feel my migraine coming on, oh heavens!

THE HOUSE SERVANT   There isn't any police right now. (*To*

Grusha) Pack up your belongings, sister, and make yourself scarce.

GRUSHA (*angrily picking up the child*) You monsters! At a time when they're nailing your heads to the walls!

THE HOUSE SERVANT (*pushing her out*) Shut your mouth. Or the old man will come, and then I pity you.

OLDER LADY (*to the younger lady*) Look and see if she hasn't stolen something!
(*While the ladies on the right search feverishly to see whether something has been stolen, the house servant steps out the door left with Grusha*)

THE HOUSE SERVANT I always say: Don't buy a pig in a poke. Next time take a look at people before you trust them.

GRUSHA I thought they'd be decent if they thought I was one of them.

THE HOUSE SERVANT That was silly of you. Believe me, nothing is harder than imitating lazy, useless people. Once they suspect you of being able to wipe your own ass or of ever in all your life working with your hands, you're done for. Wait a second, I'll get you some millet bread and a few apples.

GRUSHA Better not. I'd better go before the landlord comes. If I walk all night, I'll be out of danger, I think. (*Goes*)

THE HOUSE SERVANT (*calls softly after her*) Keep to the right at the next crossing.
(*She disappears*)

THE SINGER
When Grusha Vachnadze went northward
Prince Kazbeki's guards followed her.

THE MUSICIANS
How can a barefoot girl escape from the Ironshirts?
The bloodhounds, the setters of snares?
Even at night they hunt. Pursuers
Never get tired. Butchers
Never sleep long.
(*Two Ironshirts are trotting along the highway*)

THE CORPORAL Blockhead, you'll never amount to anything. Your heart isn't in it. A superior can tell that by the little things. When I laid that fat woman the other day, you carried out my orders, you held her husband, you kicked him in the stomach, but did you take pleasure in it like a good soldier, or did you just go through the motions? I watched you, Blockhead. You're dead wood, you're a tinkling cymbal, you'll never get a promotion. (*They go on a while in silence*) Don't think I won't remember that every move you make is a display of insubordination. I forbid you to limp. You only do it because I sold the horses because I'd never get such a good price again. By limping you wish to intimate that you don't care for hiking, I know you. It won't do you any good, it will make things worse for you. Sing!

THE TWO IRONSHIRTS (*sing*)
 To the war my weary way I'm wending
 While my sweetheart stays to mind the cattle.
 Loyal friends her honor are defending
 Till I come back from the bloody battle.
THE CORPORAL   Louder!
THE TWO IRONSHIRTS
 As into my grave instead I travel
 See my sweetheart throwing in the gravel
 Hear her say: "There go the feet with which he chased me
 There the arms that many times embraced me."

(*Again they walk for a while in silence*)
THE CORPORAL   A good soldier has to put his heart and soul in it. He'll let himself be torn to pieces for a superior. With his dying glance he takes in his corporal's nod of approval. That's all the reward he wants. There won't be any nod for you, and you'll have to kick in all the same. Damnation, how am I going to find the governor's brat with a subordinate like you, just tell me that.
(*They go on*)

THE SINGER
 When Grusha Vachnadze came to the Sirra River
 Her flight became too much for her, the helpless child too
  heavy.

THE MUSICIANS
  In the corn fields the rosy dawn
  Is merely cold to one who has not slept. To the fugitive
  The merry clatter of milk pails from the farm where the
      smoke rises
  Sounds menacing. Carrying the child, she
  Feels its weight and little else.
  (*Grusha stops outside a farm*)

GRUSHA Now you've wet yourself again and you know I
  have no diapers for you. Michael, I'll have to leave you
  now. We're far enough from the city. They can't care
  enough about a little nothing like you to follow you all
  this way. That peasant woman looks friendly, and get a
  whiff of the milk! So good-bye, Michael, I'll forget how
  you kicked me in the back all night to keep me on the
  move, and you forget the short rations. I did my best. I'd
  have liked to keep you longer because your nose is so little,
  but it can't be done. I'd have liked to show you your first
  bunny and—teach you to stop wetting yourself, but I've
  got to go back, because my sweetheart the soldier ought
  to be back soon, too, and what if he didn't find me? You
  can't ask that of me, Michael.
  (*A fat peasant woman carries a milk pail in through the
  door. Grusha waits until she is inside, then she goes
  cautiously toward the house. She steals up to the door
  and sets the child down in front of it. Then she hides behind
  a tree and waits until the peasant woman comes out again
  and finds the bundle*)

THE PEASANT WOMAN Heavens above, what's this? Husband!
THE PEASANT (*coming out*) Now what? Let me eat my soup.
THE PEASANT WOMAN (*to the child*) Where's your mother?
  Haven't you got one? It's a boy, I believe. And he's got
  fine linen, this is a noble child. And they just drop it on
  the doorstep. What terrible times!
THE PEASANT If they think we're going to feed him, they're
  mistaken. Take it to the priest in the village, and that's the
  end of it.
THE PEASANT WOMAN What would the priest do with him?
  He needs a mother. There, he's waking up. Don't you think
  we could keep him?

THE PEASANT (*shouting*)   No!

THE PEASANT WOMAN   If I bed him down in the corner beside the armchair, I'll only need a basket, and I'll take him out to the fields with me. Look, he's laughing. Husband, we have a roof over our heads, we can do it, I'm not listening.

(*She carries him in, the peasant follows protesting. Grusha comes out from behind the tree, laughs and hurries away in the direction from which she came*)

THE SINGER   Why so happy, woman returning homeward?

THE MUSICIANS

Because with a smile, the helpless child has

Got himself new parents, I am happy. Because the dear child

Is off my hands, I am glad.

THE SINGER   And why so sad?

THE MUSICIANS

Because I am free and unburdened, I am sad

As one who has been robbed

As one who has been made poor.

(*She has only gone a little way when she meets the two Ironshirts who bar the way with their pikes*)

THE CORPORAL   Young lady, you have bumped into the armed forces. Where have you come from? And why? Have you illicit relations with the enemy? Where are they? What movements are they making in your rear? What about the hills, what about the valleys, how are your stockings fastened?

(*Grusha stands stock still in a fright*)

GRUSHA   They are well-fortified, you'd better stop short.

THE CORPORAL   I always stop short, you can count on me for that. Why are you gaping at my pike? "A soldier in the field never lets his pike out of his hand." That's the regulation, Blockhead, learn it by heart. Well, young lady, where are you going?

GRUSHA   To meet my sweetheart, soldier, a certain Simon Chachava, of the palace guard in Nukha. If I write him a letter, he'll break every bone in your body.

THE CORPORAL   Simon Chachava, of course, I know him. He

gave me the key, said to look in on you now and then. Blockhead, we're getting unpopular. We'd better tell her our intentions are honorable. Young lady, I may seem to make jokes, but I'm serious underneath. So here you have it officially: I want a child from you.

(*Grusha lets out a little scream*)

THE CORPORAL Blockhead, she catches our meaning. A sweet shock, isn't it? "But first I must take the buns out of the oven, lieutenant. First I must change my torn shirt, colonel!" Joking aside, poking aside, young lady: we're combing the region for a certain child. Have you heard anything about such a child, that's turned up from the city, a noble child in fine linen?

GRUSHA No, I haven't heard a thing.

THE SINGER

Run, kind-hearted girl, the killers are coming!

You who are helpless, help the helpless child! And so she runs.

(*She turns suddenly and runs away in panic fear, toward the peasant's house. The Ironshirts exchange glances and follow her cursing*)

THE MUSICIANS

In the bloodiest times

There are kindly people.

(*In the peasant's house the fat peasant woman is bending over the child in its basket when Grusha Vachnadze rushes in*)

GRUSHA Hide him, quick. The Ironshirts are coming. I left him on the doorstep, but he's not mine, he comes of a noble family.

THE PEASANT WOMAN Who's coming? What Ironshirts?

GRUSHA Don't waste time. The Ironshirts that are looking for him.

THE PEASANT WOMAN They've no business in my house. But it looks like I'll want a word with you.

GRUSHA Take off his fine linen, it will give us away.

THE PEASANT WOMAN Don't bother me with linen. In my house I give the orders. And don't throw up on my furniture. Why did you leave it? That's a sin.

GRUSHA (*looking out*) They'll be coming out from behind the trees any minute. I shouldn't have run away, that made them angry. Oh, what should I do?

THE PEASANT WOMAN (*also peers out and is suddenly scared stiff*) Mother of God, the Ironshirts!

GRUSHA They're looking for the child.

THE PEASANT WOMAN But what if they come in here?

GRUSHA You mustn't give it to them. Say it's yours.

THE PEASANT WOMAN Yes.

GRUSHA They'll run it through if you give it to them.

THE PEASANT WOMAN But suppose they ask me for it? I've got silver for the harvesters in the house.

GRUSHA If you give it to them, they'll run it through, right here in your house. You've got to tell them it's yours.

THE PEASANT WOMAN Yes. But suppose they don't believe me?

GRUSHA If you say it like you meant it . . .

THE PEASANT WOMAN They'll burn the roof over our heads.

GRUSHA That's why you've got to say it's yours. His name is Michael. I shouldn't have told you that.

(*The peasant woman nods*)

GRUSHA Don't nod your head like that. And don't tremble, they'll notice.

THE PEASANT WOMAN Yes.

GRUSHA Stop saying "yes." I can't stand it. (*Shakes her*) Haven't you one of your own?

THE PEASANT WOMAN (*mumbling*) Gone to war.

GRUSHA Then maybe he's an Ironshirt himself. Would you expect him to run babies through? Wouldn't *you* give him a piece of your mind! "Stop poking your pike into my house, is that how I raised you? Wash your neck before you talk to your mother."

THE PEASANT WOMAN That's a fact. I wouldn't let him do that.

GRUSHA Promise to tell them he's yours.

THE PEASANT WOMAN Yes.

GRUSHA They're coming now.

(*Knocking at the door. The women do not answer. Enter the Ironshirts. The peasant woman bows low*)

THE CORPORAL That's her all right. What did I tell you?

I've got a nose on me. I could smell her. I've got a question
to ask you, young lady: Why did you run away? What did
you think? That I wanted something from you? I bet it
was something indecent. Admit it!

GRUSHA (*while the peasant woman keeps bowing*) I left milk
on the stove. I suddenly remembered it.

THE CORPORAL I thought it was because you thought I was
looking at you indecently. As if I had some idea about you
and me. Kind of a sensual look, see what I mean?

GRUSHA I didn't see anything like that.

THE CORPORAL But it's possible, don't deny it. After all, I
could be a swine. I'll be perfectly frank with you: I could
get all sorts of ideas if we were alone. (*To the peasant
woman*) Haven't you something to do in the yard? Feed
the chickens?

THE PEASANT WOMAN (*falling suddenly on her knees*) Mr.
Soldier, I didn't know a thing. Don't burn the roof over
my head!

THE CORPORAL What are you talking about?

THE PEASANT WOMAN It's got nothing to do with me, Mr.
Soldier. She left it on my doorstep, I swear it.

THE CORPORAL (*sees the child and whistles*) Oho, there's a
little fellow in the basket, Blockhead, I smell a thousand
piasters. Take the old woman outside and hold her fast.
Seems to me I've got a little interrogation on my hands.
(*Without a word the peasant woman lets the soldier lead
her away*)

THE CORPORAL So here's the baby I wanted of you. (*He goes
to the basket*)

GRUSHA Mr. Officer, it's mine. It's not the one you're looking for.

THE CORPORAL Let's have a look. (*He bends over the basket*)
(*Grusha looks about in despair*)

GRUSHA It's mine, it's mine.

THE CORPORAL Fine linen.

(*Grusha rushes at him to pull him away. He flings her off
and again bends down over the basket. She looks about
desperately, sees a big log, lifts it and brings it down on
the corporal's head from behind. He collapses. Quickly
picking up the child, she runs out*)

THE SINGER
  And fleeing from the Ironshirts
  After twenty-two days of flight
  At the foot of the Yanga-Tau glacier
  Grusha Vachnadze adopted the child.

THE MUSICIANS
  The helpless one adopted the helpless one.
  (*Grusha leans over a half-frozen stream and scoops up water for the child in the hollow of her hand*)

GRUSHA (*sings*)
  Since no one wants to take you, child
  I shall have to take you.
  Black the day as black can be
  If you're satisfied with me
  I will not forsake you.

  I have carried you so far
  Sore my feet and bleeding
  Spent such fortunes buying milk
  You've grown dear to me
  (Fondness comes from feeding.)

  I will throw your linen out
  Swaddle you in tatters
  I will wash you and baptize
  You in glacier water.
  (You'll just have to stand it.)

  (*She has taken off the child's fine linen and wrapped him in a rag*)

THE SINGER
  When Grusha Vachnadze, pursued by the Ironshirts
  Came to the footbridge leading over the glacier to the village on the eastern slope
  She sang the Song of the Shaky Bridge and risked two lives.
  (*A wind has come up. The footbridge appears in the half-light. One cable is broken and the bridge is slanting over*)

*the abyss. Peddlers, two men and a woman, are standing
undecided at the end of the bridge when Grusha arrives.
One of the men is fishing with a pole for the dangling
cable)*

FIRST MAN   Take your time, young lady, you won't get across
the pass anyway.

GRUSHA   But I have to take my baby to my brother's place on
the east side.

THE WOMAN   Have to! What do you mean have to! I have to
get across because I have to buy two carpets in Atum,
which a woman has to sell because her husband died. But
can I do what I have to do; can *she?* Andrey has been
fishing for the cable for two hours, but even if he catches
it how are we going to make it fast? Tell me that.

FIRST MAN *(listening)*   Sh-sh, I think I hear something.

GRUSHA *(in a loud voice)*   The bridge isn't all that shaky. I
think I'll try to cross it.

THE WOMAN   I wouldn't try it if the devil himself were after
me. Why, it's suicide.

FIRST MAN *(shouting)*   Ho!

GRUSHA   Don't shout! *(To the woman)* Tell him not to shout.

FIRST MAN   But somebody's shouting down there. Maybe
they've lost their way down there.

THE WOMAN   Why shouldn't he shout? Is there something
shady about you? Are they after you?

GRUSHA   I guess I'd better tell you. The Ironshirts are after
me. I hit one of them on the head.

SECOND MAN   Hide the stuff.

(The woman hides a sack behind a rock)

FIRST MAN   Why didn't you tell us right away? *(To the
others)* If they catch her, they'll make hash out of her!

GRUSHA   Get out of the way, I've got to cross that bridge.

SECOND MAN   You can't! The chasm is two thousand feet
deep!

FIRST MAN   Even if we could catch the cable, there wouldn't
be any sense in it. We could hold it in our hands, but the
Ironshirts could cross the same way.

GRUSHA   Out of my way!

(Not very distant cries: "She's up there!")

THE WOMAN   They're coming close. But you can't take your child on the bridge. It's almost sure to collapse. And look down there.

(*Grusha looks into the chasm. More cries from the Iron-shirts below*)

SECOND MAN   Two thousand feet.

GRUSHA   But those men are worse.

FIRST MAN   You can't do it. Think of the child. Risk your own life if they're out to get you, but not the child's.

SECOND MAN   Besides, she'll be heavier with the child.

THE WOMAN   Maybe she really has to get across. Give it to me, I'll hide it, and you'll try the bridge by yourself.

GRUSHA   No. Where he goes, I go. (*To the child*) We're in this together, son. (*Sings*)

> Deep is the chasm, son
> See the bridge sway
> Not of our choosing, son
> Is our way.
>
> You must go the way that
> I have picked for you
> You must eat the bread that
> I have saved for you
>
> Share the two, three morsels
> Taking two of three.
> How big or how little
> Better not ask me.

I'll try it.

THE WOMAN   It's tempting God.

(*Cries from below*)

GRUSHA   I beg you, throw your pole away, or they'll fish up the cable and come after me.

(*She goes out on the swaying bridge. The peddler woman screams when the bridge threatens to break. But Grusha goes on and reaches the other side*)

FIRST MAN   She's across.

THE WOMAN (*who had fallen on her knees and prayed,*

angrily)   It was a sin all the same.
(*The Ironshirts appear from below. The corporal's head is bandaged*)

THE CORPORAL   Have you seen a woman with a child?

FIRST MAN (*while the second man throws the pole into the chasm*)   Yes. There she is. And the bridge won't carry you.

THE CORPORAL   Blockhead, you're going to pay for this.
(*Grusha on the opposite side laughs and shows the Ironshirts the child. She goes on, the bridge stays behind. Wind*)

GRUSHA (*looking around at Michael*)   Never be afraid of the wind, it's only a poor devil like us. His job is pushing the clouds and he gets colder than anybody.
(*Snow begins to fall*)
The snow isn't so bad either, Michael. Its job is covering the little fir trees so the winter won't kill them. And now I'll sing a song for you. Listen! (*Sings*)

Your father is a bandit
And your mother is a whore
Every noble man and honest
Will bow as you pass.

The tiger's son will
Feed the little foals his brothers
The child of the serpent
Bring milk to the mothers.

4

In the Northern Mountains

THE SINGER
The sister trudged for seven days.
Across the glacier, down the slopes she trudged.

When I come to my brother's house, she thought
He will stand up and embrace me.
"Is it you, sister?" he will say.
"I've long been expecting you. This is my beloved wife.
And this is my farm, mine by marriage.
With eleven horses and thirty-one cows. Be seated!
Sit down at our table with your child and eat."
Her brother's house was in a smiling valley.
When the sister came to the brother's house, she was ill
   from her journey.
The brother stood up from the table.

(*A stout peasant couple who have sat down to eat.
Lavrenti Vachnadze already has his napkin around his neck
when Grusha, supported by a hired hand and very pale,
enters with the child*)

LAVRENTI VACHNADZE   Where have you come from, Grusha?

GRUSHA (*feebly*)   I've come across the Yanga-Tau pass,
Lavrenti.

HIRED HAND   I found her outside the hay shed. She has a child
with her.

THE SISTER-IN-LAW   Go and curry the bay. (*The hired hand
goes out*)

LAVRENTI   This is my wife, Aniko.

THE SISTER-IN-LAW   We thought you were working in Nukha.

GRUSHA (*who can hardly stand up*)   Yes, I was.

THE SISTER-IN-LAW   Wasn't it a good position? We heard it
was.

GRUSHA   The governor has been killed.

LAVRENTI   Yes, we heard there was trouble. Your aunt told
us, don't you remember, Aniko?

THE SISTER-IN-LAW   It's perfectly quiet here. City people are
always looking for trouble. (*Goes to the door and calls*)
Sosso, Sosso, don't take the cake out of the oven yet, do
you hear? Where are you anyway? (*Goes out, calling*)

LAVRENTI (*quickly, in an undertone*)   Have you a father for
it? (*When she shakes her head*) Just as I thought. We've
got to think up something. She's very religious.

THE SISTER-IN-LAW (*coming back*) Those servants! (*To
Grusha*) You have a child?

GRUSHA   It's mine. (*She slumps over. Lavrenti raises her up*)

THE SISTER-IN-LAW   Saints alive, she's got some disease. What will we do?
   (*Lavrenti starts leading Grusha to the bench by the stove. Aniko, horrified, gestures him to stop and points to a sack by the wall*)

LAVRENTI (*takes Grusha to the wall*)   Sit down. Sit down. It's only weakness.

THE SISTER-IN-LAW   What if it's scarlet fever!

LAVRENTI   There would be spots. It's weakness, Aniko, nothing to worry about. (*To Grusha, who has sat down*) Are you feeling better now?

THE SISTER-IN-LAW   Is the child hers?

GRUSHA   Mine.

LAVRENTI   She's going to join her husband.

THE SISTER-IN-LAW   Oh. Your meat is geting cold. (*Lavrenti sits down and begins to eat*) It doesn't agree with you cold, the fat is no good when it's cold. You know you have a delicate stomach. (*To Grusha*) If your husband's not in the city, where on earth is he?

LAVRENTI   He lives across the mountains, she says.

THE SISTER-IN-LAW   Oh. Across the mountains.
   (*Sits down to eat*)

GRUSHA   I think you'll have to take me somewhere to lie down, Lavrenti.

THE SISTER-IN-LAW (*continues her interrogation*)   If it's consumption, we'll all get it. Has your husband a farm?

GRUSHA   He's a soldier.

LAVRENTI   But he's inherited a farm from his father, a small farm.

THE SISTER-IN-LAW   Hasn't he gone to war? Why not?

GRUSHA (*with difficulty*)   Yes, he's gone to war.

THE SISTER-IN-LAW   Then why are you going to the farm?

LAVRENTI   When he comes back from the war, he'll go to the farm.

THE SISTER-IN-LAW   But you're going there right away?

LAVRENTI   Yes, to wait for him.

THE SISTER-IN-LAW (*screams*)   Sosso, the cake!

GRUSHA (*mumbles feverishly*)   A farm. Soldier. Wait. Sit down, eat.

THE SISTER-IN-LAW   It's scarlet fever.

GRUSHA (*starting up*) Yes, he has a farm.

LAVRENTI I think it's weakness, Aniko. Don't you want to see about the cake, my love?

THE SISTER-IN-LAW But when will he come back if what they're saying is true and the war has broken out again? (*Waddles out, calling*) Sosso, where are you? Sosso!

LAVRENTI (*stands up quickly, goes to Grusha*) We'll put you to bed right away. She's a good soul, but not until after dinner.

GRUSHA (*holds out the child to him*) Take it! (*He takes it, looking around*)

LAVRENTI But you can't stay long. She's religious, you see. (*Grusha collapses. Her brother catches her*)

THE SINGER
      The sister was too sick.
      The cowardly brother had to take her in.
      The autumn went, the winter came.
      The winter was long
      The winter was short.
      The people mustn't find out.
      The rats mustn't bite.
      The spring mustn't come.

(*Grusha sitting at the loom in the storeroom. The child is huddled on the floor. They are wrapped in blankets*)

GRUSHA (*sings while weaving*)
      The loved one prepared to go
      And his betrothed ran after him pleading
      Pleading and in tears, tearfully admonishing:

      Dearest love, dearest love
      If you must go off to war
      If you must fight in the hard battle
      Don't run ahead of the war
      And don't lag behind the war
      Up in front there is red fire

In the rear there is red smoke.
Keep in the middle of the war
Stay close to the banner bearer.
The first are always sure to die
The last are sure to be struck down as well
Those in the middle come home again.

Michael, we must be very clever. If we make ourselves as
small as cockroaches, my sister-in-law will forget that we're
in the house. We'll be able to stay until the snow melts.
And don't cry because it's cold. If you're poor and suffer
from the cold besides, people won't like you.

(*Lavrenti comes in. He sits down beside his sister*)

LAVRENTI Why are you sitting here bundled up like coach-
men? Is the room too cold?

GRUSHA (*hastily removing her shawl*) It's not cold, Lavrenti.

LAVRENTI If it's too cold, you shouldn't be sitting here with
the child. Aniko would never forgive herself. (*Pause*) I
hope the priest didn't ask you questions about the child.

GRUSHA He asked, but I didn't tell him anything.

LAVRENTI That's good. I wanted to talk to you about Aniko.
She's a good soul, but she's so very, very sensitive. If
people say the least thing about the farm, she gets upset.
You see, she takes everything to heart. One time the
milkmaid had a hole in her stocking in church, and my
dear Aniko has been wearing two pairs of stockings to
church ever since. You won't believe it, but it's in the
family. (*He listens*) Are you sure there are no rats here?
You can't stay here if there are. (*A sound is heard as of
dripping from the roof*) What's that dripping?

GRUSHA It must be a leaky barrel.

LAVRENTI Yes, it must be a barrel.—You've been here for
six months now. Was I talking about Aniko? Of course I
didn't tell her about that Ironshirt, she has a weak heart.
So she doesn't know you can't look for work, and that's
why she spoke the way she did yesterday. (*They listen
again to the dripping of the melting snow*) You can't
imagine how worried she is about your soldier. "Suppose

he comes home and doesn't find her?" she says, and lies
awake at night. "He can't be home before spring," I say.
The good soul. (*The drops fall faster*) When do you suppose he'll come, what do you think? (*Grusha is silent*)
Not before spring. Don't you agree? (*Grusha says nothing*)
I see, you've given up expecting him. (*Grusha says nothing*) But when spring comes and the snow thaws here and
on the passes, you can't stay here any longer, they're
likely to come looking for you, and people are talking
about an illegitimate child.

(*The glockenspiel of the falling drops has become loud and
steady*)

LAVRENTI   Grusha, the snow is melting on the roof; it's spring.

GRUSHA   Yes.

LAVRENTI   (*with enthusiasm*)   I'll tell you what we'll do. You
need a place to go, you've got a child (*he sighs*), so you
need a husband to make people stop gossiping. I've been
asking around—oh, very cautiously—about a husband for
you. I've found one, Grusha. I've spoken to a woman who
has a son just across the mountain, with a small farm, she's
willing.

GRUSHA   But I can't marry anybody, I've got to wait for
Simon Chachava.

LAVRENTI   Of course. I've thought of all that. You don't
need a husband in bed, only on paper. I've found the right
man. This woman I've made arrangements with—her son is
dying. Isn't that perfect? He's at his last gasp. It will be
just like we said: "A husband across the mountains." And
when you got there, he breathed his last and you were a
widow. What do you say?

GRUSHA   I could use an official document for Michael.

LAVRENTI   An official document makes all the difference in
the world. Without an official document even the shah
of Persia wouldn't dare to call himself the shah. And you'll
have a roof over your head.

GRUSHA   What does the woman want for it?

LAVRENTI   Four hundred piasters.

GRUSHA   Where did you get them?

LAVRENTI   (*guiltily*)   Aniko's milk money.

GRUSHA Over there nobody will know us.—All right, I'll do it.

LAVRENTI (*stands up*) I'll let the woman know right away. (*Goes out quickly*)

GRUSHA Michael, you certainly mess things up. I came by you as a pear tree comes by sparrows. And because a Christian bends down and picks up a crust of bread to make sure that nothing is wasted. Michael, I ought to have left in a hurry that Easter Sunday in Nukha. Now I'm the ninny.

THE SINGER

The bridegroom lay on his deathbed when the bride appeared.

The bridegroom's mother was waiting at the door and pressed her to make haste.

The bride brought a child with her, the witness hid it during the wedding.

(*A room divided by a partition: on one side a bed. Under the mosquito netting a very sick man lies motionless. The mother-in-law comes running in on the other side, pulling Grusha by the hand. After them Lavrenti with the child*)

THE MOTHER-IN-LAW Hurry, hurry, or he'll kick in on us before the wedding. (*To Lavrenti*) You didn't tell me she had a child already.

LAVRENTI What difference does it make? (*With a gesture toward the dying man*) It can't matter to him, not in his condition.

MOTHER-IN-LAW Not to him! But I'll never outlive the disgrace. We're honest folk. (*She starts to cry*) My Yussup doesn't have to marry a woman that has a child already.

LAVRENTI All right. I'll throw in another two hundred piasters. You have it in writing that the farm goes to you, but she is entitled to live here for two years.

THE MOTHER-IN-LAW (*drying her tears*) That will hardly cover the funeral expenses. I hope she'll really give me a hand with the work. But where has the monk gone now? He must have crawled out the kitchen window. Now

we'll have the whole village on our necks if they hear
that Yussup is giving up the ghost. Oh my goodness! I'll
go get him, but he mustn't see the child.

LAVRENTI I'll make sure he doesn't see it. But why a monk
and not a priest?

THE MOTHER-IN-LAW It's just as good. Except I made the
mistake of giving him half his fee before the ceremony, so
now he's gone off to the tavern. I only hope . . . (*She
runs off*)

LAVRENTI The priest was too expensive for her, the skinflint.
She's hired a cheap monk.

GRUSHA Send Simon Chachava over here if he turns up.

LAVRENTI Yes. (*Indicating the sick man*) Don't you want to
take a look at him?

(*Grusha, who has picked up Michael, shakes her head*)

LAVRENTI He doesn't even move. I hope we're not too late.
(*They listen. On the other side neighbors enter, look
around and line up along the walls. They begin to mumble
prayers. The mother-in-law comes in with the monk*)

THE MOTHER-IN-LAW (*after a moment's surprise and irritation, to the monk*) There you have it. (*She bows to the
guests*) Please be patient just a minute. My son's fiancée
has just arrived from the city and there's to be an emergency marriage. (*Goes into the bedroom with the monk*)
I knew you'd spread it far and wide. (*To Grusha*) The
marriage can take place right away. Here's the contract.
Me and the bride's brother . . . (*Lavrenti tries to hide in
the background after quickly recovering Michael from
Grusha. The mother-in-law waves him away*) Me and the
bride's brother are the witnesses.

(*Grusha has bowed to the monk. They go to the bedside.
The mother-in-law pushes back the mosquito netting. The
monk begins to reel off his lines in Latin. Meanwhile
Lavrenti tries to prevent the child from crying by showing
him the ceremony and the mother-in-law keeps motioning
him to put the child down. Once Grusha looks around
toward the child and Lavrenti waves the child's hand at
her*)

THE MONK Are you prepared to be a faithful, obedient, and

good wife to this man and to cleave to him until death
you do part?

GRUSHA (*looking at the child*)   Yes.

THE MONK (*to the dying man*)   And are you prepared to be
a good husband and provider to this woman until death
you do part?
(*When the dying man does not answer, the monk repeats
his question and looks around*)

THE MOTHER-IN-LAW   Of course he is. Didn't you hear him
say yes?

THE MONK   All right, we declare the marriage concluded.
But how about extreme unction?

THE MOTHER-IN-LAW   Nothing doing. The marriage cost
enough. Now I've got to attend to the mourners. (*To
Lavrenti*) Did we say seven hundred?

LAVRENTI   Six hundred. (*He gives her the money*) I won't
sit down with the guests. I might make friends with somebody. So good-bye, Grusha, and if my widowed sister
comes to see me one of these days, my wife will bid her
welcome, or she'll hear from me.
(*He goes. The mourners look after him indifferently as he
passes through*)

THE MONK   And may one ask who this child is?

THE MOTHER-IN-LAW   A child? I don't see any child. And you
don't see one either. Understand? Or maybe I'll have seen
certain goings-on behind the tavern. Come along now.
(*They go into the other room, after Grusha has set the
child on the floor and told him to keep quiet. She is introduced to the neighbors*)

THE MOTHER-IN-LAW   This is my daughter-in-law. She was
just in time to find our dear Yussup alive.

ONE OF THE WOMEN   He's been lying abed a whole year now,
hasn't he? When my Vassili went off to the army, he came
to the farewell party.

ANOTHER WOMAN   A thing like this is terrible for a farm, the
corn ready to reap and the farmer in bed. A good thing for
him if he doesn't have to suffer much longer is what I say.

FIRST WOMAN (*confidentially*)   At first we thought he took
to his bed to keep out of the army. And now he's dying!

THE MOTHER-IN-LAW   Do sit down and have a few cakes.
(*The mother-in-law beckons to Grusha and they both go
into the bedroom where they take pans of cake from the
floor. The guests, including the monk, sit down on the floor
and start a muffled conversation*)

A PEASANT (*the monk has taken a bottle from his cassock and
passed it to him*)   There's a child, you say? How can that
have happened to Yussup?

THIRD WOMAN   She was certainly lucky to swing it, with him
so sick.

THE MOTHER-IN-LAW   Now they've started gossiping; and
they'll be eating up the funeral cakes and if he doesn't die
today, I'll have to bake more tomorrow.

GRUSHA   I'll bake them.

THE MOTHER-IN-LAW   Last night some men rode by and I
went out to see who it was. When I came back he was lying there like a corpse. That's why I sent for you. He can't
last long now. (*She listens*)

THE MONK   Dear wedding guests and mourners! Deeply
moved, we stand before a death bed and a marriage bed, for
a woman has been married and a man is soon to be buried.
The groom has been washed and the bride is hot. For in
the marriage bed there lies a last will, which arouses the
lusts of the flesh. Dearly beloved, how various are the paths
of humankind! One dies to get a roof over his head, another
marries in order that flesh may return to the dust whence it
was made. Amen.

THE MOTHER-IN-LAW (*who has listened*)   He's getting even. I
shouldn't have taken such a cheap one, he's no better than
I paid for. An expensive one behaves. In Sura there's a priest
who's even said to be a saint, but naturally he costs a fortune. A fifty-piaster priest like this has no dignity, he's got
just enough religion for fifty piasters, no more. When I
went to get him out of the tavern, he was making a speech
and yelling: "The war is over! Beware of peace!" We'd
better go in.

GRUSHA (*gives Michael a cake*)   Here's a cake for you, be
nice and quiet, Michael. We're respectable people now.
(*They take the cake pans out to the guests. The dying man
sits up under the mosquito net, sticks his head out, and looks*)

after the two women. Then he sinks back. The monk has taken two bottles from his cassock and passed them to the peasant who is sitting beside him. Three musicians have entered; the monk grins and waves to them)

THE MOTHER-IN-LAW *(to the musicians)* What are you doing here with your instruments?

A MUSICIAN Brother Anastasius here *(indicating the monk)* said there was a wedding.

THE MOTHER-IN-LAW What's this? Three more people on my neck? Don't you know there's a dying man in there?

THE MONK A fascinating problem for a musician. Shall it be a muffled wedding march or a dashing funeral dance?

THE MOTHER-IN-LAW Play something at least, we know nothing can stop you from eating.

(The musicians play a mixture of genres. The women pass cakes)

THE MONK The trumpet sounds like a whimpering baby, and you, little drum, what is your message to the world?

THE PEASANT *(beside the monk)* Couldn't the bride give us a little dance?

THE MONK With a skeleton?

THE PEASANT *(beside the monk, sings)*

Mistress Roundass thought it was time to wed
She took an elderly man to bed
To frolic and to dandle.
Next morning she had changed her mind:
I'd rather have a candle.

(The mother-in-law throws the drunken man out. The music breaks off. The guests are embarrassed. Pause)

THE GUESTS *(loudly)* Did you hear that? The grand duke is back.—But the princes are against him.—Oh, it seems the shah of Persia has lent him a big army to restore order in Gruzinia.—How can that be? The shah of Persia hates the grand duke!—But he also hates disorder.—Anyway the war is over. Our soldiers are coming back. *(Grusha drops the cake pan)*

A WOMAN *(to Grusha)* Aren't you feeling well? It's the excitement over our dear Yussup. Sit down and rest, my dear.

(Grusha stands tottering)

THE GUESTS   Now everything will be the same as before.—Except there will be more taxes, because we'll have to pay for the war.

GRUSHA (*feebly*)   Did someone say the soldiers are coming home?

A MAN   I said so.

GRUSHA   That can't be.

THE MAN (*to a woman*)   Show her your shawl! We bought it from a soldier. It's from Persia.

GRUSHA (*looks at the shawl*)   They're here.

(*A long pause. Grusha kneels down as though to pick up the cakes. She takes the silver cross and chain from her blouse, kisses the cross and begins to pray*)

THE MOTHER-IN-LAW (*seeing that the guests are silently looking at Grusha*)   What's got into you? Can't you pay attention to our guests? What do we care about these fool rumors from the city?

THE GUESTS (*loudly resuming their conversation while Grusha kneels with her forehead to the floor*)   You can buy Persian saddles from the soldiers, some are exchanging them for crutches.—Only the bigwigs on one side can win a war, the soldiers on both sides lose it.—At least the war's over. It's something if they can't drag you off to the army any more. (*The peasant in the bed has sat up. He is listening*)— What we need is two more weeks of good weather.—Our pear trees are hardly bearing at all this year.

THE MOTHER-IN-LAW (*passing the cake*)   Have a little more cake. Help yourselves. There's more.

(*The mother-in-law goes into the bedroom with the empty cake pan. She does not see the sick man. She is bending over a full cake pan on the floor when he begins to speak in a hoarse voice*)

YUSSUP   How much more cake are you going to stuff into their bellies? Do you think I shit money? (*The mother-in-law turns abruptly and stares at him aghast. He climbs out from behind the mosquito net*)   Did they say the war was over?

THE FIRST WOMAN (*in the other room, amiably to Grusha*)   Has the young lady someone in the army?

THE MAN It's good news that they're coming home, isn't it?

YUSSUP Stop goggling. Where is this woman you've saddled me with?

(*Receiving no answer, he gets out of bed in his nightgown and staggers past the mother-in-law into the other room. She follows him trembling, with the cake pan*)

THE GUESTS (*see him and exclaim*) Jesus, Mary and Joseph! Yussup!

(*All spring up in alarm, the women rush toward the door. Grusha, still on her knees, turns her head and stares at Yussup*)

YUSSUP A funeral supper. Wouldn't that suit you! Get out before I take a whip to you.

(*The guests leave the house in haste*)

YUSSUP (*grimly to Grusha*) Upsets your little game, eh? (*She says nothing; he takes a millet cake from the pan the mother-in-law is holding*)

THE SINGER

Oh, confusion. The wife discovers she has a husband!
By day she has the child. At night she has the husband.
Day and night her beloved is on his way.
The couple look each other over. The room is small.

(*Yussup sits naked in a tall wooden bathtub and the mother-in-law adds water out of a pitcher. In the bedroom Grusha is sitting huddled over with Michael who is playing at mending straw mats*)

YUSSUP She should be doing this, not you. Where has she gone now?

THE MOTHER-IN-LAW (*calls*) Grusha! Yussup wants you.

GRUSHA (*to Michael*) Here are two more holes for you to mend.

YUSSUP (*as Grusha enters*) Scrub my back!

GRUSHA Can't the farmer do it himself?

YUSSUP "Can't the farmer do it himself?" Take the brush, damn it! Are you my wife or are you a stranger? (*To the mother-in-law*) Too cold!

THE MOTHER-IN-LAW I'll get some hot water right away.

GRUSHA Let me go.

YUSSUP   You stay right here! (*The mother-in-law runs out*)
Rub harder. And don't put on airs like you'd never seen a
naked man before. Who made your kid? The Holy Ghost?

GRUSHA   The child wasn't conceived in joy, if that's what the
farmer means.

YUSSUP (*looks around at her and grins*)   I wouldn't say that,
to look at you. (*Grusha stops scrubbing him and shrinks
back. The mother-in-law enters*) Nice work. You've married me to a cold fish.

THE MOTHER-IN-LAW   She just doesn't try.

YUSSUP   Pour, but be careful. Ouch! Careful, I said. (*To
Grusha*) I wouldn't be surprised if you'd got yourself in
trouble in the city. Or what would you be doing here? But
I won't go into that. I haven't said anything about the bastard you've brought into my house, but with you my
patience is running out. It's not natural. (*To the mother-
in-law*) More! (*To Grusha*) Even if your soldier comes
back, remember, you're married.

GRUSHA   Yes.

YUSSUP   But your soldier won't come back any more, it's no
use thinking he will.

GRUSHA   No.

YUSSUP   You're cheating me. You're my wife and you're not
my wife. Where you lie, there's nothing, but nobody else
can lie there. When I go out to the fields in the morning,
I'm dead tired; when I lie down at night, I'm as spry as the
devil himself. God made you a woman, and what do you
do? My farm doesn't bring in enough for me to buy a
woman in the city, and besides, there's the trip to think of.
A woman hoes the fields and spreads her legs, that's what
it says in our almanac. Do you hear me?

GRUSHA   Yes. (*Softly*) I'm sorry to be cheating you.

YUSSUP   She's sorry! More water! (*The mother-in-law pours
more water*) Ouch!

THE SINGER
    As by the brook she sat washing the linen
    She saw his face in the water. And his face grew paler
    With each passing moon.

When she stood up to wring out the linen
She heard his voice from the murmuring maple and his voice
   grew softer
With each passing moon.
Sighs and excuses multiplied, salt tears and sweat were shed.
With each passing moon the child grew up.

(*Grusha is kneeling by a small brook, dipping clothes in the water. A little way off some children are standing. Grusha is talking to Michael*)

GRUSHA You may play with them, Michael, but don't let them order you around because you're the smallest.

(*Michael nods and goes to the other children. They start to play*)

THE BIGGEST BOY Today we're going to play Heads Off. (*To a fat boy*) You're the prince, you're supposed to laugh. (*To Michael*) You're the governor. (*To a little girl*) You're the governor's wife, you're supposed to cry when his head is chopped off. And I'm going to chop his head off. (*He shows his wooden sword*) With this. First the governor is brought into the yard. The prince leads the procession, the governor's wife comes last. (*The procession forms, the fat boy goes first, laughing. Then come Michael and the biggest boy, then the little girl who is crying*)

MICHAEL (*stops still*) Me chop head off too.

THE BIGGEST BOY That's my job. You're the littlest. Governor is easiest. Get down on your knees and let your head be chopped off. It's easy.

MICHAEL Want sword too.

THE BIGGEST BOY It's mine. (*Gives him a kick*)

THE LITTLE GIRL (*calls to Grusha*) He won't play right.

GRUSHA (*laughs*) They say the smallest duckling knows how to swim.

THE BIGGEST BOY You can be the prince if you can laugh.

(*Michael shakes his head*)

THE FAT BOY I laugh best. Let him chop your head off once, then you chop his off and then me.

(*Reluctantly the biggest boy gives Michael the wooden sword and kneels down. The fat boy has sat down, slapping*)

his thighs and laughing loudly. The little girl is wailing.
Michael swings the big sword and cuts the other boy's head
off; he falls down in the process)

THE BIGGEST BOY   Ouch! I'll show you the right way.

(*Michael runs off, the children after him. Grusha looks*
after them laughing. When she turns back, Simon Chachava,
in a ragged uniform, is standing on the other side of the
brook)

GRUSHA   Simon!

SIMON   Am I addressing Grusha Vachnadze?

GRUSHA   Simon!

SIMON (*formally*)   God bless the young lady. I hope she is
well.

GRUSHA (*stands up happily and bows low*)   God bless you,
soldier. And thank heaven you have returned in good health.

SIMON   As the haddock said, they found better fishes, so they
didn't eat me.

GRUSHA   Bravery, said the kitchen helper; luck, said the hero.

SIMON   How have things been? Was the winter bearable,
were the neighbors kind?

GRUSHA   The winter was rather hard, Simon, and the neighbors as usual.

SIMON   May I ask whether a certain person is still in the habit
of putting her legs in the water when she washes clothes?

GRUSHA   The answer is no because of the eyes in the bushes!

SIMON   The young lady is speaking about soldiers. A paymaster is standing before you.

GRUSHA   Doesn't that mean twenty piasters?

SIMON   And lodging.

GRUSHA (*tears coming to her eyes*)   Behind the barracks,
under the date palms.

SIMON   Exactly. I see the young lady has taken a look around.

GRUSHA   So she has.

SIMON   And she hasn't forgotten. (*Grusha shakes her head*)
Then the door is still on its hinges, as they say? (*Grusha*
looks at him in silence and shakes her head again) What do
you mean? Is something wrong?

GRUSHA   Simon Chachava, I can never go back to Nukha
again. Something has happened.

SIMON   What has happened?

GRUSHA   It has happened that I hit an Ironshirt on the head.

SIMON   Grusha Vachnadze must have had good reason.

GRUSHA   Simon Chachava, my name isn't the same as before.

SIMON (*after a pause*)   I don't understand.

GRUSHA   When do women change their names, Simon? Let me
explain. Nothing has come between us, everything is the
same, you've got to believe me.

SIMON   Nothing has come between us, but something has
changed?

GRUSHA   How can I explain it so quickly with the brook between us? Can't you take the bridge and come over?

SIMON   Perhaps it's no longer necessary.

GRUSHA   It's very necessary. Come over, Simon. Hurry!

SIMON   Does the young lady mean the soldier has come too
late?

(*Grusha looks at him despairingly, her face bathed in tears.
Simon stares straight ahead. He has picked up a piece of
wood and is whittling*)

THE SINGER

So many words are said, so many words are left unsaid.

The soldier has come. Where he has come from he does not
say.

Hear what he thought and did not say:

The battle began at gray of dawn, blood flowed at noon.

The first fell before me, the second fell behind me, the
third fell next to me.

On the first I trampled, the second I left behind, the third
was run through by the captain.

My first brother perished by iron, my second brother perished by smoke.

They struck flame from my head, my hands were frozen
in my gloves, my toes in my stockings.

To eat I had aspen buds, to drink I had maple broth, I
slept at night on stones, or in water.

SIMON   I see a cap in the grass. Can there be a child so soon?

GRUSHA   Yes, Simon, there is. How could I hide it? But you
mustn't fret, it's not mine.

SIMON   They say: Once the wind starts blowing, it blows
through every crack and cranny. The lady need say no
more.

(*Grusha bows her head and says nothing*)

THE SINGER

Yearning there was, but no waiting.
Broken the oath. The reason is not reported.
Hear what she thought and did not say:

Soldier, when you were fighting in the battle
The bloody battle, the bitter battle
I found a child who was helpless.
I hadn't the heart to leave it.
I had to care for what would have perished
I had to bend down for bread crumbs on the ground
I had to tear myself to pieces for what was not mine
A stranger.
Someone must help
For a sapling needs water.
The baby calf strays when the cowherd sleeps
And the cry goes unheard!

SIMON   Give me back the cross I gave you. No, throw it in
the brook.

(*He turns to go*)

GRUSHA   Simon Chachava, don't go away, it's not mine, it's
not mine! (*She hears the children calling*) What is it, children?

VOICES   Soldiers!—They're taking Michael away!

(*Grusha stands horrified. Two Ironshirts come toward her,
leading Michael*)

IRONSHIRTS   Are you Grusha? (*She nods*) Is this your child?

GRUSHA   Yes. (*Simon goes away*) Simon!

IRONSHIRTS   We have a court order to take this child, found
in your care, to the city. There is reason to believe that it is
Michael Abashvili, son of Governor Georgi Abashvili and

his wife Natella Abashvili. Here is the order, duly signed
and sealed. (*They lead the child away*)

GRUSHA (*runs after them shouting*) Leave him, please, he's
mine!

THE SINGER

> The Ironshirts took the cherished child away. The unhappy
> woman followed them to the perilous city.
>
> The mother who had borne him demanded the child's
> return. His foster-mother appeared in court.
>
> Who will decide the case, to whom will the child be given?
>
> Who will the judge be? A good one? A bad one?
>
> The city was in flames. On the seat of justice sat Azdak.

5

The Story of the Judge

THE SINGER

> Hear now the story of the judge:
>
> How he became judge, how he passed judgment, what
> manner of judge he is.
>
> That Easter Sunday when the great uprising took place and
> the grand duke was overthrown
>
> And Abashvili, his governor, our child's father, lost his head
>
> Azdak the village scribe found a fugitive in the thicket and
> hid him in his hut.

(*Ragged and tipsy, Azdak helps a fugitive disguised as a
beggar into his hut*)

AZDAK Stop panting. You're not a horse. And running like
snot in April won't save you from the police. Stop, I tell
you. (*He catches the fugitive, who has kept going as though
to run through the opposite wall of the hut*) Sit down and
eat, here's a piece of cheese. (*He rummages through a
chest full of rags and fishes out a cheese; the fugitive starts
eating avidly*) Haven't eaten in some time, huh? (*The fugi-*

tive grumbles) What were you running for, you asshole?
The policeman wouldn't even have seen you.

THE FUGITIVE   Had to.

AZDAK   Shits? (*The fugitive looks at him uncomprehendingly*)
Jitters? Scared? Hm. Stop smacking your lips like a grand
duke or a pig! I can't stand it. We've got to take blue-
blooded stinkers the way God made them. Not you. I once
heard of a chief justice who was so independent he farted
at dinner. When I watch you eating, horrible thoughts come
to me. Why don't you say something? (*Sharply*) Let's see
your hand! Can't you hear me? I want to see your hand.
(*Hesitantly the fugitive holds out his hand*) White. So
you're not a beggar at all. A phony, a walking swindle!
And me hiding you like you were a self-respecting citizen.
What are you running for if you're a landowner? That's
what you are, don't deny it, I can tell by your guilty look!
(*Stands up*) Get out! (*The fugitive looks at him uncer-
tainly*) What are you waiting for, you peasant-flogger?

THE FUGITIVE   Looking for me. Request undivided attention,
have proposition.

AZDAK   What's that? A proposition? That's the height of
insolence. He wants to make a proposition! The victim
scratches till his fingers are bloody, and the leech makes a
proposition. Get out, I say!

THE FUGITIVE   Understand point of view, convictions. Pay
hundred thousand piasters one night. Well?

AZDAK   What? You think you can buy me? For a hundred
thousand piasters? A rundown estate. Let's say a hundred
and fifty thousand. Where are they?

THE FUGITIVE   Not on me naturally. Will send. Hope no
doubts.

AZDAK   Deep doubts. Get out!

(*The fugitive stands up and trots to the door. A voice from
outside*)

VOICE   Azdak!

(*The fugitive turns around and trots to the opposite corner,
where he stops still*)

AZDAK (*shouts*)   I'm busy. (*Steps into the doorway*) Are you
nosing around again, Shauva?

SHAUVA THE POLICEMAN (*outside, reproachfully*) You've caught another rabbit, Azdak. You promised it wouldn't happen again.

AZDAK (*sternly*) Don't talk about things you don't understand, Shauva. The rabbit is a dangerous and harmful animal that eats plants, especially the varieties known as weeds, and must therefore be exterminated.

SHAUVA Azdak, don't be so mean to me. I'll lose my job if I'm not severe with you. I know you've got a good heart.

AZDAK I haven't got a good heart. How often do I have to tell you I'm an intellectual?

SHAUVA (*slyly*) I know, Azdak. You're a superior man, you say so yourself. All right, I'm only an uneducated Christian and I ask you: If one of the prince's rabbits is stolen and I'm a policeman, what am I to do about the guilty party?

AZDAK Shauva, Shauva, you ought to be ashamed. There you stand asking me a question when a question is the worst of all temptations. Suppose you were a woman, Nunovna, for instance, the wicked slut, and you show me the upper reaches of your leg, Nunovna's I mean, and ask me: What should I do about my leg, it itches—is she innocent, behaving like that? No. I catch rabbits, but you catch men. A man is made in God's image, a rabbit isn't, you know that. I'm a rabbit-eater, but you're a cannibal, Shauva, and God will judge you. Go home, Shauva, and repent. No, wait a minute, maybe I've got something for you. (*He looks around at the fugitive who stands there trembling*) No, never mind. Go home and repent. (*He slams the door in his face. To the fugitive*) You're surprised, aren't you? That I didn't hand you over. But I couldn't even hand a bedbug over to that dumb-ox policeman, it goes against my grain. Never be afraid of a policeman. So old and such a coward. Eat up your cheese like a poor man, or they're sure to catch you. Do I have to show you how a poor man behaves? (*He pushes him down in his chair and puts the piece of cheese back in his hand*) This chest is the table. Put your elbows on the table, surround the cheese on the plate as if it might be snatched away at any moment, can you ever be sure? Hold your knife like a small sickle and don't look at the cheese so greedily, your expression should be more on the sorrowful side, because it's already vanishing, like all beauty. (*Watches him*) They're looking for you, that's in your favor, but how can I know they're not mistaken about you? In Tiflis one time they hanged a landowner, a Turk. He was able to prove that he didn't just cut his peasants in half the usual way, but quartered them. He gouged out twice as much taxes as anybody else, his zeal was above suspicion, but they hanged him as a criminal all the same, just because he was a Turk, which he couldn't help. That was an injustice. He found himself on the gallows the way Pontius Pilate found himself in the Creed. To make a long story short, I don't trust you.

THE SINGER
   And so Azdak lodged the old beggar for the night.
   When he found out that he was the grand duke in person,
      the butcher
   He was ashamed. He denounced himself, he ordered the
      policeman
   To take him to Nukha, to court, to be tried.
   (*In the courthouse yard three Ironshirts are sitting drinking. From a column hangs a man in a judge's robe. Enter Azdak bound, dragging Shauva behind him*)
AZDAK (*cries out*) I helped the grand duke, the grand thief, the grand butcher, to escape. In the name of justice I demand a public trial and a severe sentence!
THE FIRST IRONSHIRT   Who's this bird?
SHAUVA   It's Azdak, our scribe.
AZDAK   I'm a contemptible traitor, a marked man! Report, flatfoot, how I insisted on being taken to the capital in chains because I sheltered the grand duke, grand scoundrel, by mistake, which was only made clear to me later by this document that I found in my hut. (*The Ironshirts study the document. To Shauva*) They can't read. See, the marked man denounces himself! Tell them how I made you run with me half the night to clear everything up.
SHAUVA   By threatening me. That wasn't nice of you, Azdak.

AZDAK Shut up, Shauva, you don't understand. A new era has dawned, it will rumble over you like thunder, you're through, policemen will be exterminated, pfft. Everything will be investigated, brought to light. A man with any sense will turn himself in, he can't escape from the people. Report how I yelled all the way down Shoemaker Lane. (*He acts it out with sweeping gestures, squinting at the Ironshirts*) "I let the grand scoundrel escape out of ignorance. Tear me to pieces, brothers!" To forestall any questions.

THE FIRST IRONSHIRT And what was their answer?

SHAUVA They comforted him on Butcher Lane and laughed themselves sick on Shoemaker Lane, that's all.

AZDAK But you're different, I know that, you're men of iron. Where's the judge, brothers, I want to be questioned.

THE FIRST IRONSHIRT (*points to the hanged man*) There's the judge. And stop bothering us. We're touchy about that kind of thing right now.

AZDAK "There's the judge." Such an answer has never been heard in Gruzinia. Townspeople, where is his excellency the governor? (*He points to the gallows*) There's his excellency, stranger. Where is the chief tax collector? The chief recruiting officer? The patriarch? The chief of police? Here, here, here, all here. Brothers, that's what I was expecting of you.

THE SECOND IRONSHIRT That's enough! What did you expect, you clown?

AZDAK What happened in Persia, brothers, what happened in Persia?

THE SECOND IRONSHIRT What happened in Persia?

AZDAK Forty years ago. Hanged, the whole lot of them. Viziers, tax collectors. My grandfather, a remarkable man, saw it. Three whole days, all over the country.

THE SECOND IRONSHIRT But who governed if the vizier was hanged?

AZDAK A peasant.

THE SECOND IRONSHIRT And who commanded the army?

AZDAK A soldier, soldier.

THE SECOND IRONSHIRT And who gave them their pay?

AZDAK A dyer, a dyer gave them their pay.

THE SECOND IRONSHIRT   Are you sure it wasn't a carpet weaver?

THE FIRST IRONSHIRT   But why did all that happen, you Persian?

AZDAK   Why it all happened? Do you need a special reason? Why do you scratch yourself, brother? War! Too much war! And no justice! My grandfather brought back a song that tells the way it was. My friend the policeman and I will sing it for you. (*To Shauva*) And keep a good hold on the rope, that goes with it. (*He sings, while Shauva holds the rope*)

Why are our sons not bleeding any more, and our daughters weep no more?
Why is it that only the calves in the slaughterhouse have any blood left?
Why is it that only the willows on Lake Urmi are shedding tears?

The emperor stands in need of a new province, the peasant must hand over his savings.
So that the roof of the world may be conquered, the roofs of all the huts are carted off.
Our men are taken away, scattered to all four winds so that the noble lords at home may feast and revel.
And the soldiers kill one another, the generals salute one another.
They bite the widow's tax farthing to see if it is real.
The lances are broken.
The battle has been lost. But the helmets have been paid for.
Is it so? Is it so?

SHAUVA   Yes, yes, yes, yes, it is so.

AZDAK   Do you want to hear the rest?
(*The first Ironshirt nods*)

THE SECOND IRONSHIRT (*to the policeman*) Didn't he teach you the song?

SHAUVA   Oh yes, but my voice is no good.

THE SECOND IRONSHIRT   No. (*To Azdak*) Go on, go on.

AZDAK   The second stanza is about the peace. (*Sings*)
    Public offices overcrowded, officials sitting all the way out
        to the street.
    Rivers overflow the banks and devastate the fields
    Men who can't take their own pants down are ruling
        empires.
    They can't count to four but they eat eight courses.
    The corn growers look round for buyers, find only starve-
        lings
    The weavers go home from their looms in rags.
    Is it so? Is it so?
SHAUVA   Yes, yes, yes, yes, it is so.

AZDAK
    That's why our sons are not bleeding any more, and our
        daughters weep no more
    Why only the calves in the slaughterhouse have any blood
        left.
    Why it is that only the willows on Lake Urmi are shedding
        tears.

THE FIRST IRONSHIRT (*after a pause*)   Are you going to sing
that song here in town?
AZDAK   What's wrong with it?
THE FIRST IRONSHIRT   Do you see that red glow over there?
(*Azdak looks around. There is a fiery glow in the sky*)
That's out in the slums. When Prince Kazbeki had Governor Abashvili beheaded this morning, our carpet weavers
caught the "Persian disease" too and asked if Prince Kazbeki
didn't eat too many courses. And at noon today they strung
up the city judge. But we took care of them for two
piasters a weaver. See what I mean?
AZDAK (*after a pause*)   I see. (*He looks around fearfully,
slinks off to one side and sits down on the ground with his
head in his hands*)
THE FIRST IRONSHIRT (*after all have taken a drink, to the third*)

Now we're going to have a little fun.

(*The first and second Ironshirt go toward Azdak, blocking his retreat*)

SHAUVA   I don't think he's really bad, gentlemen. Steals a few chickens, maybe a rabbit now and then.

THE SECOND IRONSHIRT (*stepping up to Azdak*)   You came here to fish in troubled waters, didn't you?

AZDAK (*looking up at him*)   I don't know why I came here.

THE SECOND IRONSHIRT   Are you the kind that sides with the carpet weavers? (*Azdak shakes his head*) What about that song?

AZDAK   Got it from my grandfather. A stupid, ignorant man.

THE SECOND IRONSHIRT   Right. And what about the dyer that handed out the pay?

AZDAK   That was in Persia.

THE FIRST IRONSHIRT   And what about your denouncing yourself for not hanging the grand duke with your own hands?

AZDAK   Didn't I tell you I let him go?

SHAUVA   I'll vouch for that. He let him go.

(*The Ironshirts drag the screaming Azdak to the gallows. Then they let him go and laugh uproariously. Azdak joins in the laughter and laughs loudest. Then he is untied. All begin to drink. Enter the fat prince with a young man*)

THE FIRST IRONSHIRT (*to Azdak*)   Here comes your new era. (*More laughter*)

THE FAT PRINCE   And what might there be to laugh about, my friends? Permit me to put in a serious word. Yesterday morning the princes of Gruzinia overthrew the grand duke's bellicose government and liquidated his governors. Unfortunately the grand duke himself escaped. In this fateful hour our carpet weavers, those eternal agitators, have had the audacity to revolt and hang the city judge, a man whom everyone loved, our dear Illo Orbeliani. Ts, ts, ts. My friends, what we need in Gruzinia is peace, peace, peace. And justice! Here I've brought you my dear nephew, Bizergan Kazbeki, an able man, to be the new judge. I say: The decision rests with the people.

THE FIRST IRONSHIRT   You mean we're to elect the judge?

THE FAT PRINCE   Exactly. The people will elect an able man.

Talk it over, my friends. (*While the Ironshirts put their heads together*) Don't worry, duckling, the job is yours. And once they nab the grand duke, we can stop sucking up to the rabble.

THE IRONSHIRTS (*among themselves*) They're scared shitless because they haven't caught the grand duke.—We can thank this village scribe for letting him go.—They're not sure of themselves yet, that's why they're saying "my friends" and "the decision rests with the people."—Now he's even talking about justice for Gruzinia.—But fun is fun, and this is going to be fun.—We'll ask the village scribe, he knows all about justice. Hey, stinko . . .

AZDAK Do you mean me?

THE FIRST IRONSHIRT (*continues*) . . . would you want this nephew for a judge?

AZDAK Are you asking me? You're not asking me, are you?

THE SECOND IRONSHIRT Why not? Anything for a laugh.

AZDAK The way I see it, you want to put him to the test. Am I right? Haven't you got some criminal handy, so the candidate can show his ability? One who knows the ropes.

THE THIRD IRONSHIRT Let's see. We've got the governor's bitch's two doctors down in the cellar. Let's take them.

AZDAK No, that's no good. You can't take real criminals when the judge hasn't been confirmed in office. It's all right for him to be a jackass, but he's got to be confirmed in office, or it's an offense against the law, which is a very sensitive organ, something like the spleen, which must never be punched or death sets in. You can hang them both, that won't be an offense against the law, because no judge was present. The law must be administered with perfect gravity, because it's so stupid. For instance if a judge jails a woman for stealing a piece of millet bread for her child, and he hasn't got his robe on or he scratches himself while handing down the sentence, so that more than a third of him is naked, I mean, suppose he has to scratch the upper part of his leg, then his judgment is a scandal and the law has been flouted. A judge's robe and a judge's hat can hand down a better sentence than a man without them. Justice goes up in smoke if you're not very careful. You wouldn't test a jug of wine by giving it to a dog to drink, hell, your wine would be gone.

THE FIRST IRONSHIRT So what do you suggest, you hair-splitter?

AZDAK I'll play the defendant for you. I already know who he'll be. (*He whispers something in their ears*)

THE FIRST IRONSHIRT You?

(*All laugh uproariously*)

THE FAT PRINCE What have you decided?

THE FIRST IRONSHIRT We've decided to give it a try. Our good friend here will play the accused, and here's a seat of justice for the candidate.

THE FAT PRINCE It's unusual, but why not? (*To his nephew*) A mere formality, duckling. What have you learned? Who won the race, the slow runner or the fast one?

THE NEPHEW The stealthy runner, Uncle Arsen.

(*The nephew sits down on the seat of justice, the fat prince stands behind him. The Ironshirts sit down on the steps. Azdak enters with the unmistakable gait of the grand duke*)

AZDAK Is there anybody here who knows me? I am the grand duke.

THE FAT PRINCE What is he?

THE SECOND IRONSHIRT The grand duke. He really knows him.

THE FAT PRINCE Good.

THE FIRST IRONSHIRT Start the trial.

AZDAK Hear I'm accused inciting war. Ridiculous. Repeat: ridiculous! Sufficient? If not sufficient, brought lawyers, believe five hundred. (*He motions behind him, as though there were many lawyers around him*) Need all available seats for lawyers.

(*The Ironshirts laugh; the fat prince joins in*)

THE NEPHEW (*to the Ironshirts*) Do you wish me to try the case? I must say it seems rather unusual, in poor taste I mean.

THE FIRST IRONSHIRT Get started.

THE FAT PRINCE (*smiling*) Throw the book at him, duckling.

THE NEPHEW Very well. People of Gruzinia versus grand duke. Accused, what have you to say for yourself?

AZDAK Plenty. Naturally read war lost. Declared war only on advice patriots like Uncle Kazbeki. Demand Uncle Kazbeki as witness. (*The Ironshirts laugh*)

THE FAT PRINCE (*good-naturedly to the Ironshirts*) Quite a character, isn't he?

THE NEPHEW Motion overruled. Obviously you can't be prosecuted for declaring war, every ruler has to do that now and then, but only for conducting it incompetently.

AZDAK Nonsense. Didn't conduct it at all. Had it conducted. Had it conducted by princes. Naturally fouled it up.

THE NEPHEW Do you mean to deny that you were in supreme command?

AZDAK Certainly not. Always in supreme command. When born, bellowed at nurse. Raised to drop shit in privy. Accustomed to command. Always commanded officials to rob my treasury. Officers flog soldiers, only my command; landowners sleep with peasants' wives only my strict command. Uncle Kazbeki here has big belly only by my command.

THE IRONSHIRTS (*applauding*) He's rich. Hurrah for the grand duke!

THE FAT PRINCE Answer him, duckling! I'm with you.

THE NEPHEW I will answer him as befits the dignity of the court. Accused, respect the dignity of the court.

AZDAK Right. Command you proceed with trial.

THE NEPHEW Not taking commands from you. You claim forced by princes declare war. How then can you claim princes fouled up war?

AZDAK Not sending enough men, embezzling funds, delivering sick horses, drinking in whorehouse during attack. Move call Uncle Kaz witness.

(*The Ironshirts laugh*)

THE NEPHEW Do you mean to make the monstrous assertion that the princes of this country did not fight?

AZDAK No. Princes fought. Fought for war contracts.

THE FAT PRINCE This is too much. The man talks like a carpet weaver.

AZDAK Indeed? Only tell truth!

THE FAT PRINCE Hang him! Hang him!

THE FIRST IRONSHIRT   Take it easy. Go on, excellency!

THE NEPHEW   Silence! Pronounce sentence: must be hanged. By neck. Lost war. Sentence pronounced. Irrevocable. Take him away.

THE FAT PRINCE (*hysterically*)   Take him away! Take him away!

AZDAK   Young man, earnestly advise not fall into clipped, military delivery in public. Can't be employed watchdog if howl like wolf. Get me?

THE FAT PRINCE   Hang him!

AZDAK   If people notice princes talk same as grand duke, they will hang grand duke and princes. Moreover annul sentence. Reason: war lost, but not for princes. Princes won their war. Collected three million eight hundred sixty-three piasters for horses not delivered.

THE FAT PRINCE   Hang him!

AZDAK   Eight million two hundred forty thousand piasters for army provisions not supplied.

THE FAT PRINCE   Hang him!

AZDAK   Therefore victorious. War only lost for Gruzinia, not present in this court.

THE FAT PRINCE   I think that will do, my friends. (*To Azdak*) You can step down, gallowsbird. (*To the Ironshirts*) My friends, I think you can now confirm the new judge.

THE FIRST IRONSHIRT   I guess we can. Bring down the judge's robe. (*One of them climbs on another's back and takes off the hanged man's robe*) And now (*to the nephew*) beat it, so the right ass can sit in the right seat. (*To Azdak*) Step forward, take the seat. (*Azdak hesitates*) Sit down on it, man. (*Azdak is forced onto the seat of justice by the Ironshirts*) The judge was always a blackguard, so now let a blackguard be judge. (*The robe is put on him, a basket is set on his head*) Look at our judge!

THE SINGER

There was civil war, the ruler was insecure.

Azdak was made judge by the Ironshirts.

For two years Azdak was judge.

THE SINGER AND HIS MUSICIANS

When with flame the skies were glowing and with blood the gutters flowing

Bugs and roaches rose from every crack.
Lances were replaced by cleavers, sermons made by un-
     believers
And upon the seat of justice sat Azdak.

(*Azdak is sitting on the seat of justice, peeling an apple.
Shauva is sweeping the courtroom. On one side an invalid
in a wheelchair, a doctor who is the defendant, and a lame
man in rags. On the other side a young man accused of
blackmail. An Ironshirt bearing the banner of the Ironshirts
corps, stands at the door*)

AZDAK   Today, in view of the large number of cases pend-
ing, the court will hear two cases at once. Before I begin,
a brief announcement: I take. (*He holds out his hand.
Only the blackmailer takes out money and gives it to him*)
I reserve the right to punish one of the parties here present
(*He looks at the invalid*) for contempt of court. (*To the
doctor*) You are a doctor, and you (*To the invalid*) are the
plaintiff. Is the doctor to blame for your condition?

THE INVALID   He is. I had a stroke on account of him.

AZDAK   That would be professional negligence.

THE INVALID   Worse than negligence. I loaned him money for
his studies. He's never repaid a cent, so when I heard he
was treating patients for nothing, I had a stroke.

AZDAK   You had every right. (*To the lame man*) And what
are you doing here?

THE LAME MAN   I'm the patient, your worship.

AZDAK   I gather he treated your leg?

THE LAME MAN   Not the right one. My rheumatism was in
my left leg, he operated on the right leg, that's why I limp.

AZDAK   And he did it for nothing?

THE INVALID   A five-hundred-piaster operation for nothing!
Gratis! For a mere thank you. And I staked him to his
studies! (*To the doctor*) Did your professors teach you to
operate for nothing?

THE DOCTOR   Your worship, it is indeed customary to ask for
the fee before operating, because the patient pays more willingly before an operation than afterward. In the present
case I believed at the moment of operating that my assistant
had already collected my fee. I was mistaken.

THE INVALID   He was mistaken! A good doctor doesn't make mistakes! He examines the patient before operating.

AZDAK   That is correct. (*To Shauva*) What's the other case, Mr. Public Prosecutor?

SHAUVA (*zealously sweeping*)   Blackmail.

THE BLACKMAILER   Your worship, I'm innocent. I simply wanted to ask a certain landowner whether he had really raped his niece. He informed me most amiably that he had not; if he gave me money, it was only because my uncle wishes to take music lessons.

AZDAK   Aha! (*To the doctor*) Whereas you, doctor, can cite no extenuating circumstance for your offense?

THE DOCTOR   The most I can say is that to err is human.

AZDAK   Don't you realize that a good doctor must have a sense of financial responsibility? I once heard of a doctor who made a thousand piasters out of a sprained finger by discovering that it had something to do with the circulation, which an incompetent doctor might have overlooked, and another time by careful treatment, he turned a gall bladder into a gold mine. There's no excuse for you, doctor. Uxu, the grain dealer, had his son study medicine to learn business methods, which gives you an idea of the high standards of our medical schools. (*To the blackmailer*) What's this landowner's name?

SHAUVA   He doesn't wish to be named.

AZDAK   Then I'll hand down the verdicts. The court holds that blackmail has been proved, and you (*to the invalid*) are fined one thousand piasters. If you have another stroke, the doctor is ordered to treat you free of charge and amputate if necessary. (*To the lame man*) You are accorded a bottle of cognac in lieu of damages. (*To the blackmailer*) You will assign half your fee to the public prosecutor inasmuch as the court does not divulge the landowner's name, furthermore you are advised to study medicine because you're cut out for that profession. And you, doctor, for unpardonable professional error, you are acquitted. Next cases!

THE SINGER WITH HIS MUSICIANS
Every pleasure costs full measure, funds are rarely come by
    squarely

Justice has no eyes in front or back.
That is why we ask a genius to decide and judge between us
Which is done for half a penny by Azdak.

(*From a caravanserai on the Gruzinian military highway comes Azdak, followed by the landlord, the old man with the long beard. Behind them the hired hand and Shauva carry the seat of justice. An Ironshirt takes his stance with the banner of the Ironshirts corps*)

ADZAK   Put it here. Here at least we get some air and a bit of a breeze from that lemon grove over there. It's a good thing for justice to be conducted in the open. The wind picks up her skirts and you can see what she's got on underneath. Shauva, we've had too much to eat. These inspection trips are strenuous. (*To the landlord*) It's about your daughter-in-law?

THE LANDLORD   Your worship, it's about the honor of my family. I wish to make a complaint on behalf of my son who has gone across the mountains on business. Here is the guilty hired hand, and here is my unfortunate daughter-in-law. (*Enter the daughter-in-law, a voluptuous type. She is veiled*)

AZDAK (*sits down*)   I take. (*With a sigh the landlord gives him money*) Good. So much for the formalities. A case of rape?

THE LANDLORD   Your worship, I caught the fellow in the stable, pushing our Ludovika into the straw.

AZDAK   Yes, yes, the stable. Splendid horses. That little bay struck my fancy.

THE LANDLORD   Naturally, on behalf of my son, I raked Ludovika over the coals.

AZDAK (*gravely*)   I said it struck my fancy.

THE LANDLORD (*coldly*)   Really?—Ludovika confessed that the hired man had taken her against her will.

AZDAK   Remove your veil, Ludovika. (*She does so*) Ludovika, the court has taken a fancy to you. Tell us what happened.

LUDOVIKA (*who has learned her part by rote*)   When I entered the stable to look at the new foal, the hired hand said to me without provocation: "Warm weather we're having," and placed his hand on my left breast. I said to him: "Stop that," but he continued to touch me in an immoral manner, which aroused my anger. Before I could discern his sinful intentions, he had overstepped the bounds. The deed was done when my father-in-law entered and kicked me by mistake.

THE LANDLORD (*explaining*)   On my son's behalf.

AZDAK (*to the hired hand*)   Do you admit that you started it?

HIRED HAND   Yes, sir.

AZDAK   Ludovika, do you like sweets?

LUDOVIKA   Yes, sunflower seeds.

AZDAK   Do you like to sit a long time in the bathtub?

LUDOVIKA   Half an hour or so.

AZDAK   Mr. Public Prosecutor, put your knife on the ground over there. (*Shauva does so*) Ludovika, go pick up the public prosecutor's knife.

(*Swaying her hips, Ludovika goes over to the knife and picks it up*)

AZDAK (*pointing at her*)   Did you see that? The wiggle on her. The guilty party is discovered. Rape is proved. By eating too much, especially sweet things, by prolonged sitting in warm water, by indolence and a soft skin, you have raped that poor man. Do you think you can display a rear end like that in court and get away with it? It's premeditated assault with a dangerous weapon. You are sentenced to assign to the court the little bay that your father-in-law rides on his son's behalf. And now, Ludovika, you will accompany me to the stable, because the court wishes to inspect the scene of the crime.

(*Over the Gruzinian military highway Azdak on his seat of justice is carried from place to place by his Ironshirts. Behind him Shauva carrying the gallows and the hired hand leading the little bay*)

THE SINGER WITH HIS MUSICIANS

Times when master fights with master for the poor are no disaster

Chaos gets the tax collector off their back.

Bearing weights and measures phony, leading someone else's pony

Through the country rode the poor man's judge, Azdak.

And he took away from Croesus and distributed gold pieces
To their rightful owners gave them back.
By a bodyguard protected of the humble and neglected
Rode Gruzinia's good-bad judge, Azdak.

(*The little procession moves off*)

When you go to judge your neighbors leave at home your
    legal papers
Take a good sharp ax and you'll be on the track.
Never mind about God's thunders, axes often will do
    wonders.
Such a wonder worker is the judge Azdak.

(*Azdak's seat of justice is set up in a tavern. Three kulaks
are standing before Azdak, to whom Shauva brings wine.
In the corner stands an old peasant woman. In the open
doorway and outside, the audience of villagers. An Ironshirt
stands at the entrance with the banner of the Ironshirts
corps.*)

AZDAK   The public prosecutor has the floor.

SHAUVA   It's about a cow. For five weeks the defendant has
    had in her barn a cow belonging to the kulak Suru. She has
    also been found in the possession of a stolen ham, and some
    cows belonging to the kulak Shutev were killed after he had
    asked the defendant to pay the rent on a field.

THE KULAKS   It's my ham, your worship.—It's my cow, your
    worship.—It's my field, your worship.

AZDAK   What have you to say to all this, little mother?

THE OLD WOMAN   Your worship, one night five weeks ago,
    just before morning, somebody knocked on my door, and
    outside there was a man with a beard, holding a cow. "Dear
    lady," he said to me, "I am St. Banditus, the worker of
    miracles, and because your son was killed in the war I'm
    bringing you this cow as a souvenir. Take good care of
    her."

THE KULAKS   Irakli, the bandit, your worship.—Her brother-
    in-law, your worship! The cow-thief, the firebug!—He
    should have his head cut off!

(*A woman's scream is heard from outside. The crowd grows uneasy and moves back. Enter Irakli the bandit with an enormous ax*)

THE KULAKS   Irakli! (*They cross themselves*)

THE BANDIT   A very good evening to you, dear friends! A glass of wine!

AZDAK   Public prosecutor, a jug of wine for our guest. Who are you?

THE BANDIT   I'm a wandering hermit, your worship, and thank you for the charitable gift. (*He drains the glass that Shauva has brought him*) Another.

AZDAK   I'm Azdak. (*He stands up and bows; the bandit bows likewise*) The court bids the visiting hermit welcome. Continue, little mother.

THE OLD WOMAN   Your worship, the first night I didn't know St. Banditus could perform miracles; it was only a cow. But a few days later the kulak's hired men came and wanted to take the cow away. Outside my door they turned around and went home without my cow and great big bumps sprouted on their heads. Then I knew St. Banditus had moved their hearts and changed them into kindly men. (*The bandit laughs loudly*)

THE FIRST KULAK   I know what changed them.

AZDAK   That's fine. You'll tell us later. Continue!

THE OLD WOMAN   Your worship, the next to be changed into a good man was the kulak Shutev, a devil as everyone knows. But St. Banditus got him to remit the rent on my little field.

THE SECOND KULAK   Because somebody cut my cows' throats in the field.

(*The bandit laughs*)

THE OLD WOMAN (*at a sign from Azdak*)   And then one morning the ham came flying through the window. It hit me in the small of my back, I'm still lame, see, your worship. (*She takes a few steps. The bandit laughs*) I ask you, your worship: When did a poor woman ever get a whole ham without a miracle?

(*The bandit begins to sob*)

AZDAK (*coming down from his seat*)   Little mother, that

question goes straight to the heart of this court. Kindly be seated. (*Hesitantly the old woman sits down on the judge's chair. Azdak sits on the floor with his glass of wine*)

AZDAK   Little mother, I almost called you Mother Gruzinia, the Sorrowful

The Bereft, whose sons are in the war

Beaten with fists, hopeful

Weeping when she gets a cow.

Surprised when she is not beaten.

Little mother, deign to sit in merciful judgment upon us, the damned.

(*Bellows at the kulaks*) Admit you don't believe in miracles, you godless scum! Each of you is fined five hundred piasters for godlessness. Get out!

(*The kulaks slink out*)

AZDAK   And you, little mother, and you, pious man, share a jug of wine with the public prosecutor and Azdak.

THE SINGER AND HIS MUSICIANS

So he bent the regulations to his own interpretations

And he took the law and stretched it on a rack.

And they found out with a shock, it's men with nothing in their pockets

Who alone are able to corrupt Azdak.

Seven hundred days and twenty, he dealt justice to the gentry

And he dealt them every joker in the pack.

On the woolsack you could find him with the gallows close behind him

Passing judgments worthy of Azdak.

THE SINGER

Then the days of disorder were over, the grand duke returned.

The governor's wife returned, vengeance was taken.

Many died, again the slums were in flames, Azdak was seized with fear.

(*Azdak's seat of justice in the courthouse yard. Azdak is*

sitting on the ground, mending his shoe and talking with Shauva. Noise from outside. Behind the wall the fat prince's head is carried past on a pike)

AZDAK Shauva, the days of your bondage are numbered, the minutes for all I know. For a long time now I've led you by the iron bit of reason till you bled at the mouth, spurred you on with syllogisms and abused you with logic. You're weak by nature; if an argument is slyly tossed your way, you gobble it up, you can't control yourself. It is your nature to lick the hand of a higher being, but there are very different kinds of higher beings. Now you are going to be set free, and soon you'll be able to follow your bent, which is low, and your unerring instinct which teaches you to plant your heavy boot in human faces. For the days of confusion and disorder are past and it's too soon for the great day that I find described in the Song of Chaos, which we shall now sing one last time in memory of those glorious times. Sit down and don't tangle with the tune. Don't be afraid, let it be heard, the refrain is loved by all. (*Sings*)

Sister, veil your face, brother, go get your knife, the times are out of joint.
The masters are filled with lamentation and the little men with joy.
The city says: Let us drive the powerful from our midst.
The offices are invaded, the lists of serfs are destroyed.
The masters are harnessed to the millstones. Those who have never seen daylight come out.
The ebony poor-boxes are shattered, the sesnem wood is cut up for beds.
Those who had no bread have granaries now, those who begged for grain, now distribute grain.

SHAUVA Oh, oh, oh, oh.

AZDAK Where are you, general? Please, please, please make order.

The son of the respected lord can no longer be known. The child of the mistress becomes the son of the slave-girl.
Rich aldermen look for refuge in cold barns, and the pau-

pers who could scarcely find ditches to sleep in loll in
soft beds.

The former boatman now owns many ships. When the
owner looks for them, they are no longer his.

Five men are sent out by their masters. They say: Go yourselves, we have already arrived.

SHAUVA   Oh, oh, oh, oh.

AZDAK   Where are you, general? Please, please, please make
order!

Yes, that's what our country might have come to if law
and order had been neglected any longer. But now the
grand duke, whose life I saved like a dumb ox, has returned
to the capital and the Persians have lent him an army to restore order with. Already the slums are in flames. Bring me
the thick book I always sit on. (*Shauva takes the book from
the seat of justice and Azdak opens it*) This is the book of
the law, I've always used it, you can testify to that.

SHAUVA   Yes, to sit on.

AZDAK   Now I'd better look and see what they can pin on me.
I've connived with paupers, that will cost me dearly. I've
helped poverty up on its rickety legs, they'll hang me for
drunkenness; I've looked into rich men's pockets, they'll
get me for blasphemy. And there's nowhere I can hide,
everybody knows me, because I've helped everybody.

SHAUVA   Someone's coming.

AZDAK   (*stands up in a fright, then goes trembling to the chair*)
Finished! But I won't do anybody the favor of behaving
like a great man. I beg you on my knees for mercy, don't go
away, I'm drooling at the mouth. I'm afraid of death. (*Enter
Natella Abashvili, the governor's wife, with the aide-de-
camp and an Ironshirt*)

THE GOVERNOR'S WIFE   Who is this fellow, Shalva?

AZDAK   A fellow who knows his place, your excellency, and
yours to command.

THE AIDE-DE-CAMP   Natella Abashvili, the late governor's wife,
has just returned. She is looking for her two-year-old son,
Michael Abashvili. She has received word that the child
was carried off to the mountains by a former servant.

AZDAK The child will be brought back, your highness. Yours to command.

THE AIDE-DE-CAMP They say the woman calls the child her own.

AZDAK She will be beheaded, your highness. Yours to command.

THE AIDE-DE-CAMP That will be all.

THE GOVERNOR'S WIFE (*on her way out*) I don't like that man.

AZDAK (*follows her to the door, bowing low*) It will all be taken care of, your highness. Yours to command.

6

The Chalk Circle

THE SINGER

Hear now the story of the lawsuit over Governor Abashvili's child

And how the true mother was identified

By the famous test of the chalk circle.

(*In the yard of the courthouse in Nukha. Ironshirts bring in
Michael, lead him across the courtyard and out behind. An
Ironshirt holds Grusha back in the archway with his pike
until the child has been led away. Then she is admitted.
With her is the woman cook from the former governor's
household. Tumult and fiery glow in the distance*)

GRUSHA He's a brave boy, he can already wash himself.

THE COOK You're in luck, it's not a real judge, it's Azdak. He
drinks like a fish and he doesn't know a thing, the biggest
thieves have got off free. He gets everything mixed up and
the rich people never bribe him enough, that makes it better
for our kind of people.

GRUSHA I need luck today.

THE COOK Don't say it! (*She crosses herself*) I'd better say
another rosary for the judge to be drunk. (*She moves her
lips in silent prayer while Grusha tries in vain to get a*

glimpse of the child) The only thing I don't understand is why you're so intent on keeping him if he isn't yours. In times like these.

GRUSHA He's mine, I've brought him up.

THE COOK Didn't you ever stop to think what would happen if she came back?

GRUSHA At first I thought I'd give him back, and then I thought she wouldn't come after him any more.

THE COOK And even a borrowed coat keeps a body warm, is that it? (*Grusha nods*) I'll swear to anything you say, because you're a good girl. (*Refreshes her memory*) I was boarding the child for five piasters and then on Easter Sunday evening when the trouble broke out, Grusha came and took him. (*She sees the soldier Chachava approaching*) But you haven't done right by Simon, I've talked with him, he doesn't understand.

GRUSHA (*who doesn't see him*) I can't worry my head about him now if he doesn't understand.

THE COOK He understands that the child isn't yours, but your being married and not free till death you do part is too much for him to understand.

(*Grusha sees Simon and greets him*)

SIMON (*gloomily*) I wish to inform the lady that I am ready to swear. I am the father of the child.

GRUSHA (*softly*) That's all right, Simon.

SIMON At the same time I wish to state that this obligates me in no way. Nor the lady either.

THE COOK You didn't have to say that. You know she's married.

SIMON That's her affair, no need to rub it in.

(*Two Ironshirts come in*)

THE IRONSHIRTS Where's the judge?—Has anyone seen the judge?

GRUSHA (*who has turned away and covered her face*) Stand in front of me. I shouldn't have come to Nukha. If I run into the Ironshirt I hit on the head . . .

ONE OF THE IRONSHIRTS (*who have brought the child steps forward*) The judge isn't here.

(*The two Ironshirts go on looking*)

THE COOK I hope nothing has happened to him. With another

you won't stand any more chance than a snowball in hell.
(*Another Ironshirt enters*)

THE IRONSHIRT (*who has inquired about the judge, reports*)
Nobody there but two old people and a child. The judge
has taken a powder.

THE OTHER IRONSHIRT   Keep looking!
(*The first two Ironshirts go out quickly, the third stops still.
Grusha lets out a scream. The Ironshirt turns around. It is
the corporal, he has a scar across his whole face*)

THE IRONSHIRT IN THE ARCHWAY   What's the matter, Shotta?
Do you know her?

THE CORPORAL (*after staring at her at length*)   No.

THE IRONSHIRT IN THE ARCHWAY   They say she kidnapped the
Abashvili child. If you know anything about it, you can
make a pile of money, Shotta.
(*The corporal goes off cursing*)

THE COOK   Is he the one? (*Grusha nods*) He'll button up if
you ask me. Or he'll have to admit he was after the child.

GRUSHA (*relieved*)   I'd almost forgotten I saved the child from
them . . .
(*The governor's wife comes in with the aide-de-camp and
two lawyers*)

THE GOVERNOR'S WIFE   Thank goodness the populace haven't
come. I can't stand the smell. It gives me migraine.

THE FIRST LAWYER   Please, gracious lady, be careful what you
say until we get another judge.

THE GOVERNOR'S WIFE   I haven't said a thing, Illo Shuboladze.
I love the common people and their simple, straightforward
ways, it's only the smell that gives me migraine.

THE SECOND LAWYER   There won't be much of an audience.
Most of the people have shut themselves up in their houses
on account of the fighting in the slums.

THE GOVERNOR'S WIFE   Is that the creature?

THE FIRST LAWYER   My dear Natella Abashvili, please refrain
from invective until it's definite that the grand duke has
appointed a new judge and we're rid of the present judge
who is just about the lowest individual ever seen in a judge's
robe. Look, things seem to be moving.
(*Ironshirts enter the yard*)

THE COOK   The mistress would be tearing your hair out if she didn't know that Azdak is the friend of the poor. One look at a face is enough for him.

(*Two Ironshirts have started fastening a rope to a column. Azdak is brought in in chains. Behind him, also in chains, Shauva. After him come the three kulaks*)

AN IRONSHIRT   Thought you'd make a getaway, did you? (*He strikes Azdak*)

A KULAK   Take off his robe before you string him up!

(*Ironshirts and kulaks pull the judge's robe off Azdak. His ragged underwear becomes visible. One gives him a push*)

AN IRONSHIRT (*pushing him to another*)   Want a lump of justice? Here it is!

(*Amid cries of "You take it!" and "I don't need it!" they push Azdak from one to the other until he collapses. Then he is pulled to his feet and dragged under the noose*)

THE GOVERNOR'S WIFE (*who has been clapping hysterically during the "ball game"*)   I disliked that man the moment I laid eyes on him.

AZDAK (*covered with blood, panting*)   I can't see. Give me a rag.

THE OTHER IRONSHIRT   What do you want to see?

AZDAK   You, you dogs. (*He wipes the blood from his eyes with his shirt sleeve*) Greetings, dogs! How are you, dogs? How's the dog pack, stinking nicely? Licking the old boot again? Back at each other's throats, dogs? (*A dust-covered rider has entered with the corporal. He has taken papers from a leather pouch and looked through them. Now he intervenes*)

THE DUST-COVERED RIDER   Stop! Here's the grand duke's decree concerning the new appointments.

THE CORPORAL (*roaring*)   Attention! (*All come to attention*)

THE DUST-COVERED RIDER   Here's what it says about the new judge: We hereby appoint a man who distinguished himself by saving a life that is of the utmost importance to our country—a certain Azdak of Nukha. Who's he?

SHAUVA (*pointing to Azdak*)   The one under the gallows, your excellency.

THE CORPORAL (*bellowing*)   What's going on here?

THE IRONSHIRT   Beg leave to report that his worship was already his worship and was denounced by these kulaks as an enemy of the grand duke.

THE CORPORAL (*indicating the kulaks*)   Take them away! (*They are led off, bowing without interruption*) See to it that his worship suffers no further annoyance. (*Goes out with the dust-covered rider*)

THE COOK (*to Shauva*)   She clapped before. I hope he saw her.

THE FIRST LAWYER   This is disastrous.

(*Azdak has fainted. He is brought down, revives, and is again clothed in the robe of justice. He staggers out of the group of Ironshirts*)

THE IRONSHIRTS   No offense, your worship!—What does your worship wish?

AZDAK   Nothing, fellow dogs. An occasional boot to lick. (*To Shauva*) You're pardoned. (*He is unbound*) Get me some red wine, sweet. (*Shauva goes out*) Beat it, I've got a case to try. (*The Ironshirts go off. Shauva comes back with a jug of wine. Azdak drinks copiously*) Something for my ass! (*Shauva brings the law book and puts it on the seat of justice. Azdak sits down*) I take!

(*The plaintiffs who have been holding a worried conference smile with relief. They whisper among themselves*)

THE COOK   Oh dear!

SIMON   They say "You can't fill a well with dew."

THE LAWYERS (*approach Azdak, who looks up expectantly*)   A perfectly ridiculous case, your worship.—The defendant has abducted the child and refuses to return it.

AZDAK (*holds out his open hand, looking at Grusha*)   A very attractive young lady. (*They give him more*) I open the proceedings and demand the strict truth. (*To Grusha*) Especially from you.

THE FIRST LAWYER   High court of justice! As the people say, "Blood is thicker than water." This venerable wisdom . . .

AZDAK   The court wishes to know what counsel's fee is.

THE FIRST LAWYER (*astonished*)   I beg your pardon? (*Azdak amiably rubs his thumb and forefinger together*) Oh! Five hundred piasters, your worship, to answer the high court's unusual question.

AZDAK Did you hear that? The question is unusual. I ask you because I listen with a very different ear if I know you're good.

THE FIRST LAWYER (*bows*) Thank you, your worship. High court of justice! Of all human ties the ties of blood are the strongest. Mother and child: can there be any closer relationship? May a child be taken from its mother? High court of justice! She conceived it in the sacred ecstasies of love, she carried it in her womb, fed it with her blood, bore it in pain. High court of justice! It is common knowledge that even the ferocious tigress, robbed of her cubs, goes ranging through the mountains without rest, shrunk to a shadow. Nature itself . . .

AZDAK (*interrupting, to Grusha*) What's your answer to that and all the rest of what counsel is going to say?

GRUSHA It's mine.

AZDAK Is that all? I hope you can prove it. In any case, I suggest that you tell me why you think I should award you the child.

GRUSHA I brought him up the best I knew how, I always found him something to eat. He had a roof over his head most of the time, I let myself in for all kinds of trouble for his sake, and expenses too. I didn't worry about my own convenience. I taught the child to be friendly to everyone and right from the start to work as best he could, he's still so little.

THE FIRST LAWYER Your worship, it is significant that the defendant herself alleges no blood tie between the child and herself.

AZDAK The court takes note.

THE FIRST LAWYER Thank you, your worship. Permit a sorely bereaved woman, who has lost her husband and must now fear to lose her child, to address a few words to you. Gracious Natella Abashvili . . .

THE GOVERNOR'S WIFE (*softly*) A cruel fate, sir, compels me to plead with you to return my beloved child. It is not for me to describe the torments of a bereaved mother, the sleepless nights, the . . .

THE SECOND LAWYER (*erupting*) It is unspeakable how this

woman has been treated. She is barred from entering her husband's palace, the income from his estates is withheld from her. Without an iota of feeling they tell her the income is entailed to the legal heir, she can't do a thing without the child, she can't pay her lawyers! (*To the first lawyer who, in despair over this outburst, is motioning him frantically to keep quiet*) My dear Illo Shuboladze, why should it not be made known that the Abashvili estates are at stake?

THE FIRST LAWYER　Honored Sandro Oboladze, please! We agreed we . . . (*To Azdak*) It is true, of course, that the outcome of this trial will also determine whether our noble client obtains possession of the sizable Abashvili estates; "also," I say, and by design, for the paramount consideration, as Natella Abashvili justly pointed out in the first words of her moving plea, is the tragedy of a mother. Even if Michael Abashvili were not heir to the estates, he would still be my client's dearly beloved child.

AZDAK　Enough! The court looks upon your mention of the estates as proof that we're all human.

THE SECOND LAWYER　Thank you, your worship. My dear Illo Shuboladze, we can prove in any event that the woman who seized the child is not the child's mother! Allow me to set the hard facts before the court. By an unfortunate concatenation of circumstances, this child, Michael Abashvili, was left behind when his mother fled the city. Grusha, a kitchen maid in the palace, was present that Easter Sunday and was seen busying herself with the child . . .

THE COOK　While the lady was busy worrying which dresses to take with her!

THE SECOND LAWYER (*impassive*)　Almost a year later Grusha appeared with the child in a mountain village and concluded a marriage with . . .

AZDAK　How did you get to this mountain village?

GRUSHA　On my feet, your worship, and he was mine.

SIMON　I am the father, your worship.

THE COOK　He was boarding with me, your worship, for five piasters.

THE SECOND LAWYER　This man is Grusha's betrothed, your worship, his testimony is therefore untrustworthy.

AZDAK Are you the man she married in the mountain village?

SIMON No, your worship. She married a peasant.

AZDAK (*motions Grusha over to him*) Why? (*Indicating Simon*) No good in bed? I want the truth.

GRUSHA We didn't get that far. I married on account of the child. To give him a roof over his head. (*Indicating Simon*) He was in the war, your worship.

AZDAK And now he wants to get back with you, is that it?

SIMON I wish to state . . .

GRUSHA (*angrily*) I'm no longer free, your worship.

AZDAK And the child, you claim, comes from whoring? (*When Grusha does not answer*) Let me ask you one question: What kind of a child is it? A ragged little bastard off the streets or the child of a noble, well-to-do family?

GRUSHA (*angrily*) An ordinary child.

AZDAK I mean: did he show refined features at an early age?

GRUSHA He showed a nose in his face.

AZDAK He showed a nose in his face. I regard that as a significant answer. There's a story they tell about me; it seems that once before pronouncing a verdict I went out and sniffed at a rosebush. Little tricks like that are necessary nowadays. Now I'm going to make it short, I'm not going to listen to any more of you people's lies—(*to Grusha*) especially yours. I can imagine how you (*to the group around the defendant*) cooked this all up to pull the wool over my eyes. I know you, you're crooks.

GRUSHA (*suddenly*) I can imagine you'd want to make it short, I saw what you took.

AZDAK Shut up! Did I take anything from you?

GRUSHA (*in spite of the cook who is trying to restrain her*) Because I haven't got anything.

AZDAK Perfectly right. I don't get a thing from you down-and-outers, I could starve. You want justice, but you don't want to pay. When you go to the butcher's, you know you'll have to pay, but you go to the judge like you'd go to a wake.

SIMON (*in a loud voice*) "When the horse was to be shod, the horse fly held out his legs." As the saying goes.

AZDAK (*takes up the challenge with enthusiasm*) "Better a

treasure from the manure pile than a pebble from a mountain spring."

SIMON   "A fine day, let's go fishing, said the angler to the worm."

AZDAK   "I'm my own master, said the hired man and cut off his foot."

SIMON   "I love you like a father, said the tsar to the peasants and chopped the tsarevitch's head off."

AZDAK   "A fool's worst enemy is himself."

SIMON   But "a fart has no nose!"

AZDAK   You're fined ten piasters for indecent language in court, that'll teach you what justice is.

GRUSHA   Some justice! You throw the book at us because we don't talk refined like her with her lawyers.

AZDAK   Right. You're too dumb. You deserve to be sat on.

GRUSHA   Because you want to hand the child over to that woman who's so refined she wouldn't know how to change its diapers! You don't know any more about justice than I do, put that in your pipe!

AZDAK   You've got something there. I'm ignorant, the pants under my robe are full of holes, see for yourself. With me it all goes into eating and drinking, I was raised in a monastery. Come to think of it, I'm fining you ten piasters too, for contempt of court. What's more, you're stupid, antagonizing me instead of making eyes at me and wiggling your ass a little to put me in a good humor. Twenty piasters.

GRUSHA   You can make it thirty and I'll still tell you what I think of your justice, you drunken turnip. How dare you talk to me like the cracked Isaiah on the church window— big shot! When they pulled you out of your mother, they didn't expect you to rap her knuckles if she stole a cup of millet some place, and aren't you ashamed of yourself to see me trembling like this on account of you? You serve these people so their houses won't be taken away—because they stole them; since when do houses belong to bedbugs? But you take care of them, or they couldn't drag our men off to their wars, you flunky!

(*Azdak has stood up. He is beaming. Halfheartedly he strikes the table with his little gavel as though to obtain*

*order, but when Grusha goes on reviling him, he merely
beats time for her)*

GRUSHA   I have no respect for you. No more than I have for a
thief and murderer with a knife, he does what he pleases.
It's a hundred to one you can take the child away from me,
but I'll tell you one thing: for a job like yours they should
only pick rapists and usurers, to punish them by making
them sit in judgment over their fellow men, which is worse
than hanging on the gallows.

AZDAK   That makes it thirty, and I'm not going to wrangle
with you any more, this isn't a tavern. I'm a judge and I've
got my dignity to think of. To tell you the truth, I've lost
interest in your case. Where are those two who wanted a
divorce? *(To Shauva)* Bring them in. I'm adjourning this
case for fifteen minutes.

THE FIRST LAWYER *(as Shauva leaves)*   We can rest our case,
gracious lady, it's in the bag.

THE COOK *(to Grusha)*   You've rubbed him the wrong way.
Now he'll take the child away from you.

(Enter a very aged couple)

THE GOVERNOR'S WIFE   Shalva, my smelling salts.

AZDAK   I take. *(The old people do not understand)* I hear you
want a divorce. How long have you been together?

THE OLD MAN   Forty years, your worship.

AZDAK   Why do you want a divorce?

THE OLD MAN   We don't like each other, your worship.

AZDAK   Since when?

THE OLD WOMAN   The whole time, your worship.

AZDAK   I will take your request under deliberation and give
you my decision when I'm through with the other case.
(Shauva leads them to the rear) I need the child. *(Motions Grusha to come over to him and bends down to her
in a not unfriendly manner)* Woman, I've seen you have a
soft spot for justice. I don't believe he's your child, but supposing he were, wouldn't you want him to be rich? You'd
only have to say he's not yours. One two three he'd have a
palace, and plenty of horses in his stable and plenty of beggars on his doorstep, plenty of soldiers in his service and
plenty of petitioners in his courtyard. See? What's your

answer to that? Don't you want him to be rich? (*Grusha is silent*)

THE SINGER   Hear now what the angry woman thought and did not say: (*Sings*)

If he walked in golden shoes
Cold his heart would be and stony.
Humble folk he would abuse
He wouldn't know me.

Oh, it's hard to be hard-hearted
All day long from morn to night.
To be mean and high and mighty
Is a hard and cruel plight.

Let him be afraid of hunger
Not of the hungry man's spite
Let him be afraid of darkness
But not fear the light.

AZDAK   Woman, I think I understand you.

GRUSHA   I won't give him up. I've raised him and he knows me.
(*Shauva brings the child in*)

THE GOVERNOR'S WIFE   He's in rags!

GRUSHA   That's not true. They didn't give me time to put on his good shirt.

THE GOVERNOR'S WIFE   He's been in a pigsty!

GRUSHA (*furious*)   I'm not a pig but I know someone who is. Where did you leave your child?

THE GOVERNOR'S WIFE   I'll show you, you vulgar slut. (*She is about to fling herself on Grusha but is restrained by the lawyers*) She's a criminal! She ought to be flogged! This minute!

THE SECOND LAWYER (*stops her mouth*)   Gracious Natella Abashvili! You promised . . . Your worship, the plaintiff's nerves . . .

AZDAK   Plaintiff and defendant: the court has heard your case, but has not yet ascertained who this child's real mother is. It is my duty as judge to pick a mother for the child. I'm going to give you a test. Shauva, take a piece of chalk. Draw a circle on the floor. (*Shauva draws a chalk circle on the floor*) Put the child in the circle! (*Shauva places Michael, who is smiling at Grusha, in the circle*) Plaintiff and defendant, stand just outside the circle, both of you! (*The governor's wife and Grusha step close to the circle*) Each of you take the child by one hand. The true mother will have the strength to pull the child out of the circle.

THE SECOND LAWYER (*quickly*)   High court of justice, I object to making the fate of the large Abashvili estates, which are entailed to the child as heir, hinge on the outcome of so dubious a contest. Furthermore, my client is not as strong as this person who is accustomed to physical labor.

AZDAK   She looks well fed to me. Pull!

(*The governor's wife pulls the child out of the circle. Grusha has let go, she stands aghast*)

THE FIRST LAWYER (*congratulates the governor's wife*)   What did I say? The ties of blood.

AZDAK (*to Grusha*)   What's the matter with you? You didn't pull.

GRUSHA   I didn't hold on to him. (*She runs to Azdak*) Your worship, I take back what I said against you, I beg your forgiveness. If only I could keep him until he knows all his words. He knows just a few.

AZDAK   Don't try to influence the court! I bet you don't know more than twenty yourself. All right, I'll repeat the test to make sure.

(*Again the two women take their places*)

AZDAK   Pull!

(*Again Grusha lets the child go*)

GRUSHA   I raised him! Do you want me to tear him to pieces? I can't.

AZDAK (*stands up*)   The court has now ascertained who the true mother is. (*To Grusha*) Take your child and clear out. I advise you not to stay in the city with him. (*To the governor's wife*) And you get out of here before I convict you of fraud. The estates devolve to the city, they will be turned into a park for the children, they need it, and the park shall be named "Azdak Park" after me.

(*The governor's wife has fainted and is led away by the aide-de-camp; the lawyers have already gone*)

(*Grusha stands motionless. Shauva brings her the child*)

AZDAK   Because I'm taking off the robe of justice, it's got too hot for me. I'm nobody's hero. But I invite you all to a little farewell dance out there in the meadow. Oh, I almost forgot something, too much wine. The divorce. (*Using the seat of justice as a table, he writes something on a piece of paper and starts to leave*)

(*The dance music has started up*)

SHAUVA   (*has read the paper*) But this is all wrong. You haven't divorced the two old people, you've divorced Grusha from her husband.

AZDAK   Divorced the wrong people? That's too bad, but it sticks, I retract nothing, the law's the law. (*To the very old couple*) I invite you to my celebration instead, I'll bet you still like each other enough to dance together. (*To Grusha and Simon*) And from you two I want forty piasters.

SIMON   (*takes out his purse*) Fair enough, your worship. And many thanks.

AZDAK   (*putting the money away*) I'm going to need it.

GRUSHA   We'd better leave the city tonight, hadn't we, Michael? (*Starts to lift the child on her back. To Simon*) Do you like him?

SIMON   (*lifts the child on his back*) Beg to report: I like him.

GRUSHA   Now I can tell you: I took him because I betrothed myself to you that Easter Sunday. So it's a child of love. Michael, let's dance.

(*She dances with Michael. Simon dances with the cook. The old couple dance too. Azdak stands in thought. Soon the dancing couples hide him. He is seen from time to time, more and more seldom as more couples come in and dance*)

THE SINGER

And that night Azdak disappeared and was never seen again.
But the people of Gruzinia did not forget him, they long remembered
The days of his judging as a brief

Golden Age when there was almost justice.
(*The dancers dance off the stage. Azdak has vanished*)

And you who have heard the story of the chalk circle
Bear in mind the wisdom of our fathers:
Things should belong to those who do well by them
Children to motherly women that they may thrive
Wagons to good drivers that they may be well driven
And the valley to those who water it, that it may bear fruit.

Notes and Variants

THE VISIONS OF
SIMONE MACHARD

Texts by Brecht

The Visions of Simone Machard

Little Simone Machard works for the hostelry at a small town called Saint-Martin in central France. She is there to help out, primarily in connection with the hotel gas pump; the hotel also runs a trucking business. It is June 1940; the Nazis have taken Paris; streams of refugees are pouring across central France and passing through Saint-Martin.

Simone's seventeen-year-old brother is at the front; she loves him dearly and is sure that he is involved in the fighting. Meanwhile in the village and in the hotel she finds that at this point, in the middle of a great national disaster, high and low alike can think of nothing but themselves. It is now that she reads a book given her by her teacher, which contains the story of the Maid of Orleans, greatest of all French patriots.

During those feverish nights, with the Germans already at the Loire, she is moved by the course of events to dream that she is herself Saint Joan. An angel appears to her from the garage roof and tells her that she has been chosen to save France. He has the features of her soldier brother André. In her dream the legend of the book mingles with the reality of the little hotel. The hotel's owner is suddenly a constable of the royal court; the hotel staff, the truck drivers, and the old night porter, wear armor and form a little unit of feudal soldiery who escort her to the king; while in the king himself she recognizes the spineless local mayor.

Thereafter Simone at the hostelry undergoes a miniature

version of the terrible and uplifting fate of Joan of Arc, and again and again in her dreams she turns into the saint.

She dreams that the angel gives her an invisible drum. He tells her that this drum is the soil of France, and that in an emergency the soil of France—her drum—will resound, summoning the people to resist France's enemies. In her role as a great popular leader she then in her dream goes to the king, holds confidential talks with the king-mayor and warns him not to spend his time playing cards with his nobles, the owner-constable and the other luminaries of Saint-Martin, but instead to attend to the arming and feeding of the people. The people, for their part, are called on to fight wholeheartedly. In this way she manages to unite king, people, and nobles and to crown the king-mayor in Rheims.

In the real world of the hotel, when its owner and his drivers simply wish to run away from the Germans, she fetches the mayor and has the hotel forced to hand over its stocks of food to the municipality rather than remove them to the rear, while the drivers and their trucks are made to evacuate the refugees who are blocking the French army from using the roads. (The owner allows the child to have her way because at least this stops his hostelry from being looted, and the drivers help her because they sympathize with her anxiety for her brother at the front.)

But when she calls for the hostelry's secret stocks of gasoline to be destroyed to prevent them from falling into enemy hands she is going too far, and the owner's mother dismisses her.

That night she dreams the chapter in her book in which the Maid, following her initial victories, encounters the first problems in her own ranks. Although Paris is still in enemy hands she is not given command of a fresh army. The king-mayor and the owner-constable ennoble her, admittedly, but they take away her sword. Once more the angel appears on the garage roof and she has to tell him that she has been dismissed. Severely the angel recommends her to stick to her course and not, for instance, to let the gas fall into the hands of the Germans, or else their murderous tanks will be able to keep on thrusting ahead.

A few days later the Germans enter Saint-Martin. The

owner has fled. His mother and old Captain Beleire, a Laval supporter and vineyard owner, wish to come to terms with the victorious Germans at any price. To prove that they mean to collaborate they tell the German commandant that the gasoline is hidden in the brickyard. But the brickyard is already ablaze when the Germans get there. Simone has set fire to it. This act of sabotage threatens the new and promising Franco-German collaboration. Wanted: the incendiary.

In a disturbing dream Simone once again encounters the heroic Joan of the legend, now deserted by her own side, because the queen mother Isabeau and the duke of Burgundy have asserted themselves at court and are trying to arrange an armistice with the enemy. The queen mother looks just like the mother of the owner, while the duke of Burgundy is like the constable. Only Simone, now wide awake, cannot believe this dream. And when on the owner's return he feels sorry for her, and he and the drivers want to take her away, she insists on staying. How is her brother to find her if and when he returns? So she is denounced to the Germans and arrested.

In a final vision Simone dreams that she, Joan, has been taken captive and handed over by the enemy to an ecclesiastical court which has to decide whether the voices which she heard summoning her to resist the enemy came in fact from God or from the devil. She is tragically shocked to find that the noble judges who condemn her to the stake for having spoken with the devil's voice are all people whom she knows: the mayor, the captain, the owner, with the owner's mother putting the case for the prosecution.

Simone dreams this last dream in prison, and the following morning the Germans hand her back to the French. Her friends among the hotel staff are hopeful for her. They feel that a French official inquiry into the fire must be bound to admit the patriotic nature of her motives. But there are good reasons why the German attitude should be so generous. The Germans think it undesirable that there should have been an act of sabotage which might serve as a precedent for others. And shooting a child would jeopardize the collaboration they so badly need. So they have agreed with their French friends that the case should be sidetracked.

Simone has to hear the owner and his mother, her employ-

ers, giving evidence against her, while the mayor leaves her
to her fate. Numb with shock, she learns that a French court
finds that her action was not undertaken for patriotic reasons,
but that she caused the fire for purely personal motives, as a
mischievous act of revenge for her dismissal. She is sent to a
home for delinquent children.

The people, however, are not fooled. When the owner returns to the hostelry he finds that his staff have left. And as
Simone is being led away after the verdict Saint-Martin is
shaken by a bombing attack. English planes are carrying on
the struggle.

For Simone these explosions have a special meaning. Did her
dream angel not tell her that the soil of France was her invisible drum, whose sound would bring the sons of France
hurrying to defend it? And here is French soil reverberating.
It is the angel, her brother André, who has sent her the planes.

N.B. Interwoven with the play is the delicate story of little
Simone's relations with a wounded soldier, one of her brother's
friends.

> [GW *Schriften zum Theater* 3, pp. 1181–85. This plan
> for the play, which may have been conceived as a film
> treatment, differs from our text, particularly in its ending,
> which is unlike that in any other version. Nowhere else
> is the captain specifically described as being old, while
> the identification of the drum with the soil of France is
> also unusually clearly made. Note that there is no mention
> of the refugees in the schoolhouse.]

Working Plan

1. *the germans invade france. at the hostelry "au relais" it is
business as usual, but simone machard is reading a book of
legends.*
   (a)   two drivers see bombs, an old man mends tires, a
   soldier licks his wounds, a child reads a book.
   (b)   the colonel does not wish to be greeted.

(c) conversation about the treachery of the top people, about visions, hordes of refugees, headaches, teachers and wine.

(d) soldiers get their stew pot half-filled with lentils. simone's brother is unknown.

(e) the owner defends his stocks and tells simone to give the colonel his bill.

(f) the hotel has a star, the staff remain cool.

(g) the mayor is bawled out by the colonel because the roads are blocked.

(h) the mayor wants trucks for the refugees, the owner has no gasoline, the staff confirm it, the captain needs the trucks for his wine barrels, the war is lost.

(i) only a miracle can save france, in the mayor's view; the staff say "simone thinks one will take place."

2. *joan of arc, summoned by divine voices, crowns the king in rheims and unites all frenchmen against the hereditary foe.*

(a) the angel calls joan and gives her the task.

(b) she gets helmet and bayonet.

(c) the ajaxes escort her, and battles are won.

(d) she recognizes the king.

(e) her argument with the king.

(f) she crowns him.

3. *simone gets a hearing for the mayor, and the hotel is saved.*

(a) the germans have crossed the loire, the staff has breakfast, the owner has certain wishes, the staff has breakfast, simone disappears.

(b) the owner is horrified to find that he is not liked. simone is looked for by her parents.

(c) the mayor arrives with soldiers, having been fetched by simone. the trucks are requisitioned but the mayor weakens.

(d) simone supports him and arranges everything, aided by madame mère. the soldiers are given wine, and leave for the front. the village is given the food stocks, and simone's parents are the first.

(e) the wave of patriotism infects the owner. handshake and toast. the gasoline must be saved, as simone said.

(f)   the owner has departed. madame mère fires simone.
the mayor admires the tip.

4. *joan, rewarded by the court but dismissed in her native
village, is encouraged by her voices to continue the struggle.*
   (a)   although the enemy is still in her country, joan can get
no more troops.
   (b)   instead she is thanked for her services. she is knighted
with her own sword.
   (c)   but her sword is not returned to her; the king gives it
to the constable as a mark of gratitude.
   (d)   the angel appears and tells her to carry on the struggle.

5. *the germans occupy the village. simone sets fire to the
gasoline.*
   (a)   madame mère receives the german commandant. "he's
human like the rest of us."
   (b)   the captain harangues the staff. in future discipline will
prevail.
   (c)   simone hears the captain warning the mayor not to
conceal the existence of the gas in the brickyard.
   (d)   simone tells the mayor of her plan to set fire to the
brickyard. he seems to approve.
   (e)   the opponents also get on at a low level. the commandant's batman talks with the wounded soldier.
   (f)   the gentry enter the yard to inspect the brickyard. a
good understanding prevails.
   (g)   the brickyard is ablaze.

6. *simone is surrendered by the top people.*
   (a)   simone's parents come to thank her: as a result of her
generous action her father has got the beadle's job.
   (b)   the owner returns. he is embarrassed by the parents'
tributes: "your hotel is france in miniature." père gustave
accompanies him inside.

daydream
   (a)   the maid's messenger is kept from the king. why?
   (b)   because the english are within. and what is being
talked about?

(c)   the maid. and what else?

(d)   the fact that she is to blame for the war.

(e)   so she isn't relieved, but her troops are thrown in again and so she is captured.

(f)   but the angel appears once more and assures her that everything she did was right, and warns her to stick to her mission.

6. *simone is surrendered by the top people,* continued.

(c)   the drivers urge simone to flee. she stands by her faith in the owner.

(d)   then the owner comes out too and urges her to flee.

(e)   simone is seized by panic, and does flee.

(f)   the german commandant and the french gentry enter the courtyard and a search is made for simone. she is not there. the commandant is angry and goes back indoors.

(g)   sigh of relief from the gentry. simone is standing in the courtyard. she has come back. they implore her. she refuses to flee. the commandant arrives. simone: it's me.

7. *the english hand joan over to an ecclesiastical court consisting of frenchmen, which interrogates her about the angel.*

(a)   the english bring joan before the ecclesiastical court. they ask for a report as to whether the voices come from god or from the devil.

(b)   the constable, the burgundian, and the renegade colonel don their ecclesiastical robes.

(c)   the ecclesiastical court discusses the voices' origin with joan and finds them devilish.

8. *trial of simone machard by the authorities of her village. she is found not guilty of the crime of sabotage but is sent to the pious sisters' corrective institution on the grounds of incendiarism and vindictiveness.*

(a)   the germans hand simone back.

(b)   the commission goes out of its way to whitewash her of any accusation of sabotaging the germans.

(c)   the staff welcome this attitude on the court's part and hope for her release.

(d)   the remainder of the interrogation is devoted to

simone's attitude to her employers, particularly on the day of the great panic.

(e)   questioned about her motives for incendiarism she continues to insist that she did it for france's sake.

(f)   she is forced however to admit that she really wanted to save the gasoline from its owners.

(g)   she is therefore handed over to the pious sisters of sainte-madeleine for correction.

(h)   while she says good-bye in the yard to the staff and to her parents the commission goes off to report to the german commandant.

> [BBA 1204/1–3. This is one of the most elaborately worked-out of all Brecht's characteristic structural plans. It is mounted on a card, with scenes 1 to 8 (and their subheadings) forming eight parallel columns. There are penciled figures by Brecht giving (apparently) the estimated duration of each subscene, and it seems altogether probable that the collaborators used it as a basis for their first script.]

The Dreams

The dreams in which Simone relives the St. Joan legend can be made intelligible to audiences unaware of the legend by the large-scale projection of individual pages from the book, possibly including woodcut illustrations.

For the *first dream:* "Summoned by an angel to save France, Joan unites the French by crowning Charles VII king in the city of Rheims."

For the *second dream:* "Following some brilliant victories, Joan is ennobled. However, she has powerful enemies at court who would like to see an armistice."

For the *third dream:* "Betrayed into enemy hands, Joan is handed over to an ecclesiastical court which condemns her to death."

> [GW *Schriften zum Theater* 3, p. 1185. These captions can be compared with those in the plans quoted in the

editorial note, below. Illustrations reproduced from old illuminated manuscripts are gummed into one or two of Brecht's typescripts of the play.]

First Dream of Simone Machard (during the night of June 14)

I was addressed from the garage roof in a loud voice as "Joan!", went immediately out into the yard and saw *the angel* on the roof of the garage. He waved to me in friendly fashion and told me that I had been called to defeat France's enemies. He ordered me to go straightway to Châlons and crown the king, as I had read in the book. After the angel had disappeared once more the soldier came out of the garage towards me and handed me sword and helmet. The former looked like a bayonet. I asked whether I should clean it for him but he answered that it was against the enemies of France. Thereupon I felt as if I were standing in green countryside. A strong wind was blowing and the sky was like it is between four and five in the morning when you go to mass. Then I saw how the earth, together with all the meadows and poplars upon it, curved as if it were a ball, and how the enemy loomed up in a mighty procession without end. In front rode the drummer with a voice like a wolf and his drum was made of a Jew's skin; a vulture perched on his shoulder with the features of Farouche the banker from Lyons. Close behind him came the field marshal firebug. He went on foot, a fat clown, in seven uniforms and in none of them did he look human. Above these two devils was a canopy of newspapers, so it was easy for me to recognize them. Behind them rode the remaining executioners and marshals, with countenances for the most part like the backsides of plucked chickens, and behind them drove an endless procession of guns and tanks and railroad trains, also cars on which were altars or torture chambers, for everything was on wheels.

[BBA 118–19. More than anything else, this draft of the first dream, part of which was taken into the play (p.

19), links the "Visions" of the play's title with the series of poetic "Visions" written by Brecht from 1938 on. See the notes to the *Poems*, the section dealing with the Steffin Collection/Visions (1938–40). The drummer is Hitler, the field marshal Hermann Goering, whom the Communists held responsible for the Reichstag fire of 1933.]

Two Characters

Scene 1

SIMONE

All this being ordered hither and thither remains characteristic of the little maid-of-all-work so long as the hither and the thither are still undefined, and the hither and thither is not contrasted with something else. This would be the case were she, for instance, to be rent apart between the wishes of those above her and the needs of those below—for she is exploited from on top and from underneath—and if, to form the contrast, there were something at some particularly rending moment to be observed about TANKS that was of special worry and concern to her.

Scene 6 [*our scene 3b*]

THE OWNER

The owner can only develop into a character if he acquires an evolution of his own in this scene. His confrontation with the staff becomes manly as a result of the invasion. The invasion offers him the opportunity to score a "victory," but he shouldn't be too eager to pick up this particular laurel wreath. It is essential that he should fall into a rage on hearing that his brickyard has been destroyed; this is not the kind of war he wants to wage. Waging it in this way destroys the point of war. Patriotic feelings raise their head later, as inhibitions. How is it going to look if he hands a French citizen over to the Germans? That would be setting a bad example.

> [BBA 1190/50. For the renumbering of scenes, see the editorial note.]

Editorial Note

1. General

When Brecht and Feuchtwanger discussed collaborating on a play at the end of October 1942 they considered various possibilities before settling on a St. Joan story:

> A confused person has dreams in which the characters of the patriotic legend take on features of her superiors, and she learns how and why those superiors are waging their war, and how long for.

Thus the note in Brecht's journal, which calls the project *Saint Joan of Vitry (The Voices)*. According to Feuchtwanger's recollection many years later the heroine was originally to be called Odette, but in what must be one of the earliest plans she is Jeanne Gotard. This was for a play of eleven scenes, starting:

1. the germans attack france. jeanne gotard is given an old book with the story of joan of arc.
2. joan of arc calls on the king.
3. jeanne gotard hides the gasoline stocks from the advancing german tanks.

—and finishing:

7. incendiarism of jeanne gotard.
8. respectable frenchmen talk to respectable englishmen.
9. arrest of jeanne gotard.
10. initiation of proceedings against joan of arc.
11. condemnation of jeanne gotard by a french court.

What seems like the beginning of a treatment in Brecht's typing is headed *Saint Joan of Vitry* and goes as follows:

> In Vitry, a small town in Champagne, during the German invasion of 1940, a young girl by the name of Jeanne Gotard dreamt a strange dream lasting five consecutive nights. By day she worked her father's gasoline pump, he being a soldier serving in the Maginot Line. The schoolmaster across the way had lent her an old book with the illustrated story of Joan of Arc, and so at night she dreamt she was Joan. In her dreams however the historical events reported in the book were intermingled with memories of certain incidents at the gas station, so that the story of the saint displayed strange variations which not only made a profound impression on those listeners to whom she recounted her nightly experiences but would also certainly have interested an historian, if such a person had been present. In her dreams she appeared armed with bayonet and steel helmet, but the rest of her clothes were those that she wore every day, while the historical personalities with whom she had to deal—king, marshals, cardinals, and ordinary people—bore the faces of familiar personalities of the town of Vitry, such as visited the gas station in the daytime. Coulonge the banker merely wore a plumed hat, the mayor of the town simply a flowing cloak over his grey suit. . . .

A nine-scene version of the plan eliminates the missing scenes 4–6 of the scheme given above, and renames the heroine Michèle. Thus:

1. the germans attack france, michèle gotard reads a patriotic legend.
2. joan of arc, summoned by divine voices, crowns the king in rheims and unites all frenchmen against the hereditary foe.

3. michèle saves stocks from the advancing german tanks.
4. joan of arc, rewarded by the mighty and dismissed in her native village, is moved by the divine voices to continue the struggle.
5. michèle's incendiarism.
6. highly-placed frenchmen talk to highly-placed englishmen.
7. michèle is betrayed and is arrested by the germans; however, certain circles arrange for her to come before a french court.
8. joan is perturbed by the angel's failure to appear. the high court meets and questions her about the voices.
9. condemnation of michèle gotard by a french court.

With the much more elaborately worked-out plan given above on pp. 236–40 Michèle Gotard finally turned into Simone Machard, but the English decision to hand Joan of Arc over for trial by her own people—which Feuchtwanger saw as the pivotal point of the play—became swallowed in the next scene. Nonetheless this eight-scene version seems to have served as the basis for the actual writing of the play.

Brecht's first typescript is in eight scenes, bearing the dates December 28, 1942, at scene 5 and January 1943 near the end; a note in his handwriting calls it "first script, written in California." An almost entirely rewritten script follows, which is not in Brecht's typing and bears corrections by his and other hands; it was among his collaborator Ruth Berlau's papers and is headed "a play in two acts by Bertolt Brecht and Lion Feuchtwanger" with three suggested English titles: *Simone Hears Voices*, *St. Joan in Vichy* and *The Nights of St. Joan*. Feuchtwanger seems to have used a copy of this, lacking Brecht's last revisions, for a third, slightly modified version which he headed "a play in eight scenes by Bertolt Brecht and Lion Feuchtwanger" and sent to Elisabeth Hauptmann in Berlin a year before Brecht's death; it bears no marks by Brecht. The fourth and final script derives likewise from the rewritten version; it dates from 1946 and contains none of Feuchtwanger's modifications, but is heavily corrected by Brecht, who at some points went back to the first version. This is the script which was used for the German collected edition and accordingly is the basis of our own text. We shall refer to them respectively as the first version, the Berlau script, the Feuchtwanger script, and the 1946 or final version.

For Brecht there were two principal points of uncertainty in the writing of it. The first was the question of Simone's age; he found himself wanting to make her younger and younger ("mainly because i cannot give a motive for her patriotism," he noted in his journal), yet by doing so he destroyed her interest as a character. "The difficulty is," he noted on December 8, 1942, of his struggle with the Handshake scene,

> i'm writing the scene with no picture of the principal part, simone. originally i saw her as a somewhat ungainly, mentally retarded, and inhibited person; then it seemed more practical to use a child, so i'm left with the bare functions and nothing to offset them with in the way of individuality.

The other problem was the actual ending of the play, which is unresolved in the first script and may well have been left in some confusion when Brecht went off to New York on February 8. As will be seen from the detailed analysis that follows, he envisaged two alternative endings, arguing (in the journal entry for January 5) that

> the correct version is unperformable. in reality of course the wendells [i.e. the De Wendels of the Schneider arms firm] and pétains made use of the defeat and the foreign occupation to put down their social opponents. simone accordingly would need to be released by the germans (following false evidence by the staff of the hostelry) then handed over to the corrective institution by madame mère and captain fétain for subversive activities. in the performable version this would have to be blurred over; condemning simone for incendiarism due to her hatred of the owner means at the same time saving her from execution by the germans.

It was only in the final version that he seems finally to have settled for the less blurred alternative.

But besides these a number of other important variables can be observed in the scripts, though Brecht himself had nothing to say about them. To summarize these, they are:

(a) the identification of the angel with Simone's brother. At the beginning of the first version it is the Archangel Michael, while there is also a note saying "the angel's voice is [? the voice] of the people."

(b) the characters of Maurice and Robert, who in the first version are brothers. There they are shown shirking the call-up, and Maurice has evidently refused to help move the refugees (as is made explicit in the Berlau script). However, at the end of the Berlau (ii) and Feuchtwanger scripts they turn against the owner. Not so in the final script.

(c) the character of Père Gustave. He seems much more unpleasant in the earlier versions, bootlicking the owner and giving evidence against Simone.

(d) the rôle of the mayor, who compromises at a different stage in each version. Thus in the Feuchtwanger and Berlau (ii) versions of the fourth dream (i.e. our scene 4a) he is still defending Simone, whereas in the final text he is one of her judges.

(e) the owner's journey with the two truck drivers. In our version it is not explained how they came back, nor why they brought back the china and not the wines (initially the captain's) nor what happened to such refugees as they found room for. In the other texts the party runs into the Germans and/or breaks down, but again it is far from clear what is really supposed to have happened.

(f) the rôle of the refugees is heavily stressed in the final text, which brings in the notion of their being a "mob" quartered in the schoolhouse.

(g) Simone's escape is exclusive to the last version, though she half-tries in the Berlau and Feuchtwanger scripts.

(h) the placing of the daydream varies. This section of the play, Feuchtwanger told Brecht in a letter of March 27, 1943, had displeased all with whom he had discussed it (William Dieterle, Hanns Eisler, Oscar Homolka, and Berthold Viertel) and should therefore be cut.

Such points reflect a good deal of uncertainty in the authors' minds, and the effect is visible even in the final version, where the definition of the characters is further smudged by the occasional reallocation of lines. Besides this there is not only the altering of names—thus in the first script the mayor was Phillip (sic) Duclos, the owner Henri Champon, his mother "madame mère," and the captain Captain Bellair—but a basic insecurity about places and dates. In the earlier scripts the scope of the action embraced Saint-Nazaire, Tours, and Lyons —places several hundred kilometers apart and all of them far from the Champagne country where the previous scheme of the play was laid. Again, where the final text puts Simone's village on one of the main roads from Paris to the south, the Berlau script puts it on the Paris-Bordeaux road. The cumulative effect of all these hesitations and improbabilities helps to weaken the play.

2. Scene-by-Scene Account

The following is an account of the main changes. It uses the numbering of the final text with, in brackets, the numbers and titles of the corresponding eight-scene arrangement.

1. The Book [1]

The first version had Simone on stage from the start, reading her book; her present moves and business come from the Berlau script, which also changes the provenance of the book from "the nuns" (first version) to "the schoolmistress" and then, in Brecht's hand, to "the owner," as now. The soldier Georges's dialogue with Simone about the beauties of France was reworked more than once, and is altogether missing in the Feuchtwanger script. An addition to the Berlau script reads, in lieu of the lines from "Is that what it says in the book?" to "To the schoolhouse again today?" (p. 6):

> (*Simone nods*)
> GEORGES Perhaps they mean the cafés with their orange
>   awnings or the food markets in the early morning, full of
>   meat and vegetables.
> SIMONE What do you like best?

GEORGES   They say one's own fish, bread, and wine are best.

SIMONE   What's the most beautiful thing you've seen?

GEORGES   I don't know. In Saint-Malo, for instance, I saw the launching of the *Intrépide*, a big blue box for catching cod. We went to a bistro and drank so much framboise that my cousin Jean fell out of his swing-boat.

SIMONE   Was he hurt?

GEORGES   No, he fell on the fat proprietress. What do you like best?

SIMONE   When they give us milk rolls at school.

GEORGES   Yes, that's something that could stay the way it is. Same with playing bowls in the shade outside the town hall, wouldn't you say? And the women would be all right, particularly the girls in Lyons or Arles, say, pleasant ways they've got, but then you're not interested in that. Yes, there's quite a lot one could put up with.

SIMONE   And our hostelry?

GEORGES   Just like France. Certain people spoil the whole picture so to speak.

The reference to the engineers which follows (with the mention of Simone's brother), derives from the same script, as does also the dialogue between Père Gustave and the owner (up to the latter's exit on p. 8) and most of the ensuing detail about "the gentleman with the trout" and his meal. Only part of this is in the Feuchtwanger script, while the first script goes almost straight from Georges's attempt to take away Simone's book (p. 7) to the engineers' actual entry on p. 8 (though it does make the point that Simone is holding down her brother's job while he is at the front). The fact that the brother is Saint-Martin's only volunteer comes from the Berlau script; the phrase "And the people are the enemy" (p. 9) is from an addition to the 1946 version. Virtually everything from the colonel's exit (p. 10) to the mayor's entry (p. 12) is new in the Berlau script; in the first version the mayor arrives before the colonel leaves, and is bawled out for permitting the confusion on the roads, the colonel threatening to report him to the préfecture at Lyons.

Thereafter the first version moves straight from the mayor's request for the trucks to his formal confiscation of them (p.

12). It is at this point that the owner states his prior obligation to the captain and his wines, provoking the mayor to speak of his duty to France.

> MONSIEUR SOUPEAU Don't talk about France. You're just using an opportunity to score off the captain because he cut your wife at the préfet's ball in return for your taking Simone out of his service so she might go to school. . . .

This leads quickly into the mayor's demand for the gasoline too. From there down to Maurice's statement (p. 14) that they never heard of any gas the first version is like a draft of the final text. Thereafter:

> MAYOR So that's your answer? I see. Only a miracle can save France; it's rotten from top to bottom. (*To Simone*) You've got a brother at the front; in the south, isn't he? Do you imagine he'll have any gas for his tank? Jammed in the endless stream of refugees, he's no doubt waiting for a mortal attack by enemy dive-bombers. But I don't suppose you're any more likely than the others to tell me where I can get him some gas, eh, Simone?
> (*Simone stands motionless, then gives a dry sob and rushes away. Sighing, the mayor turns and leaves*)

Neither the Berlau nor the Feuchtwanger script has any mention of the gasoline in this scene or the dream which follows. The former has the final text from the mayor's entry to Monsieur Soupeau's "I want to talk to you in private" (p. 13); whereupon the mayor replies:

> No, Henri, we will no longer talk in private. I may be a bad mayor, I suppose, and have done wrong to shut an eye so often. But unless I can organize those twenty trucks for the refugees I don't know how I'll be able to look my son in the face when he gets back from the front. (*He notices Simone*) Sending some of your food parcels to the schoolhouse? You only filled the soldiers' pot half full. I ought to have confiscated your stocks long ago.
> MONSIEUR SOUPEAU (*threateningly*) Try it and see.

MAYOR   How can the refugees get anywhere if they're robbed of their last sou all along the line?

MONSIEUR SOUPEAU   This is a restaurant, not a charitable institution. You can go, Simone.
(*Simone starts to go*)

MAYOR (*stops her. Calmly*)   Any news from your brother?
(*Simone shakes her head*)

MAYOR   I've not heard from my son either. (*Quietly and bitterly to the others*) At this moment her brother can see the German tanks advancing towards him, Stukas above him, blocked roads behind him so that no reinforcements can get through to him; and here she is being expected to help exploit Frenchmen who are in trouble.

The owner claims that this is undermining her respect for her employer, to which the mayor replies "I see," and so on to the end as in the final version.

Simone Machard's First Dream [2]

The angel's opening speech in verse is in the first version, but not the brief dialogue between him and Simone which follows and identifies him with her brother André; a preliminary version of this is in the Berlau script. Simone's song, which had Saint-Nazaire in the first version, had Saint-Omer in the Berlau script and Rocamer in both the Feuchtwanger and the final scripts till Brecht restored Saint-Nazaire once again on the latter. The three "dream language" phrases on p. 15 ("Leftit cribble clump"), p. 17 ("Workers gobbie girl, belie!"), and p. 20 ("Clidder dunk frim, Klemp!") are pen additions by Brecht to the final script, which had already contained "Ockal grisht burlap" (p. 20). Two other nonsense remarks referred to in the stage directions were spelled out in the Berlau script: Simone's unintelligible reply on p. 17 ("Allekiwist, Maurice") and Robert's remark (p. 17) ("Wihilirichi"). In the first version the whole scene is shorter. Thus after Simone's offer to clean Père Gustave's guns for him the owner enters and Simone almost instantly beats her drum to summon the king with a version of her long speech on pp. 19–20. He thereupon enters, asks after her brother, confiscates the trucks and inquires about the gasoline (which is not mentioned in the Berlau script). Why are the drivers lying, he asks.

> SIMONE   They have to lie, or else they'll be called up, see? because Monsieur Soupeau will give up certifying that they're essential workers.

Then the engineers appear as on p. 20 and beat their stew pots like bells, and the scene ends much as in the final text.

2. *The Handshake* [3]

There is some characteristic geographical confusion in the first version, where the owner's wines and china were to go to Saint-Nazaire and the refugees to Lyons (several hundred kilometers apart); then Lyons was changed to "Vermillon," a place apparently invented by Brecht. The mayor arrives in this version not with the town police but with the sergeant from scene 1 and his two soldiers. Simone's ensuing explanation (to her mother and the owner) is not included; it was worked out on the Berlau script. Then from where the mayor weakens (p. 24) to the entry of Madame Soupeau everything is different, the drivers in particular being more uncooperative and the refugees not making an appearance:

> MAYOR (*weaker*)   Monsieur Soupeau, I'm only doing my duty. All I asked was for you to put your trucks at my disposal.
>
> MONSIEUR SOUPEAU (*yells*)   What do you want my trucks for?
>
> MAYOR   I told you. I'm going to shift the refugees.
>
> SIMONE   The old people and children anyhow, so as to clear Route 74 for the troops in Lyons to move up.
>
> MONSIEUR SOUPEAU (*stares at her, then to the mayor, nastily*)   Have you got the drivers? I'm told my men won't drive.
>
> MAYOR (*to the drivers*)   Are you really refusing to evacuate the refugees?
>
> SIMONE   No, they'll drive them. Maurice, Robert, will you drive?

MAURICE (*ironically*) If monsieur le maire orders . . .

MONSIEUR SOUPEAU Certain officials seem to be using this disastrous war as a pretext for laying down the law to the business community. But very well, then, I bow to force. My drivers can take the refugees to Vermillon.

MAYOR Not to Vermillon; that would mean using Route 74. First to Saint-Nazaire.

MONSIEUR SOUPEAU What can I have my trucks do in Saint-Nazaire? But very well, you're hiding behind your orders and the army. I'm asking the army to do something for me in return: pack up my wine reserves and the china, because that must go too.

MAYOR Why can't your men do that?

MONSIEUR SOUPEAU Because my men are on strike. I'd be within my rights if I put them up against the wall for refusing to remove French property to safety in face of the enemy. But there's no discipline left.

MAYOR (*to the sergeant*) Is that something you can put to your men, do you think? I've nothing against giving Monsieur Soupeau a hand to save his property.

MADAME MACHARD (*sees that her daughter wants to say something*) Quiet, Simone.

SIMONE But aren't the soldiers supposed to be bringing up the equipment for blowing the bridges?

MAURICE No. [illegible]

SIMONE To hold up the tanks till reinforcements come; you know. They ought to go right away.

SERGEANT We'd have been there by now if we hadn't had to wait for the field kitchen on account of their not giving us a meal. I don't see why I should fall over myself to help this gentleman and his hotel; he's the one refused to feed us.

SIMONE You'll get fed, won't he, Monsieur Henri? There'll be no room for provisions on the trucks if you're to be able to carry a proper number of refugees, will there, Maurice? I'll just get the key of the cellar.

MADAME MACHARD Simone!

MONSIEUR SOUPEAU What's got into you, Simone? I was amazed to see you bring in the mayor against me. Go indoors at once and wash your neck, you shameless ungrateful creature.

MADAME MACHARD Please excuse our daughter, Monsieur Soupeau; she has lost her head.

Monsieur Soupeau's mother, here called Madame Mère, then enters and gives Simone the key, telling her to get wine for the soldiers. There is no mention of feeding the refugees or of the danger of looting, and it is the soldiers who then help themselves to the provisions. Simone returns with the bottles and persuades Maurice and Robert to load up. German planes dive, prompting M. Soupeau to say that he must get away, as on p. 25, but his mother is also on stage and she replies contemptuously that she is staying:

> Thanks to Simone's very sensible arrangements you will get to Saint-Nazaire as planned, and Maurice and Robert will take the china and the refugees south to Lyons. Is that right, Simone?

She proposes to give the town such food stocks as cannot be moved, saying (in a line later given to the mayor) "This is a time for making sacrifices, Henri. We must let our hearts speak" (p. 29). Then they all drink as on p. 30, and the owner makes his conciliatory speech (p. 30). The drivers are told to load up with Monsieur Machard, and leave. It is then the owner himself who asks about the gasoline in the brickyard, saying:

> The Germans mustn't get it. Georges, Gustave, run down to the brickyard. Smash the pump and seal up the tank, right?
>
> MAYOR   Better set fire to it, Henri. There's an army order says all stocks of gasoline have got to be burnt. The Germans must not find a single canful in any village.
>
> MONSIEUR SOUPEAU   Burn it? Rubbish. We'll need it. How are our forces to replenish their tanks when they attack? Simone, tell the mayor that France isn't lost yet.
>
> SIMONE   That's a fact, monsieur le maire.
>
> MAYOR   But so many people are in the know, Simone.
>
> MONSIEUR SOUPEAU   No Frenchman could give away the secret. If I didn't realize that before I do now. Georges, Gustave, get moving.
>
> SIMONE (to Gustave)   I cleaned the garage out for you, Père Gustave.
>
> PÈRE GUSTAVE   Right. Patriotism seems to have become all the fashion around here.

Then the owner says good-bye to his mother (p. 31), and kisses her and Simone. The radio is heard saying that the French will counterattack and not a foot of ground is to be given up. There is no more reference to the gasoline, and madame says that she is closing the hotel. Simone is not specifically dismissed, but the last exchange between her and the mayor is as in the final text, and she picks up the owner's suitcases and slowly leaves with lowered head.

The Berlau script is approximately the same as the final version as far as the appearance of the representatives of the refugees (p. 25). Then, from the mayor's "What is it?":

ONE OF THE REFUGEES (*excitedly*) Monsieur le maire, we've heard the hotel is selling off its trucks. We insist you do something about it.
WOMAN There are sick people in the schoolhouse. We can't take our children to Bordeaux on foot.

The mayor replies "Madame, messieurs" etc. as in the final text, and is answered by the woman. Then this script cuts straight to the long stage direction on p. 26, with the difference that the main crowd of refugees does not appear. In the simultaneous dialogue which follows, the left hand column is that of the final version. In the right hand column, however, when Simone asks Robert and Maurice to take the refugees, Maurice refuses, saying "I'm not a nurse" and telling Robert "You've got no influence at the mairie. The mayor and M. Soupeau are birds of a feather; it's always us who pay the bill in the end . . . " The argument is interrupted by the announcement that the German tanks are nearly at Tours, causing the owner to complain "And my Sèvres and my vintage wines haven't yet been loaded." An approximate version of the dialogue from "SIMONE (*angrily*)" to "VOICES (*from outside*)" then follows (in the final version it comes earlier on pp. 25–26), with the difference that Simone's anger is initially against Maurice for wanting to clear out and abandon the refugees. Here madame enters and gives Simone the key (p. 27), and the ensuing dialogue down to her "Will somebody load them for us?" (p. 28) is more or less that of the final text. Thereafter:

SIMONE Of course, madame. Right, Maurice?
MAURICE Go to hell. Pack china, with the Germans arriving? High time we were off.
MADAME MÈRE (*sharply*) Nobody but the children seems to realize that French property cannot be allowed to fall into the hands of the Germans.
MAURICE (*to Robert*) All right, we can help carry out the cases. (*Goes out with Robert into the storehouse*)

It continues approximately as in the final text from "ONE OF THE REFUGEES" (p. 28) to the general dispersal on p. 30. Here Maurice, Robert, and Georges also leave; Maurice poses the question about the brickyard as he goes, after which the dialogue is a blend of the first and final versions until M. Soupeau takes his leave. Asked yet again about the gasoline (this time by the mayor) he says to ask his mother. In the Feuchtwanger script Simone then suggests getting Georges and Père Gustave and blowing it up, but in the Berlau script this is changed to a mere inquiry what should be done.

MADAME MÈRE Didn't you hear what M. Soupeau said? He asked us not to do anything precipitate. We can leave the problem of whether to destroy the gasoline till the last minute. After all, it's still my son's property we're dealing with.
SIMONE But it would be terrible if the Germans used our gasoline to fill up, like they did in Abbeville. Wouldn't it, monsieur le maire?
MAYOR It hasn't come to that yet by a long shot.

The rest of the scene is virtually as in the final text.

Simone Machard's Second Dream [4]

The first version and the Berlau script both have Père Gustave in lieu of the soldier Georges as a member of Simone's bodyguard; neither establishes the identification of the owner's mother as Queen Isabeau. When Simone calls on the angel (p. 34) both versions have her sitting on the ground and beating her drum, crying "Come here, you Frenchmen, the enemy has arrived." In the Berlau script there is no reaction; she calls Georges and drums harder, then calls on the angel. The first version makes the angel St. Michael. Also it has no mention of the mayor's dream language (pp. 33–34). The angel's song "When the conqueror" (p. 35) is slightly different in the first version, which omits the previous recitative ("Maid of France," etc., pp. 34–35) and the dialogue with Simone after that.

3. The Fire

In the first version subscene (a) bears this title and is scene 5, while subscene (b) is scene 6, The Betrayal, and is followed by the Daydream of Simone Machard. In the Berlau and Feuchtwanger scripts the Daydream is incorporated in the second of these two scenes (instead of, as now, in the first).

(a) [5. The Fire]

At the beginning of the scene the exchange where Georges suspects that Simone has been fired, the mention by Père Gustave of the "mob from the schoolhouse" (p. 37) and Simone's wondering if seeing a person in a dream means that he is dead (p. 37), are none of them in the first version, while the actual entry of the refugees (p. 38) occurs only in the final script. Thereafter there are extensive differences. In the first script the captain enters at this point, saying that the mayor will come. "And another thing. I've been told there were cases of looting and blackmail in these parts yesterday. Order and discipline are herewith reestablished: you get me, friends?" He is followed instantly by Père Gustave. The captain thereupon delivers a version of the speech which now comes just before the Daydream:

> CAPTAIN Ah, monsieur le maire, I trust your wife is in good health. I just wanted to tell you, Duclos, that France's one hope of avoiding total disaster is to collaborate as

honorably as she can with the gentlemen of the German
general staff. Paris is overrun with communists, and here
too all kinds of things occurred yesterday without the
authorities lifting a finger. To put it in a nutshell, the
commandant is fully aware of this hotel's connection
with a certain brickyard. You might like to take action
accordingly, Duclos. Wait a moment before you follow
me out, or it'll look as if I had to have you dragged down
here. (*Goes in*)

This is much the same in the Berlau script. Then Simone and
the mayor conduct their dialogue about the brickyard, from
his (present) entry (p. 39) to his exit, which in the final version becomes *He starts to go in* (p. 40), allowing the captain
to reenter with his speech roughly as above. All the present
dialogue from Madame Soupeau's entry (p. 38) to the entry
of the mayor is an addition to the final script.

In the earlier versions the dialogue with Georges and Père
Gustave which now follows the Daydream runs straight on
from the mayor's exit, with slight differences. Thereafter
from the entry of the German soldier to the end of (a) everything else is the same except that the German captain (or
commandant in the first version) says nothing. The Berlau
script however inserts the following dialogue before "So
you won't come?" (p. 43):

SOLDIER [i.e. GEORGES] What are you after? Oh, the gasoline, is it? Don't you touch it. You keep out.

SIMONE But M. Soupeau said it was up to us.

SOLDIER M. Soupeau's gone, but you're here. They'll shoot
you down like a mad dog. (*He draws her downstage.
Urgently*) Simone, promise me you'll be sensible.

SIMONE But you said yourself that they're bringing up
whole new regiments. They broke through against the
132nd, you said.

SOLDIER But not against the 7th [her brother's unit, in
this version].

SIMONE (*quietly*) That's not true, Monsieur Georges.

PÈRE GUSTAVE Don't you get mixed up with the Germans.
Sabotage can cost you your neck.

SOLDIER It all comes from that damned book of yours.

You've been reading it all day again, then you go and
imagine you're God knows who, isn't that it?

Apart from the first sentence this is not in the Feuchtwanger
script. But from then on to the end of (a) both are practically
identical with the final text.

(b)   (6. The Betrayal)
The first version specifies that this occurs three days after
(a). In all three of the early scripts the scene starts with
Georges reading the paper as the German captain saunters
across the stage and into the hotel. Simone brings a hot-water
bottle for the owner's mother, who is unwell. Then Simone
wonders about the significance of seeing a person in a dream
(the passage now near the beginning of [a]) and her parents
enter, delighted that M. Machard has got the job of bailiff.
It appears that the owner has returned; the Berlau and
Feuchtwanger scripts add that he and Maurice were held up
by German tanks. In all three versions he comes in with Robert,
looking pale and sleepless. All this is prior to the beginning
of the present subscene (b), but from then on the dialogue
continues much as in the final text up to where Simone says
that she will confess to the Germans to save the owner (p.
46). The main differences are (1) that the Machard parents
are present up to the firing of Georges; (2) that there is no
mention of the refugees in the schoolhouse; (3) that in lieu
of Père Gustave's remark about the hotel's sudden popularity
(p. 46) Robert tells Simone that the Peugeot has been stolen,
that one of the trucks has broken down and that Maurice is
bringing back the other. Thereafter, however, the scene ends
differently.
   In the first version it ends quickly, with the owner assuring
Simone that since she no doubt meant well he will stand by
her, then going into the hotel without saying whether she is
really fired or not. Robert asks if he will betray her, and
Georges says, "He can't do that. After all he is a Frenchman."
The mayor and the captain walk across the stage into the
hotel; Simone bows to the mayor, who pays no attention.
That is the end of the scene, and the Daydream follows.

Daydream of Simone Machard

In the first version there is no game of cards. The owner is present, and the captain enters later, bringing the German captain as an "unknown knight" with whom the French are invited to collaborate. He offers the mayor a cigar, but the drumming starts again and the mayor refuses. There are no references to "the mob"; madame boxes the owner's ears, not the mayor's, and the dream ends with the German captain saying, "Of course the Maid must be got rid of."

In the Berlau and Feuchtwanger scripts, after Simone has said that she will confess to the Germans (as above) Madame Machard reappears to say that the mayor has given the bailiff's job to "old Frossart" instead of to her husband, who has been "dropped like a hot potato." "The mayor," comments Georges, "is scared of his own courage." This leads straight into the Daydream. Mayor, captain, and the owner sit playing cards, and neither madame nor the German captain appears. After "So I can sell my wines" (p. 42), the owner says "Have you really decided to support her, King Charles the Seventh? And given her father the bailiff's job?" The mayor announces his determination much as in the final version, then sits down. The dream ends with the captain pointing this out to the owner and saying "There you are, Henri; France doesn't support her any more."

A quite different concluding section follows in both these scripts. After the dream Simone says she must leave, then Maurice arrives, having heard about the explosion:

MAURICE Are you crazy, Simone? How could you?

SIMONE He won't give me away.

MAURICE Get your things on at once, you must get out of here. I'll drive you. Pack up whatever she needs most, Madame Machard.

MADAME MACHARD I don't understand you people. You aren't expecting her to throw up her job?

GEORGES (*to Maurice*) You really think he might . . . ?

MAURICE (*shrugs his shoulders*) If he cares about saving his wretched hotel he'll have to. They might have used the gasoline as a way of showing how ready they are to collaborate. She's put a spoke in that. There's only one thing left for them to do: turn her in. (*With emphasis*) At this moment she's got no more vindictive enemies in the world than Madame Mère and her respected son.

ROBERT   You're exaggerating. After all, they are French.

MAURICE   Didn't you get what they were saying on the radio?

GEORGES   Wasn't listening. What was it?

MAURICE   The marshal has dissolved the government and taken over all its powers. That means open collaboration. Meantime *she's* still at war.

ROBERT   M. Soupeau said he'd stand by her.

MAURICE   He hadn't been told about the radio announcement. Get your things on, Simone.

SIMONE   (*still absent-mindedly*)   I can't leave, Maurice.

GEORGES   Ten minutes back you were saying you must.

SIMONE   That was only because I was imagining things. But M. Soupeau won't give me away.

MADAME MACHARD   But, messieurs, don't give the girl crazy ideas. She can't possibly give up her job now, when the rent's due. What with our André being away as well.

MONSIEUR SOUPEAU   (*comes out of the hotel, very excitedly*)   Simone! You've got to disappear! At once! Maurice, get her out of here! Doesn't matter where. Got that?

MAURICE   Yes sir.

MONSIEUR SOUPEAU   It's a matter of minutes. (*Goes back into the hotel*)

ROBERT   So he *isn't* going to give you away.

MAURICE   He's given her away already. Did you see how he'd been sweating? Get a move on, Simone!

SIMONE   No, no, no. I don't want to leave. He's not going to touch me. He only came out to help me.

MAURICE   He's got a bad conscience, that's all.
   (*Simone obstinately stays put*)

GEORGES   What have you got against leaving?

SIMONE   I can't. Suppose my brother comes back. I promised him I'd be here and keep his job for him.

MAURICE   That's enough. (*He seizes her, picks her up and carries her struggling into the garage over his shoulder*) Go outside the hotel, Georges, and whistle if the coast is clear. (*Goes out with Simone*)

(*Georges goes out into the road. During what follows he is heard whistling*)

MADAME MACHARD   I knew it would come to this. Her brother's to blame, and all that book-reading.

SIMONE'S VOICE (*from outside*)   I'm not going. I can't. You don't understand.

MADAME MACHARD   What have I done to deserve it?

ROBERT   Oh, do shut up. Don't you realize that she'll be shot if they catch her?

MADAME MACHARD   Simone? Holy mother of God! (*Sits distraught at the foot of the gasoline pump*)

(*Robert goes out into the garage*)

(*Enter from the hotel Monsieur Soupeau and the captain*)

MONSIEUR SOUPEAU   Simone! Père Gustave! (*To the captain*) Actually she was discharged some days ago. But went on hanging around my yard, so I've been told.

CAPTAIN (*notices Madame Machard*)   Isn't that her mother?

MONSIEUR SOUPEAU (*embarrassed*)   Ah, Madame Machard. Have you by any chance seen Simone?

MADAME MACHARD   No, Monsieur Henri, I'm looking for her myself. That girl's always doing errands for the hotel, monsieur le capitaine.

(*Père Gustave enters from the storehouse*)

MONSIEUR SOUPEAU   Oh, there you are, Père Gustave. Go and get Simone, would you?

(*Père Gustave goes obediently up the road. The whistling stops*)

MONSIEUR SOUPEAU (*to the captain*)   I just can't imagine what put the idea in her head.

CAPTAIN   It's not as hard as all that, Monsieur Soupeau. But it'll all be sorted out.

PÈRE GUSTAVE (*coming back, as Georges's whistling is heard once more*)   I can't find her, Monsieur Henri. Georges says she left half an hour ago.

CAPTAIN (*skeptically*)   Too bad that you people "can't find her," Monsieur Soupeau. (*Turns and goes into the hotel*)

MONSIEUR SOUPEAU (*mopping his perspiration*)   Thank God for that.

MADAME MACHARD   In the nick of time. The things we have to go through for our children!

(*Maurice appears at the garage door*)

MONSIEUR SOUPEAU   Why are you still here, Maurice? Shouldn't you be . . .

MAURICE   Did she come out this way? She broke away from me.

(*Simone comes in from the street, with Georges behind her*)

MONSIEUR SOUPEAU   Are you out of your mind? Quick, quick . . .

SIMONE   You aren't going to give me away, are you, Monsieur Henri?

MONSIEUR SOUPEAU   I told you to disappear. And now— (*furious gesture of helplessness*) First you set fire to my brickyard. I don't say a word, though it's *I* who have to answer for it with the Germans. And now you're being pigheaded just so as to make things harder for me. They can shoot you for all I care; I wash my hands of it.

(*The German captain comes out of the hotel in helmet and greatcoat, with the captain behind him*)

CAPTAIN   But we'll do everything we can, sir. Give us two hours.

(*Simone has instinctively tried to hide behind M. Soupeau. He steps to one side so that she is seen*)

CAPTAIN   Why, here she is. Here's our arsonist, sir.

THE GERMAN CAPTAIN   A child like that?

(*Pause*)

MONSIEUR SOUPEAU   Simone, this is a pretty kettle of fish.

All this is omitted from the final version, where the dialogue about the German poster ("It all depends on whether" p. 46 to Père Gustave's "I told you nothing of the kind" p. 47) has been brought forward from the beginning of scene 8 in the earlier versions, and the rest is new.

4.   *The Trial*

(a)   *Simone Machard's Fourth Dream*   [7]

In the first version this takes place "during the night of June 18" (i.e. three days earlier than in the final text). All three earlier scripts specify that the confused music is to "continue the motifs of the third dream." In the first version there is only one soldier with the German captain.

Down to the entry of the judges all three are more or less

the same as the final text, and the first version continues so as
far as the point where they put their heads together (p. 50).
In the Berlau and Feuchtwanger scripts, however, there are at
first only three judges, the mayor suddenly appearing beside
them "in the capacity of a defense counsel"; nor does Simone
identify them one by one as they come in but all at once
when they uncover their faces. Otherwise these two scripts
continue close to the final version down to the end of the
scene, the main later additions being the reference to the
refugees in the schoolhouse and Madame Soupeau's concluding
line. In the first version a number of the lines were differently
allotted, though their wording remains the same: thus Père
Gustave's call for accusers from the public (p. 51) and his
challenge to the angel (p. 53) were given to Simone's father,
while it was the mayor who called for a chair for Queen
Isabeau and asked Simone "Where is God? . . . " (p. 53).

   (b)   [8. The trial]
The first version gives two alternative scenes, one of them in-
complete and each differing widely from the other. The Berlau script also gives two texts, the first of which peters out
in a series of shorthand notes, while the second is identical
with that of the Feuchtwanger script. Altogether therefore
there are four main variants of this scene: the first version
(i) and (ii), the Feuchtwanger version (which seems to have
been worked out from Berlau (i) and possibly copied in
Berlau (ii)), and the final 1946 text.

   In the first version (i) there is no flag visible, and the mayor,
the owner, his mother, and the captain are on stage at the start,
as well as the four of the final version. A German soldier
marches Simone in, hands the mayor a document, salutes and
leaves. The document gives the responsibility of dealing with
Simone to the local authorities.

CAPTAIN   The tone of the document is severe, but the contents are very decent. The commandant is leaving it to the
   local authority to interrogate the incendiary. Monsieur
   le maire, do your duty by the township of Saint-Martin.
MAYOR (*sighing*)   Simone, the Germans have handed you

back to your own authorities. You are strongly suspected of sabotage, a crime for which one can be shot. However, the authorities have been able to raise some doubt as to the deliberateness of your intention to commit sabotage. Do you understand the purpose of this inquiry?

SIMONE   Yes, monsieur le maire.

MAYOR   Luckily the question is easily settled. Now listen carefully. If you caused the fire *before* the Germans put up their poster forbidding the destruction of essential stocks then it was not sabotage. Suppose you had done it after the poster, it would have been sabotage and we couldn't save you. Do you understand that? Did you see the poster?

The dialogue follows as on p. 46 (which is where it was shifted to in the final text), except that there it is Monsieur Soupeau, not the mayor, who asks the questions. After Père Gustave's "I told you nothing of the kind" (p. 47) it goes on:

MAYOR   Père Gustave, you have offered to give evidence to the effect that Simone set fire to the brickyard. But you insist that she did it before the German order?

PÈRE GUSTAVE   (*avoiding Simone's eye*)   Yes.

ROBERT   Oh, you've volunteered to give evidence, have you?

MADAME MÈRE   Quiet, Robert.

MAYOR   It's all quite clear. (*To Simone*) Will you show us where the red poster was displayed? Come along, it'll still be there.

SIMONE   But I saw it before that, monsieur le maire.

MAYOR   Don't be difficult. This is official.

(*Mayor, Monsieur Soupeau and captain leave with Simone through the gateway*)

PÈRE GUSTAVE   I had to, because of what I let out when Monsieur Soupeau drove off.

MAURICE   Shut up.

GEORGES   The mayor's a decent man. He's whitewashing her to the Germans, and they'll let her off.

MAURICE   They're a lot of crooks. All they're doing is clearing Saint-Martin of any suspicion that it has Frenchmen in it [p. 59 in our text]. They're set on collaborating

with the Germans. Simone's right. It's as though she
knew what tune they were going to play.

ROBERT   We won't have heard the last of it. You wait.

Then the party returns with Simone, and the mayor says he
thinks the Germans will agree that it was not sabotage. The
captain differs, and M. Soupeau's mother says "It was a base
act of revenge against my son and myself."

MAYOR   Revenge? What for?

MADAME MÈRE   Because we dismissed her. It's quite simple.

MAYOR   Henri, do you believe that?

MONSIEUR SOUPEAU (*forcefully*)   I refuse to stand up for
   this creature any longer. I offered her a chance to get
   away; she insisted on staying. I'm through with her. I've
   had enough to worry about.

Then Madame sends Maurice, Robert, Père Gustave, and
Georges back to their work, and they leave. She starts cross-
examining Simone, approximately as from where she *turns to
Simone* (p. 57) to Simone's "I did it because of the enemy"
(p. 58). Then she tells Thérèse to "fetch the sister" and delivers a speech that is partly the captain's "The least our
guests can expect . . ." (p. 58) and partly her own "The
child is insubordinate" etc. (p. 60) of the final text. Thérèse
returns with an Ursuline nun.

MADAME MÈRE   Sister Michèle is being so good as to take
   this unfortunate child into the educational establishment
   run by the strict sisters of St. Ursula.

SIMONE (*trembling*)   No, no! Not to St. Ursula's! I did it
   because of the Germans. I want to stay.

   (*The sister takes her arm and leads her to the gateway*)

SIMONE   André! André!

There it breaks off at the foot of a page.

   The first version (ii), headed in Brecht's hand "Second
version, January 43," likewise breaks off at the foot of a page,
this time towards the end of madame's interrogation of
Simone. It starts with Maurice, Robert, Georges, and Père

Gustave on stage, as in the final version, but with two German sentries. They are discussing Simone's examination by the mayor, which has taken place off stage and in the German captain's presence, but evidently went much as in (i). Georges says "I don't see why he doesn't do the interrogating himself, Maurice."

> MAURICE   Well, you saw how angry it made him yesterday when he heard it was a child. Shooting children doesn't go all that well with their policy of dishing out soup on the square in front of the mairie. The captain had supper with him last night. I can tell you exactly how the conversation will have gone. (*He mimics the German captain and the French captain in turn*) "Bad show. I'll have to shoot her." "That'll put the kybosh on peaceful collaboration for the next couple of years, sir."—"What's the answer?" "Collaboration, my dear captain. Leave the case to us."—"Then tomorrow up goes the water tower, eh, monsieur? Here's our radio announcing every hour that the French population is receiving us with open arms, wants nothing but peace."—"My dear captain, but whoever says the person responsible was acting against the Germans?"—"Aha . . . I see. You mean you can prove that she did it *before* . . ." So that now she did it *before* the proclamation, d'you see?

Then the owner enters and tells Père Gustave that his evidence won't be needed: "A child! What do they expect?" etc. (as on p. 55). Georges's ensuing remarks finish with him saying that someone betrayed her.

> MONSIEUR SOUPEAU   You dare to say that to me after I've stood here and told her she must get away?

He seizes the wounded Georges by the arm, and there is a struggle in which Robert joins till it is interrupted by the entry of the German captain. The captain tells the two sentries to follow him and leaves.

> PÈRE GUSTAVE   He's taking his men away. Does that mean that Simone's been let free?

MAURICE   I'd be extremely surprised.

GEORGES   Anyhow that boche with the monocle realizes that Captain Bellaire isn't the only person around here. Monsieur le capitaine has had his innings. They couldn't conceal the fact that there are still some Frenchmen in France. Ow! Even kids of thirteen can show them, eh, Maurice?

But the mayor's two policemen appear at the gate, then madame leads in Simone from the hotel, with the mayor and the captain following, and they all go into the storehouse. Maurice makes his remark about clearing Saint-Martin, and M. Soupeau angrily orders the policemen to clear the yard.

MAURICE   Let's go. There's nothing we can do here for the moment. They've got their police and they've got the Germans. (*Draws Robert and Georges away*) Poor Simone. Too many enemies.

GEORGES   (*hoarsely*) Look out, Monsieur Henri, other times are coming. And when they come we'll be asking you about Simone. (*All three go out*)

The party then emerges from the storehouse, and madame conducts her interrogation of Simone on lines rather closer to the final text, including a mention of "the mob from the schoolhouse." This version breaks off with madame's "Who told you the Germans would ever . . ." (p. 58).

Finally the Feuchtwanger script (identical with Berlau ii) starts with much the same stage direction as our text, but without Georges and with the addition of the two German sentries. It opens with Maurice's remark about the marshal; Simone, however, has not got away but is being interrogated as in the first version (ii). Georges, who has been giving evidence, comes out of the hotel to report that they are all behaving very decently, even madame and the captain. The German captain has said "that these are tragic days and he has no desire to hurt Frenchmen's feelings." He is allowing the others to establish Simone's ignorance of the poster because, as Maurice puts it, "I don't imagine they want to start off their armistice and their formal collaboration by shooting our children for us."

GEORGES (*scratching his head*)   Do you think nothing's going to happen to her?

MAURICE   That's another question.

ROBERT   If they do anything to Simone I'm coming to Algiers with you, Maurice. (*To Georges*) The radio says the old government's going to carry on the fight from there.

GEORGES (*moving his arm thoughtfully*)   That's what one ought to do.

PÈRE GUSTAVE   They talk a lot on the radio.

Then M. Soupeau enters as in the first version (ii), leading on to the struggle and a version of the ensuing dialogue as far as Madame Soupeau's entry with Simone (but no policemen) and disappearance into the storehouse.

MONSIEUR SOUPEAU (*complainingly, as he dusts down his suit*)   I gave her an opportunity to disappear. She insisted on staying. She's caused me nothing but troubles from the very first. A hundred thousand francs, she's cost me. As for the cost to my nerves, I can't count it. And now she's causing bad blood between me and my old employees. That's what comes of trying to protect her. Well, the time for sentimentality is over. I shan't interfere any more. Not that I bear you people a grudge. She upset all of us. Back to work, Maurice and Robert! (*Maurice and Robert stay put*)

MONSIEUR SOUPEAU   Didn't you hear me?

MAURICE   Robert and I will just wait and see what's happening to Simone.

The party leaves the storehouse, and this time madame's interrogation of Simone is witnessed and occasionally interrupted by Robert, Maurice, and Georges. It is longer than in the final version, though largely coinciding with it, and ends with an admission by Simone that she was acting on her own, not on the mayor's orders.

MADAME SOUPEAU   To settle a score with the hotel.

MONSIEUR SOUPEAU   And to think maman told lies to the
  Germans to make them set you free!

The two policemen enter, and thereafter the script stays close
to the final text, except that there are no nuns and the institution is the "house of correction at Tours"; (an addition to the
Berlau (ii) script in Brecht's hand introduced the "brutish
lady" and the comments indicating that this was a place for
the mentally handicapped). However, instead of fetching her
things from the storehouse, as in the final text, she says good-
bye to Georges, Maurice, and Robert until she is dragged off
calling "André! André!" There is no appearance of the angel,
and after M. Soupeau's order to resume work the ending is
different.

MAURICE   What, us? You'll find it difficult to get anyone in
  Saint-Martin to work for you after this. Come on.
  (*Maurice, Robert, and Georges turn to leave.*)

MONSIEUR SOUPEAU (*running after them*)   But Maurice! I
  haven't done anything to you, have I?—Five years we've
  been together—It was for the hotel's sake—It was for the
  sake of your jobs, for that matter—Maurice! Robert!

GEORGES (*at the gateway, turns around, hoarsely*)   You
  look out. Other times are coming. When they come we'll
  be asking you about Simone. (*Curtain*)

In the 1946 script, which our text follows, the date is given
as "Morning of June 19" (later changed to June 22). The
mayor's order to M. Machard to clear the schoolhouse is a
typed addition. The nuns are mainly handwritten amendments
(as in Berlau ii); the "brutish lady" remains in one stage direction (the published text makes her plural) but elsewhere is
amended to "the nuns" or "one of the nuns." The house of
correction is struck out, together with all references but one
to Tours (the mayor offers to give evidence there). References to St. Ursula come from the first version, those to the
mentally handicapped from the additions to the Berlau script,
reinforced by Simone's new comment "They tie you up!"
(p. 59).

3. Feuchtwanger's Novel

Simone, a novel by Lion Feuchtwanger, was published in 1944 by the Viking Press in a translation by G. A. Herrmann. It is less "the book of the play" than an independent reworking of the ideas discussed in the course of the author's collaboration with Brecht, who, as far as we know, was not involved in its composition, and it differs in various important respects. Thus out of twenty-one chapters only two contain visions (as against the much more even alternation in the play) though there are three others where Simone is shown reading the books (plural) which she has been given by an old bookbinder friend. The town of Saint-Martin in this account is a fair-sized place, a Burgundian chef-lieu d'arrondissement (i.e. of the importance, say, of Châlons-sur-Saône) where the stepuncle who corresponds to the hotel owner runs a largish trucking business, not a hotel. The refugees are in the Palais de Justice; the sous-préfet corresponds to the mayor, and the local Marquis de Saint-Brisson to the captain who wants his wines evacuated. Simone Planchard is "a tall, lanky fifteen-year-old":

> Her bony, tanned face framed with dark blond [*sic*] hair was tense; her dark, deep-set eyes under a low but broad and well-shaped forehead eagerly absorbed all that moved before her. . . . She could scarcely be called beautiful, but her intelligent, thoughtful, somewhat stubborn face with its strong chin and prominent Burgundian nose was good to look at.

Moreover, her father had been a local left-wing hero who had died in the Congo two years previously while investigating native working conditions. Madame, who corresponds to the hotel owner's mother (and like her appears as Queen Isabeau) was evidently the father's stepmother. Thanks to her, Simone's rôle in the household (the Villa Monrepos) is that of an unpaid servant.

This Simone has no brother. She has a confidant in the

secretary of the sous-préfecture and two friends of her own age—her schoolmate Henriette and Henriette's brother Étienne —though neither figures very largely in the story. Of her uncle's employees in the loading yard Maurice (there is no Robert, and Georges is a nonentity) is at first cruelly and gratuitously offensive to her; it looks as if he is meant to stand for the French communists, skeptical of the bourgeoisie and their war, and uninvolved until after the German victory. In the dream episodes he figures as the monstrous Gilles de Rais. From the first Simone seems attracted to him, and once she has set fire to the yard (trucks, gasoline, and all)—which occurs about halfway through the book, as against two-thirds of the way through the play—he starts behaving more amicably, though still in a rather condescending way. He offers to get her away on his motorcycle; but by the time she decides to accept his offer it is too late and he has already gone. She escapes by herself, but is arrested in Nevers and brought back.

Though madame and the other villains (such as the lawyer Maître Levautour) seem heavily caricatured, the stepuncle's actions are generally credible and within the bounds of reason. For much of the story he even behaves kindly. "Don't you understand," he asks her, "that I can't live without my business? I am a business man. I can't help that." And again, in explanation of his actions, "Some people are born to be artists, others to be engineers; I was born to be a business man, a promoter." To save his business and at the same time prevent the Germans from punishing the entire town he arranges with the French authorities that Simone shall confess to having caused the fire for personal reasons. This she formally does on the understanding that no proceedings will be taken against her. However, the marquis and madame see to it that she is sent away to the Grey House, the reformatory at "Francheville," the departmental capital, and "an uncouth woman" escorts her away. As she is driven off the crowd in the street makes signs to her—

Arms were raised waving to her, women and girls wept, the gendarme had come to attention, shouts sounded in

her direction: "Good-bye, Simone—good-bye, Simone
Planchard—take care of yourself, Simone—so long, Simone
—we won't forget you, Simone Planchard—we'll come
and get you, Simone."

And she rides away confident "that she would survive the
Grey House."

SCHWEYK IN THE SECOND WORLD WAR

Texts by Brecht

The Story

The Good Soldier Schweyk, after surviving the First World War, is still alive. Our story shows his successful efforts to survive the Second as well. The new rulers have even more grandiose and all-embracing plans than the old, which makes it even harder for today's Little Man to remain more or less alive.

The play begins with a

Prelude in the Higher Regions

wherein a preternaturally large Hitler with a preternaturally large voice talks to his preternaturally large police chief Himmler about the putative loyalty, reliability, self-denial, enthusiasm, geopolitical consciousness, and so on and so forth of the European "Little Man." The reason why he is demanding such virtues of the Little Man is that he has made up his mind to conquer the world. His police chief assures him that the European Little Man bears him the same love as does the Little Man in Germany. The Gestapo will see to that. The Führer has nothing to fear, and need have no hesitation about conquering the world.

1

There has been an attempt on Hitler's life. Hearty applause from the "Flagon" in Prague, where the good dog hustler Josef Schweyk and his friend Baloun are sitting over their morning drinks and discussing politics with the "Flagon's" landlady, the young widow Anna Kopecka. Fat Baloun, whose exceptional appetite presents him with special problems in these days of Nazi rationing, quickly lapses into his normal gloom. He has learned from reliable sources that the German field kitchens will dish out sizable helpings of meat. How much longer is he going to be able to hold out against the temptation simply to go and join up in the German army? Mrs. Kopecka and Schweyk are greatly disturbed by his situation. A soul in torment! Schweyk, ever the realist, suggests making Baloun swear an oath never under any circumstances to have anything to do with the Germans. Baloun reminds them that it is six months since he last had a square meal. In exchange for a square meal, he says, he would be prepared to do *anything*. Mrs. Kopecka thinks something might be arranged. She is a blazing patriot, and the idea of Baloun in the German army is more than she can bear. When her young admirer turns up, the butcher's son Prochazka, they hold a touching conversation in which she poses Cleopatra's age-old question: "If it truly is love, then tell me how much?" She wants to know if his love, for instance, would run to the scrounging of two pounds of smoked butt for the undernourished Baloun. He could take it from the paternal shop, only the Nazis have established heavy penalties for blackmarketeering. Nonetheless, seeing the way to the widow's heart open before him for the first time, young Prochazka agrees in a positive tornado of emotion to bring round the meat. Meanwhile the "Flagon" has been filling up and Schweyk has started letting all and sundry know what he thinks of the Munich plot against Hitler. Inspired by the announcements on the German radio, he plunges with foolhardy innocence into a mortally dangerous conversation with Brettschneider, who is known to all the regular customers as a Gestapo agent.

His classic driveling fails to deceive the Gestapo man. Without any more ado Herr Brettschneider arrests the amazed but obliging Schweyk.

2

Introduced to Gestapo headquarters at the Petschek Bank by Herr Brettschneider, Schweyk flings up his right hand, bawls out "Hurrah for our Führer Adolf Hitler! We're going to win this war!" and is discharged as chronically half-witted.

Hearing that Schweyk is a dog hustler, the interrogating SS officer Ludwig Bullinger asks about a pedigreed dog he has seen in the Salmgasse. "Beg to report, sir, I am professionally acquainted with the animal," says Schweyk cheerfully, and goes on to expatiate on the racial question. That spitz is the apple of Undersecretary Voyta's eye, and not to be had for love or money. Schweyk and the SS officer discuss how best to have the undersecretary arrested and expropriated as an enemy of the state; however, it turns out that he is "no yid" but a quisling. So Schweyk gets the honorable job of stealing the pedigreed spitz and showing himself to be a good collaborationist.

3

Returning in triumph to the "Flagon," Schweyk finds that a tense situation has developed. Fat Baloun is waiting for his meal like a cat on hot bricks, fully prepared at the first glimpse of the pork to abjure all intention of ever joining Hitler's army. It is now ten past twelve, and young Prochazka has not yet shown up. Schweyk has been so considerate as to bring along SS Man Müller 2 from Gestapo headquarters, with the promise that widow Kopecka will tell his future by reading his hand. At first the landlady refuses on the grounds that she has had unfortunate experiences with her predictions. Young Prochazka now finally appears, and everyone looks nervously at his music case—he is a student at the music academy—because of course the SS man must not see the meat. To get him out of the way Mrs. Kopecka sits down and reads his hand. It seems that he is destined to perform heroic deeds, and has been picked out finally for a hero's death. Depressed and demoralized, the SS man lurches out and Baloun flings himself on the music case round which he has been longingly circling for some time. The case is empty. Young Prochazka makes his miserable confession: he didn't dare steal the smoked butt because the sight of Schweyk's arrest gave him such a fear of the Gestapo. Angrily the widow Kopecka spurns him with a Biblical gesture, for he has failed the test as a man and a Czech. Despondently he leaves, but no sooner does the bitterly frustrated fat man speak slightingly of her suitor than she snaps back that the Nazis are to blame for it all. So Baloun's wrath is diverted to the oppressors of his once beautiful country, and when Herr Brettschneider the Gestapo agent comes in he starts singing the subversive song of the black radish, which must "get on out" and be "cut up and salted" till "he sweats," all of which strikes Herr Brettschneider as suspicious, but offers him no pretext to intervene.

First Schweyk Finale:
Interlude in the Upper Regions

The mighty Hitler, having encountered obstacles in his attempt to conquer the world, needs more bombers, tanks, and guns, and inquires of the mighty Göring whether the European Little Man is prepared to work for him. Göring assures him that the European Little Man will work for him just like the Little Man in Germany. The Gestapo will see to that. The Führer has nothing to fear and need have no hesitation about carrying on conquering the world.

4

Schweyk's operation against the germanophile Undersecretary Voyta's spitz takes place in the park along the Moldau,

which is where Voyta's maidservant and her friend Paula are
accustomed to take the pedigreed hound for his walkies every
evening. Schweyk and Baloun come up to the bench where the
two girls are sitting, and pretend to have erotic aims in view.
Schweyk warns the girls in all honesty that SS leader Bullinger
wants to annex the spitz for the sake of its racial purity and
have it sent to his lady wife in Cologne; he has had this on
impeccable authority. Thereupon he goes off "to meet someone at the Metropole." Baloun exchanges pleasantries with the
girls, and they are moved by the Moldau's majestic flow to
start singing a folk song. By the end of the song the dog has
gone. Schweyk has underhandedly lured it away as they were
singing. The girls rush off to the police station, and Schweyk
has just returned with the spitz to tell his friend that they
mustn't let the SS leader have it till he has put down the
money, when a sinister-looking individual appears on the
scene. Schweyk the dog-catcher has a man-catcher on his
track; the individual identifies himself as a functionary of the
Nazi labor organization whose job it is to recruit idlers and
loafers into the "voluntary labor service." Concerned for the
spitz, Schweyk and Baloun are led off for registration.

5

Noon break at the Prague freight station. Schweyk and Baloun have become railroad workers for Hitler and are waiting
under the eyes of a heavily-armed German soldier for their
cabbage soup to be sent up from the "Flagon." Today it is
widow Kopecka in person who brings their enamel dishes.
The stolen spitz left in her care by Schweyk is becoming the
focus of some intense political activity, and must be got off
the premises. The controlled press is saying that the dog's
disappearance is due to an act of vengeance by the population
against a pro-German official. Schweyk promises to come and
collect it. He is listening with only half an ear, since he is
troubled by Baloun's condition. The sentry's dinner has arrived—goulash! Trembling from head to foot, Baloun has
gone sniffing after the cauldron as it was borne past him. Now

he is excitedly asking the sentry whether the helpings in the German army are always as big as that, etc., etc., and scarcely pays attention to the imploring glances of his friends. The soldier is plunged in thought as he munches his goulash, all the while silently moving his lips between bites. He has been told to memorize the number 4268, being that of a freight car with harvesting machines for Lower Bavaria, and this is something he finds difficult. Always ready to help, Schweyk sets out to teach him a mnemonic technique which he learned from a water-board statistician who is one of the regulars at the "Flagon." By the time Schweyk has finished explaining it, the poor sentry's brain is in such a tangle that when they eventually ask him for the freight car he helplessly points to the first car he sees. Schweyk is afraid that this may mean that a carload of machine guns for Stalingrad may get sent to Bavaria in lieu. "But who knows?" he remarks consolingly to Baloun and Mrs. Kopecka. "Maybe by that time they'll need harvesting machines in Stalingrad and machine guns in Bavaria. Why not?"

6

Saturday night at the "Flagon." Dance. A morose Baloun takes the floor with the undersecretary's maidservant, who is there with her friend. The police are still interviewing the two girls about the spitz. Yesterday, however, they dropped a hint to Herr Brettschneider as to its whereabouts: at SS leader Bullinger's, possibly already in Cologne. Baloun hints that this may be his last evening at the "Flagon": he is fed up with feeling hungry. And it incidentally emerges that the noisy fun of the dance floor serves a higher purpose: covering up the sound of the news from London, which Kopecka is listening to and passing on to the guests. Enter then Schweyk, cheerfully, with a parcel under his arm: meat for Baloun's goulash. The fat man can hardly believe it; the two friends embrace most movingly. Baloun's enthusiasm is such, however, that Schweyk asks Mrs. Kopecka to put extra paprika in the goulash, since it's only horsemeat. The landlady looks quizzically at him, and he confesses that it is Mr. Voyta's spitz. A police car draws up. SS leader Bullinger enters the "Flagon," with SS men at his heels. Hue and cry for the Voyta spitz. Asked by Bullinger whether he knows the dog's whereabouts, Schweyk innocently replies that he hasn't got it. "Didn't you see in the papers, Herr SS Leader, where it said it had been stolen?" Bullinger's patience gives way. He bellows that the "Flagon" is the source of all subversive Czech subversiveness and will have to be smoked out. Moreover, the dog can only be there. The SS is starting to search the place when Herr Brettschneider arrives. Herr Brettschneider, who has long pictured himself in the rôle of protector (this is, after all, a protectorate) to the charming Mrs. Kopecka, forcefully stands up to the fuming Bullinger and invites him to Gestapo headquarters, where he has some rather revealing information about the present location of the missing dog. Mrs. Kopecka's house is above suspicion; he would go to the stake for that. Unfortunately at this very moment the gentlemen's attention is drawn to a parcel reposing on one of the tables. The wretched Baloun has been unable to keep his fingers off Schweyk's gift. A triumphant Bullinger discloses the contents of the parcel: meat. So the "Flagon" is a center of the blackmarket! At that Schweyk feels forced to admit that he put the parcel there. He claims that a gentleman with a black beard gave it to him "to hold." All those present affirm having seen the man, while Herr Brettschneider, after going to the stake on the "Flagon's" behalf, thinks it very possible that the criminal spotted the SS a hundred yards off and accordingly ran away. Nonetheless Bullinger insists on arresting Schweyk, and the gentlemen escort him out of the "Flagon"—Bullinger, with the parcel under his arm, prophesying that he will find that dog yet. Cold-shouldered by the widow, young Prochazka has spent the entire evening sitting in a corner; now he slinks guiltily out, followed by the widow's icy stare. Baloun bursts into tears. Thanks to his weakness the loving couple has been parted and his friend landed in mortal danger. The "Flagon's" landlady consoles him. In a big song she foretells that just as the Moldau washes away all the dirt, so her oppressed people's love of their country will wash away the cruelties of their invaders.

Second Schweyk Finale:
Interlude in the Upper Regions

The anxious Hitler, having been caught by the Russian winter, needs more soldiers. He inquires of the anxious Goebbels whether the European Little Man is prepared to fight for him. Goebbels assures him that the European Little Man will fight for him just like the Little Man in Germany. The Gestapo will see to that.

7

As a result of disagreements between Bullinger the crocodile and Brettschneider the tiger, and what with Hitler's screaming for fresh soldiers, the good soldier Schweyk has moved from the cellars of the Gestapo to the recruiting bureau for the German army. Among those whom he encounters there is Undersecretary Voyta, who is being sent to the front because his spitz was stolen. All the inmates are discussing what loathsome diseases they can report to the doctors at their medical inspection. Schweyk for his part feels another bout of rheumatism coming, since he has no time to travel to Russia for Hitler when "nothing's been settled in Prague." Hearing that young Prochazka is standing outside the barracks with an important message for him, he fears the worst. Happily Prochazka manages to bribe an SS man to smuggle in a note to him, and it is an encouraging one. The "Flagon" landlady's suitor writes that, having been deeply moved by Schweyk's self-sacrifice and ghastly fate, he will now supply "the desired article." At that Schweyk feels prepared to devote himself with an untroubled mind to Hitler's Russian affairs, which are said to be going none too well. Outside is heard the Nazis' notorious "Horst Wessel" song; a battalion is moving off to the East. The inmates begin singing their own version of the Nazi anthem, where "The butcher calls" and "The sheep march on," and an NCO comes in who is mistaken enough to praise them for joining in so cheerfully, then informs them that they are all undoubtedly fit to enlist and are accordingly accepted into the army. They are to be divided among different units to prevent them from getting up to any filthy tricks, so Schweyk bids a touching farewell to the undersecretary and goes off to Hitler's war.

8†

Weeks have elapsed. Deep in the wintry plains of the Russian empire Hitler's good soldier Schweyk is marching to join his unit near Stalingrad, where it is supposed to combine with other sections of the Nazi army in holding back the Red army's terrible assaults. As a result of one of his numerous misadventures he has lost contact with the rest of his draft. Untroubled by geographical preconceptions, however, and in his usual blithely trusting frame of mind, he is marching towards his allotted destination wrapped in a great bundle of assorted articles of clothing to keep out the cold. A semi-demolished signpost says that Stalingrad is 100 miles off.

While he is thus marching to Stalingrad the "Flagon" keeps looming up in a rosy light before our good Schweyk's eyes. He pictures to himself how young Prochazka lives up to his promises. The man's love of the landlady has overcome his fear of the Gestapo, and to her agreeable surprise he hands Mrs. Kopecka two pounds of smoked butt for Schweyk's unfortunate friend Baloun.

As he battles courageously against the icy blasts of the steppes, the indefatigable and utterly well-intentioned Schweyk becomes uncomfortably aware that he is getting no closer to his goal. The farther he marches, the greater the distances shown on the signposts to Stalingrad, where Hitler so urgently needs him. A thousand miles away Anna Kopecka may at this moment be singing her "Song of the Flagon," that homely and hospitable place. The voracious Baloun's long-awaited meal will have developed into a wedding feast for the landlady and young Prochazka.

Schweyk marches on. The blizzards on those interminable eastern steppes, where the distance to Stalingrad always re-

† The stage is divided in two.

mains about the same, cloak the sun by day and the moon by night from the view of the good soldier Schweyk, who set out to give the great Hitler a helping hand.

Epilogue

It is likewise deep in the eastern steppes that the good soldier Schweyk personally encounters his Führer Hitler. Their conversation in the driving snow is brief and almost entirely swallowed by the storm. The gist of this historic conversation is that Hitler is asking Schweyk whether he knows the way back.

[GW *Schriften zum Theater* 3, pp. 1186–96. Dated New York City, May 1943. This preliminary summary of the story was made for Kurt Weill, and it contains some differences from the final text. Thus the interludes balance more neatly; there is no interlude after scene 2; and Goebbels appears instead of von Bock. This is the only version which makes Prochazka a music student (scene 3) and has Schweyk preparing for an attack of rheumatism (scene 7). It omits the army chaplain and the singing of "The German Miserere," and the ending is unlike that of any of the scripts.]

Staging

The "Flagon" bar in Prague forms the center of the set. Black oak paneling, bar with brass fitting, electric piano with a transparent top in which the moon and the flowing Moldau can appear. In the third act only a part of the "Flagon" appears to Schweyk in his thoughts and dream: his own table. Schweyk's Anabasis" shown in this act; move in a circle around this part of the "Flagon." The length of his march can be indicated by such devices as having the peasants' hut roll forward or backward, growing larger or smaller in the process. —The interludes should be played in the style of a grisly fairy tale. The whole Nazi hierarchy (Hitler, Göring, Goebbels) can appear in all of them (plus Himmler and von Bock as the case may be). The satraps can accentuate the verses with shouts of "Heil!"

> [Note "Zur Inszenierung" appended to the text of the play in GW5, p. 1995.—Tr. Ralph Manheim.]

Editorial Note

1. General

Brecht's Schweyk play derives from Jaroslav Hašek's novel *The Adventures of the Good Soldier Švejk* [or Schweik] *in the World War*, or more precisely from its German translation by Grete Reiner, which was first published in 1926 and from then on remained one of Brecht's favorite books. It was promptly dramatized by Max Brod, the Prague German writer who was responsible also for the publication of Kafka's posthumous novels, and by the German humorist Hans Reimann. The resulting play was one of those chosen by Erwin Piscator for his first season with his own company in Berlin in 1927–28, when Brecht was one of his team of dramaturges, and because it seemed far too conventional and static for the form of production which Piscator had in mind, which was to make use of a treadmill stage and George Grosz projections, it was radically overhauled by this team. In Brecht's own mind, he himself was the main author of the Piscator version of this play; thus according to *The Messingkauf Dialogues* "he did Schweik for him entirely." However, all other accounts give Piscator's principal dramaturge Felix Gasbarra an equal or even greater share in the new adaptation, and there is nothing in Brecht's papers to bear him out, beyond his penciled title page to the script (the rest of which is not typed by him): "Adventures of the Good Soldier Schweik./Brecht, Gasbarra,

Piscator, G. Grosz." Nor, as far as we know, did either he or his editors subsequently consider publishing it among his own works, though these contain a number of his adaptations, notably those for the Berliner Ensemble.

This script differs from the Brod-Reimann version above all in its attempt to match the "epic" and picaresque form of Hašek's unfinished masterpiece. In his journal Brecht termed it "a pure montage from the novel." Briefly, its first part, corresponding to the novel's part I, is divided into the following short scenes (the numbers of the relevant chapters in the book being given in brackets): 1. [1] At Schweik's./ 2. [1] At the "Flagon."/3. [7] At Schweik's (where he determines to volunteer)./4. [7] Street scene (with Schweik in the wheelchair shouting "To Belgrade!")./5. [8] Recruiting office (medical inspection)./6. [8] Military hospital./7. [8] Streets in Prague (with Schweik under arrest)./8. [9] Transformation scene: detention room, chapel, and sacristy./9. [14] Lieutenant Lukaš's rooms (Katz, the chaplain, loses to Schweik at cards)./10. [14] The same (where Schweik fulfills the lady's wishes)./11. [14] The same (preparatory to the stealing of the dog)./12. Street in Prague (Schweik and sapper Voditchka as dog thieves)./13. [3 of part II] The same (Voditchka making anti-Hungarian gestures)./14. [15] Barrack square (the colonel recognizes his dog and packs Schweik and Lukaš off to the front).

The second part, drawn from parts II and III of the novel, is in a slightly confused order (e.g., the numbering of the second scene) and differs from the staged version in its ending. (Piscator himself recounts that his team suggested various alternatives, but that he finally settled for Gasbarra's idea, based on Cadet Biegler's dream in part III, chapter 1, of a scene in heaven with Schweik and war wounded parading before God; when this proved under-rehearsed, however, it was changed for the parting scene between Schweik and Voditchka, who agree to meet "at six o'clock after the war".) Again, the scenes are as follows: 1. [II/1] Transformation scene: in the train, changing to the station police office at Tábor./5. [II/2] Film, with Schweik marching (the start of Schweik's "Anabasis") and episode with the herdsman./2.

[II/2] Transformation scene: country road, then Putim police station, then film./3a. In a troop train (about Baloun and his hunger)./3b. Schweik rejoins his unit./3c. [III/2] In the train (where Baloun has eaten the sardines)./3d. [III/3] Beside the railway track (with Baloun doing physical jerks)./ 3e. [III/2] Other side of the train (with Schweik made to do the same). Schweik here tells the 4268 episode as a story./4. [III/4] Battlefield. (He gets lost, puts on Russian uniform and is taken prisoner by a Hungarian unit of his own army. A shell bursts, and he is killed.)

In returning to this material with a view to reworking it for the Second World War, Brecht found little that he could incorporate as it stood. Discussing his plan with his son on his return from New York at the end of May 1943, he realized that he was changing Schweik's character by allowing him to risk frequenting so dangerous a tavern as the "Flagon" (which figures little in the book), and to sacrifice himself for the sake of Baloun. "That indeed is where the situation is sharper than in 1914," he noted in his journal for May 27, where he reports that he has been re-reading the novel in the train on the way back:

> once again i was overwhelmed by hašek's vast panorama and the authentically un-positive point of view which it attributes to the people, they being themselves the one positive element and accordingly incapable of reacting "positively" to anything else. whatever happens schweik mustn't turn into a cunning underhanded saboteur. he is merely an opportunist exploiting the tiny openings left him.

He had already written the "Story" for Kurt Weill before leaving New York, and it seems that he soon showed this to Eisler, who commented that Schweik could not be seen as a typical "Little Man" and suggested that Brecht's play ought to end with him leading Hitler to Stalingrad, not back home. Another diary entry, of the 29th, shows that he also discussed it with Peter Lorre, whom he evidently had in mind for the title part, while again on July 12, when the first rough version was already complete, he noted that the language of the play differs substantially from that of the german hašek translation. south german elements have been worked in, and in various ways the gest is different. so it would be wrong, e.g., to speak bohemian dialect in this play; in other words the vocal inflections shouldn't be bohemian german.

Scene 2 of the first part of the Piscator adaptation is the only one to have survived in recognizable form, and even there Brecht changed the sex of the landlord Palivec, turning him (doubtless for Lotte Lenya's sake) first into Mrs. Natonek, then changing her name to Kopecka. Most of Hašek's characters, too, he abandoned, so that aside from a brief glimpse of Father Lacina (the less interesting of Hašek's two disgraceful chaplains) only Baloun and the police agent Brettschneider appear with Schweik in the play; all other characters are Brecht's or belong to history. But the basic concept and a number of subsidiary situations or elements were transplanted into the new terms: the stealing of the dog, for instance, Baloun's embarrassing appetite, the incident of freight car 4268, the notion of an "Anabasis" with its semiconscious loss of orientation, and above all the whole Schweikian approach to authority, patriotism, and war. Though the songs were mainly Brecht's, three of Schweik's chants are taken from the book— "Standing behind the gun" (p. 114) from II/2; "Onward to Jaromersh hoofing" (pp. 118–19) from III/4 (Piscator II/5); and "Thought that in the service" (p. 120) from I/8 (Piscator I/7)—while Baloun's "Beseda Song" (p. 102) can be found in III/4, where it is described as "the song the Czech regiments sang when they marched and bled for Austria at Solferino." And despite what Brecht says, Schweik's whole way of speaking derives from the novel. If at times it resembles that of Mother Courage, or Matti (in *Puntila*), or even Galy Gay (in *A Man's a Man*, another part which Brecht identified with Lorre), this is only because they too in some measure reflect the same source.

The new play was at first simply called *Schweyk*, the phrase "in the Second World War" making its appearance as an addition on the title page of what seems to be the latest of the four versions in the Brecht Archive. The other three of these all date from 1943 and consist of a bound copy in Brecht's typing, dated Santa Monica, July 1943; a largely identical Brecht typescript (but divided into acts and with a different ending) which he gave to Peter Lorre; and a fair copy not typed by Brecht. In summarizing their slight differences scene by scene we will refer to them respectively as the first script, the Lorre script, the fair copy, and the old Berliner Ensemble script (it bears that company's stamp). The first printed text appeared in volume X of the collected *Stücke* (1958), though a duplicated stage script was available from Henschel-Verlag in East Berlin in 1956.

2. Scene-by-Scene Account

Prelude in the Higher Regions

Our text is identical with the first script. The fair copy has a different version of the first three lines:

HITLER

My dear Himmler, forty-eight is the age I've now got to.
And so henceforward "now or never" must be my motto.
Accordingly I've just decided [to conquer the whole world, etc.]

This version ends, after "Where does the humble Little Man in Europe stand?":

HIMMLER

My Führer, he loves you—or that's how it's been planned
—much as the Little Man in Germany loves you too.
The Gestapo arrange all that.

HITLER

It's just as well they do.

—thus matching the last lines of the subsequent Interludes between scenes 3 and 4, and between scenes 6 and 7.

Scene 1

Virtually unchanged from the first script.

Scene 2

Virtually unchanged. The report about the banker Krusha and Bullinger's reaction to it were additions to the first script.

Interlude in the Nether Regions

Is in the first script but not in the fair copy, the old Berliner Ensemble script, or the duplicated stage script.

Scene 3

The fat lady shopkeeper is an addition by Brecht on the first script, which remained virtually unchanged.

Interlude in the Higher Regions

Unchanged. In the Lorre script this ends Act 1.

Scene 4

One or two cuts have been made since the first script, notably a characteristic Schweyk story following after "Ah yes, the Moldau" on p. 95. The *Moritat* "Henry Slept beside his Newly-wedded," unattributed by Brecht, who gives it as an appendix in the printed version, is by J. F. A. Kazner (1779): according to Dr. Sammy McLean it is also known as "Heinrich und Wilhelmine," "Die Geisterstimme von Mitternacht," and "Der ungetreue Liebhaber."

In the first script this scene was originally followed by a

second "Interlude in the Nether Regions," which Brecht cut there.

Scene 5

A speech by Schweyk about sabotage, added as an after-thought to the first script, was dropped in the fair copy.

Scene 6

All through this scene the references were to the London, not the Moscow Radio. The amendment was made on the first script, but not on the other three, nor on the duplicated stage script. Kati's remark about Schweyk's hat (p. 109) was an addition to the first script, which also lacks the "Song of the Moldau" at the end, presumably because Brecht was still re-writing it; (besides those in the other scripts, there are seven separate versions of this song).

In the Lorre script Act 2 ends here.

Interlude in the Higher Regions

Stalingrad replaced Rostov on the first script, and similarly with the numerous references that follow up to the end of the play.

Scene 7

Virtually unchanged.

Scene 8

The drunken chaplain was originally not Bullinger's brother but the Reverend Matz from Rosenberg. The relevant amendments were made on the first script, but the fair copy and the duplicated stage script still have him as Matz. A reference to the torture chambers was also added, and taken over into the fair copy; presumably it was dropped so that Schweyk should remain innocent of such things. The price specified in Mrs. Kopecka's song "Come, dear guest, and have a seat" (which was accompanied by a melody in Brecht's characteristic notation) was 80 Kreuzers in the first script; the final cry "On to Stalingrad!" was missing; and there were a number of other even smaller changes.

Epilogue

All four scripts and the duplicated stage script originally had Schweyk saying of the south (p. 132):

But there are piles of corpses there.

HITLER
    Then I'll push east.

SCHWEYK
    Then we'll have the British in our hair.

(We have omitted the stage directions.) This is changed to the present reading on the first script alone; hence it seems likely (as with the references to the London Radio) that Brecht used the bound script for his final amendments in the 1950s. In the Lorre script the ending is different from mid-scene on; thus after "And so it has done" (p. 131) there is no examination of the prospects north, south, east, and west, and instead Hitler finishes by returning to his opening theme:

HITLER
    The average German's useless without my grip to keep
    him steady.

SCHWEYK
    You kicked him too hard when he was down; he's a
    master race already.

HITLER

When I took over I found his international reputation
was sinking.

But now you're fighting side by side with him.

SCHWEYK

I'd much
rather we were drinking.

(*Schweyk picks up his rifle and shoves Hitler in front of
him. They stop at the signpost, and Schweyk turns his
torch on it. He reads "Stalingrad—30 miles," and marches
on in that direction with Hitler before him. The darkness
and the storm swallow them up*)

The final chorus is not in the fair copy.

THE CAUCASIAN CHALK CIRCLE

Texts by Brecht

Notes to *The Caucasian Chalk Circle*

1. REALISM AND STYLIZATION

Actors, stage designers, and directors normally achieve stylization at the cost of realism. They create a style by creating
"the" peasant, "the" wedding, "the" battlefield; in other words
by removing whatever is unique, special, contradictory, acci-
dental, and by providing hackneyed or hackneyable stereo-
types, the bulk of which represent no mastery of reality but
are just drawings of drawings—simple to provide since the
originals already have elements of style in them. Such stylists
have no style of their own, nor any wish to grasp that of
reality; all they do is to imitate methods of stylization. Plainly
all art embellishes (which is not the same as glossing over). If
for no other reason, it must do so because it has to link reality
with enjoyment. But this kind of embellishment, formulation,
stylization, must not involve phoniness or loss of substance.
Any actress who plays Grusha needs to study the beauty of
Brueghel's *Dulle Griet*.

2. TENSION

The play was written in America after ten years of exile, and
its structure is partly conditioned by a revulsion against the
commercialized dramaturgy of Broadway. At the same time

it makes use of certain elements of that older American theater whose forte lay in burlesques and "shows." In those highly imaginative manifestations, which recall the films of that splendid man Chaplin, the tension focused not merely on the progress of the plot (or only in a much cruder and larger sense than now), but more on the question "How?". Nowadays when we are "offered an amusing trifle" it is simply the feverish efforts of a rapidly aging whore who hopes that her graceless tricks will serve to postpone or annul the moment when her painful and frequently-operated vagina has once again to be handed over to a client. The pleasure of telling a story is hamstrung by fear that it will fall flat. Unleashing this pleasure, however, does not mean freeing it from all control. Detail will be of the greatest importance, but that does not mean that economy won't be of great importance too. Imagination can be applied to the achievement of brevity. The point is not to abandon something rich. The worst enemy of true playing is playing about; meandering is the sign of a bad story-teller, while cosiness is just self-satisfaction and to be despised as such. Direct statement is among the most important methods of epic art, and it is as fair to [speak] of epic restlessness as of epic repose.

3. THE CHALK CIRCLE

The test of the chalk circle in the old Chinese novel and play, like their Biblical counterpart, Solomon's test of the sword, still remains a valuable test of motherhood (by ascertaining motherliness) even if motherhood today has to be socially rather than biologically defined. *The Caucasian Chalk Circle* is not a parable. Possibly the prologue may create confusion on this point, since it looks superficially as if the whole story is being told in order to clear up the argument about who owns the valley. On closer inspection, however, the story is seen to be a true narrative which of itself proves nothing but merely displays a particular kind of wisdom, a potentially model attitude for the argument in question. Seen this way, the prologue becomes a background which locates the practicability and also the evolution of such wisdom in an historic setting. And so the theater must not use the kind of technique developed by it for plays of the parable type.

4. BACKGROUND AND FOREGROUND

In the English language there is an American term "sucker," and this is exactly what Grusha is being when she takes over the child. The Austrian term "die Wurzen" means something of the same sort, while in High German one would have to say "der Dumme," "the fool" (as in the context "they've managed to find somebody fool enough to . . ."). Her maternal instincts lay Grusha open to troubles and tribulations which prove very nearly fatal. All she wants of Azdak is permission to go on producing, in other words to keep on paying. She loves the child; her claim to it is based on the fact that she is willing and able to be productive. She is no longer a sucker after the trial.

5. [SETTING OF THE PLAY]

The play's setting needs to be very simple. The varying backgrounds can be indicated by some form of projection; at the same time the projections must be artistically valid. The bit players can in some cases play several parts at once. The five musicians sit onstage with the singer and join in the action.

6. INCIDENTAL MUSIC FOR *THE CHALK CIRCLE*

Aside from the few songs which can take personal expression, the story-teller's music need only display a cold beauty, but it should not be unduly difficult. Though I think it is possible to make particularly effective use of a certain kind of monotony, the musical basis of the five acts needs to be clearly varied. The opening song of Act 1 should have something barbaric about it, and the underlying rhythm should be a preparation and accompaniment for the entry of the governor's family and the soldiers beating back the crowd. The mimed song at the end of the act should be cold, so that the girl Grusha can play against the grain of it.

For Act 2 (The Flight to the Northern Mountains) the theater calls for thrustful music to hold this extremely epic act together; nonetheless it must be thin and delicate.

Act 3 has the melting snow music (poetical) and, for its main scene, funeral and wedding music in contrast with one another. The song in the scene by the river has the same theme as the Act 1 song in which Grusha promises the soldier to wait for him.

In Act 4 the thrustful, scurrilous ballad about Azdak (which would best be sung *piano*) must be interrupted twice by Azdak's two songs (which definitely have to be simple to sing, since Azdak must be played by the most powerful actor rather than by the best singer). The last (lawsuit) act demands a good dance at the end.

7. BEHAVIOR OF THE SINGER IN THE LAST SCENE OF ACT 1

The playwright's suggestion that the general principle of having the scenes embody specific passages of the singer's song in such a way that their performance never overshadows the singer's solo performance to the villagers ought to be deliberately abandoned in production.

8. CASTING OF AZDAK

It is essential to have an actor who can portray an utterly genuine man. Azdak is utterly genuine, a disappointed revolutionary posing as a human wreck, like Shakespeare's wise men who act the fool. Without this the judgment of the chalk circle would lose all its authority.

9. PALACE REVOLUTION

The curt orders given offstage inside the palace (sporadically and in some cases quietly so as to imply the palace's vast size) must be cut once they have served to help the actors at rehearsal. What is going on onstage is not supposed to be a slice of some larger occurrence, just the part of it to be seen at this precise spot outside the palace gate. It is the entire occurrence, and the gate is *the* gate. (Nor is the size of the palace to be conveyed in spatial terms.) What we have to do is replace our extras with good actors. One good actor is worth a whole battalion of extras. I.e., he is more.

> [Sections 1–6, 8, and 9 are from GW *Schriften zum Theater* 3, pp. 1204–08. The typescripts suggest that sections 1–4 belong together, and we have put them in their original, possibly accidental, but still logical order. They and section 6 are thought to date from 1944. Sections 5 and 7 are notes accompanying the first version of the script that year, 7 being taken from BBA 192/178. The last two were written nearly ten years later, 8 being assigned to about 1953 by BBA while 9 relates to a rehearsal held on December 4 of that year in preparation for Brecht's Berliner Ensemble production.]

Dance of the Grand Duke with his Bow

Oh, the green fields of Samara!
Oh, the bent backs of a warlike race!
O sun, o domination!

I am your prince. This bow they are bringing
Is elm tipped with bronze, strung with flexible sinew.
This arrow is mine, which I mean to send winging
To plunge itself deep, o my enemy, in you.

Oh, the green fields of Samara!
Oh, the bent backs of a warlike race!
O sun, o domination!

Off, off to the fight, bowstring taut. Aren't you frightened
To feel how much deeper the bronze will go worming
Its way through your flesh as the bowstring is tightened?
Fly, arrow, and cut up that enemy vermin!

So I tug, tug and tug at the bow that they made me.
How strong are my shoulders! A fraction more. Steady . . .
Why, it's broken! All lies! Elm and bronze have be-
    trayed me.
Help, help! God have mercy: my soul's so unready.

Oh, the cattle-stocked fields of Samara!
Oh, the bent backs of a warlike race!
Oh, the cutting up of the enemy!

[BBA 28/23-4. A penciled note by Elisabeth Hauptmann,
dating probably from the 1950s or later, identifies this as
material discarded from the play.]

Concerning the Prologue

Your dislike of the prologue puzzles me somewhat; it was the
first bit of the play to be written by me in the States. You
see, the problem posed by this parable-like play has got to
be derived from real-life needs, and in my view this was
achieved in a light and cheerful manner. Take away the prologue, and it's impossible to understand on the one hand why
it wasn't left as the Chinese chalk circle, and on the other why
it should be called Caucasian. I first of all wrote the little story
which was published in Tales from the Calendar. But on coming to dramatize it I felt just this lack of elucidatory historical
background.

[From Werner Hecht (ed.): Materialien zu Brecht's
"Der kaukasische Kreidekreis," Frankfurt, Suhrkamp-Verlag, 1966, p. 28. This passage is taken from a letter to

Brecht's publisher Peter Suhrkamp, and reflects a common attitude among West German critics and theater directors. The "little story" was "The Augsburg Chalk Circle," for which see p. 309.]

Contradictions in *The Caucasian Chalk Circle*

1. Main contradictions

The more Grusha does to save the child's life, the more she endangers her own; her productivity leads to her own destruction. That is how things are, given the conditions of war, the law as it is, and her isolation and poverty. In the law's eyes the rescuer is a thief. Her poverty is a threat to the child, and the child adds to it. For the child's sake she needs a husband, but she is in danger of losing one on its account. And so forth.

Bit by bit, by making sacrifices, not least of herself, Grusha becomes transformed into a mother for the child; and finally, having risked or suffered so many losses, fears no loss more than that of the child itself. Azdak's judgment makes the rescue of the child absolute. He is free to award the child to her because there is no longer any difference between the child's interests and hers.

Azdak is the disappointed man who is not going to cause disappointment in others.

2. Other contradictions

The petitioners prostrate themselves before the governor as he goes to Easter mass. Beaten back by the Ironshirts, they fight wildly among themselves for a place in the front row.

The same peasant who overcharges Grusha for his milk is then kindly enough to help her pick up the child. He isn't mean; he's poor.

The architects make utterly servile obeisances to the governor's aide-de-camp, but one of them has to watch the other two to see how they do it. They are not just natural boot-lickers; they need the job.

Grusha's spineless brother is reluctant to take in his sister, but furious with his kulak of a wife on account of his dependence on her.

This spineless brother cannot say boo to his kulak of a wife, but is overbearing with the peasant woman with whom he fixes up the marriage contract.

The motherly instincts of the peasant woman who takes in the foundling against her husband's wishes are limited and provisional; she betrays it to the police. (Likewise Grusha's motherly instincts, though they are so much greater, so very great, are limited and provisional: she wants to see the child into safety, then give it away.)

The maid Grusha is against war because it has torn her beloved from her; she recommends him always to stay in the middle in order to survive. However, on her flight into the mountains she sings of the popular hero Sosso Robakidze who conquered Iran, in order to keep her courage up.

[GW *Schriften zum Theater* 17, pp. 1208–10. Assigned by BBA to 1954. However, Brecht's concept of main and subsidiary contradictions (i.e., conflicting elements in a situation) derives from Mao Tse-tung, whose pamphlet *On Contradiction* he seems to have read in 1955.]

A Detour

P: The people at X want to cut "the way to the northern mountains." The play is a long one, and they argue that this whole act is really no more than a detour. One sees how the maid wants to get rid of the child as soon as she has got it away from the immediate danger zone; but then she keeps it after all, and that, they say, is what counts.

B: Such detours in modern plays have to be studied carefully before one makes up one's mind to take a short cut. It might prove to seem longer. Certain theaters cut one of

Macheath's two arrests in the *Threepenny Opera* on the grounds that both might have occurred because he twice went to the brothel instead of clearing out. They made him come to grief because he went to the brothel, not because he went to it too often, was careless. In short, they hoped to liven things up and finished by getting tedious.

P: They say it weakens the maid's claim to the child in the trial scene if her feeling for him is shown as subject to limitations.

B: To start with, the trial scene isn't about the maid's claim to the child but about the child's claim to the better mother. And the maid's suitability for being a mother, her usefulness and reliability are shown precisely by her level-headed reservations about taking the child on.

R: Even her reservations strike me as beautiful. Friendliness is not unlimited, it is subject to measure. A person has just so much friendliness—no more, no less—and it is furthermore dependent on the situation at the time. It can be exhausted, can be replenished, and so on and so forth.

W: I'd call that a realistic view.

B: It's too mechanical a one for me: unfriendly. Why not look at it this way? Evil times make humane feelings a danger to those who have them. Inside the maid Grusha the child's interests and her own are at loggerheads with one another. She must acknowledge both interests and do her best to promote them both. This way of looking at it, I think, must lead to a richer and more flexible portrayal of the Grusha part. It's true.

[From "Die Dialektik auf dem Theater" in *Versuche 15*, Suhrkamp and Aufbau Verlags, 1957. As with other dialogues in that collection, Brecht shows himself as B, talking with some of his young collaborators: in this case P for Peter Palitzsch, R for Käthe Rülicke, and W for Manfred Wekwerth. They were not literal transcriptions.]

Editorial Note

1. General

The Caucasian Chalk Circle brings together two threads that had been twining their way gently through Brecht's mind for several years before Luise Rainer asked him to write the play. They are of course the old Chinese story of the chalk circle, with its strong resemblance to the judgment of Solomon, and the story of the eccentric, paradoxical judge which (though one can never be certain of this) Brecht appears to have devised for himself. Of these the former probably has the longer ancestry—in Brecht's mind, that is—for Klabund's modern German dramatization was staged by Max Reinhardt at the Deutsches Theater, where Brecht had just spent a year as a junior dramaturge, on October 20, 1925. Brecht knew Klabund, or Alfred Henschke (as he was really called), from Munich as a writer and singer of ballads faintly akin to his own—he had actually replaced Brecht in the second performance of the *Red Raisin* program that followed *Drums in the Night* there—and Klabund's wife, the actress Carola Neher, was to become one of his best-loved performers. Moreover, his still earlier friend, her unrelated namesake Caspar Neher, was designer for the new play, while Elisabeth Bergner, then coming to the peak of her fame in Germany, played its leading part. "We all saw it," said Hanns Eisler later.

Described as "*The Chalk Circle*. A play in five acts from the Chinese, by Klabund," the text was published the same year (by J. M. Spaeth Verlag, Berlin). In fact it and its heroine, the prostitute Haitang, have a good deal more in common with *The Good Person of Szechwan* than with *The Caucasian Chalk Circle*, and almost certainly helped also to inspire the former play, which was already written by the time of Brecht's arrival in the U.S. Even the basic situation of the chalk circle differs from Brecht's version, in that the heroine (who naturally wins the test) is the biological mother and the false claimant a stepmother, while the symbolism of the circle is already underlined by Haitang's princely lover in the first act, as he draws one in white on a black wall, to represent the vaulted sky and the uniting of two hearts:

HAITANG   Whatever lies outside this circle is nothing. Whatever lies inside this circle is everything. How are everything and nothing linked? In the circle that turns and moves (*drawing spokes in the circle*)—in the wheel that rolls . . .

The test is conducted twice, first by the corrupt judge Tschutschu in Act 3, when Haitang loses, then again by her old lover, now become emperor, in Act 5. "Take a piece of chalk," says the emperor to his master of ceremonies:

draw a circle here on the ground before my throne, put the boy in the circle.

MASTER OF CEREMONIES   It has been done.

EMPEROR   And now, both you women,
Try to draw the boy out of the circle
At the same time. One of you take his left arm,
The other his right. It is certain
The right mother will have the right strength
To draw the boy out of the circle to herself.

(*The women do as he says. Haitang grips the boy gently; Mrs. Ma tugs him brutally to her side*) It is clear that this person (*indicating Haitang*) cannot be the mother. Otherwise she would have managed to draw the boy out of the circle. Let the women repeat the experiment. (*Mrs. Ma once again pulls the boy to her side*) Haitang, I see that you do not make the slightest effort to draw the boy out of the circle to you. What's the meaning of that?

Haitang explains that, having brought the child up, she knows that his arms are too delicate to stand tugging:

If the only way I can get my child is by pulling off his arms, then let somebody who has never known a mother's suffering for her child pull him out of the circle.

EMPEROR (*standing up*) Behold the mighty power locked in the chalk circle! This woman (*indicating Mrs. Ma*) aimed to get control of all Mr. Ma's fortune and to that end seized the child. Now that the real mother has been acknowledged it will be possible to find the real murderer . . .

for Mrs. Ma had murdered their joint husband and accused Haitang of the crime. She now confesses, and together with the judge is pardoned by Haitang, who is left alone with her son and her imperial lover as the curtain falls.

At the time this slightly sugary play provoked Brecht to parody it, making Jackie Pall in *The Elephant Calf* of 1926 (volume 2 of the *Collected Plays*) pull his mother out of a "doubtless most incompetently drawn circle" in order to prove contrariwise that he, the elephant child, is her son or alternatively her daughter. Roughly twelve years later, however, when Brecht was living in Svendborg, he took up the theme again and must have wondered whether to give it a Chinese or a European setting. The title *The Odense Chalk Circle* (Odense being the principal city of Fünen Island, where Svendborg is situated) seems to suggest the latter, but only a few fragmentary notes under this heading are left, e.g.:

> the governor who has to act like a poor man. he pretends to eat too crudely and is sharply rebuked.

—and:

> the gentry are scared because the governor has been driven out. they flee, fully expecting the peasantry to institute a bloodbath.
>
> but the peasants don't come and there is no bloodbath.
>
> by an oversight the judge appointed by the rebels is confirmed by the governor.
>
> he pronounces judgment in the case of the two mothers.

There was to be a character called Hieronymus Dan, while another note suggests accompaniment by "old and austere

music (fifes, drums, organs)." There is also, however, a
more coherent scheme headed simply *The Chalk Circle*, and
this is full of Chinese names. It appears to go thus:

I

how schao-fan gets to be a judge. he hides a hunted
man. this upsets his wedding. the bride's family withdraws.

the peasants propose schao-fan for the judge's post. laughter all round.

the governor returns to power and sends a messenger ap-
pointing a judge: schao-fan.

the wedding takes place. ([what] was taken out is
brought back in before the scene starts, silently or to a
song: love is an irresistible force, etc.) the new judge
gives judgment in a long lawsuit between the village and
the bride's family. the judge finds for the village by
sticking to the letter of the law.

II

the judge's pranks. he gets drunk in a case involving
property and makes everything depend on what shape
one of the litigants' nose is, etc.

he is put in gaol. his house is destroyed as if by a tornado.

the maid's wanderings with the child. through the dangers
of the blizzard, through the worse dangers of the slums.

she rejects good food for the child and exposes it to
hunger.

III

the mother denies the child. by acknowledging him she
would be acknowledging that she is the judge's wife.

the maid adopts it, mutely, behind her own back, like
a jackdaw whose thieving is hereditary.

IV

the judge gets his post back by mistake.

he bribes witnesses, he fails to examine them once bribed, he muddles everything, proposes marriage to a lady witness in open court and so on.

Section III was later shifted to precede Section I.

A single sample of the dialogue (BBA 128/05–06) shows how Brecht's interest was already centering on the disreputable judge, and goes on to outline a "second part" in which the heroine is again called Haitang:

PEOPLE he's a very bad judge. he breaks the law—no, he's never read it—aye, it was pure accident he got the job. he used to be a rice planter. one night an old man broke into his paddy-fields and begged him to have mercy: soldiers were after him. tao-schun was sorry for him and hid him in his hut under some old baskets. that old man was the governor of the province, and after the foiling of the plot against him that night thanks to his flight and the planter's sympathy he quickly smote down his enemies. he had the planter trained and made him a judge. but tao-schun was a great disappointment to him. he said quite openly in a bar that it just hadn't occurred to him to ask the old man what level of society he came from. and so he had treated him as a fugitive not as a governor. but for that he'd no doubt have handed him over to the soldiers. he regretted having saved one of the oppressors.—for some time they've only been giving cases to tao-schun when the senior judge is ill, like today.

PARTY WAITING (*jump up appalled*) is it really tao-schun on the bench today? if so we must have an adjournment. (*to one another*) he won't accept a penny. we're sunk.

PARTY OPPOSITE tao-schun's in charge! hear that? it's all up, then. he won't accept a penny.

PARTY OF THE FIRST PART hey, you! we've just been told one of our family's seriously ill. so we'd like to go home. would it make any difference to you if we held the case some other day? (*in an undertone*) you dirty lot of vultures!

PARTY OF THE SECOND PART it's all the same to us so long as the truth comes out.

THE FIRST FAMILY you're right there. better lose our field tomorrow than today. let's go (*exeunt*)

THE FAMILY OPPOSITE *(as they leave)* those crooks! wait
    till judge tai's recovered, that'll put an end to their claims
    even if it costs us 50 taels.
THE JUDGE, TAO-SCHUN *(sings)*
    the judge is unwell, his thumb's feeling sore
    (he pretends to count money)
    so today there's a healthier look to the law.
    but what d'you imagine a verdict is for?
    eat your fill; then you'll stink all the more.

The few notes headed "second part" follow:

> haitang is caught in the civil war. together with the
> child, she is forced to take risks for the sake of the cause.
> she exposes the child to many dangers. their journey
> through the blizzard. cheerful song. their journey through
> the slums. (more dangerous.)

> in face of a snowstorm
> i once was full of courage
> but in face of people
> i now am cowardly.
> the snowstorm will not destroy us.
> the earthquake is not avid for us.
> but the coal merchant wants money
> and the shipowner must be paid for the voyage.

Even before leaving Denmark, however, Brecht had begun
work on *The Good Person of Szechwan*, for which this last
"aria" could easily have been written, and around the same
time he seems to have set aside the oriental version of the
story and started to see the judge figure in German garb.
Thus Mother Courage, in the 1939 script of that play, re-
calls a corrupt judge in Franconia who sounds very like him
(*Collected Plays*, vol. 5, p. 399), and the following year
Brecht wrote the short story "The Augsburg Chalk Circle"
which appeared in the June 1941 issue of the Moscow *Inter-
nationale Littérature* and later in *Tales from the Calendar*. This
develops the theme a lot further in the direction of our play,
but at the same time shifts it bodily to Brecht's own home-
town and the period of the Thirty Years' War. Here the

child's mother, fleeing before the invading Catholics, spends too long packing her clothes and runs off without it. Instead Anna the maid takes charge, watching by it much as does Grusha at the end of scene 2:

> When she had spent some time, an hour perhaps, watching how the child breathed and sucked at its little fist, she realized that she had sat too long and seen too much to be able to leave without the child. Clumsily she stood up, wrapped it in its linen coverlet, took it on her arm and went out of the courtyard with it, looking shyly around like someone with a bad conscience, a thief. [pp. 160–61]

She takes it off to her brother's in the country, where he makes her marry a dying cottager with the same results as in the eventual play. When the child's mother arrives "several years" later and removes it, she sues for her boy's return. The judge is one Ignaz Dollinger, who is described as "a short but extremely meaty old man," famous for "his homely cross-examinations, with their cutting remarks and proverbs" and accordingly "praised by the lower orders in a lengthy ballad." "Is he yours?" he bellows at her, accusing her of being after the dead father's property. "Yes," she replies, ". . . If I can just keep him till he knows all the words. He only knows seven" (p. 227). So he hears the case, concludes that both mothers are lying, and makes the test of the chalk circle, in which Anna lets the boy go, so that he is jerked to his mother's side.

> Old Dollinger got to his feet.
> "And that shows us," he announced in a loud voice, "who the right mother is. Take the child away from that slut. She'd tear him cold-bloodedly in two."

Three or four years later, when Jules Leventhal commissioned him to write the play for Broadway (which may seem inconsistent with his professed "revulsion" but was not wholly so), the main structure and principal characters were ready in Brecht's mind, and the only remaining problems were

setting and framework: what period and country to pick
for it and how to relate it to the present day. The choice of
medieval Georgia and of a contemporary Soviet framework
must already have been made before he left New York in
mid-March 1944 to return to Santa Monica and work on
the script, for there is no sign of hesitation. Certainly the
resulting first script is written with great sureness and an unusual scarcity of amendments and afterthoughts, while there
are far fewer drafts and alternative versions than for some
of the less complex or elaborately developed plays. The dating
of the framework was to change; in the first script the prologue is set in 1934, without reference to the war. So were
most of the names of the characters, which started by being
mainly Russian and were Georgianized later; thus Grusha
Vachnadze was originally Katya Grusha (or at one point
Katya Kirshon), her soldier Volodya Surki, her brother Piotr,
and the lesser characters Petrov Petrovitch, Maxim Maximo-
vitch, and the like, while the princes were boyars and
Gruzinia Georgia throughout.

Just when the various alterations were made is impossible to
say. A journal entry of May 8 shows that Brecht was held
up for a fortnight while he evolved social reasons for the
judge's shabby eccentricities, grounding these ultimately in

his disappointment that the fall of the old rulers had not
introduced a new era but merely an era of new ones.
hence he goes on practicing bourgeois justice, but in a
disreputable, sabotaged version which has been made to
serve the total self-interest of the judge. this explanation
of course mustn't modify what i had previously, and is for
instance to be no excuse for azdak.

But this hitch is not reflected in the script. Nor, other than
very marginally, is the remodeling of the heroine, which another entry of August 8 says has taken him three weeks; he
may have found Katya in the first script "nicer" and not
enough like Brueghel's *Dulle Griet* (who is glued on the
title pages of the three earliest scripts), but he does not
seem to have altered her much, or provided those practical

motives for her goodness which Feuchtwanger (who found her "too holy") had asked for. Altogether the changes to his first conception were surprisingly slight.

The first script bears a note by Brecht, "first version" and is dated "Santa Monica June 5, 1944," the day when he posted it off to Luise Rainer. The second, which contains the new version of the prologue and an ad lib epilogue, is similarly called "second version"; it must have been finished early in September, and consists very largely of carbons of the first, with some retyped pages. Its title page gives the names of Eisler and Winge as "collaborators" as well as (Ruth) Berlau who figures alone in the published version; (John Hans Winge was an Austrian who had been working in a Los Angeles factory). Both scripts were bound for Brecht, and he seems to have made his amendments, e.g., of names, indifferently in one or the other. These were then taken into a third, undated script of 1944. Like the first two, this version was typed by Brecht, but this time more conventionally, using upper- and lower-case letters. The play was first actually published in English, Eric and Maja Bentley's translation appearing as one of *Two Parables for the Theater* in 1948; the first German publication being in the special Brecht issue of *Sinn und Form* (Potsdam) the following year. This in turn was amended by Brecht for publication in the *Versuche* series in 1954.

2. Scene-by-Scene Account

The following are scene-by-scene notes on the main differences:

1. The Dispute over the Valley

In all three scripts and the *Sinn und Form* version this was called "Prologue," and perhaps as a result many critics and directors have taken it as not forming an integral part of the play. However, as Brecht pointed out in his letter to his publisher Suhrkamp (p. 300), it forms the beginning of the first script and, though altered, was never thereafter omitted. In that first version, which sets the episode on Sunday, June 7, 1934, there are no references to the war damage and the scene is nearly two pages shorter. We reproduce it in full on pp. 323–27.

Another early note, which may even have preceded it, specifies:

> *scene:* in the background a school with posters and a soviet flag. a few dusty trees.

> *meeting:* the folklore not to be overdone. those present are in their sunday best, no traditional costumes. among them a soldier on leave. a woman has a child on her lap. some of the men have very short haircuts.

> *the singer* wears european garb. very comfortable; like all suits, his is somewhat crumpled. his musicians wear russian shirts; one of them has a georgian cap.

> *the tone* of the discussion is very relaxed; a general delight in argument is evident. now and again one of the young people shoots a paper dart at a girl opposite and is told to shut up.

Within three months the scene had been rewritten virtually in its final form. Only its ending was different, being taken from the first version, from its last stage direction ("As they are leaving," etc.) to the Voice's closing announcement. This was altered in 1954, after the *Sinn und Form* publication. Another minor point involved the switching of the names of the two collective farms, which was done on the second script but inadvertently overlooked in the *Sinn und Form* version. Here Hanns Eisler performed what he ironically called "one of my great services to German literature" by telling Brecht that he must not identify a goat farm with the name of Rosa Luxemburg in view of the insulting use of the term "goat" for a woman in Germany (as the English "cow").

2. The Noble Child

The scripts all amplify the opening stage direction by the words "his manner of performing shows that he has done it a hundred times before; he turns the pages mechanically, casting an occasional glance at them. By slight movements he tells the musicians when to come in." In the first script this ran on . . . "and prefixes each entry of the actors by striking the ground with a wooden mallet." See the note in Brecht's journal for July 3, 1944, which argues that the play's successive episodes are "embodiments of the main incidents in his tale" and pictures him striking the ground thus and behaving like a director at a performance. "This is necessary to avoid illusion and its intoxicating effects." This idea is abandoned in number 7 of Brecht's notes above (p. 298).

Aside from the subsequent change of names, which has already been mentioned and which gives a much more Georgian flavor, the amendments to the first script are generally minor ones. The dust-covered rider originally entered just before the governor's "Not *before* mass, Shalva," which was followed by the exchange "Did you hear that?" etc., p. 150; this was altered only in the 1950s. The references to geese in the dialogue between Grusha (Katya) and Simon (Volodya/Surki) were originally to fish, but appear in the second script. Katya's answer to the query "Is the young lady as healthy as a fish in water?" is

> Why as a fish in water, soldier? Why not like a horse at a horse market? Can it pull two carts? Can it stand out in the snow while the coachman gets drunk? Being healthy depends on not being made ill.
>
> SURKI That won't happen.

—while when he asks if she is impatient and wants apples (not cherries) in winter she retorts "Why not say 'does she want a man before she's too old?'" This and the new stress on her aptitude for the role of "sucker" ("you simple soul," "you're a good soul," "you're the boneheaded kind," pp. 158–59) represent the main differences between Grusha and the Katya of the first script.

Her song "When you come back home I'll be there" (pp.

154–55) was a response to Konstantin Simonov's war poem "Wait for Me," whose translation, by Nathalie Rene, Brecht had cut out of *Moscow News* and gummed in his journal at the time of the first work on *Simone Machard:*

> Wait for me and I will come.
> Wait, and wait again.
> Wait where you feel sad and numb
> And dreary in the rain.
> Wait, when snows fall more and more,
> Wait when days are hot . . .

etc., the "I" of course here being a soldier. The remainder of the verse in this scene is virtually unchanged from the first version, though the "temptation to do good" there was "great" and not "terrible." It is interesting perhaps that the whole line in its present form should have been very firmly written in by Brecht on the second script; he clearly felt it to be important.

3. The Flight to the Northern Mountains

Much of the unrhymed verse (which was originally not broken into lines but divided by oblique strokes) differs in the first script, where it is mainly struck out without having yet been replaced by the new versions; maybe these became detached from the script. In the second script it is all there, virtually as now. According to Rudolf Vápeník the song "To the war my weary way" of the two Ironshirts on p. 168 is translated from a Moravian folk song set (as one of his Slovak Folk Songs) by Bartók.

The first episode (Grusha getting milk from the old peasant) is one of those which Brecht retyped entirely for the second script, but despite some rewording it was not substantially changed. As revised, it ended with the words "Michael, Michael, I've certainly let myself in for something" (p. 163), followed by the stage direction:

> (*She stands up, worried, takes the child on her back and marches on. Grumbling, the old man collects his cup and looks expressionlessly after her*)

The next episode (Outside a Caravanserai), which figures in the first script, was then cut, not to be restored till the collected edition; it was not performed in Brecht's production. The brief appearance of the two Ironshirts which follows was slightly bowdlerized in the 1950s; before "He'll let himself be torn to pieces for a superior" (p. 168) it read "When he hears an order he gets a stand; when he sticks his lance into the enemy's guts he comes." The short scene with the two peasants is virtually unchanged from the first script, but once Grusha runs into the Ironshirts there are a fair number of alterations, the central part of the episode being among the passages retyped by Brecht for the second script. The gist of his changes here is to make Grusha more evidently frightened of the soldiers than was Katya in the first version, and also to make it seem less likely that she is handing the child over to the peasants for good. Thus Katya was not *"in a fright"* (p. 170) and did not *"let out a little scream"* (p. 171)—these directions appearing only from the third script on—while instead the first script made her laugh and say:

> Corporal, if you're going to question me so severely I'll have to tell you the truth: that I'd like to be on my way. How about lowering your pike?

The episode of the bridge is once again almost as in the first script, though there is one possibly significant detail: the first man originally greeted Katya's feat in exactly the words the first soldier uses of Kattrin in the drum scene of *Mother Courage* (*Collected Plays*, vol. 5, p. 208): "She's done it." Brecht changed this in the 1950s to "She's across," presumably in order not to stress the connection between the two characters, both of whom were then being played by the same actress.

4. In the Northern Mountains

Originally entitled "Katya Grusha's sojourn at her spineless brother's: her strange marriage and the return of the soldier." A number of passages here were retyped and rewritten for the second script, for instance the episode of the melting snow, starting with the singer's introduction (p. 180):

THE SINGER
> The sister was too sick. The cowardly brother had to let her stay / She lay in the storeroom. Through the thin wall she heard him talking to his wife: / "She'll / soon be gone," he said. "When she's well. How soft your breasts are. . . ." / The sister was sick till winter came. The cowardly brother had to let her stay. / The storeroom grew cold and she heard him talk to his wife. / "When spring comes she'll be gone," he said. "How firm your thighs are. . . ." / The room was cold. The road was colder. The winter was long, the winter was short. / The rats mustn't bite, the child mustn't cry, the spring mustn't come. / Where to go when the snow melts? (*Still weak, Katya squats at the loom in the storeroom. She and the child, who is squatting on the ground, are wrapped in rugs and rags against the cold. The child cries. Katya tries to comfort it*) [At this point there is a photograph of a Mongolian-looking woman at a spinning-wheel gummed into the script.]

KATYA Don't cry, or do it quietly. Otherwise my sister-in-law will hear us and we'll have to go. Cockroaches aren't supposed to make any noise, are they? If we keep as quiet as cockroaches they'll forget we're in the house. Remember the cockroaches. (*The child cries again*) Hush. The cold doesn't have to make you cry. Being poor's one thing, freezing's another. It doesn't get you liked. You keep quiet and I'll let you see the horses; remember the horses. (*The child cries again*) Michael, we have to be clever, we've no wedding lines for my sister-in-law. If we make ourselves small we can stay till the snow melts. (*She draws the child to her and looks, appalled, at one particular point*) Michael, Michael, you've got no sense. If it's on account of the rats you don't need to cry. Rats are quite human. They have families. They store up food for 500 years.

PIOTR (*slips in*) What's up? Why are you looking over at that corner, Katya? Is he frightened?

KATYA What's he to be frightened of? There's nothing there.

PIOTR   I thought I heard scuffling in the straw. I hope it isn't rats. You wouldn't be able to stay with the child here.

KATYA   There aren't any rats. It'd be impossible to get a job anywhere with him.

PIOTR   (*sits by her*)   I wanted to talk to you about Lisa-veta . . .

Piotr is Lavrenti, and Lisaveta his wife Aniko, and the conversation continues much as in our text from "She's a good soul" (p. 181) to "Was I talking about Aniko?" (p. 181), then:

You can't think how it upsets her not to be able to offer you anything better than this room. The big room above is too hard to heat. "My sister will understand": I've told her that a thousand times, but does she believe me? She even blames herself in private for not being able to stand children. That's because she hasn't any of her own. Her heart's not strong enough, you see.

Grusha's song "The loved one prepared to go" (pp. 180–81) then comes after the second "Grusha is silent" (p. 182). After the *glockenspiel of the falling drops* (p. 182) Piotr makes his proposal about the marriage, much as in our text except that Katya is to come back to live in his house again as soon as her bridegroom dies; the provision about her being entitled to live on the latter's farm for two years (p. 183) only appearing in the third script. The wedding ceremony itself was hardly changed except in this respect, thus on leaving (p. 185) Piotr/Lavrenti says "I'll wait for you by the poplar at the entrance to the village, Katya."

KATYA   Suppose it takes longer?
MOTHER-IN-LAW   It won't take longer.

The conversation among the guests (p. 187) was retyped virtually as now for the second script; in the first it ran:

THE GUESTS   (*noisily*)   There've been more disturbances in the city, have you heard?—Ay, the boyar Rajok's besieged in the palace, they say.—The grand duke is back and it's all going to be like it used to be.—Lots of them coming back all the time from the Persian war.—They even say the old governor's wife's come back, and all the palace guard with her. (*Katya drops the cake pan. People help her to pick up the cakes*)

A WOMAN (*to Katya*) You not feeling well? Too much excitement, that's it. Sit down and have a rest. (*Katya sits down*)

THE GUESTS Here today, gone tomorrow. Gone tomorrow, here today. But we still have to pay taxes.

KATYA (*feebly*) Did someone say the palace guard had come back?

A MAN That's what I heard.

ANOTHER They say, though, that boyar Rajok's green flag is still flying over the palace. But the palace is being besieged. The old governor's wife is supposed to be living in one of the houses opposite.

KATYA Who told you that?

THE MAN (*to a woman*) Show her your shawl! . . .

Thenceforward to the end of the scene the first version has been altered very little, the one significant addition (on the second script) being Grusha's explanation that she can never go back to Nukha (originally Kachezia) because she had knocked down an Ironshirt.

5. The Story of the Judge

Most of the amendments to this scene are minor ones, and a good few date from 1954; the three scripts are thus close to one another, only the episode with the fat prince's nephew having been to some extent rewritten after the first script. Already there the singer, who up to that point had only figured as such, began from the beginning of the Azdak ballad on (p. 206) to be "*the singer and his musicians*," and this is oddly enough the only hint anywhere in the play or Brecht's notes that he may be required to perform Azdak's part, though Brecht seems to have taken this for granted in the production.

The Ironshirts' action in dragging Azdak to the gallows was added in 1954; previously they had been slapping him and Shauva genially on the shoulder. The fat prince's (the boyar Rajok's) first speech was altered and expanded in the rewriting for the second script; at the same time the chatter of the Ironshirts (p. 203) emphasizing their awareness of their (momentary) political importance was also added. Some small changes were made to heighten the dialogue where the nephew pronounces his verdict (p. 206), both in the rewriting and in 1954. After the first two of Azdak's cases (respectively the doctor and Ludovika) the stage direction showing Azdak on his travels (p. 210) along the military highway and the two accompanying verses of the Azdak ballad were introduced in 1954. The presence of Ironshirts behind Azdak's throne each time, with their flag as a tangible sign of support for him, was an addition on the first script, as was also the appearance of the fat prince's head on one of their pikes (p. 214).

6. The Chalk Circle

In the first script there is a song near the beginning of the scene (after the cook starts praying, p. 216) which was thereafter omitted:

> The people say: the poor need luck
> They won't get far by using their heads.
> They won't grow fat by the work of their hands.
> Therefore, it is said
> God has devised for them games of chance
> And the dog races. Likewise God
> In his unremitting care for his poor folk
> Sees to it that the tax inspectors sometimes slip.
> For the poor need luck.

All through there are two elements missing from this version —the threat which the wounded corporal represents to Grusha (p. 218) and Simon's confession that he is the father of the child (p. 217). Instead Simon alleges that it was the son of one of his comrades. Then after the entry of the governor's wife the first lawyer goes on from his condemnation of the

judge as "just about the lowest individual ever seen" (p. 218)
to say

> I insist you settle this matter out of court.
>
> GOVERNOR'S WIFE As you wish.
>
> FIRST LAWYER In view of the size of the estate which the
> child is inheriting, what do a few piasters count here and
> there? (*On a nod from her he strolls over to Katya*) A
> thousand piasters. (*Seeing Katya's look of uncertainty*) I
> am authorized to offer you a thousand piasters if the case
> can be kept from coming to court.
>
> THE COOK Holy Mary, a thousand piasters!
>
> FIRST LAWYER (*strutting off*) You see what your friends
> think.
>
> KATYA Are they trying to offer me money for Michael?
>
> THE COOK And they'd certainly go higher.
>
> VOLODYA (*darkly*) A meal that doesn't fill you makes you
> hungry, they say.
>
> FIRST LAWYER (*coming back*) Well, what about that thou-
> sand?
>
> GOVERNOR'S WIFE Is she being brazen enough to think it
> over? (*Crosses to Katya*) You shameless person, don't
> you know you've to bow when I speak to you?
>
> KATYA (*bows deeply, then*) I can't sell him, milady.
>
> GOVERNOR'S WIFE What? You call that selling, when you've
> got to return what you stole? You thief, you know it's
> not yours!
>
> VOLODYA (*sees Katya hesitating; at attention*) I attest that
> this is the child of my comrade Illo Toboridze, Mrs.
> Anastasia Sashvili, sir.
>
> GOVERNOR'S WIFE Aren't you one of the palace guard? How
> dare you lie to me, you swine?
>
> VOLODYA Straight from the horse's mouth, sir, as the saying
> goes. (*The governor's wife is speechless. Ironshirts have
> entered the courtyard and the aide-de-camp has been
> whispering to one of them. The second lawyer tugs the
> governor's wife's sleeve and whispers something to her*)
>
> THE COOK They wouldn't be offering money if they
> weren't frightened of Azdak's favoring you. He goes by
> faces.

All this was dropped in the second script, which contained
the present short bridge passage to cover the cut.

The first part of the actual trial, up to Simon's testimony, was retyped after the first script, everything between Grusha's "It's mine" (p. 221) and the middle of the second lawyer's speech beginning "Thank you, your worship" (p. 222) being new. Originally Grusha was followed by the second lawyer saying

> Excuse me, Maxim Maximovitch, but the court wants facts. My lord . . .
>
> FIRST LAWYER My dear Pavlov Pavlovitch, I would have thought my address . . .
>
> SECOND LAWYER Is dispensable, my dear Maxim Maximovitch. My lord, by an unfortunate concatenation of circumstances, this child, etc.

This means that all reference to the Abashvili (Sashvili) estates was lacking from the original scene, since the same is true of their mention in the second lawyer's speech later on p. 227. Much of the backchat between Azdak and Grusha likewise comes from the second script, which first introduced Grusha's long diatribe starting "You drunken turnip" (p. 224) and ending "than hanging on the gallows" (p. 225). Her passage too with the governor's wife (p. 226) is a product of that script, but from then on till the final dance the first version has survived very largely intact. It ends with the singer's final verses in a slightly different line arrangement and without the ironic qualifying word "almost," which was an addition to the second script. An epilogue follows, but was evidently written later; its use was to be optional, and it is not included in the third script or any of the published versions other than the *Materialien zu Brechts "Der kaukasische Kreidekreis"* (Frankfurt, Suhrkamp-Verlag, 1966), from which the following translation has been drawn:

Epilogue
(ad libitum)

The ring of spectators from the two collective farms becomes visible. There is polite applause.

PEASANT WOMAN RIGHT   Arkadi Cheidze, you slyboots, in league with those who stole our valley, how dare you compare us members of the Rosa Luxemburg kolkhoz with people like that Natella Abashvili of yours, just because we think twice about giving up our valley?

SOLDIER LEFT (*to the old man right, who has stood up*) What are you looking over there for, comrade?

THE OLD MAN RIGHT   Just let me look at what I'm to give up. I won't be able to see it again.

THE PEASANT WOMAN LEFT   Why not? You'll be coming to call on us.

THE OLD MAN RIGHT   If I do I mayn't be able to recognize it.

KATO THE AGRONOMIST   You'll see a garden.

THE OLD MAN RIGHT (*beginning to smile*)   May God forgive you if it's not one.
   (*They all get up and surround him, cheering*)

3. Prologue from the First Script (1944)

Public square of a Caucasian market town, with peasants and tractor drivers of two kolkhoz villages seated in a circle, smoking and drinking wine; among them a delegate from the planning commission in the capital, a man in a leather jacket. There is much laughter.

THE DELEGATE (*in an effort to get their attention*)   Let's draw up an agreed statement, comrades.

AN OLD PEASANT (*standing*)   It's too soon for that, I'm against it; we haven't thrashed things out; I object on scientific grounds.

WOMAN'S VOICE (*from the right*)   Not thrashed it out? We've been arguing ten hours.

THE OLD PEASANT   And what about it, Tamara Oboladze? We've still got four hours left.

A SOLDIER   Correct. I'm surprised at you, Tamara. Who's going to get up from table when there's still a quarter of a calf left in the dish? Who's going to be satisfied with ten hours of argument if he can have fourteen?

A GIRL   We've done Cain and Abel, but nobody's even mentioned Adam and Eve yet. (*Laughter*)

THE DELEGATE   Comrades, my head's in a whirl. (*Groaning*) All this elaborate business about scientifically based goat breeding, all those examples to back it, all those subtle allusions, and then great masses of goat's cheese and endless jugs of wine to top it off! I suggest we draw up a concluding statement, comrades.

A TRACTOR DRIVER (*decisively*)   Even the best things must come to an end. Hands up those who want the discussion closed! (*The majority raise their hands*)

THE TRACTOR DRIVER   The closure's carried. Now for the statement!

THE DELEGATE   The point at issue then (*he begins writing in his notebook*) is a difference between two kolkhoz villages, the Rosa Luxemburg and Galinsk, concerning a valley which lies between them and is not much good for grazing. It belongs to the Rosa Luxemburg kolkhoz (*addressing those at his left*) and is being claimed by the Galinsk kolkhoz, that's (*to those on his right*) you people.

THE OLD MAN   Put down that we have to have the valley for raising our goats, just like we have to have other valleys, and it's always belonged to our village. (*Applause left*)

A PEASANT RIGHT   What d'you mean, "always"? Nothing's "always" belonged to anybody. You haven't even always belonged to yourself. Twenty-five years ago, Chachava, you still belonged to the grand duke. (*Applause left*)

THE DELEGATE   Why don't we say the valley belongs to you now?

THE PEASANT RIGHT   And when you say you have to have it for your goats, better put in that you've got all the pasture land you need not more than half an hour from there.

A WOMAN LEFT   Put this down. If goats are driven half an hour every day they give less milk.

THE DELEGATE   Please don't let's go through all that again. You could have government aid to build stables on the spot.

THE OLD MAN LEFT   I'd like to ask you (*addressing the peasant right*) a small personal question. Did you or did you not enjoy our goat's-milk cheese? (*On his not immediately replying*) Did you or did you not enjoy those four or five pounds you were tucking away? I'd like an answer, if you don't mind.

THE PEASANT RIGHT   The answer's yes. So what?

THE OLD MAN (*triumphantly*)   I wonder if the comrade knows why he enjoyed our goat's-milk cheese? (*Pause for effect*) Because our goats enjoyed the grass in that particular valley. Why isn't cheese just any old cheese? Eh? Because grass isn't just any old grass. (*To the delegate*) Put that in your book.

(*Laughter and applause right*)

THE DELEGATE   Comrades, this isn't getting us anywhere.

THE PEASANT RIGHT   Just write down why we think the valley ought to be made over to us. Mention our expert's report on the irrigation scheme, then let the planning commission make up its mind.

THE DELEGATE   The comrade agronomist!

(*A girl stands up right*)

NATASHA   Put me down as Nina Meladze, agronomist and engineer, comrade.

THE DELEGATE   Your native village of Galinsk sent you to technical school in Tiflis to study, is that right? (*She nods*) And on getting back you worked out a project for the kolkhoz?

NATASHA   An irrigation scheme. We've a lake up in the mountains that can be dammed so as to irrigate 2,000 versts of barren soil. Then our kolkhoz can plant vines and fruit trees there. It's a project which can only be economic if the contested valley is included. The yield of the land will go up 6,000 percent. (*Applause right*) It's all worked out here, comrade. (*She hands him a file*)

THE OLD MAN LEFT (*uneasily*)   Put in a word to say that our kolkhoz thinks of going in for horse breeding, will you?

THE DELEGATE   Gladly. I think I've got it all now. There's just one more suggestion I'd like to make if I may, comrades. It would please me very much if I could add a footnote to my report saying that the two villages have come to an agreement after having heard all the arguments put forward this day, Sunday, June 7, 1934.

(*General silence*)

THE OLD MAN LEFT (*tentatively*)   The question is, who does the valley belong to? Why don't we have another drink or two and talk it over? There are still some hours to go. . . .

THE PEASANT RIGHT   All right, let's take our time over the footnote, but do let's close the discussion as decided, specially as it gets in the way of our drinking, eh, comrades?

(*Laughter*)

VOICES   Yes, close the discussion. How about a bit of music?

A WOMAN   The idea was to round off this visit by the planning commission's delegate by listening to the singer Arkadi Cheidze. We've been into it with him. (*While she is speaking a girl runs off to fetch the singer*)

THE DELEGATE   That sounds interesting. Thank you very much, comrades.

THE OLD MAN LEFT   But this is off the point, comrades.

THE WOMAN RIGHT   Not really. He got in this morning, and promised he'd perform something which had a bearing on our discussion.

THE OLD MAN LEFT   That'd be different. They say he's not at all bad.

THE PEASANT RIGHT (*to the delegate*)   We had to telegraph to Tiflis three times to get him. It nearly fell through at the last minute because his chauffeur caught a cold.

THE WOMAN RIGHT   He knows 21,000 verses.

THE PEASANT RIGHT   It's very difficult to book him. You people in the planning commission ought to see he comes north more often, comrade.

THE DELEGATE   I'm afraid we're mainly involved with economics.

THE PEASANT RIGHT (*with a smile*)   You sort out the distribution of grapes and tractors; why not songs too? Anyhow here he is.

(*Led by the girl, the singer Arkadi Cheidze enters the circle, a thickset man with simple manners. He is accompanied by four musicians with their instruments. Applause greets the artists*)

THE GIRL (*introducing them*)   This is the comrade delegate, Arkadi.

THE DELEGATE (*shakes his hand*)   It is a great honor to meet you. I heard about your songs way back as a schoolboy in Moscow. Are you going to give us one of the old legends?

THE SINGER   An extremely old one. It's called "The Chalk Circle" and comes from the Chinese. We perform it in a somewhat altered version of course. Comrades, it's a great honor for me to entertain you at the end of your day of strenuous debates. We hope that you'll find the old

poet's voice doesn't sound too badly under the shadow of
Soviet tractors. Mixing one's wines may be a mistake, but
old and new wisdom mix very well. I take it we're all
having something to eat before the performance begins?
It's a help, you know.

VOICES   Of course. Everyone into the club.

(*As they disperse the delegate turns to the girl*)

THE DELEGATE   I hope it won't finish too late. I have to go
home tonight, comrade.

THE GIRL (*to the singer*)   How long will it take, Arkadi?
The comrade delegate has got to get back to Tiflis tonight.

THE SINGER (*offhandedly*)   A matter of a few hours.

THE GIRL (*very confidentially*)   Couldn't you make it
shorter?

THE SINGER (*seriously*)   No.

VOICE   When you've finished eating, Arkadi Cheidze will
give his performance out here on the square.

(*All go off to eat*)

> [From Werner Hecht (ed.): *Materialien zu Brechts "Der
> kaukasische Kreidekreis,"* Frankfurt, Suhrkamp-Verlag,
> 1966. This comes from the first script of the play, which
> was finished by June 1944. The inconsistency in the girl
> agronomist's name (which is Kato in the final version)
> is due to its being Georgianized from Natasha Borodin in
> course of many similar amendments to this script.]

APPENDIX

The Duchess of Malfi

Edited, with notes

by A. R. Braunmuller

Introductory Note

Nearly every aspect of Brecht's adaptation of John Webster's *Duchess of Malfi*— the text, the collaborators' shares, the dates of composition and revision, even the spelling of the title itself—offers puzzles and confusions almost impossible of certain solution. The text printed on pp. 335–417 approaches as nearly as possible what can be reconstructed of Brecht's version of the play, or rather, the version over which he seems to have exercised the most influence and on which he expended the most care.

Both the origin of the project to adapt the play and the process of that adaptation helped ensure that the result would be neither a full-scale reworking (on the order of *Edward II* or *Coriolanus*) nor a purely Brechtian enterprise. Elisabeth Bergner, the actress, and her husband, the producer Paul Czinner, suggested the play as suitable material for Brecht's attention and Miss Bergner's talents. Around April or May 1943, work on the project began in New York. H. R. Hays, Brecht's early translator, also worked on the adaptation at this time. From this period dates *The Duchess of Malfy . . . An Adaptation for the Modern Stage* copyrighted June 26, 1943, by Brecht and Hays, and a variety of drafts in the Brecht Archive in Berlin. Many sheets from this copyrighted version became the basis for Brecht's further work.

Late in 1943, W. H. Auden joined the effort, and shortly thereafter Hays withdrew. Bergner and Czinner seem to have suggested about this time that an effort be made to incorporate material from Webster's other tragedy, *The White Devil*, into the new adaptation, and some subsequent drafts show an increasing use of scenes and lines from this play (see the editorial notes to Act 1, scene 2 and Act 2, scene 4). The *Duchess* appears in Brecht's journal as a finished work on July 21, 1943, probably a reference to the Brecht-Hays copyrighted version. Brecht continued to work on it, however, for another journal entry covering his next New York visit (November 1943 to March 1944) describes it as "not completely finished," while as late as June–July 1945 it is only described as finished "in the rough."

Although Brecht continued to write, Auden's name alone appears on a text, copyrighted October 24, 1945, which is largely reworked Webster with an excellently concise first act (apparently by Auden, but following Webster's text closely). Brecht reappears with Auden in a version copyrighted on April 4, 1946, and continued his association with the project at least through the trial performances in Providence, Rhode Island (September 20, 1946) and in Boston. The play opened on Broadway October 15, 1946. Although the programs and advertisements for the trial productions mention "Bertold [*sic*] Brecht" along with Auden, Brecht's name appears nowhere in the New York program or in the generally condemnatory reviews. The final Broadway version had returned to Webster's original with some revisions and modernization; it even includes part of the "Julia" subplot which had been excised from all but one of the now surviving versions.

It is not easy to make a precise statement of Brecht's practical contribution to adapting the *Duchess*. Certainly, he made important decisions about restructuring the play and rearranging large units of Webster's original. These decisions led him to write new scenes, such as the battlefield scene (2,1) and the Cardinal's murder (3,1), and to rewrite the play's conclusion. At one point, his interest in a conversation between Bosola and the old woman (2,2) nearly reverses the general reduction which he makes in Bosola's part. Brecht made many smaller and more detailed contributions as well. He understood Webster's English well enough to rearrange the play without having always to pass through a German version first. For example, having decided to increase the economic motive for Ferdinand's murder of his sister, Brecht adds (in English) some lines from Webster's IV.ii to his own 1,2. For longer passages, sometimes sandwiched between pieces of Webster or of translated Brecht, he often used German. In the version of 2,6 which we follow, for instance, the Duchess' reading of Ferdinand's letter appears in German in the text with two marginal translations, one quite literal and another, a replacement, more fluent and in near-blank verse. At another point, opposite an English speech near the end of the echo scene, appears the note, "Brecht's rough translation" (see the editorial notes on 3,2), suggesting that Brecht may have occasionally translated his own German. In one of the drafts for Ferdinand's concluding speech to 3,3 (see the notes), some of the English spellings suggest Brecht's mental translation from German cognates or his use of similar sounds. H. R. Hays also testifies to Brecht's ability to read and write English, when he wished. Thus, while it might be accurate to say that Brecht's chief contribution lies in his wholly original scenes, the rearrangement of Webster's original, and some very clear-sighted choices of omissions and new emphases, it must be added that he often dipped into the minutiae of the play. He had the ability and the interest to work over single lines and short speeches.

The text which follows has been constructed from the following Brecht Archive sources: "Dramatis Personae" (1174/02); "Prologue" (1174/68–69); 1,1 (1419/06–13 and 1174/03–07); 1,2 (1174/08–13); 1,3 (1419/25–26, 1174/154–157, and 1174/18–20); 1,4 (1174/21–23); 2,1 (1174/25–28); 2,2 (1174/29–30 and 1174/162); 2,3 and 2,4 (1174/31–44); 2,5 and 2,6 (1419/64–74); 3,1 (1174/185–187); 3,2 through 3,5 (1174/45–63); 3,6 (1174/64 and 1419/107–108); "Epilogue" (1176/109). Manuscript corrections and changes have been incorporated into the text; obvious typographical errors and misspellings have been silently corrected. Brecht Archive sources for material in the editorial notes are cited in the appropriate places.

(The editor of this text gratefully acknowledges the help of Lee Bliss and Edward Mendelson, and the financial support of the University of California Research Committee.)

The Duchess of Malfi

(After John Webster)

CHARACTERS

(In order of their appearance)

DELIO BOLOGNA

ANTONIO BOLOGNA

BOSOLA

CARDINAL OF ANCONA

DUKE FERDINAND

CASTRUCHIO

CARIOLA

ATTENDANT

DUCHESS OF MALFI

FIRST OFFICER

SECOND OFFICER

FIRST SERVANT

SECOND SERVANT

NEGRO PAGE

MONK

THIRD OFFICER

FOURTH OFFICER

COURTIERS, GENTLEMEN, MEN AT ARMS, STANDARD BEARERS, LADIES

Prologue

Friar's Cell.

Friar and Duke Ferdinand.

FRIAR (*cries out in horror*)
No more, young man, no more! I dare not hear it!

FERDINAND
Gentle father,
To you I have unclasped my burdened soul,
Emptied the storehouse of my thoughts and heart
That I might have the comfort, now to ask you:
Must I not do what all men else may,—love?

FRIAR
Why, foolish madman—

FERDINAND
Shall, then, for that I am her brother born,
My joys be ever banished from her bed?

FRIAR
Have done, unhappy man! For thou art lost!

FERDINAND
So tell me, holy man,
What cure shall give me ease in these extremes?

FRIAR
Art thou, my son, that miracle of wit,
Who once, within these three years, wert esteem'd
A wonder of thine age, throughout the world?
How did the [people (?)] of Italy applaud

Thy government, behavior, learning, speech, and all that
   could make up a man!
O Ferdinand, why hast thou left the school
Of knowledge, to converse with lust and death?
For death waits on thy lust. Look through the world,
And thou shalt see a thousand faces shine
More glorious than this idol thou ador'st:
Leave her and take thy choice.

FERDINAND
It were more easy to stop the ocean
From floats and ebbs, than to dissuade my vows.

FRIAR
Thou must.

FERDINAND
      I can not, holy father.

FRIAR
Then I have done, and in thy wilful flames
Already see thy ruin; Heaven is just.—
Yet hear my counsel.
Hie to thy house, and lock thee fast
Alone within thy chamber; then fall down
On both thy knees, and grovel on the ground;
Cry to thy heart; wash every word thou utter'st
In tears (and if't be possible) of blood:
Beg heaven to cleanse the leprosy of lust
That rots thy soul; acknowledge what thou art,
A wretch, a worm, a nothing; weep, sigh, pray
Three times a day and three times every night.

FERDINAND
That I have done to no avail.
If you can not absolve me, holy father,
Then I am lost. Therefore I am determined
I'll to the war in Cyprus.
And may that conflict drown the earth in blood,
I'll be content if I do not return.

FRIAR
Pray for thyself, abroad,
Whilst I pray for thee here—away!
My blessing with thee! We have need to pray!

ACT ONE

1

Presence Chamber in the Palace of the Duchess of Malfi.

Delio and Antonio are on. Bosola lurks in the background.

ANTONIO
    In these unruly times you are welcome, cousin Delio.
    I fear my letter drew you rudely
    Out of sweet France. How did you like it there?

DELIO
    'Tis still a land of sunshine. You will spend
    In a fortnight what you may scarcely win there
    In a twelve-month. The French are exceeding skillful
    In the arts, not those of love alone
    But likewise martial stratagem. In Paris
    I have studied their new fashion of gunnery.

ANTONIO
    New come from Paris, how doth Malfi please you?

DELIO
    So well that I am sorry I shall straightway
    Be leaving it. I thank you, dear Antonio,
    For my preferment with Lord Ferdinand.
    'Tis agreed I follow him to the wars.
    (Indicating Bosola)
    What doth this fellow seek here?

ANTONIO
    I know not. One of those parasites

That breed in princes' palaces. Here comes
The Cardinal.

(*Enter the Cardinal of Ancona with a monk who is his chaplain and secretary and several other gentlemen. Bosola immediately crosses to the Cardinal*)

BOSOLA

I do haunt you still.

CARDINAL So.

BOSOLA I have done you better service than to be slighted thus. Miserable age where the only reward of doing well is the doing of it.

CARDINAL You enforce your merit too much.

BOSOLA I fell into the galleys in your service, where for two years together I wore two towels instead of a shirt with a knot on the shoulder after the fashion of a Roman mantle. Slighted thus? I will thrive some way.

CARDINAL Would you become honest!

BOSOLA With all your divinity do but direct me the way to it. I have known many travel far for it yet return as arrant knaves as they went forth because they carried themselves always along with them.

(*The Cardinal moves away brusquely and begins to talk to his secretary*)

Are you gone? Some fellows, they say, are possessed with the devil but this great fellow were able to possess the greatest devil and make him worse. Could I be one of their flattering panders, I would hang on their ears like a horse leech, 'til I were full and then drop off.

DELIO (*to Antonio*) He hath denied him some suit. I knew this fellow seven years in the galleys for a notorious murderer and 'twas thought
In the Cardinal's pay. He was released
By the French general, Gaston de Foux
When he recovered Naples.

ANTONIO

Here comes the great Calabrian Duke.

(*The Duke Ferdinand enters with Castruchio, courtiers, men at arms, standard bearers, all the appurtenances of a princely train. He is in armor*)

FERDINAND
  Are the galleys come about yet?

CASTRUCHIO   They are, my lord. But methinks you should not
  desire to go to war in person.

FERDINAND   Now for some weighty reason. Why not?

CASTRUCHIO   It is fitting a soldier should rise to be a prince
  but not necessary that a prince should descend to be a captain.

FERDINAND   No?

CASTRUCHIO   No, lord, he were far better do it by deputy.

FERDINAND   This war too nearly touches mine honor. Since
  the old Duke of Malfi fell, I have sworn to defend my sister
  Duchess in his stead. While I live she need fear no foe.

CASTRUCHIO   Believe my experience. That realm is never long
  quiet where the ruler is a soldier.

FERDINAND   Who was it tamed the Arab stallion and broke
  him to his paces?

CASTRUCHIO   Antonio Bologna.
  (Ferdinand crosses to Antonio)

FERDINAND
  Matchless Antonio, great master of our sister
  Duchess' household!
  (He nods to Delio)
                         Your cousin pleases me.
  His skill in this new science of gunnery
  From France we'll soon know how to use in Cyprus.
  (Crowd noises without)

CASTRUCHIO   My lord, the people line the streets awaiting your
  progress to the haven. You may hear their lusty shouts.
  *(Ferdinand moves off toward the window to observe the
  crowd)*

DELIO *(To Antonio)*
  The presence begins to fill. You promised me
  To make me partaker of the natures
  Of some of your great courtiers.

ANTONIO   Well, there's the cardinal—

DELIO   What's his temper? They say he's a great scoundrel.

ANTONIO   He should have been pope but did bestow bribes too
  impudently. Some good he hath done.

DELIO   What's his brother, my new master?

ANTONIO The Duke, there? A most perverse and turbulent
nature.

DELIO Twins?

ANTONIO In quality. The Cardinal and his brother, the Duke,
are like plum trees that grow crooked over standing pools.
They are rich and o'erladen with fruit but none grows; pies
and caterpillars feed on them.

DELIO
What of their sister, the fair Duchess?

ANTONIO
You never fixed your eye on three fair medals
Cast in one figure of so different temper.
For her discourse it is so full of rapture
You will only begin then to be sorry
When she doth end her speech and wish, in wonder,
She held it less vainglory to talk much.
She throws upon a man so sweet a look
That it were able to raise one that lay
Dead in a palsy but in that look
There speaketh so divine a continence
As cuts off all lascivious and vain hope.
Her days are practiced in such noble virtue
That sure her nights, nay more her very sleeps,
Are more in heaven than other ladies' shrifts.
Let all sweet ladies break their flattering glasses
And dress themselves in her.

DELIO
                                          Fie, Antonio,
Have you turned scholar studying of her virtues?

ANTONIO
I'll case the picture up. Only this much—
All her particular worth grows to this sum.
She stains time past, lights the time to come.

FERDINAND (*as the Cardinal joins him*) A word with you,
brother. Have you bethought you concerning the protection
of our widowed sister in mine absence at the wars? How
like you my proposal that she dwell with thee at Ancona?

CARDINAL I like it not. If you think my palace is a cloister
you are deceived. She shall abide at Malfi. You worry more

than is a brother's duty. And are you doubtful of her virtue, though I think she hath given thee no cause, hire an intelligencer.

FERDINAND (*silent*)

CARDINAL   There is a fellow plagues me, one Daniel de Bosola, who hath had practice in this trade.

FERDINAND   Would not Antonio, the master of her household, be far fitter?

CARDINAL   His nature is too honest for such business. I'll send Bosola to thee.

(*Cariola, waiting woman to the Duchess, and attendant enter*)

ATTENDANT (*announcing*)   Her grace the Duchess of Malfi will be here anon.

CARIOLA (*crosses to Antonio*)   You must attend my lady in her chamber half an hour hence. She hath business with thee.
(*She exits*)

DELIO (*to Antonio*)   What's this, you blush?

ANTONIO   Nay, 'tis surely the matter of my accounts. I'll go fetch my books.
(*He exits*)

BOSOLA (*approaching Ferdinand*)   I was lured to you.

FERDINAND   My brother, here, the Cardinal, could never abide you.

BOSOLA   Never since he was in my debt.

FERDINAND   Maybe some oblique character in your face made him suspect you?

BOSOLA   He did suspect me wrongfully.

FERDINAND (*giving money*)   There's gold.

BOSOLA   What follows? Whose throat must I cut?

FERDINAND

I give you that
To live i' the court here and observe the Duchess,
To note all particulars of her behavior,
What suitors do solicit her for marriage
And whom she best affects. She's a young widow.
I would not have her marry again.

BOSOLA

No, sir?

FERDINAND
　　　　Do not you ask the reason but be satisfied.
　I say I would not.

BOSOLA
　　　　　　It seems you would create me
　One of your familiars.

FERDINAND
　　　　　　Familiar? What's that?

BOSOLA
　Why,
　An intelligencer.

FERDINAND
　　　　Such a kind of thriving thing
　I would wish thee and ere long thou mayest arrive
　At a higher place by 't.

BOSOLA (*offers to give back money*)
　　　　　　Take your devils
　Which hell calls angels. These cursed gifts would make
　You a corrupter, me an impudent traitor
　And should I take these they'll take me to hell.

FERDINAND (*imperiously*)
　Sir, I'll take nothing from you I have given.
　There is a place I shall procure for you,
　The provisorship o' th' horse.

BOSOLA
　　　　　　The provisorship
　O' the horse? Say then my corruption
　Grew out of horse dung. I am your creature.

ATTENDANT
　Her grace, the noble Duchess of Malfi.
　(*Enter the Duchess with her ladies. Her brothers greet her
　formally*)

FERDINAND
　Sister, I have a suit to you.

DUCHESS
　　　　　　To me, sir?

FERDINAND
　A gentleman here, Daniel de Bosola,
　A worthy fellow, pray let me entreat for him
　The provisorship of your horse.

DUCHESS
   Your knowledge of him
   Commends him and prefers him.
CARDINAL
   We are now to part from you and your own discretion
   Must be your director.
   (*The court withdraws*)
FERDINAND
                    You are a widow;
   You know already what man is and therefore
   Let not youth, high promotion, eloquence—
CARDINAL
   No, nor anything without the addition, honor,
   Sway your high blood.
FERDINAND
                    Marry? They are most lascivious
   Will wed twice.
CARDINAL
              O fie!
FERDINAND
                    Their livers are more spotted
   Than Laban's sheep.
DUCHESS
                    Diamonds are of most value,
   They say, that have passed through most jewelers' hands.
FERDINAND
   Whores, by that rule, are precious.
DUCHESS
                         Will you hear me?
   I'll never marry.
CARDINAL
                 So most widows say,
   But commonly that motion lasts no longer
   Than the turning of an hourglass, the funeral sermon
   And it end both together.
FERDINAND
                 Now hear me:
   You live in a rank pasture here in the court.
   There is a kind of honeydew that's deadly.
   'Twill poison your fame; look to it; be not cunning.

Nor they whose faces do belie their hearts
Are witches, ere they arrive at twenty years,
Aye, and give the devil suck.

DUCHESS

This is terribly good counsel.

FERDINAND

Hypocrisy is woven of a fine small threat,
Subtler than Vulcan's engine; yet believe it
Your darkest actions, nay your privatest thoughts,
Will come to light.

CARDINAL

You may flatter yourself
And take your own choice privately to be married
Under the eyes of night.

FERDINAND

Think it the best voyage
That e'er you made, like the irregular crab,
Which though it goes backward, thinks it goes right
Because it goes its own way, but observe;
Such weddings may more properly be said
To be executed than celebrated.

CARDINAL

The marriage night
Is the entrance into some prison.

FERDINAND

And those joys,
Those lustful pleasures are like heavy sleeps
Which do forerun man's mischief.

CARDINAL

Wisdom begins at the end. Remember it.
(*Cardinal exits*)

DUCHESS

I think this speech between you both was studied.
It came so roundly off.

FERDINAND

You are my sister,
This was my father's poignard, do you see?
I'd be loath to see't look rusty 'cause 'twas his.
I would have you give over these costly balls.
A visor and a mask are whispering rooms

That were never built for goodness. Fare ye well.
And women like that part which, like the lamprey,
Hath never a bone in't.

DUCHESS

Fie, sir.

FERDINAND

Nay,
I meant the tongue, variety of courtship.
What can not a neat knave with a smooth tale
Make a woman believe? Farewell, lusty widow.
(*He exits*)

DUCHESS

Shall this move me? If all my royal kindred
Lay in my way unto this marriage,
I'd make them my low footsteps. And even now,
Even in this hate, as men in some great battles
By apprehending danger have achieved
Almost impossible actions (I have heard soldiers say so)
So I, through frights and threatenings will assay
This dangerous venture. Let old wives report
I winked and chose a husband, Cariola,
To thy known secrecy I have given up
More than my life, my fame.

CARIOLA

Both shall be safe
For I'll conceal this secret from the world
As warily as those that trade in poison
Keep poison from their children.

DUCHESS

Have you spoke with Antonio?

CARIOLA

He attends you.

DUCHESS

Good, dear soul, now leave me. But go
And place yourself behind the arras of my chamber
Where thou mayest overhear it. Wish me godspeed.
For I am going into a wilderness.
(*Cariola exits*)
Oh the misery of us that are born great, for thus
We are forced to woo because none dare woo us.

2

Boudoir of the Duchess of Malfi.

Duchess on stage.

DUCHESS (*enter Antonio*)
  I sent for you; sit down;
  Take pen and ink and write: are you ready?
ANTONIO
                                        Yes.

DUCHESS
  What did I say?
ANTONIO
                    That I should write somewhat.
DUCHESS
  Oh, I remember:
  After this farewell and this large expense,
  It's fit (like thrifty husbands) we inquire
  What's laid up for tomorrow.
ANTONIO
  So please your beauteous excellence.
DUCHESS
                                    Beauteous?
  Indeed I thank you: I look young for your sake.
  As my steward you have taken my cares upon you.
ANTONIO
  I'll fetch your grace the particulars,
  Of all your revenues and your expenses.
DUCHESS
  Oh, you are an upright treasurer; but you mistook
  For when I said I meant to make inquiry
  What's laid up for tomorrow, I did mean
  What's laid up yonder for me.
ANTONIO
                        Where?

DUCHESS

                                    In heaven,
I am making my will (as 'tis fit princes should
In perfect memory), and I pray, sir, tell me
Were it not better to make it smiling, thus,
Than in deep groans and terrible ghastly looks
As if the gifts we parted with procured
That violent distraction?

ANTONIO

                              Oh, much better.

DUCHESS

If I had a husband now this care were quit:
But I intend to make you overseer.
Lend me a hand!
What virtue shall I claim in my account with heaven?

ANTONIO

If you want me to write down
Now all your virtues, I must beg your pardon
For having not provided enough material.

DUCHESS

Thank you.
But I was thinking of but one:—obedience.
I practiced that one when my forceful brothers
Picked my husband for me. Do write down obedience.
Hold! Now I do not know for certain, if it's to be written
To my credit or to my debit, sir.

ANTONIO

Who knows how they are reading accounts up there?

DUCHESS

Down here I'd put it on the debit side.
What do you think of marriage?

ANTONIO

I take it as those that deny purgatory,
It locally contains or heaven or hell;
There's no third place in it.

DUCHESS

                              How do you like it?

ANTONIO

My loneliness, feeding on my melancholy,

Could often reason thus—

DUCHESS

Pray let's hear it.

ANTONIO

Say a man never marry, nor have children,
What takes that from him? Only the bare name
Of being a father, or the weak delight
To see the little wanton ride a cock-horse
Upon a painted stick or hear him chatter
Like a taught starling.

DUCHESS

Fie, fie, what's all this?
One of your eyes is bloodshot. Use my ring to it.
They say 'tis a good remedy. 'Twas my wedding ring
And I did vow never to part with it
But to my second husband.

ANTONIO

You have parted with it now.

DUCHESS

Yes, to help your eyesight.

ANTONIO

You have made me stark blind.

DUCHESS

How?

ANTONIO

There is a saucy and ambitious devil
Is dancing in the circle.

DUCHESS

Remove him.

ANTONIO

How?

DUCHESS

There needs small conjuration when your finger
May do it; thus, is it fit?

ANTONIO

What said you?

(*He kneels*)

DUCHESS

Sir,

This goodly roof of yours is too low built;
I cannot stand upright in't, nor discourse
Without I raise it higher: raise yourself,
Or if you please, my hand to help you: so.

ANTONIO

Ambition, madam, is a great man's madness.
Conceive not I am so stupid but I guess
Whereto your favors tend: but he's a fool
That, being acold, would thrust his hands in the fire
To warm them.

DUCHESS

        So, now the ground's broke,
You may discover what a wealthy mine
I make you lord of.

ANTONIO

        O my unworthiness!

DUCHESS

You were ill to sell yourself.
This darkening of your worth is not like that
Which tradesmen use i' the city; their false lights
Are to rid bad ware: and I must tell you
If you will know where breathes a complete man
(I speak it without flattery), turn your eyes
And progress through yourself.

ANTONIO

Be it so.
I have long served virtue
And never taken wages of her.

DUCHESS

        Now she pays it.
And as a tyrant doubles with his words
And fearfully equivocates, so we highborn ladies
Are forced to express our violent passions
In riddles and in dreams and leave the path
Of simple virtue which was never made
To seem the thing it is not. Go, go, brag
You have left me heartless; mine is in your bosom.
I hope 'twill multiply love there. You do tremble.
Make not your heart so dead a piece of flesh

To fear more than to love me. Sir, be confident.
What is it distracts you? This is flesh and blood, sir;
'Tis not the figure cut in alabaster
Kneels at my husband's tomb. Awake, awake, man,
I do here put off all vain ceremony
And only do appear to you a young widow
That claims you for her husband, and like a widow,
I use but half a blush in it.
(Antonio remains silent)
And now that you shall not come to me in debt
(Being now my steward), here upon your lips
I sign your quittance. This you should have begged now:
I have seen children oft eat sweetmeats thus
As fearful to devour them too soon.

ANTONIO

But for your brothers?

DUCHESS

Do not think of them:
All discord without this circumference
Is only to be pitied and not feared!
It's true, they had a hope
Had I continued widow to have gain'd
An infinite mass of treasure by my death.
Yet could they know it, time will easily
Scatter the tempest.

ANTONIO

These words should be mine,
And all the parts you have spoken, had not my tongue
Been too long used to servitude.

DUCHESS

Kneel.

(Both kneel)
(Enter Cariola)

ANTONIO

Hah!

DUCHESS

Be not amazed, this woman's of my counsel:
I have heard lawyers say a contract in a chamber,
Per verba presenti, is absolute marriage.
Bless, heaven, this sacred knot, which no violence

Ever untwine!
What can the church force more?

ANTONIO

May fortune know no accident
Either of joy or sorrow to divide
Our fixed wishes!

DUCHESS

        How can the church build faster?
We now are man and wife and 'tis the church
That must but echo this. Maid, stand apart;
I now am blind!

ANTONIO

        What do you mean by this?

DUCHESS

I would have you lead your fortune by the hand
Unto your marriage bed:
(You speak in me in this, for we now are one)
We'll only lie and talk together and plot
To appease my passionate kindred: and if you please,
Lay a naked sword between us, keep us chaste.
Oh let me shroud my blushes in your bosom,
Since 'tis the treasury o' all my secrets!
(*Duchess and Antonio exit*)

CARIOLA

Whether the spirit of greatness or of woman
Reign in her most, I know not, but it shows
A fearful madness. I owe her much of pity.

3

A Room in the Duchess' Palace. Some Months Later.

Enter Bosola with a book. He encounters an old woman.

BOSOLA   And who would you be?
OLD WOMAN   It's not your business, young man.

BOSOLA   So you do not know that I make it my business to
note down address, name and color of hair of all beauties? I
did it from the cradle, lest I run out of opportunities.

OLD WOMAN   Put me on your last page, young man. I am the
last stage of all opportunities. See you at the end, young
man, see you at the end.

(*Exit*)

BOSOLA

I hope not. A mountain of ugliness! And covered in mystery.
We account it ominous
If nature do produce a colt or lamb,
A fawn or goat in any limb resembling
A man and fly from it as a prodigy.
Man stands amazed to see his own deformity
In any other creature but himself.
But in our own flesh, though we bear diseases
Which have their true names only taken from beasts
And the most ulcerous wolf and swinish measle;
Though we are eaten up of lice and worms
And though continually we bear about us
A rotten and dead body, we delight
To hide it with rich tissue. All our fear,
Nay all our terror is lest our physician
Should put us in the ground to be made sweet.
But I have work on foot: I observe our Duchess
Is sick a days, she pukes, her stomach seethes,
The fins of her eyelids look most teeming blue,
She wanes in the cheek and waxes fat in the flank
And, contrary to our Italian fashion,
Wears a loose-bodied gown; there's somewhat in it.
I have a trick may chance discover it—
A pretty one—I have bought some apricots,
The first our spring yields.

(*Enter Antonio*)

ANTONIO (*pointing to book*)   You are studying to become a
great wise fellow?

BOSOLA   Let me be simply honest.

ANTONIO   Who would not be so?

BOSOLA   Oh sir, I look no higher than I can reach. You are
lord of the ascendant, chief man with the Duchess. Search

the heads of the greatest rivers of the world, you shall find
them but bubbles of water. Some would think the souls of
princes were brought forth by some more weighty cause
than those of meaner persons. They are deceived, there's the
same hand to them, the like passions sway them; the same
reason that makes a vicar go to law for a tithe-pig and undo
his neighbors makes them spoil a whole province and batter
down goodly cities with the cannon.

(*Enter Duchess and ladies of her court*)

DUCHESS

Your arm, Antonio: do I now grow fat?
I am exceeding short-winded. Bosola,
I would have you, sir, provide for me a litter,
Such a one as the Duchess of Florence rode in.

BOSOLA

The Duchess used one when she was great with child.

DUCHESS

I think she did.

(*To lady*)

　　　　　　　Come hither, mend my ruff,
Here, when? Thou art such a tedious lady
And thy breath smells of lemon peels—would thou hadst
　　done!
Shall I swoon under thy fingers? I am
So troubled with the vapors!

BOSOLA (*aside*)

　　　　　　　　　I fear too much.

DUCHESS

I have heard you say the French courtiers
Wear their hats on fore the king.

ANTONIO

I have seen it.

DUCHESS

　　　　　In the presence.

ANTONIO

　　　　　　　　Yes.

DUCHESS

Why should we not bring up that fashion?
'Tis ceremony more than duty that consists
In the removing of a piece of felt.

Be you the example to the rest o' th' court.
Put on your hat first.

ANTONIO

You must pardon me.
I have seen in colder countries than in France
Nobles stand bare to the prince: and the distinction
Methought showed reverently.

BOSOLA

I have a present for your grace.

DUCHESS

For me, sir?

BOSOLA

Apricots, madam.

DUCHESS

O sir, where are they?
I have heard of none to year.

BOSOLA *(aside)*

Good, her color rises.

DUCHESS *(as they are brought on)*

Indeed I thank you; they are wondrous fair ones.
What an unskilful fellow is our gardener!
We shall none this month.

BOSOLA *(as she bites into one)*

Will not your grace pare them?

DUCHESS

No, they taste of musk methinks; indeed they do.

BOSOLA

I know not; yet I wish your grace had pared them.

DUCHESS

Why?

BOSOLA

I forgot to tell you the knave gardener,
Only to raise his profit by them sooner,
Did ripen them in horse dung.

DUCHESS

O you jest.

You shall judge. Pray taste one.

ANTONIO

Indeed, madam,

I do not love the fruit.

DUCHESS

        Sir, you are loath
To rob us of our dainties. 'Tis a delicate fruit;
They say they are restorative.

BOSOLA

          'Tis a pretty
Art, this grafting.

DUCHESS

       'Tis so; a bettering of nature.

BOSOLA

To make a pippin grow upon a crab,
A damson on a blackthorn—
(*Aside*)

        How greedily she eats them!
A whirlwind strike off these bawd-farthingales!
For, but for that and the loose-bodied gown,
I should have discovered apparently
The young springball cutting a caper in her belly.

DUCHESS

I thank you, Bosola, they were right good ones,
If they do not make me sick.

ANTONIO

        How now, madam?

DUCHESS

This green fruit and my stomach are not friends—
How they swell me!

BOSOLA (*aside*)

      Nay, you are too much swollen already!

DUCHESS

Oh, I am in an extreme cold sweat!

BOSOLA

        I am very sorry.

DUCHESS

Lights to my chamber! O, good Antonio,
I fear I am undone!
(*Exit with her ladies except Cariola. Bosola follows her*)

ANTONIO

     We are lost, Cariola,
We are lost. I fear me she has fallen in labor.
And there is no time for her remove.

CARIOLA
   I had prepared those ladies to attend her.
   Let us give out that Bosola had poisoned
   Her with those apricots. That will give color
   For her keeping close.

ANTONIO
                    No, no, the physicians
   Will then flock to her. I am lost in amazement.
   I know not what to think on't. Oh we must
   Straightway hit upon some stratagem.
      (*Exeunt*)

   (*Re-enter Bosola*)

BOSOLA   So, so. There's no question but her tetchiness and
   most vulturous eating of the apricots are apparent signs of
   breeding. The experiment worked.
      (*Enter Old Woman with linen over her arm*)
   Now!

OLD WOMAN   Nay, I am in haste.

BOSOLA   Nay, nay, methinks you are in time. Yes, go, give
   your foster daughters good counsel. Tell them the devil
   takes delight to hang at a woman's girdle, like a false and
   rusty watch that she cannot discern how the time passes.
      (*She exits. Enter Antonio and two palace officers*)

ANTONIO
   Shut up the court gates.

FIRST OFFICER
                    Why, sir? What's the danger?

ANTONIO
   Shut up the posterns presently and call
   All the officers of the court.

FIRST OFFICER
                    I shall instantly.
      (*He exits*)

ANTONIO
   Who keeps the keys o' the park gate?

SECOND OFFICER
                    Forobosco.

ANTONIO

Let him bring it presently.

(*Exit*)

(*Enter first officer with servants*)

FIRST SERVANT

Oh, gentlemen o' th' court, the foulest treason!

BOSOLA (*aside*)

If that these apricots should be poisoned now,
Without my knowledge?

FIRST SERVANT   There was taken even now a Switzer in the
Duchess' bed-chamber.

SECOND SERVANT   A Switzer?

FIRST SERVANT   With a pistol in his great codpiece.

BOSOLA   Ha, ha, ha!

FIRST SERVANT   The codpiece was the case for't.

SECOND SERVANT   There was a cunning traitor. Who would
have searched his codpiece?

FIRST SERVANT   True, if he had kept out of the ladies' chambers. And all the moulds of his buttons were leaden bullets.

SECOND SERVANT   Oh wicked cannibal! A firelock in's codpiece!

FIRST SERVANT   'Twas a French plot upon my life.

SECOND SERVANT   To see what the devil can do!

(*Enter Antonio*)

ANTONIO

All the officers here?

SERVANTS

We are.

ANTONIO

Gentlemen,

We have lost much plate, you know, and but this evening
Jewels to the value of four thousand ducats
Are missing in the Duchess' cabinet.
Are the gates shut?

FIRST SERVANT

Yes.

ANTONIO

'Tis the Duchess' pleasure
Each officer be locked into his chamber

Till the sunrising and to send the keys
Of all their chests and of their outward doors
Into her bedchamber. She is very sick.

SECOND OFFICER
At her pleasure.

ANTONIO
                    She entreats you take it not ill. The innocent
Shall be the more approved by it.

BOSOLA (*to servants*)
Gentlemen o' th' woodyard, where's your Switzer now?
(*All exit except Antonio*)

ANTONIO
Fear presents me somewhat that looks like danger.
How superstitiously we mind our evils!
The throwing down salt or crossing of a hare,
Bleeding at the nose, the stumbling of a horse,
Or singing of a cricket are of a power
To daunt the whole man in us.

CARIOLA (*enters with linens over her arm*)
Sir, you are the happy father of a son.
Your wife commends him to you.

ANTONIO
                    Blessed comfort!
For heaven's sake tend her well. I'll presently
Go set a figure for his nativities.

4

The Court of the Palace.

Enter Bosola with a dark lantern.

BOSOLA
Sure I did hear a woman shriek

And the sound came, if I received it right,
From the Duchess' lodgings. There's some stratagem
In the confining all our courtiers
To their several wards. I must have part of it;
My intelligence will freeze else.
It may be 'twas the melancholy bird,
Best friend of silence and of solitariness,
The owl that screamed so. Hah! Antonio?

ANTONIO (*enters with a candle and his sword drawn*)
I heard some noise. Who's there? What art thou? Speak.

BOSOLA
Antonio? Put not your face nor body
To such a forced expression of fear.
I am Bosola, your friend.

ANTONIO
                              Bosola?
(*Aside*)
This mole does undermine me—Heard you not
A noise even now?

BOSOLA
                    From whence?

ANTONIO
From the Duchess' lodging.

BOSOLA
                          Not I. Did you?

ANTONIO
I did or else I dreamed.

BOSOLA
Let's walk towards it.

ANTONIO
                      No; it may be 'twas
But the rising of the wind.

BOSOLA
                        Very likely.
Methinks 'tis very cold and yet you sweat.
You look wildly.

ANTONIO
              I have been setting a figure
For the Duchess' jewels. They are stolen.

BOSOLA

And what have you discovered?

ANTONIO

        What's that to you?
'Tis rather to be questioned what design,
When all men are commanded to their lodgings,
Makes you a night walker?

BOSOLA

       In sooth I'll tell you.
Now all the court's asleep, I thought the devil
Had least to do here. I came to say my prayers.

ANTONIO (*aside*)

I fear this fellow will undo me.
(*To Bosola*)
You gave the Duchess apricots today.
Pray heaven they were not poisoned.

BOSOLA

Poisoned? A Spanish fig
For the imputation.

ANTONIO

      Traitors are ever confident
Till they are discovered. There were jewels stolen, too.
In my belief none are to be suspected
More than yourself.

BOSOLA

     You are a false steward.

ANTONIO

Saucy slave! I'll pull thee up by the roots.
You are an impudent snake indeed, sir.
Are you scarce warm and do you show your sting?
You libel well, sir!

BOSOLA

     Now, sir, copy it out
And I will set my hand to it.

ANTONIO

My nose bleeds.
(*Takes out handkerchief and drops paper as he does so*)
One that were superstitious would count
This ominous, when it merely comes by chance.

Two letters that are wrought here for my name
Are drowned in blood. Mere accident. For you, sir,
I'll take order. This door you pass not.
I do not hold it fit that you come near
The Duchess' lodgings till you have quit yourself.
(*Exits*)

BOSOLA

Antonio here did drop a paper—
(*Raises lantern*)
Some of your help, false friend—Oh, here it is. What's here?
A child's nativity calculated?

> "The Duchess was delivered of a son 'tween the hours
> twelve and one in the night, Anno Dom. 1504."

That's this year—

> "decimo nono Decembris,"

That's this night—

> "Taken according to the meridian of Malfi."

That's our Duchess. Happy discovery!

> "The lord of the first house being in the ascendant signi-
> fies short life; and Mars being in a human sign joined
> to the tail of the Dragon, in the eighth house, doth
> threaten a violent death. Caetera non scrutantur."

Why, now 'tis most apparent this precise fellow
Is the Duchess' pimp. I have it to my wish.
This is news indeed.
Our courtiers were cased up for it. It needs must follow
That I must be committed on pretense
Of poisoning her which I'll endure and laugh at.
If one could find the father now! But that
Time will discover. Let me be dismissed.
I'll bear intelligence of this to the Duke
Shall make his gall overflow his liver.
Though lust do mask in ne'er so strange disguise,
She's oft found witty but is never wise.

CURTAIN

ACT TWO

1

The Duke of Calabria's Tent.

Ferdinand attended by a Negro page who hands him his armor onstage. Offstage a soldier sings.

SOLDIER (*sings song offstage*)
  I wrote my love a letter
  When we entered fair Milan:
  Oh the war will soon be over
  For the cook has lost his coppers
  And the captain's lost his head
  And we've shot away our lead.

FERDINAND
  Methinks this war, like a long winter, hath no end
  And spring, frost-bitten, waits on victory.
  (*To page*)
  My corselet.
  (*Page begins to buckle it on*)
  How now, boy? How fares it with your love?

PAGE   She is well save for the stripes she hath earned from my rival. She hath an eye like a dark lantern for its light is securely hidden.

FERDINAND   'Tis time you rid her of the scurvy knave.

PAGE   How can I? I am so small a thing she cannot see me. 'Tis e'en the same to her an' I had not been born.

FERDINAND   And you born for her!

PAGE   She hath received no intelligence of it. Or mayhap she
puts no credence i' th' stars.

FERDINAND   A tragedy.

PAGE   If she but knew it.

SOLDIER (*entering*)
A gentleman would see the Duke.

FERDINAND
His name?

SOLDIER
Bosola.

FERDINAND
Bosola here? I'll see him.
(*To page*)
Now my beaver.
(*Soldier exits and Bosola enters*)

BOSOLA (*travel-stained and ragged*)   Your Grace.

FERDINAND   How fares the Duchess?

BOSOLA   Sir, I am worn out in your service. 'Tis two years
since I left Malfi. There are rewards for horses and dogs but
for a faithful servant only a sore breech from riding, these
several scars, and scarce enough rags to cover my flesh.

FERDINAND   How fares the Duchess?

BOSOLA   Your Grace, I was pitifully misdirected. I have been
robbed, lain in prison, took sick of the plague and like to
have died only to bring you intelligence shall earn your ingratitude. I am like a raven of ill omen that endures a score
of tempests, twoscore snowstorms, eludes the hawk and the
fowler, to croak a message against which all would stop
their ears. Thus I am very industrious to work my own ruin.

FERDINAND
I said: how fares the Duchess?

BOSOLA
Excellently. She hath a son.
(*Ferdinand stands amazed*)
I said she hath a son.
(*Ferdinand half draws his sword*)

BOSOLA (*quickly hands him a paper*)
Read this nativity. It speaks for me.
(*While Ferdinand reads the paper the soldier sings offstage*)

SOLDIER

But when we left the city
A second war began
Though the first was scarcely over
And I'll drink a thousand beakers
With a whore upon my knee
Till my love again I see.

FERDINAND (*reads*)

The Duchess was delivered of a son . . .
(*Reads on, then speaks slowly*)
Mars joined to the dragon's tail doth prophesy
Short life, a violent death.—Although ere now
I put but little faith i' the stars, this forecast
I'd believe—could I believe thee, lying knave!
(*Suddenly*)
Who is the man?

BOSOLA

I know not.

FERDINAND (*violently*)

Uncase me, slave!
Unmarried then!
(*He begins to tear off his armor. Outside alarms and sounds of battle*)
Ho, send me Delio. He shall command for me. I am off for Malfi.
(*Delio enters. He is bleeding*)

DELIO   Your Highness, the enemy hath surprised us. They fall upon us mightily with a great body of fresh horse. The Duchess' great standard hath been taken.

FERDINAND

No matter.
We give you our command. I am for Malfi.
You shall lead our troops.

DELIO

Alas, I can not.

(*He falls*)

FERDINAND

What's this? Delio's hurt? We are undone!
(*A soldier rushes in*)

SOLDIER
   Sir, you are sorely needed.
   (*Ferdinand snatches up his armor and rushes out buckling
   it on. The sound of battle grows. Ferdinand turns back sud-
   denly and speaks to Bosola*)
FERDINAND
   Thou villain, 'tis false! Thy paper is counterfeit.
   Yet I'll come in a fortnight, depend upon it—
   I'll come shortly. Late or soon I'll come
   And should this bloody war endure ten years
   Or e'en a score of years I'll come thereafter
   And should I fall my vengeful ghost will come
   To set our house in order. Breathe no word of this.
   Meanwhile do you return and this I charge you:
   Find out the father!
   (*He exits clapping his visor shut. All during the end of this
   scene a monotonous trumpet call has been playing outside*)
BOSOLA   What's the matter with him? Why should she not
   bear a son? Her brother steals enough land for five sons. Yet
   the Duke's eyes did start from his head to hear it. 'Twas
   as if a Calabrian knight in Turkey should hear his betrothed
   lies with another and be denied a furlough. Yet all this is
   but policy for a gentleman like him was never in such a
   sweat over less than a dukedom.

2

A Room in the Duchess' Palace. Music.

Enter Antonio and Delio.

ANTONIO
   Beloved Delio! The god of war
   Has taken his time to give me back my friend!

DELIO

    Let me behold your face: it's somewhat leaner.
    Lord Ferdinand has been most eager
    To revisit Malfi and twice made ready
    To return and twice he could not. In the end
    The victory was greater. But how fares
    Your noble Duchess?

ANTONIO

                She is well.

DELIO

                      I think
    You hold your tongue in check. Speak freely.
    I'd say, you look pale.

ANTONIO

    Oh cousin Delio, I fear some great
    Misfortune threatens. Since you saw the Duchess,
    She has had three children, two sons and a daughter.

DELIO

    How? Is she married?

ANTONIO

                No, 'tis all in secret.

DELIO

    But is't known?

ANTONIO

             The rumor spreads apace.

DELIO

    What say the common people?

ANTONIO

                The rabble
    Do directly say she is a strumpet.

DELIO

    And your graver heads; what is their opinion?

ANTONIO

    They are politic and say nothing.

DELIO

    But who, then, is the father?

ANTONIO

    Oh Delio, cousin, I've almost forgotten
    How 't is to have a confidant. My mouth

Has long been locked.
I am the father of her children.

DELIO

Antonio!

ANTONIO

     Tell me, Delio, swiftly,
Hath not this gossip yet arrived to the ear
Of the Lord Ferdinand? For you must know
Both brothers, for reasons best known to themselves,
Will not allow their sister to remarry.

DELIO

You stun me with your news, Antonio.
How very great must be your passion
To dwarf your reason thus. Lord Ferdinand? His bearing
Altered while he tarried in the field. He grew
So quiet towards the end, he seemed to sleep
The tempest out as dormice do in winter.
I could now believe some rumor reached him
For houses that are haunted are most still.

ANTONIO   The banquet is over. Here come the Duchess and
her brother.

3

The Bedchamber of the Duchess.

Enter Duchess, Antonio, Cariola.

DUCHESS

Bring me the casket hither and the glass.
You get no lodging here tonight, my lord.

ANTONIO

Indeed I must persuade one.

DUCHESS

           Very good.
I hope in time 'twill grow into a custom

That husbands shall come with cap and knee
To purchase a night's lodging of their wives.

ANTONIO
I must lie here.

DUCHESS
                    Must? You are lord of misrule.

ANTONIO
Indeed my rule is only in the night.

DUCHESS
To what use will you put me?

ANTONIO
                              We'll sleep together.

DUCHESS
Alas, what pleasure can two lovers find in sleep?

CARIOLA
Good sir, I lie with her often and I know
She'll much disquiet you.

ANTONIO
                          See, you are complained of.

CARIOLA
For she's the sprawlingest bedfellow.

ANTONIO
I shall like her the better for that.

CARIOLA
Sir, shall I ask you a question?

ANTONIO
I pray thee, Cariola.

CARIOLA
Wherefore still when you lie with my lady
Do you rise so early?

ANTONIO
                       Laboring men
Count the clock oftenest, Cariola,
Are glad when their task's ended.

DUCHESS
                            I'll stop your mouth.

(*Kisses him*)

ANTONIO
Nay, that's but one, Venus had two soft doves

To draw her chariot. I must have another.
(*Kisses her again*)
When wilt thou marry, Cariola?

CARIOLA

I wouldn't know. I pray you tell me,
If there were proposed me wisdom, riches and beauty
In three several young men which should I choose?

ANTONIO

'Tis a hard question. This was Paris' case
And he was blind in it and there was great cause
For how was it possible he could judge right,
Having three amorous goddesses in view
And they stark naked?

DUCHESS

If I were to choose 'tween wisdom, riches and beauty,
I'd choose love. Even so, you shall not sleep here.

CARIOLA

'Tis well, for the silkworm is accustomed
To fast every third day and the next following
Spins the better for it.
(*They laugh*)

DUCHESS

I pray thee tell me
When were we so merry? My hair tangles.

ANTONIO (*takes Cariola aside*)

Pray thee, Cariola, let's steal forth the room
And let her talk to herself. I have diverse times
Served her the like when she hath chafed extremely.
I love to see her angry. Softly, Cariola!
(*They tiptoe out*)

DUCHESS

Doth not the color of my hair 'gin to change?
When I wax gray, I shall have all the court
Powder their hair with orris to be like me.
You have cause to love me, I entered you into my heart
(*Enter Ferdinand unseen*)
Before you would vouchsafe to call for the keys.
We shall one day have my brothers take you napping.
Methinks his presence, being now in court,
Should make you keep your own bed. But you'll say

Love mixed with fear is sweetest. I'll assure you
You shall get no more children till my brothers
Consent to be godfathers. Have you lost your tongue?
Or have I angered you? Forgive me, husband,
You shall sleep here. In truth I fear nothing
For I have tasted so much joy that now,
Whether I am doomed to live or die,
I can do both.
(*Ferdinand discloses himself and gives her a poignard*)

FERDINAND

           Die then, quickly.
Virtue, where art thou hid? What hideous thing
Is it that doth eclipse thee?
(*Duchess stands transfixed*)
Or is it true thou art but a bare name
And no essential thing?

DUCHESS

              Sir—

FERDINAND

                 Do not speak.

DUCHESS

                      No sir.

FERDINAND

Oh most imperfect light of human reason
That mak'st us so unhappy to foresee
What we can least prevent! Pursue thy wishes
And glory in them. There's in shame no comfort
But to be past all bounds and sense of shame.

DUCHESS

I pray, sir, hear me. I am married.

FERDINAND

               So!

DUCHESS

Perhaps not to your liking but for that,
Alas, your shears do come untimely now
To clip the bird's wings that's already flown.
Will you see my husband?

FERDINAND

               Yes, if I could change
Eyes with a basilisk.

DUCHESS
                    Sure, you came hither
By his confederacy?

FERDINAND
                              The howling of a wolf
Is music to thee, screech owl—prithee peace.
Whatever thou art that hast enjoyed my sister,
For I am sure you hear me, for thine own sake
Let me not know thee. I came hither prepared
To work thy discovery yet am now persuaded
It would beget such violent effects
As would damn us both. I would not for ten millions
I had beheld thee. Therefore use all means
I never may have knowledge of thy name;
And for thee, vile woman,
If thou do wish thy lecher may grow old
In thy embracements, I would have thee build
Such a room for him as our hermits
To holier use inhabit. Let not the sun
Shine on him till he's dead. Let dogs and monkeys
Only converse with him and such dumb things
To whom nature denies use to sound his name.
If thou do love him, cut out thine own tongue
Lest it betray him.

DUCHESS
                    Why might not I marry?
I have not gone about, in this, to create
Any new world or custom.

FERDINAND
                              Thou art undone.
Thou has ta'en that massy sheet of lead
That hid thy husband's bones and folded it
About my heart.

DUCHESS
                    Mine bleeds for it.

FERDINAND
Thine? Thy heart?
What should I name it unless a hollow bullet
Filled with unquenchable wildfire?

DUCHESS

You are in this
Too strict and, were you not my princely brother,
I would say too wilful. My reputation
Is safe.

FERDINAND

Dost thou know what reputation is?
I'd tell thee—but to no avail since th' instruction
Comes now too late. And so for you I say
You have shook hands with reputation,
He's left you for good. So fare you well.
I will never see you more.

DUCHESS

Why should I,
Of all the other princes of the world
Be cased up like a holy relic? I have youth
And a little beauty.

FERDINAND

So you have some virgins
That are witches. I will never see thee more.
(*Exits*)
(*Enter Antonio with a pistol and Cariola*)

ANTONIO

We are betrayed.
(*To Cariola*)
I should turn
To thee for that.

CARIOLA

But I am innocent.

ANTONIO

How came he hither?

CARIOLA

That gallery gave him entrance.

ANTONIO

I would this terrible thing would come again
That, standing on my guard, I might relate
My warrantable love.
(*Duchess silent*)
There is a weapon, little used but mighty

Even against the mightiest. Let us employ it:
Let us oppose your brother. And against his frenzy
Hold up the Gorgon-head of reason, and make him see:
He strives 'gainst nature who opposes love.

DUCHESS

You must leave me.
I stand as if a mine beneath my feet
Had been blown up.

ANTONIO

Methinks some strange enchantment, sprung
From ties of blood hath bewitch'd thee. You seem
Transfixed and can hear your husband's voice no more.
The great Lord Ferdinand is a mighty warrior, but
I have heard soldiers speak of a brave captain
Who cried: I'm powerless to defend myself, so I'll
Attack. This is my counsel: Let's call the officers
Of your palace, bid them renew their oaths
Of loyalty and attend you closely to prevent
All dark designs upon your person. Having armed
Our arguments with these precautions,
We'll speak with your too hasty brother and unfold
The history of our honorable marriage.
(*Knocking within*)
How now? Who knocks? More earthquakes?

CARIOLA

It is Bosola.

DUCHESS (*to Antonio*)
                    Away! You must instantly part hence.
I have fashioned it already.

ANTONIO (*sadly*)

I would you had given me leave to defend you
As any fishmonger would strike a blow
To shield his dear ones. But do not spare me.
Great adversaries now do menace you,
Let's put an end to strife between us two.
(*Exit Antonio. Enter Bosola*)

BOSOLA

The Duke, your brother, is ta'en up in a whirlwind,
Hath took horse an's rid post to Rome.

DUCHESS

So late?

BOSOLA

He told me, as he mounted into the saddle,
You were undone.

DUCHESS

Indeed I am very near it.

BOSOLA

What's the matter?

DUCHESS

Antonio, master of our household,
Hath dealt so falsely with me in's accounts:
My brother stood engaged with me for money
Ta'en up of certain Neapolitan bankers
And Antonio let the bonds be forfeit.

BOSOLA

Strange! This is cunning.

DUCHESS

And hereupon
My brother's bills at Naples are protested
Against. Call up our officers.

BOSOLA

I shall.

(*He exits*)
(*Antonio enters*)

DUCHESS

The place that you must fly to is Ancona.
'Tis the diocese of my brother, the Lord
Cardinal. Surely he will be merciful
And give us shelter, and even sanctify
Our marriage for we may bribe him.
He is covetous. I'll feign a pilgrimage
To Our Lady of Loretto. We shall meet there.
Hire a house and I'll send after you
My treasure and my jewels. Our weak safety
Runs upon ingenious wheels. Short syllables
Must stand for periods. I must now accuse you
Of such a feigned crime as is a noble lie
Cause it must shield our honors. I'll give out

You have dealt falsely with me in your accounts.

ANTONIO

'Tis a good stratagem. But if I do so—
At your request not fight for you—I fear
That you yourself may learn to scorn me
When I am gone for you'll have many teachers.
Say what you will but stop your ears with wax.

DUCHESS

Dear friend, I'll love no one that hates thee.
Lacking your sweet presence, I'll gaze upon
Your portrait oftener than my looking glass.
Hark, they are coming.
(*Enter Bosola and gentlemen*)

ANTONIO

                    Will your grace hear me?

DUCHESS

I have got well by you, you have yielded me
A million of loss. I am like to inherit
The people's curses for your stewardship.
You had the trick in audit time to be sick
Till I had signed your quietus and that cured you
Without the help of a doctor. Gentlemen,
I would have this man be an example to you all
So you shall hold my favor. Pray observe him,
For he has done that, alas, you would not think of
And, because I intend to be rid of him,
I mean not to publish. Use your fortune elsewhere.

ANTONIO

I am strongly armed to brook my overthrow
As commonly men bear with a hard year.
I will not blame the cause on it but do think
The necessity of my malevolent star
Procures this not her humor. O the inconstant
And rotten ground of service! You may see
'Tis even like him that in a winter night
Takes a long slumber o'er a dying fire,
As loath to part from it, yet parts thence as cold
As when he first sat down.

DUCHESS

                    We do confiscate,

Toward the satisfying of your accounts,
All that you have.

ANTONIO

                    I am all yours and 'tis very fit
All mine should be so.

DUCHESS

                    So, sir, you have your pass.

ANTONIO

You may see, gentlemen, what it is to serve
A prince with body and soul.
(*Exits*)

BOSOLA   Here's an example for extortion; what moisture is drawn out of the sea, when foul weather comes, pours down and runs into the sea again.

DUCHESS   I would know what are your opinions of this Antonio.

SECOND OFFICER   He could not abide to see a pig's head gaping. I thought your grace would find him a Jew.

THIRD OFFICER   I would you had been his officer for your own sake.

FOURTH OFFICER   You would have had more money.

FIRST OFFICER   He stopped his ears with black wool and to those that came to him for money said he was thick of hearing.

SECOND OFFICER   Some said he was a hermaphrodite for he could not abide a woman.

FOURTH OFFICER   And how scurvy proud he would look when the treasury was full! Well, let him go.

FIRST OFFICER   Yes, and the chippings of the buttery fly after him to scour his golden chain.

DUCHESS   Thank you, gentlemen; you may leave now.
(*Exeunt officers. Bosola remains*)
What do you think of these?

BOSOLA

These are rogues that in his prosperity
Would have prostituted their daughters to his lust,
Made their first-born intelligencers; and do these lice
Drop off now!—Alas, poor gentleman!

DUCHESS

Poor! He has amply filled his coffers!

BOSOLA

Sure he was too honest.

DUCHESS

I did not know you were his friend.

BOSOLA

Let me show you what a most unvalued jewel
You have in a wanton humor thrown away,
To bless the man shall find him. He was an excellent
Courtier and most faithful; a soldier that thought it
As beastly to know his own value too little
As devilish to acknowledge it too much.
Hath his virtue and his form deserved a far better fortune;
His breast was filled with all perfection,
And yet it seemed a private whispering room,
It made so little noise of it.

DUCHESS

But he was basely descended.

BOSOLA

Will you make yourself a mercenary herald
Rather to examine men's pedigrees than virtues?
You shall miss him;
For know an honest statesman to a prince
Is like a cedar planted by a spring;
The spring bathes the tree's root, the grateful tree
Rewards it with his shadow. You have not done so.
I would sooner swim to the Bermudas on two politicians'
Rotten bladders, tied together with an intelligencer's heart-
    string
Than depend upon so changeable a prince's favor.
Fare thee well, Antonio! Since the malice of the world
Would needs down with thee, it can not be said yet
That any ill thing happened to thee, considering thy fall
Was accompanied with virtue.

DUCHESS

Oh you render me excellent music!

BOSOLA

Say you?

DUCHESS

This good one that you can speak of is my husband.

BOSOLA

Do I not dream? Can this ambitious age
Have so much goodness in it as to prefer
A man merely for worth, without those shadows
Of wealth and painted honors? Possible?

DUCHESS

I have had three children by him.

BOSOLA

Fortunate lady!
For you have made your private nuptial bed
The humble and fair seminary of peace.
And the neglected poets of your time
In honor of this trophy of a man
Raised by that curious engine your white hand
Shall thank you in your grave for it; and make that
More reverend than all the cabinets
Of living princes. For Antonio,
His fame shall likewise flow from many a pen
When heralds shall want coats to sell to men.

DUCHESS

As I taste comfort in this friendly speech,
So I would find concealment.

BOSOLA

Oh, the secret of my prince,
I'll wear it on the inside of my heart!

DUCHESS

You shall take charge of all my coin and jewels
And follow him for he retires himself to Ancona—

BOSOLA

So?

DUCHESS

Whither within a few days I mean to follow him.
(*Duchess exits*)

BOSOLA

What rests but I reveal all to my lord?
Now for this act I am certain to be raised
And men that paint weeds to the life are praised.

4

A Room in the Cardinal's Palace.

On stage Cardinal and Ferdinand with a letter.

FERDINAND
  She's loose in the hilts;
  Grown a notorious strumpet.

CARDINAL
                    Speak lower.

FERDINAND
                              Lower?
  Read here what's written by my intelligencer.
  A servant, her own steward!

CARDINAL (*reads letter*)
                    Can this be certain?

FERDINAND
  Rhubarb, oh for rhubarb
  To purge this choler! Here's the cursed day
  To prompt my memory and here it shall stick
  Till of her bleeding heart I make a sponge
  To wipe it out.

CARDINAL
            Why do you make yourself
  So wild a tempest?

FERDINAND
                Would I could be one
  That I might toss her palace 'bout her ears,
  Root up her goodly forests, blast her
  And lay her general territory as waste
  As she hath done her honor.

CARDINAL
                    Shall our blood,

The royal blood of Aragon and Castile
Be thus attained?

FERDINAND

                  Apply desperate physic,
We must not now use balsamum but fire,
The smarting cupping glass for that's the means
To purge infected blood, such blood as hers.
There is a kind of pity in mine eye—
I'll give it to my handkerchief and now 'tis here.
I'll bequeath this to her bastards.

CARDINAL

                          What to do?

FERDINAND

Why to make soft lint for their mother's wounds
When I have hewed her to pieces.

CARDINAL

Cursed creature.

FERDINAND

                  Methinks I see her laughing,
Excellent hyena! Talk to me somewhat quickly,
Or my imagination will carry me
To see her in the shameful act of sin
With everyone! With some strong-thighed bargeman!
Or one o' the woodyard that can quoit the sledge
Or toss the bar, or else some lowly squire
That carries coal up to her private lodging!

CARDINAL

You fly beyond your reason.

FERDINAND

                    Go to, mistress!
'Tis not your whore's milk that shall quench my wildfire,
But your whore's blood.

CARDINAL

How idly shows this rage, which carries you
As men conveyed by witches through the air
In violent whirlwinds! This intemperate noise
Fitly resembles deaf men's shrill discourse,
Who talk aloud, thinking all other men
To have their imperfection.

FERDINAND

Have you not
My palsy?

CARDINAL

Yes, but I can be angry
Without this rupture.
(*Looks at letter*)

She will visit Ancona.

FERDINAND
You shall not receive her!

CARDINAL

I will think upon it.

FERDINAND
I could kill her now,
In you or in myself, for I do think
It is some sin in us heaven doth revenge
By her.

CARDINAL

Are you stark mad?

FERDINAND

I would have their bodies
Burnt in a coal pit with the ventages topped
That their cursed smoke might not ascend to heaven;
Or dip the sheets they lie on in pitch of sulphur,
Wrap them in it and then light them like a match;
Or else boil their bastards to a cullice
And give it to their lecherous father to renew
The sin of his back.

CARDINAL (*coldly*)

I'll leave you.

FERDINAND

Nay, I have done.
I am confident that had I been damned in hell
And should have heard of this, it would have put me
Into a cold sweat. In, in! I'll go sleep.
Now that I know who leaps my sister
I'll find scorpions to string my whips
And fix her in a general eclipse!
(*Ferdinand exits*)

5

The Shrine of Our Lady of Loretto in Ancona.

Enter two pilgrims.

FIRST PILGRIM
  We are fortunate our pilgrimage brings us
  Here today. The Cardinal himself conducts
  The service for his sister, the Duchess
  Who hath arrived from Malfi to pay her vow
  At the shrine of Our Lady of Loretto.
SECOND PILGRIM
  She hath much need to pray. 'Tis whispered
  Through all Ancona that she came seeking shelter
  For her steward lover and her bastards.
FIRST PILGRIM
  Is not this a grievous sin in the eyes of the church?
SECOND PILGRIM
  Not if it be performed in the bedchamber
  Of a palace.
FIRST PILGRIM
                Who would have thought
  So great a lady would have matched herself
  Unto so mean a person.
SECOND PILGRIM
                          Nay, lechery
  Is a great equalizer. 'Tis blind to rank.
FIRST PILGRIM
  The ceremony begins.
  (*Sound of organ music and chanting*)
SECOND PILGRIM
  'Tis strange so many monks in yon procession.
FIRST PILGRIM
  Who is that woman, clad like a penitent;
  It seems she hath a man and three small children by her side.

SECOND PILGRIM
  'Tis the Duchess, I saw her
  As she drove along the streets of fair Ancona.

FIRST PILGRIM
  Meseems she's very pale.

SECOND PILGRIM
                    Here comes the Cardinal
  From out the sacristy. What is that parchment
  He carries in his hand?

VOICE OF CARDINAL Herefore, through the authority of the
  Almighty God, Father of Heaven, and His Son, Our Savior,
  I, Cardinal of Ancona, denounce, proclaim and declare
  Angelica Teresa, Duchess of Malfi, and her paramour, Antonio Bologna, together with their children, anathema by
  the avise and assistance of our Holy Father, the pope, and
  all bishops, abbots, priors, and other prelates and ministers
  of our Holy Church, for her open lechery and sins of the
  flesh.

FIRST PILGRIM He hath excommunicated her!

VOICE OF CARDINAL I curse her head and the hairs of her head,
  her eyes, her mouth, her nose, her tongue, her teeth, her
  neck, her shoulders, her breast, her heart, her arms, her
  legs, her back, her stomach, her womb, and every part of
  her body from the top of her head to the soles of her feet.

SECOND PILGRIM There hath been no rumor she was to be
  judged.

FIRST PILGRIM And to think 'twas said she came here for
  sanctuary!

VOICE OF CARDINAL I dissever and part them from the church
  of God and likewise from contracts and oaths of law. I forbid all Christian men to have any company with them and
  all her earthly goods I seize in the name of the Holy
  Church. And as their candles go from our sight so may their
  souls go from the visage of God and their good fame from
  the world.

SECOND PILGRIM
  Then she is no longer Duchess of Malfi!

FIRST PILGRIM
  By what justice hath her brother
  Seized her estates?

SECOND PILGRIM
> Sure I think by none.

FIRST PILGRIM
I have not seen a goodlier ceremony than this
Though I have visited many.

SECOND PILGRIM
What was it with such violence he took
From off her finger?

FIRST PILGRIM
> 'Twas her wedding ring.

6

A Road Near Loretto.

Enter Antonio, Duchess, children, Cariola, servants.

DUCHESS
Banished from Ancona!

ANTONIO
> And what is worse, our love
Is named a sin and published throughout all Italy
That all may shun us and you are ravished of your goods.

DUCHESS
Is all our train shrunk to this poor remainder?

ANTONIO
These poor men which have got little in your service
Vow to take your fortune; but your wiser birds,
Now they are fledged, are gone.

DUCHESS
They have done wisely.

ANTONIO
> Right the fashion of the world.
From decayed fortunes every flatterer shrinks;
Men cease to build where the foundation sinks.

DUCHESS
I had a very strange dream last night.

ANTONIO
   What was it?

DUCHESS
                    Methought I wore my coronet of state
   And on a sudden all the diamonds
   Were changed to pearls.

ANTONIO
                         My interpretation
   Is you'll weep shortly for to me the pearls
   Do signify your tears.

DUCHESS
                    The birds that live in the field
   On the wild benefit of nature, live
   Happier than we for they may choose their mates
   And carol their sweet pleasures to the spring.
   Dear Antonio, I've dragged you into this
   And I am sorry.

ANTONIO
                    You are not the cause.
   For since that hour—scarcely now remembered,
   For 'tis obscured by so much later sorrow—
   When, standing in your chamber, I betrayed
   Plain reason urging me to fight for thee
   And went for cunning stratagems, I have lost
   Myself.
   (*Enter Bosola with a letter*)

BOSOLA
                    You are happily o'ertaken.

DUCHESS
   From my brother?

BOSOLA
   Yes, from the Lord Ferdinand, your brother
   All love and safety.

DUCHESS
                    Thou dost blanch mischief,
   Wouldst make it white.

BOSOLA   His Lordship has had word about the outrageous
   treatment his beloved sister met with at the shrine of Loretto. His Lordship will take it up with the Cardinal.

DUCHESS (*Reads*)   "Dear sister, Why do you not come back
to Malfi? Bring the right worshipful Antonio Bologna with
you. I want his head in a business." Strange words.
(*She shows the letter to Antonio*)

BOSOLA

Strange? Antonio is an upright treasurer.

DUCHESS

He is. I perceive my brother's meaning. (*To Antonio*)
He does not want your counsel, but your head.
That is, he cannot sleep till you are dead.
And here's another pitfall that's strew'd o'er
With roses; mark it, 'tis a cunning one:
(*Reads*)
"I have discharged the Neapolitan bonds and am satisfied
he was falsely accused in this matter. Thus I have made
sure of his honest service to you, my sister. Let not the
money trouble him, I had rather have his heart than his
money."
And I believe so too.

BOSOLA
                          What do you believe?

DUCHESS

That he so much distrusts my husband's love
He will by no means believe his heart is with him
Until he see it: the devil is not cunning enough
To circumvent us in riddles.

BOSOLA
                     Does that mean,
You will reject that noble and free offer?

DUCHESS

Yes.

BOSOLA (*to Antonio*)
        And what from you?

ANTONIO
                    Thus tell him: I will not come.

BOSOLA

This proclaims your breeding.
Every small thing draws a base mind to fear
As the adamant draws iron. Fare you well, sir;

You shall shortly hear from's.
(*Exit*)

DUCHESS

Dear husband,
If the Lord Cardinal treat us so harshly,
I fear my brother Ferdinand still more.
Therefore by all my love I do conjure you
To take our eldest son and fly towards Milan.
Let us not venture all this poor remainder
In one unlucky vessel.

ANTONIO

You counsel safely.
Best of my life, farewell. Since we must part,
Heaven hath a hand in it, but no otherwise
Than as some curious artist takes in sunder
A clock or watch, when it is out of frame,
To bring it to better order.

DUCHESS (*to eldest son*)

I know not which is best,
To see you dead or part with you. Farewell, boy;
Thou art happy that thou hast not understanding
To know thy misery, for all our wit
And reading brings us to a truer sense
Of sorrow.
(*Pause, she draws the boy back*)
No, give me back my son.
He is weak in the lungs. He'll take some harm.
(*To second son*)
Go, thou, with thy father. Alas, thou art so small.
Haply wilt cry for thy mother i' th' night.
Yet thou art stronger and thou hast far to go.
In the eternal church, sir, I hope we do not part thus.

ANTONIO

Do not weep.
Heaven fashioned us of nothing and we strive
To bring ourselves to nothing. Farewell, Cariola,
And thy sweet armful.
(*To the Duchess*)
If I do never see thee more,

Be a good mother to our little ones
And save them from the tiger. Fare you well.

DUCHESS   Let me look upon you once more, for that speech
came from a dying father.
(*Kisses him*)
Fare you well.
(*He goes out with second son*)
My laurel is all withered.

CARIOLA
Look, madam, what a troop of armed men
Make toward us, with their visors closed.
Why do they hide their faces? They are brigands surely.
(*Enter Bosola, helmeted with a guard*)

DUCHESS
O they are very welcome!
I would have my ruin be sudden
I am your adventure, am I not?

BOSOLA
                    You are.

DUCHESS
Come, to what prison.

BOSOLA
                    To none.

DUCHESS
                              Whither, then?

BOSOLA   To your palace. Your brother means you safety.

DUCHESS   Safety! With such safety men preserve alive
Pheasants and quails when they are not fat enough to be
eaten.

BOSOLA   These are your children?

DUCHESS
Yes. And their father is a steward.
They were born accursed.

BOSOLA
                    Fie, madam!
Forget this base, lowborn fellow.

DUCHESS
                              Were I a man,
I'd beat that counterfeit face into thy other.

SON

My father is not lowborn, he is great.

CARIOLA

Do not speak.

DUCHESS

Why not?
I prithee, who is greatest? Can you tell?
Sad tales befit my woe: I'll tell you one.
A salmon, as she swam unto the sea,
Met with a dog-fish, who encounters her
With this rough language: "Why art thou so bold
To mix thyself with our higher state of floods,
Being no eminent courtier, but one
That for the calmest and fresh time o' th' year
Dost live in shallow rivers, rank'st thyself
With silly smelts and shrimps? And darest thou
Pass by our dog-ship without reference?"
"Oh," quoth the salmon, "sister, be at peace:
Thank God we both have passed the net!
Our value never can be truly known,
Till in the fisher's basket we be shown:
I' th' market then my price may be the higher,
Even when I am nearest to the cook and fire.
So to great men the moral may be stretched;
Men oft are valu'd high, when they're most wretched."—
But come, whither you please. I am arm'd 'gainst misery;
Bent to all ways of the oppressor's will.
There's no deep valley but near some great hill.

(*Exeunt*)

ACT THREE

1

A Room in the Cardinal's Palace.

The Cardinal is reading a book. A monk sits near him telling his beads.

CARDINAL
  I am puzzled in a question about hell.
  (*Looks at book*)
  He says in hell there's one material flame
  And yet shall not burn all men alike.
  Let him by.
  (*Closes book*)
            How tedious is a guilty conscience!
  When I look into the fish pond in my garden,
  Methinks I see a thing armed with a rake
  That seems to strike at me.
  (*Enter Ferdinand and his Negro page with two swords*)
                          How, now, Ferdinand!
  Thou lookst ghastly.
  There sits in thy face some great determination.
  What is it?
FERDINAND
            I am come to punish thee.
  Call your collegium!
CARDINAL
                    Collegium? What for?
FERDINAND
  'Cause you have published our sister's shame

And publicly dishonored her. And I demand
that now in midst of your collegium
You publicly recant your accusations
in thy dome of Loretto.

CARDINAL

                              Hast thou gone mad, brother?
Thou thyself didst rage against her most
Intemperately. 'Twas you did call her strumpet.

FERDINAND

I did. But not i' th' market place.
You have so wrought it that the rabble shall soil
Her charms in the tavern and in the baths.
They'll reckon whether her breasts be large or small.
For this you shall pay in full.

CARDINAL

                              Shall you defend her?

FERDINAND

I shall defend and I shall punish her.

CARDINAL

These are strange words indeed. Why should our sister be
More your concern than mine? As if she were
A rotten tooth in your mouth and not in mine?
Now in her lamentable cause
'Twas not I but my holy office did constrain me:
She has sinned.

FERDINAND

                  I think your purse constrained you.
You have stolen her lands!

CARDINAL

I see what irks you. Pray hold your temper
And I will faithfully divide revenues with you.

FERDINAND

Thy prayers and proffers are both unseasonable.
Call your collegium.

CARDINAL

                  In the midst of night?

FERDINAND

Repentance must not wait for sunrise. And
Confessions are worked out best in these quiet

Last hours of the night, and, brother, confess you shall
That thou hast falsely indicted the Duchess of Malfi,
Our sister, out of greed.

CARDINAL

Now you are mad indeed.

FERDINAND

And you will do more. You will ask the pope to lift
That crooked ban from off her shoulders and you will re-
store the duchy
And all her rich estates to our sister.
And if you will not do so, I shall kill you.

CARDINAL

That means extortion and I will not stand for't.

FERDINAND

It means extortion and you will stand for't,
Recant or take this sword and draw.
(*He throws one sword upon him and takes the other*)

CARDINAL

I am a churchman. And I will not fight.
(*Holds up the book like a sword*)
This holy book is my defense. Pierce it and thou darest.
(*Ferdinand strikes it aside with his sword*)

FERDINAND

Will you fight or die like a poltroon?
(*He attacks the Cardinal*)

CARDINAL (*leaping up and snatching sword*)

Help!—Help!—Our guard!

MONK

Ho, guards! Guards!

FERDINAND

You are deceived.

They are out of reach of your howling!
Recant or die!

CARDINAL

I'll not recant.

FERDINAND

Die then!
(*Ferdinand wounds the Cardinal. The Cardinal drops his
sword*)

CARDINAL
   Thou hast hurt me!
FERDINAND
                    Not enough.
   (*Drives him back and stabs him*)
CARDINAL
                             Oh justice! I am done.
   I suffer now for what hath former been;
   Sorrow is held the eldest child of sin.
   (*He dies*)

2

A Ruin near Milan.

*Enter Antonio and his son. They hold their cloaks close
against them as if walking against the wind.*

ANTONIO
   Yonder lie the ruins of a noble abbey.
   When'er we tread upon these ancient stones
   We set our foot upon some reverend history.
   Here in this open court that now lies naked
   To the injuries of the stormy weather
   Some men lie interred who loved the church so well
   And gave so largely to it,
   They thought it should have canopied their bones
   Till doomsday. But all things have their end.
   Churches and cities, which have diseases like to men,
   Must have like death that we have. Come, boy, we must
      make haste,
   Until we reach Milan.
BOY
   Why can't we stay with mother?

ANTONIO

  We are too small to live with greatness.
  Our littleness is crushed between the millstones
  Of their intemperate actions.

BOY

  Shall we not see her more?

ECHO

                        Not see her more.

BOY

  Oh hark to the pretty echo from the ruin!

ECHO

  Ruin!

ANTONIO

      Two hundred steps, no more, will bring us, son,
  To the dreary valley's end, where you will see
  The towers of Milan.
  Poor boy, well do I know your feet are blistered
  Yet we must fly from danger. Do not stay!

ECHO

  Do not stay!

BOY

        If we run fast, father, think you we will yet die?

ECHO

  Yet die.

BOY

      What does the echo say?

ANTONIO

  It seems to tell us, boy, what is the fate
  Of him who is forbid to fight. Alas
  Now I remember once, ahawking with my father
  Upon the plains of Brittany, our falcon
  Spied a hare and coursed it till the poor beast
  Was wearied unto death and so, despairing
  Turned upon its back and with its stony feet
  Hardened by a whole life of timid flight
  Beat in the falcon's breast. Yet we must fly.
  Although you'll find it to no avail to fly your fate.

ECHO

  O fly your fate!

3

A Room in the Duchess' Palace.

Enter Ferdinand and Bosola.

FERDINAND
How doth our sister Duchess bear herself
In her imprisonment?
BOSOLA
                    Nobly: I'll describe her
She's sad as one long used to it and she seems
Rather to welcome the end of misery
Than shun it; a behavior so noble
As gives a majesty to adversity.
You may discern the shape of loveliness
More perfect in her tears than in her smiles.
She will muse for hours.
FERDINAND
Her melancholy seems to be fortified
With a strange disdain.
BOSOLA
                    'Tis so and this restraint,
Like English mastiffs that grow fierce with tying,
Makes her too passionately apprehend
Those pleasures she is kept from.
FERDINAND
                                Curse upon her!
Doth she inquire for her steward-husband and her cubs?
BOSOLA
Call them her children.
For though our national law distinguishes bastards
From true legitimate issue, compassionate nature
Makes them all equal.
FERDINAND
                    Doth she weep for them?

BOSOLA

Aye, for she is ignorant if they be safe or no.

FERDINAND

She shall learn. Bring her my gift.
She shall be distracted from her sorrow.
Unseen I'll mark how deeply her lecherous sin
Is rooted in her mind.
(*Ferdinand hides upon the balcony. Duchess and attendants
and Cariola enter*)

BOSOLA

All comfort to your grace!

DUCHESS

I will have none.
Prithee why dost thou wrap thy poisoned pills
In gold and sugar?

BOSOLA

Your brother,
The Lord Ferdinand, is come to visit you.
In proof that he hath sealed his peace with you, meanwhile;
For your diversion and to cure you
Of your melancholy study of what's past,
The Lord Ferdinand presents you with a rare
And precious gift.

DUCHESS

It is not gifts I'd have
My brother send me. The noblest boon within
His power to grant is friendship to my friends.

BOSOLA

Bring on the gift.

DUCHESS (*to Cariola*)

Methinks I hardly know my brother now
Yet once he loved me well.
(*The servants bring on a huge carved chest. They are
preceded by a flute-player playing on his instrument*)

BOSOLA

Here is the key.

CARIOLA

'Tis a costly gift.

DUCHESS

Set it in my bedchamber.

BOSOLA

There's more within.

DUCHESS

Do I open it?

BOSOLA

Aye.

(*She slowly goes to it, unlocks the doors. The bodies of Antonio and her child fall out. Cariola screams. Duchess stands frozen with horror*)

Your brother does present you this sad spectacle
That, now you know directly they are dead,
Hereafter you may wisely cease to grieve
For that which can not be recovered.

(*The Duchess faints. Flautist suddenly perceives what has happened and stops abruptly. Bosola raises Duchess*)

Come, you must live!

(*They try to revive her*)

Remember you are a Christian!
Leave this vain sorrow!
Things being at their worst begin to mend.
The bee when he has shot his sting into your hand
May then play with your eyelid.

CARIOLA

Good comfortable fellow,
Persuade a wretch that's broke upon the wheel
To have all his bones new set!

(*The Duchess faints again*)

My lady! Help! No, don't recall her spirits yet.
This faint is charitable. Help me carry her to her room!

FERDINAND (*from the gallery*)

She is lost! I can not save her.

BOSOLA

Why do you do this?
She hath suffered much.

FERDINAND (*coming down*)

Base varlet, there's too much pity in thy pleading!

BOSOLA

Sir, I have served you well. I have rather sought
To appear true than honest. I swear to you
She hath had eyes for no one but her husband.
Faith, end here. And go no further in your cruelty.
Pray, furnish her with beads and prayer book
And let her save her soul.

FERDINAND

                    Damn her, that body of hers,
While that my blood ran pure in it, was worth more
Than that thing which thou wouldst comfort, called a soul.
I see her sin sits deeper than I thought.
To this vile appetite for her own steward
She now adds shameful tears and mourns his death
And in her lecherous grief she naked stands,
The widow of a sweaty stableboy.
To cure such maladies the surgeon's knife
Must cut until it pricks the patient's life.
Your work is almost done.

4

The Courtyard of the Duchess' Castle.

Enter Delio, a physician, and Ferdinand's Negro page.

DELIO

I, Delio Bologna,
Cousin to the late Antonio Bologna
Who was husband to the former Duchess of this realm,
—She, as you know, is kept prisoner within these walls—
I hire you to examine His Lordship, the Duke Ferdinand,
Now lawless ruler of his sister's duchy,
Since of his state of mind the most extraordinary
And damnable rumors shake the ear.

PHYSICIAN

Is the Duke of a melancholy or choleric humor?

DELIO

Here the Duke's page will tell you all he knows.

PAGE

He oft hath had these violent fits of late.

DELIO

On the morrow of his brother, the Cardinal's, strange
And sudden death, this boy found him
All in a cold sweat and altered much in face
And language.

PAGE

Since when he hath grown worse and worse
And yet, at times, he seems himself again.

PHYSICIAN

What other symptoms
Doth his disposition show?

DELIO

One met the Duke 'bout midnight in a lane
Behind St. Mark's church.
And he howled fearfully,
Said he was a wolf, only the difference
Was a wolf's skin was hairy on the outside,
His on the inside, bade them take their swords
Rip up his flesh and try.
Does it not seem a fearful madness?

PHYSICIAN

Let me hear more. I must sound the depths
Of his distraction.

PAGE Once I did ask him why he loved solitariness. And he
replied that eagles commonly fly alone. They are doves,
crows, and starlings that flock together. And on a sudden
he started most fearfully and cried "What follows me?"
And then he flung himself upon the ground and said he
would throttle his shadow.

PHYSICIAN 'Tis most grave.

PAGE Straightway he sprung up violently and stared about
him and cried out, "Rogues, knaves, bawds! Oh the world
is sick. I think only the cold tomb can cure it. Blood's the
potion for this disease." Then he laughed horribly. Then

he drew his sword, howling, "Hence, hence! There's nothing left of you but tongue and belly, flattery and lechery!" And all must flee before him.

PHYSICIAN   This seems madness indeed.

DELIO (*to the page*)   And what of the book?

PAGE

The Lord Ferdinand did inquire concerning
A certain apothecary who 'tis whispered
Poisoned his mistress with a book.

DELIO

I like it not. I do fear for the Duchess.
So, while you try sound out the Duke, I'll make
Haste to Cortezza there to gather troops and officers
With whom I am popular since the Cyprian war
And who, I know, are loyal to the Duchess.
With them and with your expert statement, I will
Arrest the Duke and boldly free the Duchess.
God's speed! I will be back by daybreak.
(*Exeunt*)

5

A Room in the Duchess' Palace.

Onstage, Duchess and Cariola.

CARIOLA

What think you of, madam?

DUCHESS

Of nothing.
When I muse thus, I sleep.

CARIOLA

Like a madman with your eyes open?

DUCHESS

Dost thou think we shall know one another
In the other world?

CARIOLA
                    Yes, out of question.
DUCHESS
  Oh that it were possible we might but hold
  Some two days' conference with the dead!
  From them I should learn somewhat, I am sure,
  I never shall know here.
  What make you of my brother's rage, Cariola?
CARIOLA
  He did not like Antonio for your husband.
  But you must not think so much.
DUCHESS
                    Ay, I must.
  It's not like him
  As I remember him. When we were children
  Playing lovers in the park, cutting each other's
  Throats with the wooden knives, Ferdinand never was
  The highborn rightful groom, but always was
  The outlaw highwayman, the brigand dragging
  Me from some princely altar. He bore
  No pride in his birth. So, why he rages thus,
  Against mild-mannered Antonio, my husband,
  I can not tell.
  (*Enter Bosola*)
BOSOLA
  All comfort to your grace!
DUCHESS
                    I will have none.
BOSOLA
  Come, madam, be of cheer, I'll save your life.
DUCHESS
  Indeed, I have no leisure to tend so small a business.
BOSOLA
  Now, by my life, I pity you.
DUCHESS
                    Thou art a fool then
  To waste thy pity on a thing so wretched
  As can not pity itself. Knave, tell my brothers

That I perceive death, now I am well awake,
Best gift that they can give or I can take.

BOSOLA

Does not death fright you?

DUCHESS

                 Who would be afraid on't,
Knowing to meet such excellent company
In th' other world?

BOSOLA

             Come, you must live.
Who speaks of death? Surely your brother
Would have you live, my lady. He thinks of naught
Save your welfare and desires of you
But one thing, that you should swear
Upon this prayer book never to marry again.
Here is the book and you must kiss it.

DUCHESS

This were easily done. My heart is but
A dead piece of flesh and there is not
'Twixt heaven and earth one wish I'd stay for now.
Only I have two children still. Will not
My brother come and cut their throats?

BOSOLA

Can they prattle?

DUCHESS

        Yes.

BOSOLA   Then he can not call them young wolves. Anyway, he
should consider it a deal without more bargaining. This oath
will satisfy your brother. Kiss the book.

DUCHESS

If it is so
I'll swear it gladly I'll never marry.
Because I hope to meet my husband soon
In heaven, where my brothers can not interfere
With our pleasures. For they'll howl in hell.
To this I swear and kiss the book. Amen.
(*Kisses the book*)

BOSOLA

By this he doth make sure you shall not break your oath.

DUCHESS

What more?

BOSOLA

Your brother, the Lord Duke,
Now you have brought to rest his mind in this
Most deplorable case, wants to restore to you
What never should be taken away, your duchy.
(*Noise from outside; drums and marching*)

CARIOLA

My lady, you are free!

FIRST WOMAN (*at the window*)

The palace guard that held my lady prisoner
Is marching off.

SECOND WOMAN

And her standard flies once more
From the tower.

BOSOLA

Please don your ducal robes, my lady.
(*Four waiting women enter bringing robes of state and coronet*)

Please, be robed.

CARIOLA

My lady, can you stand?

DUCHESS

What matter? I'll tell thee a miracle:
I am not mad yet, to my cause of sorrow.
I am full of daggers, yet I am not mad.
What noise is that?
(*Bells. A priest has entered. He reads a Latin proclamation lifting the excommunication and restoring her estates*)

DUCHESS

What means this?

BOSOLA   At the instigation of the Duke, your brother,
The pope has revoked your excommunication
And restored your estates.

DUCHESS

Can this mean, the Holy Church's
Ban is lifted from me and mine?

BOSOLA

'Tis so.

DUCHESS

And my authority restored?

BOSOLA

You are Duchess of Malfi once more.
(*He bows. Exit priest*)

DUCHESS

What says the Cardinal to this?

BOSOLA

                    Corpses do not speak.

DUCHESS

Ay, but what says the Cardinal?

BOSOLA

His holiness, the Lord Cardinal, prince of Ancona, is dead.

DUCHESS

                    Dead?

BOSOLA

                    The Lord Ferdinand
Would not forgive his publishing of your
Misfortunes.

DUCHESS

            Bosola, is my brother mad?

BOSOLA

Only in what concerns you.

DUCHESS

My brother, slain by my brother.

BOSOLA

Executed.
Your brother, the Lord Duke, will visit you shortly
And kiss your hand and reconcile himself.
(*Exit. The Duchess stands, frozen*)

CARIOLA

My lady, do not grieve so deeply at your brother's
Violent death.

DUCHESS

            I can not grieve.
I have wept my tears. Forgive me if I do not mourn
As would be natural or seemly. Far more
Am I concerned for my brother Ferdinand,
And his coming hither.
If but this drowsiness did not weigh

So heavily upon me. But I must act
And speedily, now I am reinstated,
To defend the living and to bury my dead.
For, now the ban is lifted, I may pick them
From the dunghill and lay them
In consecrated ground and I'll prepare
A princely funeral for my beloved Antonio and my son
And in my widow's weeds I'll walk behind
Their coffins i' th' teeth of all the world.
Teresa, go fetch my children. 'Tis my wish
That they be clad in seemly fashion
To mourn their father. But since I am to meet
A perilous guest to whom the aspect
Of my children may not be pleasing, prithee,
Mariana, seek out the captain of my guard.
Bid him come hither with a score
Of armed men. And since the guest
Comes to forgive me, offering his hand,
—Alas, dripping with blood—and since I myself
Can not forgive him, fetch me from my chamber the poi-
    gnard,
Once given me by my most capricious brother:
May thus the tiger meet his sister tigress.

CARIOLA
My lady, I rejoice to see you thus determined.

DUCHESS
Yet I can scarcely stand, Cariola. And
One question goes round in my poor head
For which I have no good answer: Why
Did he kill his own brother? Because
He insulted and robbed me?

CARIOLA
                            That is right.
I marvel greatly he hath taken your part.
'Tis clear he hates you.

DUCHESS
                    Oh Cariola,
I wish I could myself think over it
In such a simple way. Alas, I can not.

My mind is full of shadows. There are wondrous
Questions from early times and half forgot,
And never answered,
Which do concern my brother Ferdinand.

CARIOLA
My lady, you look pale.

DUCHESS
          Methinks I do begin
To know somewhat I never knew before.
O my poor brother! Cariola, there are sins
With deeper roots than hate.

CARIOLA
              My lady, you are sick.
Such thoughts are bred of sickness.
When you are sound again, they'll fly out by the window.

DUCHESS
Ay, and I grow sicker, Cariola. Let me be seated.
I think I must die shortly.

CARIOLA
'Tis a denial of God's mercy to speak so.

DUCHESS
My legs grow numb. 'Tis not pain I feel, yet my foot
Seems to be sleeping.

CARIOLA Surely you have eaten somewhat that sits ill upon
your stomach. I will chafe your legs. My lady, you are cold.
(*Suddenly as she kneels to do so*)
The book you kissed! 'Twas the book! Villains! Poisoners!
Murderers!

DUCHESS
          My oath!

CARIOLA
The oath! He has made sure you will not break it!
(*To the women*)
My lady is stricken. Cry out for help!

DUCHESS
What witchcraft does he practice?

CARIOLA (*as other waiting women rush on*)
Heat water. Fetch some cordial.
The Duke has done this. Fetch water, wine.

My lady is poisoned. Quickly seek a doctor!

DUCHESS

There is none for me. My sickness is mortal.
Methinks I know his secret now. Methinks
I do perceive the cause of this enforcing
Of my chastity and more.

CARIOLA

What speak you, madam?

DUCHESS

This feverish law, put o'er me not to marry,
This spying on me! This tearing off my sheets!
This present in the chest!
And this distracted slaughter of his brother
Who bared my woes in public. All this fury,
His cruelty and his despair! And now the poison
To punish me 'cause I had shared my bed.
'Tis but a fever, unknown to a brother,
'Tis but a fever only lover knows.
Alas, my brother!
He has no friend but death to do his wooing.

CARIOLA

Pray, drink this cordial.

DUCHESS

To what end?
Nay, give it to me for I must live until
My brother comes that I may speak to him
And tell him what I know.
For I do feel such pity with the man
That all is washed away, the ruin he has wrought
My sorrow and his own. Alas
I am so weary I would rest a while.

CARIOLA

No, no, my lady,
From this slumbrous poison no one wakes again.

DUCHESS

Why then I must not sleep. Help me, Cariola.
Let's walk and never let me rest. Thy promise!
I must not die before I meet my brother.
(*She is helped up and begins to walk about, supported by*

Cariola and the weeping women)
Let someone watch to tell me if the Duke be come.
Make haste. My time is short.
(*Women go to the window to watch*)

                Do not weep so loud.
I'm not deaf yet and this noise distracts me.
(*To Cariola*)
I pray thou givest up my little boy
Some syrup for his cold and let the girl
Say her prayers ere she sleep. But I must walk
And when I falter, do thou urge me on. Cry loudly
In my ear: "His soul is lost because he loved you so!"
Oh, I grow giddy.

CARIOLA

            Lean on me, my lady.

DUCHESS

Now all the coldness
Of this too icy world creeps in about my heart.
My brother is too slow. Tell him, I could not wait.
(*She dies. Women wail. One of the women rushes out.
Shouting from outside, then drums*)
(*Enter Bosola with executioners*)

BOSOLA

Some other strangle the children.
(*Two of the executioners leave*)

CARIOLA

               Oh, you are damn'd
Perpetually for this! My turn is next;
Is't not so ordered?

BOSOLA

            Yes, and I am glad
You are so well prepar'd for't.

CARIOLA

            You are deceived, sir,
I am not prepar'd for't, I will not die;
I will first come to my trial, and know
How I have offended.

BOSOLA

         Come, dispatch her,—

You kept her counsel; now you shall keep ours.

CARIOLA

I will not die, I must not, I am contracted
To a young gentleman.

BOSOLA

Here's your wedding ring.

CARIOLA

Let me but speak with the Duke: I'll discover
Treason to his person.

BOSOLA

Delays:—throttle her.

FIRST EXECUTIONER

She bites and scratches.

CARIOLA

If you kill me now
I am damn'd; I have not been at confession
This two years.

BOSOLA (*to executioner*)

When!

CARIOLA

I am quick with child.

BOSOLA

Why, then,
Your credit's saved.
(*They strangle Cariola*)
Bear her into the next room.
(*He points to the Duchess*)
Let this lie still.
(*Drumming stops. Enter Ferdinand*)

FERDINAND

Is she dead?

BOSOLA

She is what
You'd have her. Fix your eye here.

FERDINAND

Constantly.

BOSOLA

Do you not weep?
Other sins only speak; murder shrieks out.

The element of water moistens the earth,
But blood flies upwards and bedews the heavens.

FERDINAND

Cover her face; mine eyes dazzle: she died young.

BOSOLA

I think not so. Her infelicity
Seemed to have years too many.

FERDINAND

She and I were twins. She was born some minutes
After me and died some minutes sooner.
Let me see her face again.
(*To Bosola*)
Why didst thou not pity her? What
An excellent honest man mightst thou have been,
If thou hadst borne her to some sanctuary!
Or, bold in a good cause,—oppos'd thyself
Between her innocence and my revenge!
I bade thee, when I was distracted of my wits,
Go kill my dearest friend, and thou hast done't.
For let me but examine well the cause:
Her marriage that drew a stream of gall quite through my
    heart.
Of course, I must confess, I had a hope,
Had she continued widow, to have gain'd
An infinite mass of treasure by her death.
This has an evil sound yet not so evil
As some other reason I'll not speak of.
We'll say the cause was my ungoverned passion,
My cruelty and spite. Only I fear
It is not true.
(*To Bosola*)
                As to thee, I hate thee for it.
Get thee into some unknown part of the world
That I may never see thee.

BOSOLA

Sir! Let me quicken your memory, for I
Perceive you are falling into ingratitude.
I challenge the reward due to my service.

FERDINAND (*more and more provocatively*)
  I'll tell thee what I'll give thee: a rope.
  And thou shalt hang.

BOSOLA
                    Ha!

FERDINAND
  Ay. Like a bloody fool thou'st forfeited thy life
  And thou shalt die.

BOSOLA
  Is that my pension, scoundrel?
  Draw then or have thy payment too.
  (*Ferdinand does not move. Bosola wounds him*)

FERDINAND
  That was mortal.
  Thou hast done much ill well.
  My sister, oh my sister!
  Here is the cause on it.
  (*He dies*)

BOSOLA (*unbelieving*)
  Didst thou not fight?
  Methinks, I was thy tool in this once more.
  That was the purpose and thy cunning wit
  That I should kill thee, and I did.

6

The Courtyard of the Duchess' Castle.

Enter Captain, Delio, with Duchess' eldest son and soldiers.

DELIO
  Where is the Duchess?
  (*Soldiers come out of the palace, dragging with them
  Bosola*)

SOLDIER

The Duchess of Malfi lies within
Murdered by her brother, the Lord Ferdinand,
Slain by this knave.

BOSOLA

'Twas more a deed of mercy
Done by a fool unwittingly for nothing.
I served his tyranny, and rather strove
To satisfy him than all the world, believe me, sirs.
For though I loath'd the evil, yet I lov'd
Him that did counsel it.

DELIO

'Twas him that slew my cousin too.
His measure is full—
Let him be hanged.

BOSOLA

Dear sir, my estate is sunk
Below the degree of fear.
Let worthy minds ne'er stagger in distrust
To suffer death or shame for what is just:
Mine is another voyage.
(*A soldier leads him out*)

CAPTAIN

Good Delio, we come too late.

DELIO

Did you find the Duchess' little daughter?

SOLDIER

Alas—but dead.

DELIO

Thus of this mighty family remains
This child, dragged out of the tumult by a servant.
These wretched eminent things
Leave no more fame behind 'em, than should one
Fall in a frost, and leave his print in snow;
As soon as the sun shines, it ever melts,
Both form and matter.—Let's make noble use
Of this great ruin and join all our force
To establish this young and hopeful gentleman
In his mother's right.

CAPTAIN

> Yet I have heard
> He is not wholly of noble birth?

DELIO

> An idle rumor,
> As ill founded as all which has befallen those
> Within these ancient and too firmly mortared walls.
> And, were it true, if here should spring
> A new shoot from a hundred-years-old tree
> Whose trunk too long hath twined upon itself
> It were a hopeful portent. Let us now
> Convey to bury these unhappy brethren.
> From hidden causes their misfortunes grow;
> We'll pity when the cause we can not know.

Epilogue

DELIO

> May these deaths enacted here
> Purge by pity and by fear
> Till each chastened conscience be
> From all fatal passions free.
> Hidden hatreds, loves obscure
> Fevers living could not cure
> Pride and jealousy and lust
> Ruined these to squandered dust.
> Here their greatness ended: May
> This portent teach us to survey
> Our progression from our birth.
> We are set, we grow, we turn to earth
> Courts adieu and all delights
> All bewitching appetites!
> Sweetest breath and clearest eye
> Like perfumes go out and die,
> Praise and conversation

Fall silent as we die alone.
Vain the ambition of kings
Who seek by trophies and dead things
To leave a living name behind
And weave but nets to catch the wind.

Notes and Variants

Texts by Brecht

Brecht's version of Webster's *Duchess of Malfi*

1. Backed by his brother the Cardinal, the Duke of Aragon, prior to going to war on her behalf, forbids his widowed sister ever to remarry, and places a spy in her household.
2. Hardly has her brother left than the Duchess tells her steward that she loves him, and they go to bed.
3. The spy discovers this when she becomes pregnant, and he sends a letter to the Duke.
4. The Duke gets the letter just before a battle. Confused by the idea of having to hurry back, he fights badly and is taken prisoner. (Deviation.)
5. After spending some years in captivity the Duke returns and finds that his sister has remarried. He bombards her with threats. The Duchess turns down the steward's offer to fight for her, seeing this as an interference in her dispute with her princely brother; she decides to take refuge with her brother the Cardinal. (Deviation.) Nonetheless she is moved to confide her plan to the spy by his praise for her beloved.
6. The Duke denounces his sister to the Cardinal as a whore. The Cardinal decides to excommunicate her and confiscate her duchy. He recommends a cooler approach to his brother, whose passion astounds him.
7. Having fled to the Cardinal, the Duchess and her family are excommunicated by him and banished.
8. Fleeing once more, and free as a bird, the Duchess comes to realize that her brother the Cardinal acted out of avarice, but fails to understand the Duke and his motives. A letter from him shows her what a deadly hatred he bears her husband, and she sends the latter ahead with one of the children. She is arrested. (The Duchess' uncertainty about the Duke is a deviation.)

9. In his flight the steward complains to his young son about the fate of those who let themselves be persuaded not to fight. (Deviation.)

10. The Duke has the dead bodies of her husband and little son shown to the Duchess. Deeply wounded by her despair, he decides to use the surgical knife to cut deeper. (Deviation.)

11. On seeing her executioners, the Duchess realizes that her brother's pronouncement of the death sentence is a declaration of love, and expresses her sympathy with him. Over her coffin the Duke threatens the executioner for having put his sentence into effect. (The Duchess' realization, a deviation.)

12. Arriving posthaste after hearing of the Duchess' murder, the Cardinal finds the Duke close to madness. During a memorial service organized by the Duke, the Cardinal, to stop him blaming himself, reminds him that the Duchess was no better than a whore, and the Duke kills him for the insult. He in turn is killed by his lieutenant, who has provoked his hostility by a cynical remark. (Deviation.)

[BBA 500/47–49, original in German.]

How *The Duchess of Malfi* ought to be performed

The model to be followed is the Broadway musical which, thanks to certain fiercely competing groups composed of speculators, popular stars, good scene designers, bad composers, witty if second-rate song writers, inspired costumiers, and truly modern dance directors, has become the authentic expression of all that is American. Alienation effects are extensively used by the designers and dance directors, the latter deriving theirs from folklore. The painted backdrops which constitute the main scenery reflect the influence of modern painting, including good surrealist ideas. In the dance numbers, some of them intelligently worked-out mimes, one now and again finds gestic elements of the epic theater. The plot is strongly outlined and provides a sturdy scaffolding for the various insertions.

Unless the groupings in *Malfi* have as much meaning as the dispositions in a musical, and the delivery of the verse arias the . . . .

> [From *Schriften zum Theater* 4, p. 196. The typescript ends thus at the foot of a page so that it is not clear if Brecht left it unfinished or if the rest has been lost.]

Letter to Paul Czinner

Dear Dr. Czinner,

Herewith a few points as to essential alterations.

1. The lighting needs to be much brighter, since long passages spoken in verse are virtually unintelligible.

2. The grouping of the actors should at least be changed so as to prevent them having to deliver scarcely intelligible (and sometimes imperfectly spoken) passages with their backs to the audience.

3. It is essential to return to the adaptation provided by Auden and myself. No cuts should be made without the agreement of both of us. Nor should additional passages from Webster be introduced without our being consulted, since the adaptation consists in a series of carefully considered cuts which were thoroughly and frequently discussed with Elisabeth Bergner, who approved them.

4. Not enough thought has been given to the casting of Ferdinand, as Elisabeth herself says. What is more, the director's conception of the part is a wrong one, as you and Elisabeth both say—so wrong as effectively to obscure and distort the whole sense of the play. You must engage a different Ferdinand.

5. Almost every scene needs to be redirected so as to make the story intelligible to the audience. I suggest that for this you should engage a fresh director. The present director has ignored the adaptation and seems quite incapable of directing in such a way as to allow the audience to follow the plot. (I

understand that the London critics likewise complained of the "obscure plot" in his direction of the original Webster version.)

Would you let me know by Monday, September 30, what you propose to do about these points?

Yours,

Bertolt Brecht

[BBA 1175/01–02. Copy of a letter dated "Boston, September 26, 1946." These appear to represent the changes which Brecht felt were needed before the Boston production could move on to New York.]

Attempted Broadway Production of *The Duchess of Malfi*

The adaptation of John Webster's *Duchess of Malfi* was undertaken at the request of an émigré German actress who had had success on the English stage. The additional verses were translated by Auden, who also saw to it that the original was not unduly maltreated. The actress feared that the New York critics might be provoked by the amputation of a literary monument. However, it turned out that the critics in question were little concerned about careful restoration and largely ignorant of the work (not a single comparison being made with any passage of the original). The production was supervised by an English director and involved old-style declamation in accordance with that so-called Shakespearean tradition whose style derives from the nineteenth century and has of course nothing to do with the Elizabethan theater. The shortcomings of this tradition could be clearly observed. The story narrated by the play was not performed; wherever it came through nonetheless everything possible was done to damp down its startling twists. The characters were flattened out by the pernicious practice of stressing the "eternally human" element, while the shabby attempt to make each event a typical case purged of any operation of chance, so that the audience might blindly follow the workings of "fate," stripped those events of all reality. The actors clung to their purple passages, their arias, for dear life, but without being able to ground them in the action (and for that matter without knowing how to sing). The leading actress refused to let the Duchess' experiences determine her character, nor on the other hand did she stick to one kind of character throughout; thus up to a given scene it was Countess Mitzi and thereafter Mary Queen of Scots. The line taken in the adaptation was that the Duchess' brothers were using her bourgeois love affair as the rope with which to hang her (the Duchess embarks on a bourgeois marriage), but the production saw the "master of the Duchess' household" as a comely princeling, and cut the scene where she tells her bourgeois husband not to interfere in the dispute between her and her noble brothers. The steady aggravation of the tortures to which she is subjected by Ferdinand, himself in love, lost all meaning because his helplessness was not portrayed; while in the final act the actress rejected a scene where the Duchess sees that her death sentence is also her brother's declaration of love. This sprang from a lack of intelligence and stature, and still more from a technical inability to play such episodes. This was something which she shared with the American Antonio and the English Ferdinand. Trained at the Munich Kammerspiele at the end of the First World War and subsequently at Reinhardt's and Barnowsky's theaters in Berlin, she did not command the technique of the German epic theater. As for the rest of the cast, they lacked (and no doubt despised) that of the American musical, which may be entirely phony and provide nothing but empty entertainment in greedy obedience to the fashions of the day, but has nevertheless managed to evolve certain primitive epic methods which could at least serve to present the great Elizabethans in something halfway resembling a contemporary manner.

[From *Schriften zum Theater 4*, pp. 194–6. Not included in GW. The Broadway production opened on October 15, 1946.]

Editorial Note

1. General

The Brecht Archive contains no fewer than five complete or near-complete texts of the play, as well as more entries for subsidiary materials than for any other of Brecht's works apart from *Galileo*. Two of these texts (BBA 144 and 146) predate the 1943 copyrighted version or belong to that immediate period; a third (BBA 1167) has a notation by Elisabeth Hauptmann, "Auden"; a fourth (1177) is a major revision of the 1943 copyrighted text and has manuscript additions and changes most of which have been incorporated in the typed text called "Exemplar Barbara B" (BBA 1419). This last text, then, in the possession of Brecht's daughter, seems to be the one most likely to summarize Brecht's contribution; it shows many signs of his revision, mostly in deleting and adding lines and speeches, tightening scenes and shortening them. The mass of material numbered 1174, however, contains more than two acts of a freshly typed text which includes all of Brecht's changes in 1419 and which apparently was meant to depend upon 1419's unchanged portions to form a complete play. In this text (1174), the manuscript modifications are fewer, though single sheets and groups of sheets following the coherent revised section (1174/01–64) reveal subsequent modifications and/or alternate versions of material in earlier parts of 1174 or in the formerly unchanged parts of the Barbara Brecht script.

Although no certain dates can be put on these last two texts (they are demonstrably later than mid-1943 and were typed by the same New York firm which typed the 1945 and 1946 copyrighted texts), both show careful work by Brecht and represent his continued, perhaps his conclusive, work on the play. Significantly, neither relies very extensively on *The White Devil*: whether this situation indicates that both texts date from a period before (or after) such insertions were contemplated or that Brecht decided not to attempt the amalgamation cannot be judged. Certainly the inclusion of material from *The White Devil*, having been considered by the collaborators part way through their work, was eventually dropped. Possibly the Barbara Brecht script and more probably BBA 1174 date from the latter part of the period during which Brecht is shown by his journal to have worked on the play (i.e., 1945 or early 1946). We have chosen to print as much of BBA 1174 as forms a coherent text and to fill in the gaps with the Barbara Brecht script, modified in places by changes preserved on single sheets in BBA 1174.

The draft plan entitled, "Brecht's version of Webster's *Duchess of Malfi*" (pp. 421–22) gives a general view of Brecht's design for the play and his attitude towards his work on it. Although this story cannot be directly linked with any one of the surviving texts (for example, paragraph 5 describes Ferdinand's captivity whereas all the surviving texts account for the passage of time by delaying Bosola's arrival with news of the Duchess' marriage), most of the major points of Brecht's adaptation appear in the list. Brecht apparently criticizes himself with the word "deviation," specifically the muting of Ferdinand's incestuous jealousy of the Duchess. Each time the action provides an opportunity for explicit recognition or statement of this motive, the characters turn aside. The very basic decision to emphasize this motive (in the original it remains implicit and one among several possibilities) eventually led to the introduction of a prologue (partly from John Ford's *'Tis Pity She's a Whore*) in the Barbara Brecht script and to many other interpolations throughout the play. Brecht later decided to give both the Cardinal and Ferdinand an economic motive (possession of the Duchess' estates) and there are increasingly frequent references to this mercenary incentive from the time of the 1943 copyrighted version (where it is barely mentioned) to our composite text.

A second, more structural, change comes with the very end of the play. Webster's controversial decision to place the Duchess' death in the fourth, rather than the final, act is replaced by a conclusion in which the deaths of brother and sister occur closer together and nearer the play's end. This second modification meant recasting material from the original fourth and fifth acts and also required several adjustments in earlier scenes. Webster's Act IV (all citations in roman numerals refer to J. R. Brown's "Revels" edition of *The Duchess of Malfi*, Methuen, 1964) consists almost entirely of a powerful scene in which Bosola half-tortures, half-comforts the Duchess before executing her. In Act V, interest shifts to Bosola and to an extraordinary series of ironic reversals, unintentional murders, and plans gone astray. While originally he retained a modified version of Webster's Act V (see BBA 1177/84), Brecht finally creates a crescendo of deaths: the Cardinal murdered by Ferdinand (3,1); the Duchess by Bosola, acting for the Duke (3,5); Ferdinand himself by Bosola (3,5). It remains for Delio, in a concluding scene (3,6) to order Bosola's execution and the restoration of the Duchess' surviving son as duke.

Carrying out this second decision had two chief effects: it greatly reduced Bosola's part and led Brecht to create a new scene (3,1) in which Ferdinand kills his brother out of an irrational rage at the excommunication which he himself had proposed and engineered. Through Brecht's drafts, this scene develops from a crudely direct murder (in BBA 1177) to a complicated statement of the Cardinal's remorse and Ferdinand's insane jealousy (in the version here printed). The proper use of Webster's extensive psychological analysis of Bosola puzzled Brecht throughout his work. Eventually, Bosola becomes a much less fully developed character, almost purely the Duke's tool; lingering traces of Webster's treatment occasionally blur his characterization in Brecht's play. An example will clarify Brecht's difficulties and decisions. Immediately after Webster's "excommunication scene" (III.iv), Bosola makes two entrances, the first with an equivocal letter from Ferdinand, asking for Antonio's "head in a business," and the second (after Antonio has escaped) as the leader of a military guard come to arrest the Duchess and her commoner-husband. Brecht appears to have liked the letter episode, and BBA 1177 shows him employing first one of the entrances and then the other, trying to simplify the scene and yet retain Ferdinand's duplicity. Ultimately, in a part of the Barbara Brecht script which shows signs of continued indecision (2,6), Brecht retains Webster's organization, though Bosola's double entrances clearly distressed him. How to dispatch Antonio also posed a problem. In Webster's play, Bosola kills Antonio unintentionally (V.iv), having mistaken him for Ferdinand. This solution Brecht could not use, for it had been decided that the Duchess must receive (as Ferdinand's gruesome "gift") a chest containing the bodies of her husband and child (see 3,3; Webster's analogous scene, IV.i, uses wax-works). Moreover, a remorseful or partially penitent Bosola was not part of Brecht's conception. Many early versions (1177, for example, and the Barbara Brecht script until a manuscript cancellation by Brecht) conclude the "echo scene" (3,2) with Bosola's pursuit of Antonio. In the final version printed here, Antonio's death is neither shown nor implied, merely reported as part of Delio's accusation against Bosola (3,6).

Having diminished Bosola's role, Brecht could write a first act much less complicated than Webster's, although the introduction of set-speech portraits of the major characters still provided problems; the various versions reveal Brecht's experiments in conveying this material. Brecht was more interested than Webster in Duke Ferdinand's foreign wars, and he uses them to explain the curiously long gap (more than two years) between Bosola's discovery of the Duchess' pregnancy and the Duke's return to Malfi. Webster actually mentions two series of battles (in I.i and III.iii), but shows neither; Brecht amalgamates these occasions and suggests a parallel between the Duke's making war for his sister and making war on her. Act 2, scene 2, rather truncated in the version presented here, originally (in BBA 1177, for example) concluded with a more elaborate discussion of war's significance and of Ferdinand's attitudes towards both it and his sister.

Brecht omits completely Webster's subplot, which involves the Cardinal's mistress, Julia. On this point, too, he seems to have wavered: the 1943 copyrighted version omits her; some relevant sections of the next version (1177/56–58) append a conversation between the Cardinal and Julia to the present text's 2,4; the Barbara Brecht text and BBA 1174 make no mention of her. Brecht did, however, salvage one episode from the subplot: Webster's Cardinal murders Julia by demanding that she confirm an oath by kissing a book whose cover has been poisoned (V.ii). Brecht specifies a "prayer book" and employs this device as Ferdinand's weapon against the Duchess (3,5). While Webster's Pescara (a reasonably "good" nobleman who survives the débâcle) and Malatesta (the foolish second husband proposed for the Duchess) both disappear from the adaptation, Delio is given a larger role than in Webster's play. Delio's final restoration of order and especially the epilogue make Brecht's conclusion rather more optimistic than Webster's.

2. Notes on Specific Scenes

The notes on specific scenes in the text which follow offer rejected versions of speeches or portions of scenes, as an illustration of Brecht's methods and evidence of alternatives which he thought promising enough to develop quite fully. In this second regard, BBA 1177 is extremely suggestive. Like 1174, it opens with a coherent and carefully revised partial text, in this case based on the 1943 copyrighted text (thus postdating July 1943) and then becomes a series of loosely related working drafts of scenes and speeches. These working papers reveal more clearly than the analogous material in 1174 just which parts of the play gave Brecht trouble and which interested him most as a field of adaptation and modification. One further textual oddity must be mentioned. File 1178 contains a note by Ruth Berlau: "Material not used—the remainder having been used for complete new script." This note may indicate that an entire text (composed in unknown proportions by Brecht and Auden) has not survived or yet been identified. On the other hand, the note may refer to the 1946 copyrighted version. In any case, the text here printed aims to represent the latest version overseen by Brecht himself. The adaptation seems to have moved along a parabola from Brecht's and Hays's work (revision, rewriting, and addition) to a stretch of Auden's work (including use of *The White Devil* and represented by the 1945 copyrighted text) and a period in which Brecht continued to rework the play. Through various production decisions, with which Brecht disagrees in his letter to Paul Czinner, the final Broadway version returned to almost pure Webster, reduced and clarified with relatively little of the work Brecht had done before Auden's participation and after he joined the project.

Prologue

Most of the material for this prologue comes from John Ford's *'Tis Pity She's a Whore*, which opens with a conversation between a friar and Giovanni (who loves his sister, Annabella). The passages used by Brecht follow (quoted from N. W. Bawcutt's edition, University of Nebraska Press, 1966); all of Brecht's texts for this prologue omit certain inappropriate details from Ford's play, but make no substitutions (see 1.1 49–50, below).

FRIAR
        . . .
    No more; I may not hear it.

GIOVANNI
                                Gentle father,
    To you I have unclasp'd my burdened soul,
    Emptied the storehouse of my thoughts and heart,
        . . .
    And yet is here the comfort I shall have,
    Must I not do what all men else may, love?   (I.i.12–19)

FRIAR
    Why, foolish madman—   (I.i.24)
        . . .

GIOVANNI
    Shall then, for that I am her brother born,
    My joys be ever banish'd from her bed?   (I.i.36–37)
        . . .

. . . tell me, holy man,
What cure shall give me ease in these extremes.

(I.i.40–41)

FRIAR

Art thou, my son, that miracle of wit
Who once, within these three months, wert esteem'd
A wonder of thine age, throughout Bononia [Bologna]?
How did the university applaud
Thy government, behavior, learning, speech,
Sweetness, and all that could make up a man! (I.i.47–52)

. . .

O, Giovanni, hast thou left the schools
Of knowledge to converse with lust and death?
For death waits on thy lust. Look through the world,
And thou shalt see a thousand faces shine
More glorious than this idol thou ador'st:
Leave her, and take thy choice, 'tis much less sin. . . .

(I.i.57–62)

GIOVANNI

It were more ease to stop the ocean
From floats and ebbs than to dissuade my vows.

FRIAR

Then I have done, and in thy wilful flames
Already see thy ruin; Heaven is just.
Yet hear my counsel

. . .

Hie to thy father's house, there lock thee fast
Alone within thy chamber, then fall down
On both thy knees, and grovel on the ground:
Cry to thy heart, wash every word thou utter'st
In tears, and (if't be possible) of blood;
Beg Heaven to cleanse the leprosy of lust
That rots thy soul, acknowledge what thou art,
A wretch, a worm, a nothing: weep, sigh, pray
Three times a day, and three times every night.

(I.i.64–77)

The text which Brecht adapted omits the reference to
Bologna since Antonio and Delio are both of that city, omits
the reference to "the university" since Ferdinand is supposedly
an older man, and omits the word "sweetness" as (presumably)

inappropriate to the Duke. No substitutions have been made, though "Italy" has been tried and rejected as a replacement for "Bologna."

Act One, scene 2

After this scene, several versions (the very early 146 and the late text copyrighted by Auden and Brecht in 1946) insert the dirge from Webster's *White Devil*, here employed as an "interlude." The following text comes from 1174/87:

INTERLUDE

Song by Cariola

Call for the robin red breast and the wren
Since o'er shady groves they hover,
And with leaves and flowers do cover
The friendless bodies of unburied men,
Call unto his funeral dole
The ant, the field-mouse, and the mole.
To rear him hillocks that shall keep him warm,
And (when gay tombs are robbed) sustain no harm:
But keep the wolf far thence, that's foe to men,
For with his nails he'll dig them up again.

Act Two, scene 1

The German text of the soldier's song ("I wrote my love a letter") is in Brecht's GW *Gedichte*, p. 879. Our text gives only the first verse, without its refrain, and the third; the translation is presumably by Auden. The missing portions read approximately:

I never got an answer
And the war went on five years

But that wasn't so surprising.
So I drank instead, supposing:
There she lies, in the embrace
Of the man who took my place.

And we burnt the town around us
When we captured fair Milan
Till its palaces were gutted
And for seven days we looted
And we raped them old and young
For we knew they'd done us wrong.

How could she go on waiting
With the nights becoming lighter and the spring wind
    blowing fresh?
Now it's time I found a lover
He can't make me wait for ever—
Women have such itching flesh.

One of the odd links between the plays in this volume is
the Schweyk song "Onward to Jaromersh hoofing," which not
only appears in Brecht's Schweyk play but evidently inspired
both the present song and Simone Machard's "On my way to
Saint-Nazaire." Nor is Grusha's "Four old commanders/Set
out for Iran" in scene 3 of *The Caucasian Chalk Circle* all that
remote. The two further poems which follow "Als wir vor
Milano kamen" in GW also relate to the Duchess, though they
were not meant for use in the play. Of these the second,
"Light, as though never touching the floor," will be found in
the selected *Poems*.

Act Two, scene 2

This scene ends rather abruptly, with the unexplained arrival
of "the Duchess and her brother" in both BBA 1419 and 1174.
Brecht may have intended some further action in this very
short scene, since he never announces Ferdinand's return from
the wars, but merely introduces him in 2,3. In BBA 1177/35–

36, Antonio does not reveal his marriage, and the scene continues:

DELIO
  But who, then, is the father?
ANTONIO
  I can not tell you. Tell me, Delio,
  Hath not this news arrived yet to the ear
  Of the Lord Ferdinand?
DELIO
                Meseemed his bearing
  Altered the longer he tarried in the field.
  He grew so quiet that he seemed to sleep
  The tempest out as dormice do in winter.
  I could now believe some rumor reached him
  For houses that are haunted are most still.
ANTONIO   Hark, the procession comes.
  (*The sound of cheering multitudes is heard outside. The
  two men go toward the window in order to look down at
  the street. They are obliged to speak loudly to be heard
  above the tumult*)
DELIO   The Duke brings home the realm of Cyprus as booty
  and the people rejoice as if the tailors and pastrycooks were
  to get some of it.
ANTONIO   What are those wooden beams that stand so high?
DELIO   Prows of Turkish ships our Duke hath set upon carts
  for the crowd to gape at. Well he knows how the rabble
  love a brave show.
ANTONIO   'Tis a very forest of captured standards yonder!
DELIO   Ay, they serve well to hide the worn faces of our
  soldiers. Methinks their joy would have been greater had the
  war been shorter.
ANTONIO   Enough of this victory. I'd sooner hear the women
  laugh and jest as they hang upon their husbands' arms and
  lift their children for a father's kiss.
DELIO   Be still! Here comes the Duke.
  (*Enter Ferdinand, Duchess and Bosola*)

The scene then ends with III.i.38–86 of Webster's play.

Act Two, scene 4

In another version, which apparently never developed into an entire text, this scene is followed by a trial, modeled closely on the trial of Vittoria Corombona in Webster's *The White Devil*. Almost an entire scene (also called 2,5) appears on 1174/124–30, at the end of which the Cardinal excommunicates the Duchess and removes her wedding ring. The scene emphasizes the economic motives for the Cardinal's and Ferdinand's deposing the Duchess, but also lightly touches on Ferdinand's incipient madness and his great love for his sister. The following speech (from 1174/131) seems intended to replace Ferdinand's last speech of 2,4 as a preparation for the trial:

CARDINAL   Come, put yourself in tune. It seems she can not be saved. It's a scandal that will shake all Italy. It's up to us, her brothers, to look after her dukedom. We must not hide anything, but proceed openly and fairly. I'll instantly solicit a clerical court and I'll invite all the lieger ambassadors. She is unworthy: her dukedom must be taken away from her and put in the custody of the Holy Church. Brother, let's in to make our preparations.

Act Two, scene 5

BBA 1174/124–30 gives an alternate version of this scene, based upon the trial scene in Webster's *The White Devil*. This alternate version follows; use of this scene would require substituting the speech quoted above in the note to 2,4.

(*Enter French and English ambassadors*)

FRENCH AMBASSADOR
  They have dealt discreetly to obtain the presence
  Of all the grave lieger ambassadors to hear the Duchess' trial
  Trusting our approbation to the proof

Of her black lust shall make her infamous
To all her neighboring kingdoms.

ENGLISH AMBASSADOR

But I would ask what power have the state
Of Ancona to determine a free prince.

FRENCH AMBASSADOR

This is a free state, sir, and her brother, the Cardinal,
Forehearing of her looseness, took occasion
Of their pilgrimage hither to arrest them all,
Duchess and steward and the indeterminate fruit
Of their mismatching, and is in haste
To bring them straight to judgment.

ENGLISH AMBASSADOR

But by what justice?

FRENCH AMBASSADOR

Sure, I think, by none.
These factions among great families are like
Foxes, when their hands are divided
They carry fire in their tails and all the country
About them goes to wrack for them.

ENGLISH AMBASSADOR

Still, she has offended. Who would've thought
So great a lady would [have] matched herself
Unto so mean a person.

FRENCH AMBASSADOR

They that are
Great women of pleasure are oft sudden in their wills
And what they dream they do.
(*Enter officer*)

OFFICER

Pray, silence in the court, their lordships do convene.
(*Enter Ferdinand, Cardinal, guards leading the Duchess,
Antonio, and children into the dock*)

OFFICER (*to Antonio*)   Sirrah, stand off and take your proper
station. This court is not the Duchess' bedchamber. But the
home of justice where you may not stand beside your
betters.

FRENCH AMBASSADOR   Certain people should travel as Dutch
women go to church, bear their stools with them.

OFFICER   The court's in session, signior.

CARDINAL   Stand to the table, gentlewoman, now signior, fall
to your plea.

LAWYER   Domine judex, converte oculos in hanc pestem,
mulierum corruptissimam.

DUCHESS
What's he?

FERDINAND
           A lawyer that pleads against you.

DUCHESS
Pray, my lord, let him speak his usual tongue.
I'll make no answer else.

FERDINAND
Why, you understand Latin.

DUCHESS
I do, sir, but mongst the auditory
Which come to hear my cause, the half or more
May be ignorant in 't.

CARDINAL
Go on, sir.

DUCHESS
          By your favor
I will not have my accusation clouded
In a strange tongue: all this assembly
Shall hear what you can charge me with.

FERDINAND
Pray, change your language.

CARDINAL
Oh, for God's sake, gentlewoman, your credit
Shall be more famous by it.

LAWYER
Well, then, have at you.
Most literate judges, please your lordships
So to connive your judgments to the view
Of this debauched and diversivolent woman;
Who such a black concatenation
Of mischief has affected, that to extirp
The memory of it, must be the consummation
Of her, and her projections—

DUCHESS
    What's all this?
LAWYER
                    Hold your peace!
    Exorbitant sins must have exulceration.
CARDINAL
    I shall be plainer with you, and paint out
    Your follies in more natural red and white
    Than that upon your cheek.
DUCHESS
    Oh, you mistake!
    You raise a blood as noble in this cheek
    As ever was your mother's.
CARDINAL
    Observe this creature here, my honor'd lords . . .
DUCHESS
    My honorable lord
    It doth not suit a reverend cardinal
    To play the lawyer thus. If you be my accuser,
    Pray, cease to be my judge! Come from your bench!
CARDINAL
    You see, my lords, what goodly fruit she seems.
    Yet like those apples travelers report
    To grow where Sodom and Gomorrah stood
    I will but touch her, and you straight shall see
    She'll fall to soot and ashes.
DUCHESS
    O poor charity!
    Thou art seldom found in scarlet.
CARDINAL   I pray thee, mistress, are you to deny that you did
    use our most unfortunate absence to lead a vicious and
    lascivious life?
DUCHESS
    You are deceived: 'twas marriage. 'Twas a contract
    In a chamber per verba presenti.
CARDINAL
    I am resolv'd
    Were there a second paradise to lose
    This devil would betray it.

DUCHESS

Terrify babes, my lord, with painted devils.
I'm past such needless palsy. For your accusations
Of "vicious" and "lascivious": they proceed from you
As if a man should spit against the wind:
The filth returns in 's face.

CARDINAL   Does it? Pray you, mistress, satisfy me one question: While we were absent did nothing leak into the open,
blemishing the noble house of Malfi?
(*To Antonio*)
Who made you overseer?

ANTONIO

Why, my honesty; my honesty, I think.

CARDINAL   Your lust. And while you were the master of her
household, didn't you deal falsely with her in your accounts?
(*Antonio remains silent. Cardinal turns to Duchess*)
Stood not your brother Ferdinand engaged with you
For money
Ta'en up of certain Neapolitan Jews?
And did he not let the bonds be forfeit?

DUCHESS

He did not.

CARDINAL

And whereupon, as you didst testify yourself, our
Brother's bills at Naples were protested?

DUCHESS

They were not.

CARDINAL

But didst say so before your officers.

DUCHESS

To save my husband's life.
Condemn you me for that I do love him?

CARDINAL

And look upon this creature was her husband.

DUCHESS

Had he been in the street
Under my chamber-window, even there
I should have courted him.

CARDINAL   Hear you, my lords, how she calls lechery love, a

life in sin she calls a solemn marriage. This whore, foresooth
is holy.

DUCHESS

Ha! Whore! What's that?
(*Murmurs in the court. Ferdinand rises and comes down
slowly to confront the Duchess. Sudden silence*)

ENGLISH AMBASSADOR

There is that in his look
Would wither all that's green, deform all music
Into a witch's whisper.

FERDINAND

What's that? What's that?
Shall I expound whore to you? sure I shall;
I'll give their perfect character. They are first
Sweetmeats that rot the eater, in man's nostrils
Poison'd perfumes. They are cozening alchemy;
Shipwrecks in calmest weather. What are whores?
Cold Russian winters, that appear so barren
As if that nature had forgot the spring.
They are the true material fire of hell.
What are whores?
They are those flattering bells have all one tune
At weddings, and at funerals. They are worse,
Worse than dead bodies which are begg'd at gallows
And wrought upon by surgeons to teach man
Wherein he is imperfect. What's a whore?
She's like the gilt counterfeited coin
Which, whosoever first stamps it, brings in trouble
All that receive it.

DUCHESS

This character 'scapes me.

FERDINAND

But you shall not escape
What you have made yourself. There is no court
Can punish what you are. Had I a sister?
I have a limb corrupted to an ulcer.
And I will cut it off.
(*Exit Ferdinand*)

ENGLISH AMBASSADOR

Some horrid thing
Glared through his human windows as he spoke.
I wish I had not seen it.

FRENCH AMBASSADOR

'Tis said he loved her
Dearer than life. The question of her shame
Wrecks his proud soul. There are your true pangs of death,
The pangs of life that struggle with great spirits.

ENGLISH AMBASSADOR

Hush! The Duchess is about to speak.

DUCHESS

I have no writ to rend
Such incantations save they mean
Like you, grave reasoners, to undo me,
Whose hates are plain. Brother, you had a hope
Had I continued widow to have gained
An infinite mass of treasure by my death.

CARDINAL

See, my lords,
She scandals our proceedings.

DUCHESS

I have houses,
Jewels, and a poor remnant of crusadoes.
Would these make you charitable?

CARDINAL

Hark, with what insolence she offers bribes
To hush the voice of justice. Get this down
In evidence against her plea of innocence.

DUCHESS

Humbly thus,
Thus low, to the most worthy and respected
Lieger ambassadors, my modesty
And womanhood I tender, but withal
So entangled in a curs'd accusation
That my defense must personate masculine virtue.

CARDINAL

This is the tedious prolixity of guilt.
Have done.

DUCHESS

> Find me but guilty, sever head from body
> We'll part good friends: I scorn to hold my life
> At yours or any man's entreaty, sir.

CARDINAL

> Speak no more for our opinions are concluded
> Hear then, Giovanna, your public fault
> Join'd to th' condition of the present time
> Takes from you all the fruits of noble pity
> Such a corrupted trial have you made
> Both of your life and beauty, and been styl'd
> No less an ominous fate than blazing stars
> To princes. Attend your sentence.
>
> (*The Cardinal and the clerical judges rise, so do the rest at a hint of the Cardinal. The Duchess, Antonio and the children are placed before him*)

CARDINAL   Herefore, through the authority of the Almighty God, Father of Heaven and His Son, Our Savior, I, Cardinal of Ancona, denounce, proclaim and declare Giovanna Teresa, Duchess of Malfi, and her paramour, Antonio Bologna, together with their children, anathema by the advice and assistance of our Holy Father, the pope, and all the bishops, abbots, priests, and other prelates and ministers of our Holy Church, for her open lechery and sins of the flesh.

FRENCH AMBASSADOR   He hath excommunicated her!

CARDINAL   I curse her head and the hairs of her head, her eyes, her mouth, her nose, her tongue, her teeth, her neck, her shoulders, her breast, her heart, her arms, her legs, her back, her stomach, her womb, and every part of her body from the top of her head to the soles of her feet.

DUCHESS

> A rape! A rape! Yes, you have ravished justice
> Forc'd her to do your pleasure.

CARDINAL   I dissever and part thee from the church of God and likewise from contracts and oaths of law. I forbid all Christian men to have any company with thee and all her earthly goods I seize in the name of the Holy Church. And as their candles go from our sight so may their souls go from the visage of God and their good fame from the world.

Away with her!
(*Cardinal steps down from the bench*)
(*To an official*)
Take her right hand and raise it!
(*Cardinal takes something off the Duchess' finger*)
(*Exeunt Cardinal and the clerical judges*)

ENGLISH AMBASSADOR
What was it with such violence he took
Off from her finger?

SPANISH AMBASSADOR
'Twas her wedding ring.

Act Three, scene 2

This "echo" scene exists in several versions, all differing from Webster's in the major respect that his scene is between Antonio and Delio. The version included here shows the most signs of Brecht's direct involvement; he certainly accepted it at one stage of the revision. BBA 1177/70 concludes this scene (substantially as it is printed above) with an entrance by Bosola and two murderers. Bosola ends the scene with, ". . . though they fare fast yet death is speedier than they." BBA 1419/83 originally kept this entrance, but then cancels it. Another, different version appears in the text copyrighted by Auden and Brecht in 1946; Brecht did less work on this one, and much is probably Auden's revision of Webster. This alternative scene is printed below.

SON
Father, when shall we rest?

ANTONIO
Courage, dear son,
'Tis but an hour's journey to the inn
Where we may eat and sleep.

SON
My legs refuse
To bear me longer. Let me sit a while,
A little while.

ANTONIO

> Poor child! One moment then,
> Longer we dare not. We must haste. The day
> Already wears its hunted twilight look,
> Come, dry your tears and listen. This fortification
> Grown from the ruins of an ancient abbey
> Gives the best echo you have ever heard
> As plain in the distinction of the words
> As if a spirit answered. You may make it
> A huntsman or a falconer, a musician
> Or a thing of sorrow.

ECHO

> A thing of sorrow.

ANTONIO

> There, did you hear it, son? So soon asleep!
> Sweet innocent who playest in thy dream
> With tops and spangles not those deadly toys
> That princes skirmish with and canst not spell
> The puzzle of these ruins. Here in this court
> Which now lies naked to the injuries
> Of stormy weather, some men be interred
> Loved the church so well and gave so largely to't
> They thought it should have canopied their bones
> Till doomsday; but all things have their end:
> Churches and cities which have diseases like to men,
> That have like death that we have.

ECHO

> Like death that we have.

ANTONIO

> O fearful echo that accuses my life
> Of its long weakness; that has not made its path
> By definite steps but sought its shelter
> In the strong wills of others. Now
> I am caught between their fighting stars, a clerk
> Unpracticed in the sword. O my soul,
> Is't still impossible to fly your fate.

ECHO

> O, fly your fate.

ANTONIO

> Unmoving stones, would you give such counsel

To a bold nature. Echo, I'll not talk with thee
For thou art a dead thing.

ECHO
Thou art a dead thing.

ANTONIO
My Duchess is asleep now
And her little ones, I hope sweetly: O Heaven
Shall I never see her more?

ECHO
Never see her more.

ANTONIO
O dreadful repetition
Methought that on the sudden a clear light
Presented me a face folded in sorrow.
Come, boy, awake. We have delayed too long.

SON
Let me sleep, mother. Kiss me once more.

ANTONIO
Dost thou dream of her
Forgetting where thou art? I'll carry thee
Sleep on, beloved child, believing 'tis her arms
Not thy poor father's.
(*Echo of galloping hooves is heard*)
O hark, the walls
Echo to baying hooves. Where shall the quarry
Turn for salvation now? The hunt is up
And we are gone forever.
(*Exeunt*)

BBA 1174/107 has another version with the note, "Brecht's rough translation" opposite Antonio's last speech:

ANTONIO
O fearful echo that accuses my life
Of its long weakness; that has not made its path
By definite steps but sought its shelter
In the strong wills of others. Now
I am caught between their fighting stars, a clerk
Unpracticed in the sword.

SON

   Why can't we go with mother?

ANTONIO

   We are too small to live with greatness, son.

SON

   Shall we not see her more?

ECHO

   Not see her more.

SON

   Why does the echo say so, father?

ANTONIO

   It tells us, son, how bitter is the fate
   Of him who is not allowed to fight. The whole day
   (Which now will be ended soon) I have been thinking
   Of another day, when I went ahawking with my father
   Upon the plains of Brittany, and saw our falcon spying a
      hare
   And coursing it till the poor beast
   —Since flying is much easier than running—
   Was wearied unto death and, despairing utterly,
   Turned upon its back and with its stony feet
   Hardened by a whole life of timid flight
   Hammered to pieces our falcon's chest. Lucky hare!
   O 'tis impossible to fly your fate.

ECHO

   O, fly your fate.

Act Three, scene 3

BBA 1174 has variants of the concluding exchange between
Bosola and Ferdinand, showing the way in which Brecht reduced Bosola's express motives and justifications for his actions. Three versions will illustrate Brecht's working methods:

FERDINAND

   Damn her! that body of hers,
   While that my blood ran pure in't, was more worth

Than that which thou wouldst comfort, called a soul.
Curse upon her!
I will no longer study in the book
Of another's heart

BOSOLA
Must I see her again?

FERDINAND
Your work is not yet ended.
To cure such maladies the surgeon's knife
Must cut until it pricks the patient's life.
(*Exeunt*)   (1174/75)

BOSOLA
Right. Give me that scholarship
You promised me and I'll be off to Bologna
And never see her again.

FERDINAND
Your work is not yet ended.
I found her sin sits deeper than I thought.
Vile appetite has turned to lecherous grief.
Such mourning is unbearable.
To cure such maladies the surgeon's knife
Must cut until it pricks the patient's life.
(*Exeunt*)   (1174/80)

BOSOLA
Right. Give me my scholarship and I'll go
To complete my education, never see her again.

FERDINAND
Your work is not yet ended.
I found her sin sits deeper than I thought.
Vile appetite has turned to lecherous grief
With pallidness hardly hidden, impudent [*sic*] tears.
Such mourning is imbearable [*sic*]. Nacked [*sic*] she stands
The widow of a sweaty stableboy.
To cure such maladies the surgeon's knife
Must cut until it pricks the patient's life.

                                                  (1174/79)

Between this scene and the following one, the 1946 text

copyrighted by Auden and Brecht inserts an "interlude" by Bosola. The text comes from Webster's play (IV.ii.178–95) and is spoken by Bosola in an attempt to bring the Duchess "By degrees to mortification." It is cited here from 1174/85:

INTERLUDE

BOSOLA

Hark, now everything is still
The screech-owl and the whistler shrill
Call upon our dame aloud,
And bid her quickly don her shroud!
Much you had of land and rent;
Your length in clay's now competent:
A long war disturbed your mind;
Here your perfect peace is signed:
Of what is't fools make such vain keeping?
Sin their conception, their birth weeping,
Their life a general mist of error,
Their death a hideous storm of terror.
Strew your hair with powders sweet,
Don clean linen, bathe your feet,
And (the foul fiend more to check)
A crucifix let bless your neck.
'Tis now full tide 'tween night and day;
End your groan, and come away.

This text also appears on 1174/109 and 123.

Epilogue

The second half of this epilogue comes from a passage in Webster's *The Devil's Law Case*, slightly modified to suit its new context. The original follows, quoted from Frances A. Shirley's edition (University of Nebraska Press, 1972):

All the flowers of the spring
Meet to perfume our burying:
These have but their growing prime,

And man does flourish but in his time.
Survey our progress from our birth:
We are set, we grow, we turn to earth.
Courts adieu, and all delights,
All bewitching appetites;
Sweetest breath, and clearest eye,
Like perfumes, go out and die;
And consequently this is done,
As shadows wait upon the sun.
Vain the ambition of kings,
Who seek by trophies and dead things
To leave a living name behind,
And weave but nets to catch the wind.   (V.iv.128–43)

Dear Mom,

We knew your present would work! That book
You Don't Have To Stay Single finally got you a
great guy! Tom's really nice, and he could make
a great dad. And a good husband for you, of
course. He could take us to football games, have
barbecues, help us with our homework and help
you tuck us in at night. And Sarah says he's really
good-looking, too!

So, if he *does* ask you to marry him, you'll know
what you should say…right?

Love,

Sarah and Chris

Please address questions and book requests to: Silhouette Reader Service
U.S.: 3010 Walden Ave., P.O. Box 1325, Buffalo, NY 14269
Canadian: P.O. Box 609, Fort Erie, Ont. L2A 5X3

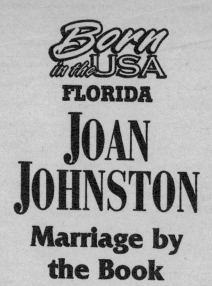

Born in the USA

FLORIDA

JOAN JOHNSTON

Marriage by the Book

Silhouette Books

Published by Silhouette Books

America's Publisher of Contemporary Romance

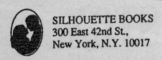

SILHOUETTE BOOKS
300 East 42nd St.,
New York, N.Y. 10017

ISBN 0-373-47159-9

MARRIAGE BY THE BOOK

Dear Readers,

Although this book in the BORN IN THE USA series doesn't have a baby in it, it does have two charming kids (patterned after my own) who help their mother find a new life partner. In 1987, when I wrote *Marriage by the Book*, I had recently become a single mom. I hadn't dated for nineteen years, and I was looking for advice about how it was done. There were lots of "self-help" books on the market that told me how to find and marry the perfect mate. In *Marriage by the Book* I had fun imagining what would happen if both the man and woman followed the advice in a "self-help" book to guide them at the beginning of their relationship, with amusing results.

The heroine's two children in *Marriage by the Book* are the same age and sex as my two children were in 1988, when the book was first published. It was easy to write dialogue for an eight-year-old boy and a fourteen-year-old girl. All I had to do was listen at the supper table!

You may notice that this book was and is dedicated to my daughter, Heather. At twenty-two, she is still bright and beautiful. My belief in her sense of style has been proven true. After graduating from the University of Florida this year with a degree in magazine journalism and attending New York University's publishing course this past summer, she recently started work at *South Florida* magazine as a graphic artist.

My sixteen-year-old son, Blake, is a junior in high school. He is as precocious now as he was then. Believe it or not, he wants to be a writer!

It's fun to look back at where we were and compare where we are now. I'm happily single, but I wouldn't turn down the right man if he showed up on my doorstep! Hope you are all doing equally well.

Best always,

Joan Johnston

For my daughter, Heather Lynne Johnston,
who is bright and beautiful
and has a great sense of fashion.

With love,
Mom

One

Her Book: *YOU DON'T HAVE TO STAY
SINGLE*
His Book: *HOW TO MARRY THE WOMAN OF
YOUR DREAMS*

"Where do you want to do it?" he asked.

"In the shower," she answered with a shy
smile. "It's always been a fantasy of mine, if you
want to know the truth."

She led him to the maroon-and-gray-tiled bathroom. A blush rose on her cheeks as she quickly
stripped the sheer panties and lace bras from the

towel rack where she'd left them to dry. "Sorry about that."

He grinned in that sexy way that had charmed her from the first moment she'd seen him. His green eyes were lambent with passion. "You're so beautiful," he murmured. "I want to see all of you." He tried pulling her T-shirt over her head, but it got caught.

"Wait! Wait! It's stuck on my nose!" She pried the T-shirt off and found his gaze, hot and hard on her. She felt her blood heating up like a prairie fire out of control and thought it was probably a good thing they were getting into the shower. She swallowed over the lump in her throat and said, "Your turn."

He reached down to pull his cotton shirt up and off. At the same time, she reached over to help. His balled fist caught her under the chin, jamming her lower teeth into her lip.

"Ow!"

"Sorry, sweetheart." He couldn't reach out to her because his arms were trapped inside his shirt. "Are you all right?"

She tasted blood, but didn't want to spoil the mood. "It's nothing. Maybe we should undress ourselves."

"Anything you say, darling."

He was out of his tight-fitting jeans and standing naked and ready at the back of the tub by the time she slid out of her short shorts and joined him. Since she was closer, she turned on the shower—which sent out a jet of ice cold water. She yelped and stepped back, slamming an elbow into his stomach.

"Ooomph!"

"Oh, I'm sorry." She stuck her head, sodden hair and all, back under the spray and reached to adjust the temperature, which by now was almost scalding. Finally she got it right and turned to face him, a game smile on her face.

He pressed her up against the tile wall, his strong, muscular body conforming to her soft curves.

She gasped and instantly arched her back so her breasts were forced against the crisp black hair on his chest.

"Whoa, baby," he murmured. "Take it easy. We've got all night...or at least until we run out of hot water."

"The wall's freezing!"

"Oh." He stepped back. "How about if I pick you up?" He cupped his hands around her thighs and heaved, but couldn't lift her.

"Must have been that last taco I ate," she teased.

He bent his knees and tried again. This time he got one leg up, but not the other.

"Ow!" she cried.

He quickly released her. "What's the matter now?" he asked, a glint of humor in his eyes.

Chagrined, she admitted, "I got a cramp in my leg."

"Let me help you rub it out."

The sensation of his large hands caressing her leg made her knees feel rubbery. "Uh, keep that up and I'm liable to become a puddle at your feet."

"While we make sure your cramp has gone away for good, how about if I soap you up a bit," he suggested.

"That sounds like fun."

And it was. At last, something that felt as good as she'd imagined. His thumbs grazed her nipples, bringing them erect. His hands curved down over her flat belly and into the nest of curls below. After a heart-stopping foray, they slid back up and around to her buttocks.

"How about giving it another try?" he rasped in her ear. "Ready for me to lift you up?"

She nodded, too breathless to speak.

This time when he reached for her hips he couldn't get a grip at all. Her body was too slippery from soap.

They both laughed. He turned and backed up a little so she could rinse herself off—and hit his head on the shower spigot.

"Ouch!" He let go of her to rub his head.

"Let me help." She reached up toward his temple, but her soapy hand brushed against the edge of his eye.

He quickly squinted and gave a cry of alarm. "Have you got a dry cloth? I've got soap in my eye."

"Just a second and I'll get a towel." She stepped out of the shower with the distinct feeling she'd just escaped from a war zone...until she slipped on the tile floor and nearly went flying. She grappled for the towel rack and barely managed to remain standing.

"Hey! Wake up out there! Where's my towel?"

Megan Padget felt a hand grab her shoulder and shake it. "Wake up! Wake up!"

"I'm awake," she replied, blinking as a piercing light hit her eyes.

"Happy thirty-ninth birthday, Mom!"

Megan sat up abruptly and looked around her. She wasn't anywhere near the shower. She was sitting in the cushioned cane chair in her living room. It had all been a weird, crazy dream. She yawned and rubbed the crick in her neck.

"We finished the dishes, Mom," her fourteen-year-old daughter, Sarah, said.

"And we have a surprise for your birthday," her eight-year-old son, Christopher added.

"You're not going to believe the present we got for you, Mom," Sarah said. "You'll really be surprised!"

"I'm sure you're right." Megan was having a little trouble leaving her dream behind. No one could have that much misfortune in a single attempt to make love with a man in the shower. No wonder she'd never attempted it in real life. Still, it *was* a fantasy of hers.... She'd just have to make sure it never came true in quite that way. Her grin widened as she thought of all the ridiculous things that had gone wrong. She felt the crinkles appear beside her large hazel eyes and around her wide, full mouth. Character lines. A sign of a life well and happily lived, she thought. Even if she never had made love in the shower.

"Hurry up, Mom," Chris urged, pulling her out of the chair. "We made a cake for you. C'mon and light the candles."

As she followed her children into the dining room, Megan ran a hand through her shoulder-length, golden brown hair. In the past year she'd noticed some gray here and there. Yes, she was definitely going to be thirty-nine this year. She took the book of matches Sarah handed to her. "This is a beautiful chocolate cake, Sarah. Did you make it all by yourself?"

"I helped with the icing," Chris said.

Sarah grimaced at her brother. "Right. He licked the eggbeaters clean."

"Aw, Mom!"

Megan reached over and ruffled Chris's tow-head of hair, a legacy from his father. Sarah's hair was equally straight and blond, thanks to the hours she spent in the warm Miami sun. Megan's children were beautiful, bright and precocious, and she felt a swell of pride and love that they'd remembered her birthday in such a special way.

"Thanks to both of you for cleaning up the kitchen while I napped. And you've made me a beautiful chocolate cake! This has been the best birthday ever."

"You haven't even opened your present yet," Sarah protested.

"I'm sure I'll love whatever you two got for me."

Unable to sit calmly any longer, Chris got up from his chair and came to stand beside her. His face flushed as he handed her an elaborately wrapped gift. "Open it, Mom."

"It feels heavy," Megan said. "I wonder what it could be."

"It's a book!" Chris blurted out.

"Shut up, Chris! Mom, he always spoils everything!"

"I do not!"

"You do so!"

"That's enough, Sarah."

"Do not!" Chris retorted one last time.

Megan waited until Chris was seated at the table again before she said, "Nothing is spoiled, Sarah, because I don't know which book you two have bought for me. Do you want me to guess before I open it?"

"You'll never guess in a million years," Sarah said, the beatific smile returning to her face.

"Yeah, never in a million years," Chris agreed.

"Chris," Sarah warned.

"I never said anything!"

Megan ignored the sibling argument and concentrated on the weight of the hardbound book in her hands. She couldn't help but wonder what her children had chosen for her. She'd been reading a lot of bestsellers lately, and she suspected they'd purchased the latest spy thriller.

"It's a suspense novel," Megan guessed.

"Wrong!" Sarah said with a pleased giggle.

"Hurry up and open it, Mom. I can't wait to see what you think."

Megan tore the paper off, genuinely curious to see what Sarah and Chris had bought. "Oh, my God! Sarah, this is...this is..."

"It's a book about how to find a husband, Mom. See?"

Megan saw only too well. *YOU DON'T HAVE TO STAY SINGLE* was staring at her in bold print and capital letters. Megan didn't know what to say. She was flabbergasted. She'd had no idea her children still had hopes of her marrying and providing them with a father. She'd divorced Gary five years ago, and in the years since then the right man had never come along. After literally thousands of dates—well, perhaps only sixty-three or so, but who was counting?—she'd thought her children had become as discouraged as she was. Apparently not.

She realized she still hadn't thanked her children. Luckily, Sarah was so excited she was still talking nonstop.

"...So you see, Mom, you've been going about this husband-hunting business all wrong. This book has step-by-step instructions, and there's even a money-back guarantee if you aren't married within a year of the date you purchased the book."

Megan felt an envelope being pressed into her hand.

"The receipt for the book is in this envelope," Sarah explained. "But I'll bet anything you never have to send it in."

"You gotta read this book, Mom," Christopher piped up. "'Cause I just gotta have someone besides my mom to play football with me. I mean, how's it gonna look when I'm in junior high school someday and still tackling you?"

"All right," Megan said with a rueful smile. "I promise to read it." She flipped open the book and began perusing the chapter headings. She flushed when she read the title of Chapter Five, "Sex—Don't Jump the Gun."

"Sarah, how much of this did you read before you wrapped it up?"

Sarah grinned. "I checked it all out, Mom. *Especially* Chapter Five."

"You're too young—"

"Jeez, Mom. We've had sex education in school. There wasn't anything there that I didn't already know. But there were a few suggestions—"

"That'll be all for now, young lady," Megan said, taking note of her wide-eyed, big-eared son.

"Sure, Mom," Sarah said. "And when you

read Chapter Two I'd really like to talk with you. I think I could be a big help."

Megan looked down at the heading for Chapter Two, "Dressing for *Sex*cess," and flushed again. But she had to agree her daughter was probably right. Sarah spent hours poring over the fashions in her teen magazines and eagerly put the ideas she read about into practice. Megan had often marveled at how Sarah could take a blouse, a belt, a scarf, floppy-topped socks and a pair of jeans and turn the ensemble into a fashion statement.

It was hard to accept the fact that her daughter wasn't a child anymore. In just four years she'd be going off to college. It wouldn't be long before Chris would follow in her footsteps. Was it possible Sarah had worried that her mother would be alone in the years to come and had sought a way to remedy that situation? Sometimes Sarah acted so…adult.

Megan set the book down on the table before she stood and pulled Chris into her arms for a quick hug. He resisted the closeness, as Megan had known he would. Sarah was only slightly more cooperative when her turn came.

"Thanks, honey," Megan said. "I mean it. I'm going to start reading tonight, and when I get to Chapter Two I'll let you know."

"You still haven't lit the candles," Chris said, holding up the box of matches.

Thirty-nine candles created quite a blaze, and by the time Megan got the last one lit the first had started to leave a large wax puddle on the icing.

"Quick! Make a wish and blow them out!" Sarah said.

Megan closed her eyes and wished for "the right man" to come along. Then she took a deep, hopeful breath and blew hard.

"You got 'em all, Mom!" Chris shouted. "Every last one!"

"What did you wish for?" Sarah asked.

"You know you can't tell a wish or it won't come true," Chris countered. "What *did* you wish for, Mom?"

Megan smiled broadly. "You know I can't tell you that."

Her children settled for a piece of cake topped with ice cream, and by the time they got the dishes done and the wrapping paper and ribbon picked up it was late.

"I think you two had better think about getting to bed," Megan said. "You've both got school tomorrow."

"Aw, Mom."

"Bed, Christopher," Megan said firmly.

"Good night, Mom," Sarah said. "I've got

some more studying to do before I turn out the light, but will you come and tuck me in?''

Megan smiled. There was still a little bit of the child left in Sarah and she'd gladly nourish it for as long as it lasted. ''Sure, honey. Just give me a call when you get your contact lenses out and your glasses on.''

Christopher had already disappeared into his room when Megan called after him, ''Don't forget to brush your teeth, Chris.''

''Aw, Mom.''

''Teeth, Christopher.''

In a very short time Sarah was tucked in and the house was dark and quiet. Doing the last minute straightening around the house, Megan came across *YOU DON'T HAVE TO STAY SINGLE* on the dining-room table. As an educator, she was the first to acknowledge the power of books to alter viewpoints, increase knowledge and shape attitudes and opinions. But reading a book to find out how to land a husband seemed to be carrying things a bit too far.

''But I promised I'd look at it,'' she said with a disbelieving shake of her head, ''and I will.''

She carried *YOU DON'T HAVE TO STAY SINGLE* with her to her femininely-decorated bedroom and set it on the table beside the bed. She debated whether or not to wear the sexy nightgown her best friend, Stephanie Stobs, had given her for her birthday, but finally gave in to the need to feel the cool, silky fabric against her skin. She pulled down the sheets and climbed into the same queen-size bed she'd slept in for the last five years of her marriage and the five years since. It sagged a little in the middle, but there was no one to run into when she landed in the center at night, so she couldn't see replacing it.

She fluffed up her two pillows and leaned back against the headboard with the book in her lap. She perused the chapter headings again: "Meeting Your Man"; "Dressing for *Sex*cess"; "You *Can* Ask Him Out!"; "Sex—Don't Jump the Gun"; "Meeting His Mother" and "Getting Him to Pop the Question." It all looked pretty harmless. But was it going to be helpful?

Megan paged through the introduction and dedication until she got to Chapter One. She read:

You go exploring for oil in a place where you expect to find it. The same holds true when looking for "the right man."

The most common place for a woman to meet the man she will marry is the workplace. It stands to reason that a woman who works in a career that attracts men will have the best chance of meeting "the right man."

Megan laughed aloud as she perused the list of suggested occupations: plumber, telephone lineman, elevator inspector, men's shoe salesman, IRS agent, automobile salesman, boat-repair-and-service technician and politician.

"What's so funny, Mom?" Sarah called from her bedroom.

"Nothing, honey. I just thought of a joke I heard today." She didn't have the heart to tell Sarah how ridiculous the book was. She swallowed her own disappointment as she put it on the bedside table and turned off the lamp.

Yanking the covers up over her bare shoulders she thought about her job at St. Mark's University. She was a good teacher and her responsibilities as chairman of the science department challenged her. The atmosphere at the university was friendly and supportive. But the St. Mark's faculty left a lot to be desired as a source of eligible males. She was a lot more likely to find a *father* on campus than a *husband!*

Thomas Steele eyed the thirty-five flaming candles on his birthday cake with something less than enthusiasm.

"All right, Tom. Make a wish and blow them out," his older brother, Randy, urged.

"Wish for something good," Randy's wife, Irene, added.

Tom stood for long seconds thinking what he wanted most out of life—and came up with a blank. He liked making love at dawn, sailing in a storm, popcorn and beer, sleeping late in the rain with the feel of a soft woman curved against his hard body, and slow, deep kisses. The problem was he felt a vague sense of dissatisfaction with his life and couldn't seem to locate the source. When the candles began to puddle on the cake he gave up and blew them out without deciding on anything.

"What did you wish for?" Randy asked.

"A hundred-foot yacht and the time and money to sail it to Tahiti," Tom quipped with a grin.

It had been a longstanding dream for the two brothers to sail away into the sunset. Their lives had been grim enough to demand a dream to sustain them. Their alcoholic father had regularly beaten their mother, and when he was finished with her he'd started on them. When the policeman had come to the door to report their father's death in a drunk driving accident, their mother had wept, and so had Tom and Randy. The policeman had been sympathetic to what he supposed was their grief. But fourteen-year-old Tom and seventeen-year-old Randy had been shedding guilty tears of relief.

Tom had sworn then that he'd never hurt a woman the way his father had hurt his mother. And he hadn't. His initial solution to the problem had been to avoid women altogether. During his adolescent years, the time when most young men honed their skills in male-female relationships, Tom hadn't dated. As he'd matured, however, his dark good looks had drawn women to him like metal filings to a magnet. Tom had accepted their freely offered feminine gifts, but he'd been careful never to lose control of his emotions with a woman. The fear was always there that if he did, he might discover he was capable of the same destructive violence as his father.

When the time had come to marry, he hadn't been a good husband. He'd learned too late that he kept too much of himself hidden away from his wife. Sally had begged him to let go, to share his thoughts and feelings, but he hadn't been able to do it. When Sally had divorced him he'd been forced to admit that his fierce control on his emotions had made him seem cold to her when she needed him most—because the times when he was feeling the most were the times when the fear he might do violence to his wife rose up to haunt him. It didn't seem to matter that he'd never raised a hand to her. The fear was there.

Unfortunately, his efforts in adolescence to avoid his fear by avoiding women, had created another problem that was equally frustrating to Tom. For what appeared on the surface to be simple reserve with women, was in fact, painful shyness. To his utter chagrin, his tongue was tied by adolescent awkwardness when he attempted a conversation with a woman to whom he was deeply attracted.

"Hey, what's got you so serious?" Randy asked, chewing a mouthful of the cake Irene had served to him. "I'd give my eyeteeth to have looked half as good as you do now when I was thirty-five."

Tom flushed. "Cut it out, Randy."

Randy leaned back in the large, comfortable chair in Tom's living room and took a sip of his beer. "Face it. You're a hunk."

"He's right," Irene seconded from her seat on the couch. "You've got those sexy green eyes and that wavy black hair. You're tall, with broad shoulders and lean hips."

"Cut it out, Irene. You're embarrassing me," Tom said.

"Don't try to pretend you don't know you're good-looking. We're not going to buy it," Randy said. "If I were you—and I weren't already married to a wonderful woman—I'd be taking a little more advantage of all that female attention."

Tom's lips twisted in a sardonic smile. "You'd be amazed what a difference it makes to a woman when she realizes I'm not interested in a long-term relationship."

"How well I remember." Randy reached out to grasp Irene's hand. "That's why Irene and I got you a very special birthday present this year—something that's going to change your life."

"Oh, yeah? If it isn't season tickets for the Miami Dolphins, forget it." Tom put his feet up against the edge of the ancient Formica dining-room table that had come with the furnished apartment he'd rented when he'd arrived in Miami two weeks ago. He leaned back until his chair rested on only two of its aluminum legs.

Randy retrieved a hastily wrapped gift from the table in front of him and threw it across the room to his brother. "Here. Open it."

Tom took his time opening the present. When he had enough wrapping paper removed to see what was in his hands his facial muscles tightened. His feet came off the table and the chair clunked down on all four legs. "What the hell is this?"

"Now don't get upset," Irene said soothingly. "Randy and I were only thinking—"

"It's pretty clear from this gift what you were thinking. But you were wrong." Tom threw the half-unwrapped book on the table. "I'm not interested in finding a wife now or in the future."

"I know you think you failed Sally," Randy said. "And you got burned pretty badly by your breakup with Maryanne."

"To a crisp."

"That's no reason to give up on everything marriage has to offer. I made a mistake the first go-around, too." Randy's hand tightened around Irene's. "But I found that things were different with the right partner. It's high time you found yourself a good woman and settled down."

"I haven't had the time—or the inclination—since Maryanne turned down my proposal."

"You can't keep running from marriage, Tom."

"I'm not running from anything. Has it occurred to you that I've just never found the right woman?"

Randy's jaw dropped open and a grin split his face. "Well, well, well. Then Irene and I have chosen a good present after all. This book is *guaranteed* to help you marry the woman of your dreams." He handed Tom an envelope. "The receipt's in here. Just hang on to it for a year, and if you aren't married you get a full refund. How about that for a deal?"

Tom laughed. "I give up. Give me the damn thing."

Randy picked up the book and held it out to Tom.

Tom shook his head in disbelief as he accepted the birthday gift from his brother. *"HOW TO MARRY THE WOMAN OF YOUR DREAMS.* Pretty heady stuff. You don't honestly believe that a book like this is going to make a difference, do you?"

Randy grinned and winked at Irene. "Sure I do. It worked for me."

Tom gaped at Randy. "You used this to find Irene?"

"He had Chapter Three down pat," Irene said. "I fell for him hook, line and sinker."

Tom perused the chapter headings until he found the one Irene had referred to: "Sex—When to Make Your Move." When he looked back up Irene was blushing.

Randy pulled his wife to her feet. He wrapped his arms around her and gave her a crushing squeeze. "God, I love you, woman!" Randy kept his arms around Irene as he turned and spoke to Tom. "I can't make you read that book. But as your older brother I'm giving you some good advice. Don't knock it till you've tried it. Now I think it's time we headed for home.''

He kept an arm around Irene's waist as he walked over to lay a hand affectionately on Tom's shoulder. "Happy birthday. It's great having you here in Miami, even if it's only for the next nine months. I'll call you later this week and we'll get together for lunch. I want to hear how you like your new job.''

"Sounds good to me.'' Tom rose and gave his sister-in-law a kiss on the cheek. "Thank you both. I appreciate you baking a cake for me, Irene.''

"I enjoyed it, but maybe this time next year you'll have your own special someone to bake one for you.''

Tom's lips flattened. "Yeah. Sure.''

"Read it!'' Randy called over his shoulder as he and Irene stepped out the door.

When they were gone, Tom looked down at the book in his hand. Well, it couldn't hurt to glance at it. Then he could face Randy with a clear conscience.

He carried the book over to the one chair in the living room, a huge, overstuffed corduroy monstrosity, and sat down, putting his bare feet up on an equally huge ottoman in front of it. He quickly reviewed the chapters: "Where to Meet Your Dream Woman"; "That First Fabulous Date"; "Sex—When to Make Your Move"; "What Do Her Criticisms Mean?"; "Avoiding Cold Feet When It's Time to Commit" and "Putting the Ring on Her Finger."

He had to admit there appeared to be a lot of useful information in the book. He resisted the urge to check out the chapter on sex, and began reading at the beginning.

Women are everywhere.

Tom laughed aloud. He didn't need a book to tell him that.

The problem is how to make contact with them. You'll do best opening a conversation with a woman if you have a reason for speaking to her. Thus service industries make excellent occupations for single men anxious to meet a prospective wife.

Tom read through the list of industries that put a man in contact with women and had to laugh again. Vacuum-cleaner salesman, hairdresser, manicurist, women's shoe salesman, principal, aerobics instructor—he couldn't fault the list, but where did that leave him? He taught college classes in political science and advised a lot of high-powered politicans. Unfortunately his female students were all much too young for him, and the vast majority of the politicans he advised were male.

He didn't want to change his job. He liked his work, and he was looking forward to his new position as a visiting professor in the political science department at St. Mark's University. He closed the book and tossed it onto the coffee table. He leaned back in the corduroy chair and crossed his forearms over his brow.

He wasn't averse to the idea of marriage, but the truth was he had too much trouble talking with women to hope that he'd be successful finding a wife on the basis of what he learned in a book. In fact, the idea of using a book to find the woman of his dreams struck him as ridiculous. Except that, as a teacher, he knew that only a fool discounted the power of the printed word. Besides, it had supposedly worked for Randy.

He remembered the feeling of dissatisfaction that had plagued him lately. Was it a *woman* that was missing from his life? Maybe it was. He toyed with the idea of taking this book seriously, then shook his head in chagrin. He couldn't believe how far he'd let his whimsy carry him.

Maybe he'd find the woman of his dreams at St. Mark's, but it was more likely she'd remain a figment of his imagination.

He forced himself to get up and go into the bedroom to sleep. Not that there was anyone to know or care where he spent the night, but he'd found it was easier to rest if he maintained a semblance of normalcy. He fell asleep almost immediately. And he dreamed. There was a woman with warm, brown eyes, laughing delightedly, her face tilted up for his kiss...and they were in the shower.

Two

Her Book: "Meeting Your Man"
His Book: "Where to Meet Your Dream
Woman"

"**Y**our children got you *what* for your birthday?"

"Keep your voice down, Stephanie. Somebody's likely to hear you." Megan looked around the room filled with professors who'd gathered for the annual welcome address by the president of St. Mark's University. There were more than a hundred members of the faculty and staff stuffed in the small auditorium like candy in a kid's mouth.

Stephanie Stobs was an associate professor in the art department and Megan's closest friend. One of the things Megan liked most about her was her vivacious personality, but Stephanie had a distinctive voice and it carried easily. Megan leaned over and whispered in her friend's ear, "You heard me. I said they bought me a book called, *YOU DON'T HAVE TO STAY SINGLE.*"

"Lordy, Lordy! I didn't know you were still looking for a husband."

"Shh! I'm not. At least, I wasn't until I got this book. Now I have to at least make a token effort at dating or I'm going to hurt their feelings. The book is full of how-to advice you wouldn't believe."

"I hope you're planning to share all the good stuff with me," Stephanie said with a grin.

"I'm not sure how much good stuff there is. Unless you'd like to consider becoming a men's shoe salesman."

Stephanie frowned, perplexed. "A men's shoe salesman?"

At that moment Steven Sawyer, the dean for academic affairs, called the meeting to order. For the next two hours they sat through mundane announcements about what had happened over the past summer and what the administration planned for the coming year. The president, Father John O'Hara, gave an inspirational speech designed to get everyone off on the right foot, and the morning session ended with the introduction of each new member of the faculty.

Megan was half paying attention, doodling daisies on her notepad, when Stephanie jabbed her in the ribs. "Will you look at that!"

Megan stared at the man standing toward the front of the auditorium. He was tall and lean, and had dark hair that just trailed over the collar of his pale pink, short-sleeved shirt. He wore form-fitting gray trousers that, from the back, left little to the imagination. Not the typical St. Mark's professor. Not at all!

At that moment he turned to gesture toward the man sitting beside him and Megan got a good look at his face.

"Lordy, Lordy!" Stephanie chanted. "Where did he come from?"

Megan couldn't answer because all the air had just been sucked from her lungs. He couldn't be as good-looking as she thought he was. She blinked her eyes, but he remained just as striking. His strong profile showed a once-straight nose that looked as though it had been broken several times, the slightly jutting chin of a man used to getting his way, high, sharp cheekbones and half of a wide, friendly smile that was devastating even from where she sat.

"Who is he?" Megan asked. "Did you hear his name?"

"Tom, I think," Stephanie murmured. "I can't believe a gorgeous guy like that is joining our faculty. I'll bet he's married. No guy that good-looking is still single. Unless he…no, he's just got to be straight. He's too good to be true! I can't wait to meet him."

"And Tom will be a visiting professor this year," Dean Sawyer intoned. "He comes to us from Washington, D.C., where he's the chairman of the political science department at Georgetown University. Tom is frequently called upon as a consultant to the U.S. State Department for his expertise on South American affairs. We're proud and pleased to welcome Tom to the faculty of St. Mark's for the coming year."

"I should have known," Stephanie grumbled. "He's only visiting." Then she grinned. "But he's here for a whole year. That means I've got a shot at convincing him that Miami has a lot to offer a man—starting with me!"

Megan realized that Stephanie was exactly the sort of woman a hunk like Tom Whatever would go for. She was dark eyed, dark haired and dazzling. Megan, at thirty-nine, didn't even put herself in the same class with Stephanie, who was ten years younger. And if Stephanie had set her sights on Tom Something-or-Other, the chances were good that she would land him. From Stephanie's next words, it was clear she was already plotting her seduction.

"Look, the whole faculty's supposed to have lunch in the cafeteria," she said. "Let's make sure we sit at the same table as Tom."

"I already promised to sit with Dean Sawyer," Megan replied, unable to completely keep the disappointment from her voice. "I need to talk with him about some budget matters. I guess you're on your own—you and the rest of the single female faculty."

Stephanie's eyes sparkled with mischief. "Think I'm gonna have some competition?"

"Don't you?"

"Yeah. But I'm up to the challenge."

Megan couldn't disagree. Stephanie was dressed in a bright blue silk dress that emphasized her small waist and generous bosom. She wore sexy high heels to compensate for her lack of height. Add dynamite looks to Stephanie's outgoing personality and what man could resist her? Certainly not Tom What's-His-Name, she thought glumly.

"I'll see you later," Stephanie said as the crowd began to disperse for lunch. "I've got to get going so I can be somewhere near him in the serving line."

Megan sighed. She looked down at her own attire and felt a sense of futility. The cotton knit dress had been washed so often that the vibrant primary colors in the print were faded. The dress fit, but with the bloused bodice it completely hid a more than respectable figure. The midcalf length of the skirt left no more than five or six inches of her legs visible. She'd long ago eschewed sexy high heels for comfortable pumps. She looked downright...dowdy.

She grimaced at the thought of how she must be flunking the chapter on "Dressing for *Sex*-cess" in her birthday book. Her daughter had been right to think that she might need some help. The question was whether it was too late to put all that excellent advice to good use.

Megan joined Dean Sawyer's table with her lunch tray and argued with him for most of the lunch hour over the money she needed for some lab equipment. Her diplomatic skills had helped her become chairman of the science department, and she'd used them to good effect over the past few years to keep the department's resources up-to-date. But this time Dean Sawyer wasn't cooperating.

"If we don't get those new filters, the microsensors we have are going to wear out much sooner. It makes good sense to order the filters now instead of waiting," Megan said.

"I understand your position," Dean Sawyer replied, "but I have other priorities right now."

Megan felt herself losing her temper, but couldn't seem to get control. "You're making a big mistake, and you're not going to appreciate it in a year when—"

"I've made my decision, Megan. It's final."

"Damn, damn, damn!" Megan muttered under her breath. She could feel the tears behind her eyelids. Why was she getting so upset over some lousy equipment? At that moment she looked away and straight into Tom What's-His-Name's eyes.

He was staring at her with green-gray orbs the color of a deep, sunlit sea. He seemed to be searching her face for answers. *And I don't even know the questions.* She examined his face for some sign of his reaction to her and was surprised to find desire—and distrust.

She couldn't look away from him. His lashes were long and too lush for a man's. His brows were straight with only a slight curve at the ends that forced her attention back to those enigmatic eyes. Despite the fact that the day was only half-done, a light shadow of beard defined his jaw. She wanted to look away, but couldn't.

She felt her heartbeat kick into high gear as his gaze moved to her lips. She let her glance drift to his mouth and saw that it was wide, with slightly full, parted lips.

She imagined those lips on hers, felt the soft pressure of that wide mouth closing over her own, imagined his tongue sliding along her lips to tease and taunt her. Her whole body shivered with pleasure at the thought. She watched as his mouth curved into a knowing smile.

Her gaze slid back to his lambent eyes, now the deep, dark green of a stormy sea. Mortified, she realized that he'd guessed her thoughts. She blushed bright red as she looked down at the food left on her tray. Had she actually been imagining a perfect stranger's lips on her own? What in the world was the matter with her?

In the first place, Stephanie had already staked her claims on the man. She would be a fool to try and compete with the younger woman. And speaking of younger, Tom Whoever-He-Was certainly didn't look thirty-nine. How could she be having such carnal thoughts about a younger man? She sneaked a peek at him from under her lashes and saw that he'd turned his attention to his companion on the left—who just happened to be Stephanie. Stephanie spoke animatedly to him and he was nodding and smiling in return.

Forget it, Megan. You're asking for trouble if you even look at the man again.

But dear God in heaven, when was the last time she'd felt anything so sexually enticing, so wickedly wonderful, when she'd simply looked at a man? She was actually considering competing with Stephanie for his attention. And why not? He was certainly worth it. The first thing she was going to do when she got home was check out Chapter Two of her birthday book. Just see if she didn't provide a little competition for Stephanie when she was dressed for *sex*cess!

When Stephanie joined Megan again for the afternoon session in the auditorium, she was full of compliments for Tom, whose last name she'd learned was Steele.

"He's got the sexiest voice. It's low and quiet, but he doesn't use it often. What I mean to say is, he doesn't talk much. All I could find out is that he plans to take advantage of his South American contacts here in Miami for some paper he's working on this coming year. He wasn't wearing a ring, but I asked him if he was married, anyway."

Stephanie paused and turned to Megan, who waited with bated breath until her friend said, "He's divorced. But he didn't volunteer any other information about himself. He's kind of quiet for being such a hunk. But that only makes him more attractive, don't you think?"

"He is attractive," Megan admitted. "In fact, I think he's the most attractive man I've seen in a long time."

Stephanie's brows rose. "Oh? Well, I think the feeling is mutual."

"What?"

"I said I think he finds you attractive, too."

"How can you say such a thing," Megan chided. "He was sitting with you."

"But he was looking at *you*," Stephanie pointed out. "In fact, he couldn't take his eyes off you. He even asked me your name."

Megan felt the color rising in her cheeks. "He did?"

"Uh huh."

"Oh."

"I saw you staring at him, Megan. It was love at first sight. You're crazy about him already, aren't you?"

"So what if I am?" she answered defensively. "What's wrong with that?"

"Why, nothing. I say go for it."

Megan wrung her hands in her lap. "But I thought you planned...uh...wanted—"

"Look, Megan, you know how it is. Either the chemistry's there or it isn't. I think Tom's a great-looking guy. I'd give it a go, but it's plain as the cute little nose on your face that he's not the least bit interested in me. Anyway, while I was eating I got a good look at the new football coach. Ooo la la! So I wish you the best with Tom. In fact, if there's anything I can do to help things along, just let me know."

"Um, well, there is something, actually."

"Name it."

"I may need your help doing some clothes shopping this weekend. You see there's this chapter in my birthday book on how to dress especially to attract a man. I'd appreciate your input when I'm ready to hit the stores."

"Sure. I'm free on Saturday. We have that faculty reception at the president's house on Sunday. You'll want to wear something stunning when you talk with Tom for the first time."

"Maybe he won't be there," Megan said.

"He'll show. It's required for new faculty. It's a come-and-go affair, though, so we'll have to be sure to get there early so you don't miss him."

Megan shook her head in disbelief. "I don't believe I'm doing this."

"It's about time. You've been out of action long enough. Megan Padget rides again!"

"Good grief, Stephanie. You make me sound like the Lone Ranger."

"Well, it's going to take more than a silver bullet to get this man. Something tells me Thomas Steele is more elusive than your ordinary bachelor."

At that moment Dean Sawyer called the afternoon session to order. Megan was grateful for the interruption because she didn't want to think about how hard it was going to be to garner Thomas Steele's attention. After all, it wasn't as though she really had hopes of developing a serious relationship with him. He was only going to be in Miami for a year. And it had been so long since she'd gone out on a date she'd probably forgotten all the rules. But at least if she saw him once or twice and nothing came of it her children would be convinced that she'd given it her best shot and allow her to send in her birthday book receipt for a refund. Then she could buy the latest mystery bestseller and retire to her comfortable bed for an exciting night of reading.

Tom had found out the woman's name was Megan Padget. He hadn't wanted to ask too many questions, because he didn't want to make his interest in her more obvious than he feared it already was. Truthfully, he found her more than a little intriguing. He'd felt her eyes on him a couple of times before he'd finally found her in the crowd at the dean's table. There was something about her that called to his senses. Her eyes were large and brown, like milk chocolate. Her hair was kind of a dark honey blond with curls that bounced when she talked. Strawberry-pink lips pouted slightly, and her complexion was pure whipped cream. Chocolate. Honey. Strawberries. Whipped cream. His mouth watered just thinking about her. He'd always had a sweet tooth, and God, she was bound to taste delicious!

Before he could start daydreaming about her again he picked up the phone in his living room and dialed Randy's number. Irene answered and he gave her an abbreviated version of the day before Randy came on the line.

"So, did you meet the woman of your dreams today?"

"Yes."

There was a stunned silence on the phone as Randy absorbed what his brother had said before the receiver erupted in Tom's ear. "I'll be damned, little brother! When you make up your mind to do something you don't fool around, do you?"

Tom stood there grinning like an idiot, glad Randy couldn't see the silly expression on his face. "It's hardly as though I went searching for the woman, Randy. She was just there."

"I assume she teaches at St. Mark's?"

"She's the chairman of the science department."

"Science, huh? Do you suppose she likes experimenting with new things?" Randy asked, his voice full of innuendo.

Tom felt warmth rising on his face as he remembered that he'd already imagined Megan Padget wrapped around him a dozen different ways. He cleared his throat and said, "Don't get your hopes up, Randy. She's probably married with a couple of kids."

"You mean you didn't ask her?"

"I haven't even spoken to her yet."

There was a dead silence on the phone. Finally Randy said, "You must have it bad, little brother, if you can call her the woman of your dreams when you haven't even exchanged the time of day. She must be a real stunner."

"She's got luscious features, but it was hard to tell about her figure or her height. The only time I saw her she was sitting down. I waited as long as I could for her to stand up, but I had to leave with the crowd at lunch or it would have been obvious that I was looking at her. When I tried to find her later she was gone.''

"When are you going to see her again?"

"There's a faculty reception at the president's house on Sunday. I suppose I'll see her there.''

"Are you going to ask her out on a date?"

This time it was Tom's end of the line that remained silent. Was he going to pursue Megan Padget? He thought of how sweet she'd looked. Then he thought of how quickly things had gone sour with Sally and Maryanne. Was the promise of a good marriage worth the risk of pain if he let himself get involved with the woman? He sighed and answered, "I don't know.''

"Look, I hate to sound like a broken record," Randy said, "but there's more to life than politics and sailing. You're by yourself too much, Tom, and that isn't healthy.''

"I'm sure I'll make friends I can spend time with.''

Randy snorted. "And a lot of those 'friends' will be female. Don't think I don't know it. But I'm talking about the kind of woman you seek out when you think about having a family, making a home for yourself. You must have wanted it once upon a time or you wouldn't have been so torn up when you lost Sally and Maryanne got away.''

"Randy, I—''

"All I'm asking is that you think about it," Randy said. "Don't judge every woman by your experience with those two. All women are not the same. Take it from me."

Tom brushed a hand through his thick black hair, thrusting it from his forehead. "All right, Randy. I'll think about it."

"That's all I'm asking. Just imagine spending the rest of your life with the woman of your dreams."

Tom hung up the phone and sagged into his chair. What could it hurt to ask her out on a date? Still, he knew he was going to have trouble talking to her. He was too attracted to her for it to be otherwise. Maybe he'd just put the moves on her, take her to bed and get her out of his system, as he had done with the others in the years since Maryanne. Hell, anything more than that was asking for trouble.

But the vague sense of dissatisfaction prickling at his neck bothered him. He brushed a hand through his rumpled hair as though to wipe the feeling away. Then he picked up *HOW TO MARRY THE WOMAN OF YOUR DREAMS* from the spooled coffee table and paged through it until he got to the chapter entitled, "That First Fabulous Date." He settled back in the comfortable corduroy chair and started to read.

Three

Her Book: "Dressing for *Sex*cess"

Megan was frantic. How could she have let her daughter talk her into this? Sarah's arguments had seemed perfectly rational at home. It was only now that she'd taken an assortment of clothing into the dressing room that she began to realize the true folly of this whole scheme. She couldn't shop for sexy clothes with her fourteen-year-old daughter! What kind of message would that send to Sarah's tender young psyche? But when Stephanie had called to say she had some kind of stomach flu, she'd told Megan to go shopping without her. And Sarah, who'd overheard the conversation, had insisted that she could do as good a job as Stephanie at helping her mom find just the right kind of outfits to be dressed for *sex*cess.

"Are you ready yet, Mom?"

"I'll be out in a minute, Sarah."

Megan looked down at the bright red silk confection she was wearing. Her birthday book had suggested she buy only primary colors. Red sent a pretty basic message, all right. Hot, it said. Ready for sex, it said. I'm woman enough for your man, it said. Megan rolled her eyes. She wasn't sure she was ready to handle the kind of sexual action this dress promised to get for her.

She buttoned up the form-fitting bodice and looked at herself in the mirror. She recalled her birthday book's advice:

Always buy clothing that looks easy to remove. Watch for items that have buttons or laces or zippers down the front. Leave a button or two undone. That way a man can easily imagine himself undressing you. Of course, a T-shirt without a bra has its own allure. Everyone knows how quickly a T-shirt can hit the floor.

She wasn't about to wear a T-shirt to the faculty reception, but then she wasn't so sure about this red dress, either. Tentatively she unbuttoned the first button, and then the second. The dress fell open provocatively. She swung her hips and the full skirt flowed around her. Lord in heaven! She actually looked...sexy.

Her book had also suggested buying touchable fabrics such as silk, wool and cotton. She fingered the silky material, pressed it down across her body, felt its smoothness against her skin. She had to admit it felt sensual. The book had said:

You want a man to imagine his fingertips roaming the territory. What is he going to feel? Your clothing should suggest the softness of skin, the textures of sex.

The textures of sex? Sex wasn't always the texture of silk to Megan's way of thinking. The act of love grew out of the feelings two people had for one another—and as a woman who'd been married for ten years, she knew that often sex between two people reflected feelings that weren't the least bit silky.

Sometimes it was rough, but fun, like terry cloth, a roller coaster of ups and downs like Harris Tweed or rich and full like brocade. There were other times it was adventuresome, like dungaree. There was a definite difference between sex that was soft and delicate like velveteen, and sex that was soft and wild like doeskin. Megan remembered a few snug fits—like banlon, and embraces tight as corseting. Then there were the warm and tender moments like flannel. She'd had her share of stiff buckram sex, too. But her favorite...her favorite sex was cotton. It was natural and honest and durable. And it lasted forever with care.

"Mom? Did you fall asleep in there?"

"I'll be out in a second." But it was several minutes before Megan finally made it out of the dressing room. "Here I am. Well, what do you think?"

"I think you look fantastic."

Megan whirled to find the source of the deep masculine voice. She stared unbelievingly at Tom Steele leaning casually against a wall of the department store. A sleeveless gray T-shirt revealed his muscular arms and the strength of his equally muscular chest. His lean, jeans-clad legs were crossed at his bare ankles, his feet encased in well-worn dock-siders.

"What are you doing here?" she demanded.

"Shopping."

"In ladies clothing?" Megan was upset because she'd dressed to attract him, and didn't know how to handle herself now that he'd shown up in the flesh. It had been over a year since she'd last flirted with a man.

The grin that spread across his face was one of pure male appreciation as he straightened and walked toward her. "I came to pick up my sister-in-law, Irene. She's here somewhere trying on a few things."

Megan hadn't realized how totally focused she'd been on Tom until she realized Sarah had disappeared. She looked around and saw her daughter on the far side of the store talking with one of her girlfriends from school.

"We haven't been formally introduced. I'm Tom Steele."

Megan held her breath in anticipation as Tom extended his hand to her. His large, callused palm surrounded hers and his fingers grasped hers firmly for a moment before he released his grip. The shock was electric and raced up her arm. It was all she could do not to jerk her hand away.

"I'm Megan Padget. It's nice to meet you, Dr. Steele."

"Tom."

"Tom." Megan's lips curved in a smile of genuine pleasure.

Then Tom and Megan just stood and stared at one another. His gaze rested on her face for a moment before it drifted down to her throat. The red dress bared her to his gaze. She groped self-consciously for the buttons she'd unfastened. As she fingered one of the few still buttoned, it slipped loose and the dress fell even further open, revealing the rounded flesh of her breasts. She immediately grabbed a handful of the silk in a wad at her throat. Surely he didn't think she'd done that on purpose!

Tom's eyes took on a hooded look as his glance slid back to her face. His gaze was intense, his eyes dark. She wondered if he was imagining himself undressing her, as the book had said he would. How did he see her?

She felt her nipples pucker beneath the silk, painfully aware that with the new sheer bra she'd bought her arousal must be showing through the dress. Her lips opened to sip a shallow breath of air. She was caught up in a sensual fantasy that could have only one ending.

Megan caught a glimpse of Sarah across the store, sorting through a table of designer blue jeans, and stiffened. How could she have so completely forgotten her daughter's presence! This was no time to let her imagination run amok. As much as she was enjoying it, she needed to get this meeting over with before Sarah returned and started asking embarrassing questions.

"It's..." Her voice was a croak. She cleared her throat and tried again. "It's an honor to have someone with your credentials teaching at St. Mark's this year. You mentioned you're meeting your sister-in-law. Does that mean you have family living here in Miami?"

"My brother, Randy, and his wife."

"She's the one you're meeting?"

"Yes. Is your husband shopping somewhere in the mall?" Tom could have kicked himself for asking such an obvious question. Where was his savoir faire? Not to mention his subtlety. It had been a long time since he'd been so attracted to a woman, and naturally, his brain couldn't seem to get an intelligent message to his mouth.

"Um...my ex-husband died two years ago. I'm not married." Megan groaned inwardly. Dumb, dumb, dumb! Of course she wasn't married if Gary was her *ex*-husband. Did she have to announce her availability so clumsily?

"Are you shopping for something special?" he asked.

"I'm looking for something to wear to the faculty reception. What do you think?" She held the full red skirt away from her hips. That necessitated releasing the bodice, which fell open with a vengeance.

His lips quirked. "I think you'll make quite a splash."

Megan was basking in Tom's approval, thinking that maybe she hadn't forgotten how to flirt after all, when a petite, blond woman appeared at Tom's elbow.

"There you are, Tom. I found what I was looking for." The woman peeked around his shoulder and saw Megan. "It looks like you have, too," she teased.

Tom chuckled as Megan blushed. "Irene Steele, this is Dr. Megan Padget. Megan is chairman of the science department at St. Mark's."

"Ohh." Irene gave the word a wealth of meaning.

Megan wondered if Tom could possibly have mentioned her to his family. How could he? They hadn't even met until today. She was aware of Irene's surreptitious inspection of her, but never guessed what was coming.

"My husband and I are having a cookout tonight, Dr. Padget," Irene said. "Can you join us?"

"Please call me Megan." Megan dearly wanted to spend more time getting to know Tom Steele, but it couldn't be tonight. "I appreciate the invitation, but—"

"It's just a casual family get-together," Irene said in an attempt to head off Megan's refusal.

"I'd love to come, but I already have plans for tonight."

"Oh?" Irene said in a way that asked for an explanation.

Megan didn't want to explain that her activities included providing the centerpieces and dessert for her son's Boy Scout beginning-of-the-year banquet, because she wasn't ready to admit yet that she had a son. She settled for saying, "I made a commitment to...to someone, and I wouldn't feel right breaking it."

Tom had felt a distinct and pleasant relief to discover Megan was unmarried. Now it appeared there was a man in her life, after all. Which was probably just as well, because the woman intrigued him far too much for his own peace of mind.

"I'm sorry to hear that," he said with a shade of irritation in his voice that he wasn't able to control.

"No, I'm the one who's sorry." Megan met Tom's eyes and let her regret show. "Maybe another time."

"Sure," Irene said. "How about next Saturday?"

"You're having another cookout next Saturday?'' Megan asked, astonished at having a second invitation issued so promptly.

Irene grinned and laughed, ignoring the way Tom's arm tensed under her hand. ''Well, we weren't. But we are now.''

Tom was ready to throttle his sister-in-law. It was bad enough that she'd invited Megan once, but the second cookout made her matchmaking attempts too obvious for comfort. It was one thing to buy him a book called *HOW TO MARRY THE WOMAN OF YOUR DREAMS*. It was quite another to calculatingly invite the woman of his dreams to dinner. He was perfectly capable of doing his own wife hunting, if he wanted a wife. Which he didn't!

''I hope you weren't thinking of including me in that invitation next Saturday,'' he said, his jaw tight with restrained anger. ''I have other plans.''

Irene pursed her lips. ''Oh, but of course I was. If you can't come...''

Megan saw that Irene was well and truly caught. It was plain she'd only issued the invitation as a way of bringing Tom and her together. Under the circumstances it would be awkward for everybody if she accepted Irene's invitation. Reluctantly Megan said, ''I'm afraid I have plans for next Saturday, too. But thanks for the offer.''

Hearing Megan was busy the following Saturday as well only confirmed Tom's belief that she was involved with another man. "Are you ready to go, Irene?"

Irene responded to the warning tone in Tom's voice by slipping her arm through his. "Sure. It was nice meeting you, Megan. I'll see you again soon, I hope."

Tom took off with his sister-in-law hanging on to his arm. She turned back to wave and smile as he dragged her away.

Sarah crossed Tom's path on her way back to her mom. "Wow!" she said, staring after him. "Did you see that hunk, Mom? Imagine if you found a guy to marry who looks like that! Think how goggle-eyed the girls would be if I introduced *him* as my new stepfather."

"Looks aren't everything, Sarah. It's more important what kind of person you are."

"Yeah, I know. But he sure looks like he'd be a nice person, doesn't he?"

Megan brushed the bangs away from Sarah's forehead. "You're probably right, honey." Megan had to agree with her daughter's taste in men. Tom Steele was gorgeous; there was no denying it. But she'd meant what she'd said to Sarah. Looks weren't everything. No matter how attracted she was to Tom Steele, and she admitted it was quite a lot, she wasn't going to let herself get emotionally involved with him until she knew whether he was the kind of man who would accept another man's children. She'd met too many men who didn't want a ready-made family.

On the other hand she wasn't willing to tell Tom about Sarah and Chris yet. She wanted to take the time first to find out whether they were compatible as a couple, whether they had interests in common and whether he was the kind of man who could make her laugh, before she took the step of letting him meet her children. She knew her decision was the right one, especially in light of Sarah's adolescent remark about having a stepfather who looked like Tom. It would be infinitely worse if Sarah introduced Tom to all her friends, only to have him disappear when the time came to make a commitment.

Eventually the day of reckoning would come. When it did she was counting on a man as intelligent as Tom had to be to recognize what an asset her two wonderful children were. And if he didn't...well, she had no use for him. None at all.

"Hey, that dress looks really great, Mom. I'll bet any man would take a second look. Are you ready to try on another one?"

The last thing Megan felt like doing was trying on more sexy clothes. But fingering the buttons that lay undone at her throat she admitted that the dress had had an effect. And tomorrow when she showed up at the faculty reception she was determined to finish the job!

Megan spent the rest of Saturday evening after the banquet reading *YOU DON'T HAVE TO STAY SINGLE* and looking for clues as to what she should do and say when she met Tom again on Sunday afternoon. She read the same paragraph over and over.

> *Be sure to let him do all the talking. Listen to what he says. Make certain you would seriously consider marrying this man before you invest time telling him about yourself.*

She felt vindicated in her decision to keep the knowledge of her children to herself. After all, the idea was to vet a man first before revealing everything about yourself. The fact that she was a mother could wait for later meetings when she was sure Tom was real marriage material.

Megan shut her birthday book and placed it on the table beside her bed. She plumped the pillows up behind her and leaned back to think. She'd never really looked on finding a husband as something that could be reduced to cold, calculated planning. She'd fallen in love with Gary in college and had never looked at another man. She hadn't much cared what occupation he chose, how much he liked to talk, how he felt about religion or money. Those were all issues *YOU DON'T HAVE TO STAY SINGLE* had suggested she broach with a prospective husband.

Yet having lived through a not-so-idyllic marriage with Gary she could see how if she'd asked some of those questions in the first place, she and Gary might have been saved a lot of heartache. Once the rosy blush had worn off their marriage, they'd fought constantly about money, about how much time they spent at their respective jobs and even about how many children they should have. Their lack of honest communication had resulted in painful years of isolation and loneliness, and finally in divorce. Marriage wasn't something she would ever wander blindly into again.

She had scoffed at the idea of taking advice from a book on how to find a husband, but so far everything she'd read in *YOU DON'T HAVE TO STAY SINGLE* was proving to be correct. Tomorrow would be another test. She'd ask the questions she was supposed to ask and see how Tom answered. That would tell her whether he was more than a handsome face and a tantalizing body.

Stephanie came to pick her up a little early on Sunday afternoon, and Megan was still dressing.

"Come on into my bedroom, Stephanie," Megan called out. "I'm just about ready."

"Lordy, Lordy! Look at you! What have you got on there? Can that possibly be a garter belt?"

Megan fought a blush. "Advice from page twenty-three. 'Sexy starts from the inside out.'"

"And you shopped for this stuff with Sarah?"

"Uh, not for this. I sent Sarah off with money to buy some jeans while I went to lingerie." Megan pulled on a silk stocking and hooked it to the lacy white garter belt.

"Stand up and let me see you," Stephanie said.

Megan stood and looked at herself in the full-length mirror attached to her closet door. She was wearing a lace bra with insets that revealed a great deal of flesh, but concealed the nipples. Her underwear and garter belt matched her bra in that they "teased," but didn't "go all the way." Megan pulled on a sheer half-slip that was decorated in equally sexy lace, then slipped her dress over her head.

"That dress isn't like anything I've ever seen you wear before," Stephanie said. "It's more…"

"Suggestive?"

Stephanie shook her head. "Not exactly. More like promising. It says come take a look. But it doesn't say touch. Some guy is going to go crazy when he finds all that lace underneath that come-hither dress.''

Megan smoothed the clingy white cotton knit over her stomach and hips. She reached up to fasten only two of the six or seven tiny buttons in the front, letting the soft cotton top fall open in a deep V that revealed the shadow between her breasts.

"Boy, when you go to school you learn your lessons well," Stephanie said. "I can't believe the difference a dress makes."

"Then you like it?"

"The question isn't whether I like it. It's whether Tom is going to like it."

"And?"

Stephanie laughed. "He's going to like it."

Megan slipped tiny pearl earrings into her pierced ears, recalling that her book had said:

The less jewelry you wear the better. Remember to keep earrings small so he can see they won't get in his way if he wants to nibble. Don't wear any jewelry that looks like it might have been given to you by another man. That means no rings and no pendant necklaces.

Megan took off the diamond necklace that she'd had made from the engagement ring Gary had given her so many years ago. She really thought this was going too far, but now that she'd committed herself to following the book's advice, she might as well go whole hog.

She slipped into the three-inch taupe heels she'd bought to complement the dress and grabbed a matching clutch purse. "We'd better get going."

The president's house was done in elaborate Spanish-style architecture that was popular in parts of Miami. It had numerous arches, tile floors, stucco walls and wrought iron framing the large windows. There was a tile fountain in the center of the rear patio where most of the faculty had congregated. The backyard bordered on Biscayne Bay and there was a dock where a boat could be moored. Even though the late August day was hot, the breeze off the bay made it seem cooler than it was.

"This is lovely," Megan said to Stephanie, her nose turned into the wind, her hair streaming out behind her. "I'd love to live on the water like this. Wouldn't you?"

"Yes, I would."

Megan turned, somehow not surprised that the

voice that had answered her was Tom's and not Stephanie's.

"Your friend went to get some more punch. Can I get you anything?"

"No, I'm fine."

They took a moment just to enjoy looking at one another. Megan couldn't take her eyes off Tom's face. His green eyes sparkled with pleasure, his lips curved with delight, and she knew without having to be told that he admired what he saw. But he didn't leave her to guess what he was thinking.

"You look lovely today." Tom heard the compliment roll off his tongue and knew it was a line he'd used a hundred times with other women. He'd wanted to say something different to Megan. Something special. "You look...nice," he told her at last, helpless to speak what he really felt.

"Thank you. You look very nice yourself," she responded.

Tom had donned a pale yellow short-sleeved shirt with a rep stripe tie and form-fitting navy slacks that emphasized his lean waist and flat belly. She fought a smile as she admitted that the view from the front was equally as enticing as the one she'd had from the back at the first faculty meeting. Her gaze caught on one of his muscular forearms, which were covered with a light dusting of black hair. She followed an enlarged vein down his arm to a strong wrist and finally to the large hand that grasped a bottle of beer. The fingers of his other hand caressed the bottle, and Megan shivered at the thought of those hands smoothing along her perspiration-glazed skin.

She looked up into Tom's eyes and knew their physical attraction was mutual. *Looks aren't everything,* she warned herself. It was time to get to the business of finding out more about Tom.

"Is your home in Washington anything like this?" She gestured toward the Spanish mansion.

"No. Everything in my neighborhood is Colonial."

"Which do you like better?"

"I can see how the high ceilings and large windows this house has would be an advantage in a place as warm as Miami. But I have to admit that something draws me to a brick house. Maybe it all goes back to the days when my mother told me the story of the Three Little Pigs."

Megan quirked a brow in bemusement.

Tom groaned inwardly. *You idiot! The Three Little Pigs?!* He ground his teeth. Determined to try to salvage the situation he explained, "The wisest pig had a house of brick. I guess that's why a brick house has always seemed like a smart investment to me."

Megan laughed. "I hope all your economic decisions aren't based on fairy tales."

"Hardly." *Good God, man! Look what you've got her thinking now!* "I admit I have my share of dreams about how I'd spend a fortune if it dropped into my lap."

"Such as?"

For a minute Megan thought he wasn't going to answer her. His gaze skipped out to follow a sailboat on the bay.

"I'd buy a boat and sail around the world," he said.

Megan felt her heart dropping to her shoes. He was a wanderer. A wanderer would make a terrible husband and an even worse father. "Do you do a lot of sailing?" she forced herself to ask.

"Not as much as I'd like. To be honest, I'd be content to sail closer to shore if I just had the time to do it."

Megan breathed a sigh of relief.

Ask her something, Steele. "What about you? What do you dream of, Megan Padget?"

"I guess I'm more the practical type. I try to do the best with what I have, rather than dream about what I can never have."

"It's the dreamers who shape the future," he said.

"It's the practical people who make those dreams a reality," she countered.

Talk with her; don't argue. "I'll concede one is as necessary as the other," he said with a wry smile, "which shows you how much of a politician I've become over the years in D.C."

"I've often wondered—"

"I'm sorry to interrupt," Dean Sawyer said, putting a hand on Megan's shoulder, "but Tom has a call from Washington. It seems there's some emer- gency—"

"Which phone?" Tom asked.

"You can take it in the president's study. I'll show you the way."

Tom turned to Megan. "Will you excuse me?"

"Of course." What else could she say?

He was gone a moment later. Megan had been amazed at the instant change in Tom's demeanor. His laid-back manner clearly hid an astute advisor. She wondered what other deceptive coloring he'd used to disguise the real Tom Steele.

"Well, do you have a date with Tom?"

Megan hadn't seen Stephanie coming and her friend's hand on her shoulder had startled her so she spilled her wine. "No, I do not have a date with Tom."

Stephanie looked disappointed. "I was sure he would ask you out."

"We were interrupted when he got called away to the phone."

"Maybe he'll be coming back out to find you later."

"Maybe," Megan said. "But I wouldn't count on it."

"What makes you say that?"

Megan shrugged. "I don't know. It's just a feeling I have."

"So where do you go from here?"

"I don't know."

"What's the next chapter in your book?" Stephanie asked.

"I think it's called, 'You *Can* Ask Him Out.'"

"There you have it then. The problem is solved."

"What problem and how is it solved?"

"Why, the problem of how to get Tom to ask you for a date," Stephanie said. "You simply ask him first."

Megan laughed out loud. "You've got to be kidding. I've never asked a man out in my life. And to start with a man like Tom Steele...I just couldn't do it. Besides, in our society it's the man who does the pursuing. It's hardly romantic if the woman has to do the asking."

Stephanie sighed loudly. "Think how great it would be if we could. Of course it's up to you, but I'd think from Tom's point of view, it would be romantic to be asked out by a beautiful woman. I mean, imagine what an awful burden it is for a man to always have to make the first move, to have to be the one to set himself up to be rejected. This way at least he'll know you're interested in him."

"Then I'm the one who's setting herself up for rejection!"

"You've got as much information to go on as he does. Is he interested in you?"

"I think so," Megan replied hesitantly.

"Do you think he thinks you're interested in him?"

"I think so," Megan repeated.

"So what's the problem? If it's custom you're worried about, customs are changing all the time. If the book says it's all right to do it, try it. At least think about it."

"Sure," Megan said. "I'll think about it."

But there was no way on earth she was ever going to come up with the courage to ask Tom Steele out on a date.

Four

His Book: "That First Fabulous Date"

The first few weeks of school were always hectic, and Megan didn't even have time to think about Tom Steele, let alone work up the courage to ask him out. But they did cross paths several times on campus. Tom was always cordial, though not particularly talkative. Megan wondered if her intuition had been wrong. Maybe he hadn't been attracted to her after all. Maybe it had been wishful thinking on her part. For a woman who had touted herself as a realist, rather than a dreamer, she was holding on to some pretty farfetched hopes where Tom Steele was concerned.

"Hello there."

At first she thought she'd imagined Tom's voice. But when she looked up she saw that she had very nearly run right into him. She hugged her textbooks closer to her for security. "Hi."

"Fancy meeting you here," he said.

"Yeah, fancy that."

Tom looked at the woman before him and felt a frustration he couldn't voice. Why couldn't he manage to sound like something other than a tongue-tied adolescent whenever he got near her?

"How are your classes going?" she asked.

"Fine," he answered. "How about yours?"

"Fine."

Megan looked at Tom and wondered why it was that their conversations on campus always seemed so stilted. And yet neither of them made any move to leave.

"So, what have you been doing lately?" he went on.

"Not much. And you?"

"Me neither."

They both stood silent a moment until Tom thrust a hand brusquely through his hair, said, "I'll be seeing you around," and stalked off.

This is damned ridiculous, he thought as he pictured the look of confusion on Megan's face when he'd turned tail and run from her. When he reached the sanctuary of his campus office he closed the door and leaned back against it. He was an intelligent, educated, internationally known authority on South American politics. But he could write what he knew about women on the head of a pin. His father hadn't been any kind of role model to follow where behavior with women was concerned, and if Sally hadn't been so persistent during his college years and done most of the talking it was likely they would never have married. Now that he thought about it, Maryanne had done most of the talking, too. It was a miracle he'd managed to get by for so long without anyone ever discovering his secret.

Everyone, men and women both, always assumed that a man like him must have had a lot of experience with women. After all, they assumed, his looks could get him anyone he wanted. Tom shook his head in disgust. It was true he was a good lover. But only because he'd cared enough to take the time to learn how to please the few partners he'd had. He'd said no a lot more times over the years than anyone might suspect. And when he'd been ready to say yes there'd been more than enough willing women eager to fill his needs. He hadn't had to say anything. The women had been glad to do the asking.

This time he wanted to do the pursuing. But it wasn't as simple as he'd thought. Although he wanted to ask Megan out for a date, he couldn't seem to come up with the right words. Hell, to tell the truth, he couldn't seem to come up with *any* words. But for the first time in his life he wanted to do something about it.

His eyes landed on the copy of *HOW TO MARRY THE WOMAN OF YOUR DREAMS*. He'd brought it into the office in case he got bored during the day and needed a laugh. Right now he didn't feel much like laughing. He crossed to his swivel chair, grabbing the book on the way. He leaned back and opened the book to the second chapter, ''That First Fabulous Date.''

First impressions are everything. You must plan your initial outing with the woman of your dreams very carefully. Try for something original, and make it an event that offers many opportunities to talk.

''In other words, don't take her out to dinner and the movies,'' Tom murmured aloud. He kept reading, finding the dating suggestions he was certain would be there.

Go to a museum opening.

He always felt a sense of reverence whenever he was in a museum that forced him into silence. He had enough trouble making conversation without that inhibiting factor.

Take a walking tour of the city.

He was sure he would enjoy such a tour, but from what he'd been able to determine, Megan was already familiar with the area. She'd end up carrying the conversation, and that was exactly what he was trying to avoid.

Attend a lecture.

He thought that sounded more promising. He sought out the *Miami Herald* he'd brought with him that morning and paged through the entertainment section to see what he could find. Unfortunately the only two talks being held over the weekend related to South American politics. He'd end up lecturing to Megan before the date was over, and he didn't want that. He went back to his birthday book for another idea.

Go to the zoo.

Tom leaned back in his chair, put his feet up on his desk and laced his hands together behind his head. When was the last time he'd gone to the zoo? Not for years. He'd tried to convince Maryanne to go with him to see the pandas at the National Zoo, but she hadn't been interested.

He picked up the entertainment section of the newspaper again. He thought he remembered seeing an advertisement for the zoo, and sure enough he found it. Miami's Metrozoo boasted a new Australian exhibit that featured koalas. He smiled. Well, they weren't pandas, but they were equally exotic and cuddly looking. He read the rest of the ad, which mentioned there was an outdoor amphitheatre. He and Megan could take a picnic and eat while listening to a popular rock group.

The more Tom read, the more sure he was that he'd stumbled upon the perfect First Fabulous Date. It would be fun, and the antics of the wild animals would hopefully provide lots of conversational material. He sighed with relief. He could see now how his birthday book might have some value after all.

He kept looking to see if the book offered any advice on actually conducting the date. Sure enough, there it was: "Dating Protocol." He grinned. He was an expert on protocol, so this should be a cinch. His grin faded as he kept reading.

Many women today insist on taking their share of the financial burden of dating, and actually disapprove of a man who wants to pay for everything.

Tom's lips pursed thoughtfully. Surely Megan wouldn't expect to pay if he asked her out on a date. Maybe he was old-fashioned, but that was the way he felt. He hadn't thought of himself as a chauvinist, either, but maybe he was. *Or maybe it's just that you have to be in control.*

The flash of insight rocked Tom back in his chair. Was that really why he thought a man had to pay…to stay in control of the situation? He shook his head, unwilling to accept that explanation of his motives. He'd surely gotten past that after losing Sally. Anyway, Megan hadn't struck him as the sort of woman who'd insist on paying her own way. And if she did… He sighed and admitted that if she did, his beliefs were going to be put to the test.

He forced himself to keep reading, and groaned aloud when he read the last two paragraphs in the chapter.

It's important to use your time together to find out whether or not you're compatible. This means asking probing questions and demanding honest answers. Will you still want to be married to this woman in a year? Five years? Twenty-five years? The questions you ask on this First Fabulous Date should be focused to answer these questions.

He'd never been one for finding out the intimate details of a woman's life. But this book seemed to suggest that the secret to a successful marriage, the key to marrying the right woman in the first place, was as simple as asking questions before you committed yourself. He was just going on a *date* for pete's sake, not to a summit conference! But all the same, he thought of several things it would be nice to know about Megan Padget. Maybe he could just work them casually into the conversation.

Megan was in the kitchen fixing supper when the phone rang. "Will you get that, Sarah?" she called to the living room.

"Sure, Mom."

At that instant it occurred to Megan that it might be Tom on the line—and she hadn't told him she had children. She raced her daughter to the phone, notwithstanding the meat-loaf mixture coating her hands, and caught Sarah just before she lifted the receiver. "I've got it. I just remembered I'm expecting a call." She waited for Sarah to walk away before she picked up the phone, praying it wasn't one of Sarah's many friends, after all.

"Hello. Padget residence."

"Is that you, Megan?"

"Tom. Hello. Yes, it's me." Megan couldn't help the smile on her face, which came out as pleasure in her voice. He'd called. She hadn't realized how much she'd been hoping he would until now.

"Um…"

Megan waited, but when he didn't say anything she asked, "Was there something you wanted to talk with me about, Tom?"

"Yes. I…um…" Tom suddenly had second thoughts about asking Megan to the zoo. Maybe that wasn't the sort of thing women did nowadays. But it was too late to come up with anything else, so he said, "Would you like to go the zoo with me on Saturday?"

"The zoo? Saturday?"

Tom cursed under his breath. For crying out loud! How could he have thought she'd want to go to the zoo? "That is, unless—"

"I'd love to go... Are you still there, Tom?"

"I'm here. That's great. I'll pick you up early, say eight in the morning?"

Megan searched her mind to think of a way she could keep Tom from coming to the house. Sarah was bound to remember him from the department store, and that would lead to speculation by her daughter that could only cause problems if things failed to develop between her and Tom.

"Uh... why don't we meet for breakfast on Saturday?" Megan countered. "I know a lovely Jewish deli that has every kind of fresh bagel your heart desires."

Tom felt a rippling unease about Megan's counter-proposal, then shrugged and said, "That sounds good. I'll pick you up—"

"No! I mean, it's on my way to Metrozoo and there's no sense you driving out of *your* way. Nell's is on U.S. 1, south of the city. The exact address is in the phone book. I'll meet you there at 8:00 a.m. sharp on Saturday. Is there anything I can bring?"

"No. I'll take care of lunch," Tom said firmly. "See you on Saturday."

Megan didn't arrive at Nell's until 8:45 a.m. At the last minute Sarah and Chris had gotten into an argument and she hadn't wanted to leave until it was settled. She'd just turned onto I-95 when her left rear tire had gone flat. Megan had never changed a tire so fast in her life. She looked down at the smudges on the clingy pink T-shirt and white shorts that she'd donned this morning to be dressed for *sex*cess. It couldn't be helped. At least she was here. She took a deep, calming breath and let it out. Now if only Tom had waited for her.

Nell's was crowded, as she'd expected it to be. She searched for a familiar set of broad shoulders and a head of wavy black hair, but didn't see them. Her heart sank. A man like Tom Steele probably wasn't used to waiting for a woman. She could hardly blame him. After all, she was forty-five minutes late. Then she spotted him waving at her. She crossed quickly and joined him in a booth at the rear of the deli.

"I'm sorry I'm late," she said breathlessly.

"It was worth the wait." His approval of her attire was clear in his green eyes. "I must admit I've already succumbed to a bagel with my cup of coffee. What would you like?"

"I'll have a cinnamon-raisin one." Megan couldn't believe how understanding he'd been. He hadn't even forced her to resort to excuses, although she felt compelled to explain, "I had a flat tire. That's why I was so late."

"In that case, congratulations for getting here

as soon as you did. Did you have any problems getting it changed?''

"I had a little trouble with the lug nuts, but otherwise it was a breeze. I'm afraid I came out a little the worse for wear, though. I—"

"You changed the tire yourself?"

Megan laughed at the astonished look on Tom's face. "Of course. Why wouldn't I? You're not one of those men who thinks a woman should depend on a man for everything, are you?"

Tom took so long answering her question that Megan feared he was going to say he was. She rushed to fill the dead air with, "I'm not a feminist or anything. At least I don't think I am. But I do believe women today have to learn to be self-sufficient. Don't you agree?"

Before Tom could formulate an answer for an issue he'd never confronted in the past, she'd continued, "Although I wish that being self-sufficient didn't sometimes mean having to get dirty." She slid around the curved booth closer to Tom. "Just look at my T-shirt and shorts."

All Tom saw were the long, slender thighs coming out of the shorts, and the pattern of lace in Megan's bra under her T-shirt—which he guessed he could have off her in two seconds flat. He tamped down his libido and said, "I'm glad to see you dressed for the heat. I understand there isn't a lot of shade at the zoo.''

''How true. I went there a month or so ago with—'' Megan stopped herself just in time from admitting she'd gone to the zoo with her children. ''With a friend of mine.''

Tom heard the same implication he'd heard before—that Megan was involved with another man. He told himself it didn't matter. She was here today with him, wasn't she? And almost too close for comfort. Her thigh was only inches from his own, and since he'd worn shorts, too, it wouldn't have taken much to press his hard, hairy leg against her soft, smooth one. He reached over for a packet of sweetener for his coffee and edged away slightly. Better to remove temptation altogether.

But he was tempted. More than he cared to admit. He told himself she was just another beautiful woman. After what he'd been through with Sally and Maryanne, he would be crazy to let himself get emotionally involved with her. He would accept what she had to offer physically and that would be that. Anyway, all they were going to do today was enjoy each other's company. This was just a simple date.

''Don't eat too many bagels,'' he warned. ''I've packed us a pretty large lunch.''

"Don't worry," Megan said with a grin. "As big as Metrozoo is, we'll walk breakfast off without any problem."

Megan ate quickly. When the waitress brought the check she leaned over to look at it. "Let's see. My half of the bill—"

"I'll get it." Tom lifted the check out of her reach.

"Then I'll leave the tip."

"I said I'll get it."

Megan cocked her head at Tom's curtness. Maybe he was more upset about her lateness than he'd let on. She hoped he wasn't going to let that affect their day. But as soon as he'd paid the check his good humor returned.

"What animals do you want to see most?" he asked as they walked out to his car.

"The ones closest to the main gate," she teased.

Tom laughed.

"You think it's funny now. Let's see how you feel in a couple of hours. That zoo has got *miles* of walkways. I hope you don't mind driving. I've got the spare on one wheel and it's not in very good shape."

Tom was startled again that she'd even considered taking her car. "I invited you. I'll drive."

"Golly, look at this!" she exclaimed when he

opened the door to a dark blue, shiny, late-model American sedan. "It looks brand new!"

"I take good care of my car. I'm glad to see it shows."

"It does." She sat carefully on the plush seats so the spots of grease on her shorts didn't touch the upholstery. "It's absolutely immaculate."

Megan was thinking how the exterior of her car hadn't been waxed once in the two years since she'd bought it secondhand with a dent. And how the interior, while uncluttered, had that lived-in look that comes from hauling loads of eight-year-old boys to baseball games and fourteen-year-old girls to cheerleading practice. Their cars were definitely not a compatible facet of their life-styles.

She wondered whether he kept his house as clean as his car. Surely not. But she might as well know now as later. "Are you as conscientious with your house as you are with your car?"

"Hell, no!" He flashed a self-deprecating grin. "I mean, I'm not a total slob at home, but I like things comfortable, and that means accessible. I've got a lady who comes in to clean my place in D.C. I've been looking for someone to do the same here. Do you know anybody?"

"Afraid not," Megan said, a cheerful smile on her face now that she knew that not only didn't he expect an immaculate house but he also was willing to hire a maid to clean. "I do my own housekeeping. But I'll ask around for you."

Megan's earlier words regarding the miles of walkways at the zoo turned out to be more true than Tom could have imagined. Metrozoo had gone beyond steel bars and concrete cages. He and Megan had to literally hike between the enormous natural habitats that had been created for the various species of wild animals.

As they watched some white tigers wind around the East Indian statuary within their area Megan said, "I worked for a boss once who paced like that."

"Oh? A professor?"

"No. I used to be a loan officer with a bank in downtown Miami."

"Why did you quit?"

I got pregnant with Sarah. "Oh, you know how those things go. I needed a change."

"It was fortunate for me that you turned to education."

His voice was low and husky and when Megan looked up into his eyes she saw the warmth of desire. She tried to stay relaxed when Tom slipped his arm around her waist to head her toward the next exhibit.

"Shall we go see the koalas now?" he said.

"Although I don't see how they could be any softer than you are."

Megan felt a shiver of excitement course down her spine as Tom's fingers caressed her waist. "The koala exhibit sounds good," she said, her voice breathless. "Let's go."

Tom's arm stayed around her during the entire walk to the koala exhibit, and Megan enjoyed the feel of his tall, male body aligned with hers. Her arm had gotten in the way between them until he'd finally wrapped it around his waist. She could feel the hard muscle beneath the cotton shirt, and she would have given anything if she could have touched his bare skin.

The koalas were so adorable they could have been posing for Australian tourist posters. Tom and Megan spent a lot of time smiling and laughing as they walked from place to place. Despite the advice they'd both received from their respective birthday books, the talk between them stayed trivial, fun—and safe.

Megan was having such a wonderful time she had to remind herself that she was supposed to be vetting Tom as a prospective husband. She racked her mind to think what subjects she ought to cover, and mentally flicked through them: attitudes toward money, goals, needs in a mate...

According to her birthday book, the key to

knowing who Tom was lay in the activities and events that had shaped him as a youth. All her questions were supposed to be aimed at his past. Megan felt a twinge of guilt for what she was about to do. However, if she and Tom were incompatible it was important to find that out before they'd spent too much time together. The answers Tom gave her now should tell her a lot about the man he was.

She took a deep breath and asked, "Do your parents live in Miami, too?"

"My father is dead," he said flatly. "My mother has remarried and lives in San Antonio."

She couldn't believe the harshness in Tom's voice. "How old were you when your father died?"

"Fourteen."

Megan could feel the tension radiating from him. This was not a subject she wanted to pursue, but his reaction made her sure it was an important one.

"It must have been awful to lose your father so young."

"On the contrary. His death was a blessing."

Megan stopped and pulled from Tom's embrace to face him. "You can't mean that!"

"Oh, but I do."

"Why?"

His eyes lit with anger as he spoke. "He was an alcoholic. When he was drunk—and I don't even remember him sober—he beat my mother, and when he was done with her he started in on me and my brother."

Megan had no experience with the kind of childhood Tom was describing. She could only empathize with the little boy who'd apparently been brutalized by his father. "I'm sorry. It must have been terrible for you all."

"I've always been afraid I'd turn out like him."

Megan stiffened. "Do you have a drinking problem?"

"Of course not!"

"Have you ever hit a woman?"

"Never! I wouldn't lift a finger—"

"Then why on earth would you compare yourself to your father?" Megan said.

"I know it isn't rational. It just doesn't seem to be something I can control."

Tom was upset that he'd said as much as he had, and even more amazed that he'd said anything at all. "Look, let's talk about something else, shall we?"

Megan slipped her arm back around his waist in an unconscious effort to comfort him and waited until he'd put his arm around her again to start talking. "Did you play any sports in high school?"

"I was one of those tiny ninety-pound weaklings you read about on the back of comic books," he admitted ruefully. "But I ran cross-country for a couple of years."

"I can't imagine you skinny." She eyed his broad shoulders and muscular arms.

"Believe it," he said. "You wouldn't have looked twice at me if you'd seen me in the ninth grade."

"What happened to change you?"

He grinned. "I took the comic book's advice and started lifting weights. In fact, lifting weights and running have both stayed with me to this day."

"Well, may I say they've stood you in good stead?" A twinkle of admiring humor lit Megan's eyes as she ran a hand across his broad chest and patted his flat stomach. She felt him suck in an abdomen that rippled with muscle and her eyes met his, the humor quickly turning to something else. She cleared her throat and looked away from the sensual fire in his green eyes. Sexual attraction was fine when you were considering an affair. However, sex alone was not enough on which to base a marriage. She forced her thoughts to the questions she knew she should be asking.

"So how did a jock like you end up an expert on South American politics?"

"If you really want to know, I'll tell you," he said as they arrived at the amphitheatre. "But why don't we talk over lunch?"

That was easier said than done. The band was louder than Tom had expected, and the conversation he'd hoped for over a lunch of fried chicken, potato salad and fresh fruit was curtailed by the rhythmic pounding of a bass guitar and drums.

Megan was glad for the hiatus in their discussion. She had a lot to think about. Tom's background was not the sort she would have guessed for a man who'd made such a success of himself. It was impossible to imagine him suffering so much physical punishment and emotional abuse as a child, or to imagine him as unattractive as he said he'd been. Supposedly a man's image of himself was formed in adolescence. Did that mean Tom still perceived himself as unwanted? Or, even more unbelievable, that he perceived himself as unattractive to women, despite what must be overwhelming evidence to the contrary any time he looked into the mirror?

"What are you thinking?" Tom asked when there was a break in the music.

What an enigma you are. "How much I'm enjoying your company." She smiled up at him. "What do you think of the band?"

"They're loud."

Megan laughed.

"Let's get out of here," he shouted to her. "This is a little more than I can handle on a full stomach."

As they walked, Megan tried to think of another topic of conversation recommended by her birthday book, mentally listing the ones she'd covered and the ones she hadn't. Ah, yes...goals.

"I understand you came to St. Mark's because you could have access to primary South American research materials here in Miami. Are you working on anything special?"

"As a matter of fact, I am. I'm looking for a solution to the current political unrest in Central America."

Megan whistled long and low. "That's a pretty tall order. Is there a solution?"

"That's what I'm going to try to find out. Plain old economics is at the root of a lot of the evils being committed. The rich want to keep what's theirs and the poor want a share of what they haven't got. Each side is attempting to kill off the other to solve the problem. Whether any kind of real social, economic and political reforms can be implemented while there's such a grueling war of attrition going on is debatable.''

Megan chewed on her lower lip as she thought over what he'd said. "So it's a 'which comes first, the chicken or the egg' kind of problem, right? You can't stop the war without reforms, and you can't have reforms while there's a war going on.''

"You're very perceptive.''

"It's the first time anyone's explained the problem to me in such understandable terms. I hope you do find a solution. What happens when your year here is up?''

"I go back to Washington.''

"Would you ever consider staying in Miami?'' Megan held her breath for his answer.

Tom linked his arm around her waist and pulled her into the small shade created by a palm tree along the path. He turned to face her, his hands framing her waist, his thumbs nearly meeting at her belly button. "I have to admit it would be nice to live closer to Randy and Irene. But it would mean doing a lot of extra flying to give advice on the Hill. There'd have to be a pretty compelling reason to stay.''

How about marriage? she thought.

"What about you?'' Tom asked, his thumbs tracing Megan's ribs. "Have you ever wanted to live anywhere else?

Megan struggled to control an involuntary shiver as Tom's thumbs caressed her through the soft cotton T-shirt. "I sometimes dream about living in the mountains out west. Maybe in Colorado or Wyoming or Montana. At least that's where I take my vacation every year."

"Is there anyone who'd miss you if you left Miami?"

"Uh...no."

Tom wanted to make sure once and for all that there was no other man in her life. So he pressed her by asking, "Then there's been no one to take the place of your husband?"

Megan couldn't breathe. Weren't these rather personal questions for a first date? But then she'd been asking some pretty personal questions herself, and she supposed she owed him an honest answer. "I...uh...haven't exactly been looking for someone to replace Gary."

"Oh? Why not?"

"I guess I should say I did look, but I stopped." *Until my daughter gave me this book....*

"And why was that?"

"I couldn't find anyone who...seemed... right."

"No? And what were you looking for that you couldn't find?"

His thumbs had tightened on her waist and he applied pressure to her back with his fingers to angle her hips toward him. She kept her eyes focused on the tuft of black hair that showed at the open collar at his throat. Since he wasn't wearing an undershirt she could see that his whole chest was covered with hair. She wanted to thrust her hands into it, to feel the texture of his skin. Unaware that her thoughts showed in her eyes, she met his intense gaze. "Uh, what was that you said?"

Tom exerted great effort to control the heated arousal caused by her glance, and said in a voice that he hoped didn't reveal the extent of his inner turmoil, "I asked what you were looking for in a husband."

"Companionship, for one thing."

"You haven't been able to find a man to keep you company?"

"Not one who..." *Not one who wanted both me and my children.*

"Not one who what?"

"One who was willing to share everything about my life, both the good times and the bad."

He stopped fighting his inclination and pulled her closer, bringing their hips into shocking contact, fitting his hardness to her softness. She cradled him intimately, and he felt the tension as he strove to keep himself still against her. The slight breeze carried the scent of gardenias, which he realized was coming from the woman in his arms. "What else do you—did you—want from a prospective husband?" he demanded, his voice a harsh whisper in her ear.

"A satisfying...physical relationship...is important."

"You mean making love?"

"Yes. Loving. Touching." She grasped his arms, fighting the urge to arch her breasts into his chest.

"What else?"

His voice was low, husky, his lips so close to her ear she could feel his warm breath. She could hardly think for the sensations rocketing through her body. "Someone who loves kids...please...I can't think with you so close."

But she did nothing to pull away from him.

And he did nothing to separate their bodies.

It was the sound of a little girl calling to her mother that finally broke the spell between them. Megan jerked backward, and the sudden movement caused Tom to release her.

All at once Megan was aware of the heat. Her T-shirt stuck to her skin and her arms and legs felt slick with sweat. She held her top away from her body and shook it a couple of times so the breeze could reach her skin.

"Goodness. It's really too hot to be out here this time of day. Maybe we should check out the aviary. It's like a jungle, cool and dark."

Tom's initial inclination was to demand more answers from Megan. But the truth was, he already knew a great deal more than he'd expected to find out. He'd learned two very important things today. First, that Megan Padget wanted the same things he did from a spouse. And second, that he wanted to know her better.

They spent the rest of the day until dusk walking without doing much talking. Megan was too caught up in the overwhelming response she felt for Tom to carry on an intelligent conversation. The thing that frightened her was the knowledge that she could easily forget all the things she'd learned about Tom's upbringing that might not make him good husband material in favor of the physical satisfaction she was almost certain she would find in his arms.

Megan didn't want the pain that inevitably accompanied a brief sexual fling. She'd gone through that stage when she'd first divorced and found it so unpleasant she hadn't ever had the inclination to repeat her one experience. But with Tom... She found herself looking forward to the end of the day because she hoped he would take her in his arms and kiss her. And Tom didn't disappoint her.

It was nearly dark when they reached Nells. Tom had already learned not to expect her to wait for him to help her out of the car. He quickly caught up to her and placed an arm around her waist to escort her to her car. "I've had a wonderful time today, Megan."

"I have, too," she answered, her voice low and throaty. Megan chastised herself for getting excited over what was probably going to be a goodnight peck on the cheek. But her breathing was already erratic and there wasn't much she could do about it.

Tom didn't intend to do more than touch his lips to Megan's. He left his hand loosely around her waist when he leaned down and brushed her mouth with his. But her lips were soft and sweet, and he went back for another taste. His mouth lingered on hers, and without conscious thought his tongue slipped out to taste the underside of her lip.

He felt his body tensing and fought against it. He lifted his head, his eyes hooded, his breathing harsh. But at the sight of Megan's mouth, glistening with moisture from his tongue, he lowered his head again, his other arm going around her as well, drawing her into the V created by his wide-spread legs. Although he pulled her tightly into his embrace, his lips were gentle, seeking.

Megan opened to him like a flower to a spring rain. He felt his heart go wild, felt his blood start rushing. His mouth slanted urgently against hers, and she met his lips eagerly. He used his teeth, nipping at her lip, then soothed the hurt with his tongue. Eventually his tongue slid deep inside her mouth. From that instant he was lost in a vortex of pleasure. His hands roamed her body as his lips and tongue plundered her mouth. And yet he wasn't taking, he was giving.

He heard the purr in Megan's throat and groaned in response. He grasped her buttocks with his hands and arched her against him, his tongue miming the movements of long-time lovers. He had her T-shirt half-off when the sound of raucous laughter and the slam of a car door brought him abruptly from the well of passion into which he'd fallen. He realized they were standing in the middle of a parking lot.

He tried to speak, but his voice was too hoarse. He cleared his throat and said, "I'll follow you home to make sure you get there safely."

For obvious reasons, none of which she could explain to Tom, Megan couldn't let him do that.

"There's really no need." She turned quickly and ran to her car.

"Wait. I—"

Megan couldn't afford to take the chance he'd follow her. She waved out the window as she backed from her slot.

"See you next week!" she yelled as she shot by him.

Tom stood watching her with his hands balled in fists by his sides. His body was throbbing with need. He was so hard he hurt, and he'd only intended to kiss her goodnight. What had happened? How had things gone awry? *How had he so completely lost control?*

He turned and walked toward his car, stunned to realize how strongly he'd responded to Megan's sensual allure. He'd broken a promise he'd made to himself at fourteen, not to ever allow his emotions free rein. If he could so easily lose himself with this woman with a mere kiss, what might he do when they finally made love? The discussion he'd had with Megan was little comfort. He'd never yet been violent like his father, but then he'd never let himself lose control with a woman, either. The thought was chilling—frightening rather than exciting. The safe course of action—the only sane course of action—was clear to him.

Stay away from Megan Padget.

Five

Her Book: "You *Can* Ask Him Out!"

Megan hadn't seen or heard from Dr. Thomas Steele for weeks. She knew that was partially due to the fact that he'd been called to Washington. But she could find no explanation for the fact that she hadn't even seen him on campus upon his return, except that he didn't want to see her. Like a lovesick teenager she'd waited by the phone night and day for Tom to call. She'd replayed every moment of their date in her head, trying to remember if she'd said anything, or done anything, that might have caused him to avoid her. But nothing came to mind. She hadn't even told him she had two kids! She'd followed her birthday book's advice down to the last comma and period, apparently to no avail.

This morning she'd finally accepted that he wasn't ever going to call. Disillusioned, disgusted and distressed, she'd tossed *YOU DON'T HAVE TO STAY SINGLE* into the trash.

"It's like he disappeared from the face of the earth," she said to Stephanie as they walked through the faculty dining hall line together.

Stephanie grimaced as she slid a soggy burrito onto her plate. "You'd think with a man named Ramon Gonzales in charge of food services here the Mexican cuisine would be a little better."

"Ramon is Cuban."

"That explains everything."

"Have you heard a word I've said about Tom?" Megan asked.

"Sure. You had one wonderful date—including a devastating goodnight kiss—and you haven't seen or heard from him since. You could always call him, you know."

"Call him?"

"Yeah, you know, pick up the phone, dial seven numbers, wait for the ring and when he answers say, 'Hello, this is Megan Padget. I'm dying to jump your bones. Why the hell haven't you called me?' ''

Megan laughed. "You're crazy. You know that?"

"Of course. That's why you like me so much." Stephanie heaped her plate with an unappetizing mixture of string beans, onion rings and mushroom sauce. "I'm not kidding. I think you should call him."

"Women don't call men."

"Are we back to that again? This is the eighties. Of course women call men. We call them jerks. We call them slobs. We call them—"

"Enough! Enough! You're no help at all."

"I've given you my best advice. If you choose not to take it, what can I say? Does that birthday book your kids gave you have anything in it to cover this situation?"

"I threw it in the trash this morning."

"That's wasteful. The least you could have done was send it back for a refund."

Megan snorted inelegantly.

"Well, before you threw it out, did you read anything in it that covered this situation?"

Megan gnawed her lip for a moment before she admitted, "Yes."

"Well?"

"It says that this is the eighties and I should call him."

Stephanie chuckled. "Look, what have you got to lose? All he can say is that he never wants to see you again."

Stephanie turned to her friend to see if she'd appreciated her wit only to find Megan's face white, her eyes bleak. Stephanie set her tray down on the closest table and turned to slip an arm around Megan's shoulder. "Hey, you really have got it bad, haven't you? Sit down. We need to talk."

Stephanie maneuvered the two of them to an isolated corner of the dining room. "Now, tell Mama Stephanie. I've seen lovesick before, but this is ridiculous."

"I've never felt like this before, Stephanie, ever. Not even when I was sixteen and Jimmy Storey gave me his letter jacket. I've been absolutely obsessed with thoughts of this man. I go to sleep thinking about him, I dream about him and he's the first thing on my mind in the morning. I don't like it," she said, biting off the words in anger. "It isn't normal. All the time there's this awful tightness inside. If this is love then you can have it! It hurts. It isn't comfortable. It's damned frightening."

"I can understand it hurts, and it's uncomfortable,'' Stephanie said. ''But frightening? How so?''

Megan closed her eyes and folded her hands together in her lap, feeling again the tension that had her sleeping with her shoulders hunched tensely every night. ''I'm afraid that it really is all over. That I'll never see him again.''

''I see. Well, then, you don't have a choice then, do you? You'll have to do it.''

''Do what?''

''Call up Tom Steele.''

Tom was miserable and he had no one to blame but himself. He leaned back in the corduroy chair in his living room and put his feet up on the ottoman. Dusk had come, but he hadn't turned on the lights. He liked it better in the dark. He didn't have to acknowledge that the room was empty...as empty as his life. He laid his hand on the phone that he'd perched on the broad arm of the chair.

Call her, you jerk. So what if you lost control. It was a temporary situation. Now that you know what happened you won't have the same problem.

He snickered. He was just kidding himself. He ached for her now and he hadn't seen her for weeks. And speaking of that, how was he going to explain the fact he hadn't called? He didn't like feeling vulnerable. He didn't like feeling out of control. But he also didn't like the feeling of loneliness that was pervading his life. Maybe it was time to let go of the past. Maybe it was time to take a chance and let himself lose control. Maybe Megan was right, and he really wasn't like his father.

He picked up the phone, dialed three numbers and slammed it down again.

What if she said no?

If you won't take a chance you'll never find a wife. Besides, could the pain of rejection be any worse than what you're already feeling?

He sighed. The past few weeks had been hell. He'd seen Megan on campus several times, but had always managed to avoid her. He supposed he wasn't acting like the typical macho hero in the movies. Those guys always went after the woman they wanted and everything else be damned. It was humbling to admit that he was an ordinary man whose only resemblance to those heroic characters was his looks. They were cardboard characters. He was flesh and blood. His pain was real...but so was his need.

Call her.

He took a deep breath and exhaled.

All right. I will.

The jangle of the ringing phone pierced the

quiet of the small living room and startled Tom so much that he knocked the phone off the arm of the chair. The receiver went flying and he grappled around in the dark searching for it. When he finally found it, his voice revealed his irritation.

"Hello. Who is it?"

"Tom?"

"Megan?"

The phone was silent for so long Tom thought he must have imagined her voice. "Megan?"

"Yes. Hello, Tom. How have you been?"

"Fine." *Damn! Think of something to say!* "How are you?"

"Fine."

"Uh...look, Megan, I've been meaning—"

"Wait! Before you say anything I want to ask you something."

"Sure. Anything."

Megan swallowed over the lump in her throat, held her hand over a heart that was threatening to burst, it was beating so hard and forced herself to speak calmly. Even so, she choked on her first attempt to speak. She swallowed and tried again. "I...I wondered if you'd like to go to a Halloween party with me. On Halloween. Uh, it's on Saturday night this year, you know."

"I know." Tom was smiling. He couldn't help himself.

"Uh…well…will you?"

"Yes."

Megan felt her heart thumping madly under her trembling hand. She closed her eyes to fight the dizziness that threatened. "Uh…I'll call you later with the details. Think about what costume you want to wear and maybe we can come up with something that matches. All right?"

"Sure."

"Goodbye, Tom."

"Goodbye, Megan."

When Tom heard the phone click at Megan's end he flicked on the lamp, found his phone and set the receiver back in the cradle. Megan had asked him out on a date. And this time he would do things right. He would— Good grief, what kind of protocol applied when the woman asked the man out? Would she let him pay? Should he offer to drive? Should he invite her back to his apartment, or wait for her to invite him to her home? And what if she didn't?

He searched through the stack of papers on the spooled table looking for *HOW TO MARRY THE WOMAN OF YOUR DREAMS*. What the hell had he done with it? It suddenly dawned on him. He'd thrown it in the garbage yesterday! Would it still be there?

He scrambled out of his chair so fast it scraped

six inches backward. He stumbled over the spooled coffee table and banged his hip on the edge of the dining-room table on his way out. What day was garbage pickup?

Please be there.

He jerked the lid off the trash can, which was illuminated by a streetlight in the alley. There it was. Right on top. *HOW TO MARRY THE WOMAN OF YOUR DREAMS.* He tenderly rescued it from its place on a pile of old newspapers and tucked it under his arm. Once back inside, he turned on every light in the house, settled into the corduroy chair and opened the book. There was bound to be something in here to cover his date with Megan.

Several hours later he set the book down on the coffee table and rubbed his eyes with the heels of his hands. He'd found nothing that was the least bit helpful regarding dating protocol when the woman asked the man out, except the statement that this occurred occasionally, and it was the lucky man who found a woman smart enough to know her own mind and courageous enough to take the risk of rejection on her shoulders. And what lovely shoulders they were, Tom mused. Thanks to a short excursion into the chapter, "Sex—When to Make Your Move," he hoped to see those shoulders quite soon.

* * *

Megan felt the devil dancing in her stomach. Any moment Tom Steele was going to arrive at her door for their second date. She had her best friend and her daughter to thank for this. The same day she'd spoken to Stephanie she'd come home to find Sarah waiting for her at the door with *YOU DON'T HAVE TO STAY SINGLE* gripped tightly in her hand.

"Look what I found in the trash." Sarah's voice had quivered with hurt. "Don't you want to find a husband? Don't you want to get married?"

"Sweetheart, it's more complicated than you think."

"You didn't even try! You didn't even give it a chance!"

Since she hadn't told Sarah about her date with Tom she had no comeback for her daughter's accusation.

"If I gave up this quickly on my homework I'd get a two-hour lecture from you," Sarah had railed.

"It's not the same," Megan had countered.

"What makes this situation any different? You have to keep trying. You have to make an effort. Nobody said it was going to be easy. Does any of that sound familiar?"

It was the beginning of the lecture Megan had

given Sarah when her daughter had been stumped by a new math concept.

Sarah thrust *YOU DON'T HAVE TO STAY SINGLE* toward her mother. "It wasn't only for mine and Chris's sake, you know, that we bought this book. It was for your sake, too. Sometimes I see you look at another couple, like when we're in line at the movies and some guy will hug his girl and give her a kiss, and you…you look so lonely, Mom. I don't want you to be lonely anymore."

"Oh, Sarah." Megan had held her arms out and Sarah had flown into her embrace. She'd hugged her daughter hard as she'd fought the sob rising in her throat. She'd pushed Sarah away and said, "Give me that book. I'm going to do something about this right now."

That very evening she'd called to ask Tom Steele out on a date. And he'd accepted.

"What's he look like?" Sarah had asked, when Megan had admitted she had a date for the church Halloween party.

"Do you remember that hunk you saw when I went shopping for clothes?"

"Sure. How could I forget him? Is your date that good-looking, Mom?"

"That's the man I have a date with."

"You're kidding!"

"No, I'm not."

"But Mom, he's a real hunk!"

Megan didn't know whether to feel insulted or not. "And what makes you think I couldn't attract a hunk?"

Sarah had grinned. "I didn't mean it that way. Or if I did, I take it back. You deserve a hunk. Wait until the girls hear—"

"Sarah, I'd rather you didn't say anything to any of your friends just yet."

"Why not?"

"We're just going out on a date, Sarah. It may not come to anything."

"But—"

"No buts. Promise me you won't say anything just yet."

"All right, Mom. Golly, I can't believe this. This is too much. I gotta go write all this down in my diary."

Megan knew she'd taken a chance telling Sarah about Tom. Tonight she was going to take another chance and tell Tom about her children. If the existence of Sarah and Chris was going to be a problem for him, she needed to know it. She'd suggested he pick her up here at the house thinking that would be the easiest way to break the news, but as it turned out, both children were spending the night with friends. In retrospect she

was glad she'd be able to pick the moment to tell
Tom she was a mother.

The sound of the doorbell startled Megan from
her reverie. When she opened the door Tom stood
before her dressed in the tailored black suit and
white clerical collar of a priest. He looked divine,
all right, but in a strictly earthly way. She couldn't
take her eyes off him.

"May I come in?"

"Oh, I'm sorry," Megan said. "Please do. I'm
nearly ready. I just have to get my cape."

Megan was self-conscious about her outfit,
which was a form-fitting, sequined, red devil costume that just happened to zip down the front to
a spot somewhere below her belly button. She
swirled the black cape around her, trying to arrange it on her shoulders.

"Let me help." Tom came up behind her and
adjusted the padded shoulders of the cape and the
high, stiff collar that framed her face. She'd put
her hair up in a knot on her head, leaving wisps
trailing down her neck and at her temples. A
headband held two red horns in place. Leaving
his hands resting on her shoulders, Tom leaned
down and kissed her cheek.

"May I say you look devilishly lovely tonight," he said with a chuckle.

"If I may say you look 'holy' delightful!"

Tom groaned. "That was awful."

"It was, wasn't it?" Megan said, unrepentant. "I must say I'm impressed with your ingenuity. When I said I'd be coming as a devil it never occurred to me that you'd dress as a priest."

"What did you expect?"

"I don't know. Something equally satanic, I suppose. There's a certain irony in us showing up together like this at a *church*-sponsored Halloween party that I don't even want to think about."

For a moment Megan stared up at him, a silly grin on her face. But as he lowered his head again, the grin faded. When his mouth was only an inch away from hers, he paused.

"Megan?"

He was giving her a chance to say no. But Megan was equally tempted and didn't want to be saved. She turned her face up and stood on tiptoe, meeting his mouth and pressing her lips against his, which were firm and unyielding for a moment, but only a moment. As their lips met, her mouth opened to his searching tongue. His arms reached out to pull her into his embrace. Megan was lost in a euphoric daze. Her whole body trembled with excitement. It was their first kiss all over again. The last time this had happened he'd stolen her senses and disappeared from her life…and she still didn't know why.

She felt her knees giving way and struggled against the haze of pleasure. When she pulled her mouth away Tom immediately sought out the racing pulse at her throat with his mouth as his hands moved over her rib cage and upward toward her breasts.

"Tom! Please!" She wasn't sure whether she was asking him to stop, or go on. She grabbed his wrists in an attempt to hold his hands in place below her breasts. But her strength wasn't enough to keep him from reaching his goal. She gasped as his hands cupped her breasts, his thumbs caressing the tips, which immediately hardened under his touch. She could feel herself succumbing to his tender persuasion. She was lost...unless she could somehow reach him with words.

"Tom, please...stop."

The sound of Megan's distraught voice shook Tom from the spell that had gripped him.

"Megan?..." He rested his forehead against hers and sucked in several breaths of air, trying to regain his composure.

"Oh, Tom, what makes this happen between us?" she whispered. "I don't understand.... When you touch me I...can't resist."

He lifted his head and when he saw where his hands were, he jerked them away from her body and staggered backward. He thrust his fingers through his hair leaving it rumpled and wild-looking. "I don't...I can't..." He ground his teeth together. How could he explain what had happened? He'd been completely out of control. He'd hoped this couldn't happen again. What was it about this woman that caused him to lose all sense of time and place when he held her in his arms?

"Are you all right?" she asked.

"I'm the one who should be asking that, I think," he said with a rueful grimace.

"We should have expected it."

"Oh?"

Megan smiled tentatively. "Look at the costumes we chose to wear. It's a wonder we weren't struck by lightning when we kissed."

Tom managed a chuckle. "I don't know about you, but I think I was."

"Maybe we'd better get to the church party. It'll be safer there."

"For whom?" he said, a grin coming back to his face now that it was apparent Megan was going to give him another chance to show that he could act civilized in her presence. "You're dressed as Lucifer, if I'm not mistaken. That could mean we're in for a hellish evening."

Megan took a step toward Tom, then reached

out and slowly entwined her fingers with his. "I happen to believe in a very forgiving God."

"Damned good thing," he muttered as they stepped out the door and into the dark night together.

The church party was being held at Viscaya, an Italian Renaissance-style villa that had been turned into a museum. Tables loaded down with fresh fruit and cheese hors d'oeuvres had been set up outside on the patio that bordered Biscayne Bay. A band was playing golden oldies and gondola rides were being offered for those who chose to take them.

Megan had been a little nervous about how Tom would react when she paid for the tickets, since he'd seemed reluctant to let her use her own money on their first date. However, he said nothing when she handed over her check to Mary Beth Prescott at the table that had been set up for dispensing tickets. Mary Beth, unfortunately, wasn't equally discreet.

"Why, Megan Padget, this is the first man I've seen you with in two years. I must say the wait was worthwhile. Introduce me to the padre."

Furious that Mary Beth would reveal such a thing, even if it was the truth, Megan replied, "This is Father Steele. Father, this is our church secretary, Mary Beth Prescott."

"You mean you're not wearing a costume? You're really a priest?" Mary Beth demanded, shocked.

Tom winked. "What do you think?"

"If it isn't a costume, I think it's a crying shame," Mary Beth said, laughing good-naturedly.

Megan grabbed Tom's hand and hauled him away. "You keep listening to Mary Beth and you're going to get a swelled head." They walked through the crowd and ended up on the stone steps that led to the water. Megan sat and pulled Tom down beside her. "I can't believe how lucky we were with the weather. It's warm tonight, but thanks to the breeze off the bay, not too warm. And the moon is so big and bright we hardly need the paper lanterns."

Megan realized Tom's attention was elsewhere. She followed his gaze to a woman who was wearing a harem costume. "It looks like she forgot a few of her seven veils."

"What? Oh." Tom flushed. "Sorry. I was wondering how someone could wear an outfit like that to a church party."

Megan laughed. "We only sponsored the party. It's open to the public. We're trying to earn some money to help support our new family-counseling center."

She found her own attention wandering as she spied a man wearing a safari outfit, who had a live parrot on his shoulder. "I recognize him!" she said with a squeal of delight. "He's one of the professors at St. Mark's."

Tom felt himself bristling with antagonism until he noticed that the man Megan had been so delighted to see had his arm around a woman dressed as a French maid. He forced himself to relax, uncomfortably aware that he was exhibiting all the classic signs of a jealous male. Jealousy was an emotion he hadn't experienced in the past, and one with which he had no desire to become familiar. "Would you like something to drink?"

"Yes. I'll go with you. If we get separated in this crowd we'll never find each other again."

That made as good an excuse as any to slip her arm around Tom's waist, and Megan took it. She'd never been jealous before, but she recognized the symptoms in herself. As they stood in line at the cash bar Megan tried to figure out what was causing the feeling. Possessiveness, for one thing. Had she ever felt possessive of Gary? Yes, but there was something else that was needed for jealousy to exist. Distrust. She had no reason to distrust Tom, no reason to believe he would seek out another woman while he was with her. But the problem wasn't with Tom. It was with the extraordinary good looks that caused women to approach him, whether he wished them to do so or not.

Megan examined Tom's chiseled profile. Could she spend a lifetime with a man whom other women found fascinating? Even if she could believe enough in his love to think he would never look at another woman, could she trust other women not to put irresistible temptation in his path? He was only human, after all. Her eyes dropped to the collar at his throat. His saintly appearance was just a costume. All men could be tempted.

She touched Tom's cheek with her fingertips and he turned to look down at her.

"It won't be long now," he said. "Getting thirsty?"

"A little." She reached out to a nearby buffet table and picked up a fresh strawberry. She took a bite from it and felt the juice on her lips. She watched Tom's eyes darken as she licked the juice away. Then she held the berry up to his lips. "Take a bite. It's delicious."

He bit off the berry so his teeth and lips nipped her fingers. She dropped the leafy stem in surprise. "Oh."

"Did I hurt you?" He took her hand in his and

brought her fingertips to his lips, kissing them softly. "I didn't mean to."

She pulled her hand from his, shaken by how quickly she'd become aroused. "We're next."

"What would you like?" he asked, his voice husky.

"Bourbon. A double."

He looked at her in surprise, but when she didn't change her mind he ordered it for her, and a beer for himself. When she reached for the money she'd tucked in a small pocket in her outfit he put a hand to stop her.

"I've got it. Are you sure you want this?" he asked as he handed her the double bourbon.

"Yes." She knew she needed something to rouse her from the sexual spell that had been cast. She took a large swallow of the drink, coughing and sputtering when the fiery liquid hit her throat. "God, that's awful!"

"Why did you order it then?"

Megan laughed, a slightly hysterical sound. *I needed something to shock me to my senses.* "I thought it would taste better than it does."

"Would you like to dance?"

Megan looked up at Tom for a moment, wondering how wise it would be to put herself in his embrace. She took another swallow of the bourbon, coughed again and said, "Sure. Why not?"

Tom set his plastic cup of beer on a stone ledge and Megan put her drink beside it.

"Come on." He placed his hand on the small of her back to head her in the right direction. He followed her back up the stairs to the patio just outside the villa and took her in his arms. As they began a slow dance their bodies melded together from breasts to thighs.

"Oh, Lord," Megan mumbled. "I knew it."

"Knew what?" he whispered in her ear.

"That it would feel like this."

Tom didn't reply, merely pulled her closer into his arms, tucking her head against his shoulder, leaning his head down close to hers so he could enjoy the scent of gardenias in her hair.

Neither of them spoke again for the next hour until the band took its break. Megan hardly knew where she was when she felt Tom's hands on her shoulders.

"Megan. The music's stopped."

She looked up into Tom's slightly hooded eyes and knew he was as aroused as she was. It was a pleasant feeling, one of expectation, of anticipation.

"What time is it?" she asked.

"Time to take a walk."

Megan didn't protest when Tom linked their arms and led her away from the villa into the intricate formal gardens. There were other couples wandering the stone pathways, but Tom found a shadowy arbor that was isolated from the noise of the crowd and turned her into his arms.

"Megan, I need you."

His lips claimed hers fiercely, passionately, and Megan willingly opened her mouth to his plundering tongue. His hands skimmed down her back and captured her hips, pulling them into the waiting cradle created by his widespread legs. She could feel the hard length of him, aroused, ready, with only two thin layers of cloth separating their eager bodies. One of his hands grasped her buttocks while the other laid claim to her breasts— first freeing them by making use of the zipper down the front of her form-fitting costume.

Megan arched upward as she felt Tom's warm, wet mouth replace his hand on her breast. Her fingers reached up to clutch his hair.

At that moment the sound of female voices intruded on their idyll. Both Tom and Megan stiffened in the darkness.

"Did you see that man with Megan tonight?"

"Some kind of body on him, huh? His face isn't half-bad, either!"

"You're telling me. I'd like to catch him on one of these paths."

"Good luck beating me to him! She's gotta leave him alone sometime tonight. And then..."

The other woman's drunken giggle made Megan shudder. Her breath rasped in her throat as she shoved her face into Tom's shoulder.

Jealousy. It burned like a fire inside her.

Her hands slipped from Tom's hair and clutched the front of her costume together. She struggled to pull the zipper back up, but it was stuck.

"Help me!" she whispered, resisting the urge to say anything more until she was clothed again and could escape Tom's embrace.

Tom lifted her hands away from the garment and slowly eased the zipper upward. He knew Megan couldn't have helped overhearing the two women. "They were just making talk. It didn't mean anything."

With the zipper back in place, Megan turned her back on Tom and walked a few steps away from him, giving her racing pulse a chance to slow down. "Are you saying strange women don't make passes at you?"

"Not as often as you seem to think," he said, his voice brusque.

She turned to look at him, but his face was hidden in the shadows. She took a deep breath.

"I'm sorry. It's just...what they said bothered me."

"I figured as much."

"You might be tempted—"

"I'm not interested in another woman, Megan. I want you. Only you."

He'd taken two steps toward her, and Megan could feel the tension radiating from him. "But what if—"

Tom's mouth came down on hers in a searing kiss that cut her off and left no doubt in her mind that she was the one he wanted. When he finally released her she had to hang on to him to keep from falling.

"I think it's time to leave," she managed to say.

"If that's what you want."

"It's what I want."

She needed time to think, and she couldn't do it this close to Tom. It wasn't until they were driving back up I-95 that Megan realized she'd never told Tom she had children. She wasn't sure how to broach the subject. Finally she said, "Have you ever thought about having children?"

He turned to look at her briefly. He opened his mouth to tell her about his son, but the whole subject was too painful...and ironic. He was the one who'd wanted children and yet it was Sally who'd taken Todd when they'd divorced—taken him across the country to California, where it was difficult, if not impossible to visit him.

He turned back to Megan, unaware of the ferocious scowl on his face. "I always wanted kids. A son who looked like me, and a daughter who..." He forced his thoughts away from the painful past and said curtly, "It was Sally who didn't want children."

"Sally?"

"She was my wife. I'm divorced. I thought you knew."

"I did."

Megan was devastated by what she'd just found out. *A son who looked like me.* She could never give him that. She was glad now that she hadn't introduced him to Sarah and Chris. Because unless he changed his mind about wanting children, it would be fruitless to see Tom Steele again.

Six

His Book: "Sex—When to Make Your Move"
Her Book: "Sex—Don't Jump the Gun"

"Aren't you going to invite me in?" Tom asked.

"No."

"Why not?"

"You know why not." Megan put a hand on Tom's chest to keep him from stepping over the threshold. "All we have to do is touch one another and neither one of us can think straight."

"Is that so bad?"

Tom's lazy grin stole Megan's breath. She

thought back to the chapter in *YOU DON'T HAVE TO STAY SINGLE* entitled, "Sex—Don't Jump the Gun."

A man judges a woman by how quickly she joins him in bed. No matter how urgently he insists he'll respect her in the morning if she succumbs to their mutual desire—he won't. So think first, and make love only when the time is right for such a commitment.

This was only her second date with Tom and the temptation to let things happen between them was strong. In fact, she knew that if they'd been anywhere near a bed on their first date they'd have landed in it.

Megan felt sure that tonight was too soon to take such a step. There were a lot of issues yet to be settled between them before they were ready to move their relationship any closer to commitment, not the least of which was the existence of her two children and the fact she couldn't give Tom any more.

"Please, Tom, I'm very tired." It was an excuse, and she knew he knew it. Still, she hoped he would accept it.

Tom couldn't help recalling the words in the

chapter of his birthday book entitled, "Sex—
When To Make Your Move."

*It's not always easy to judge when a woman
is ready to include sex in your relationship.
There are times when she'll say no and mean
it. Learn to recognize the signs of such a
refusal. She'll resist your touch, and stiffen
in response to any physical contact with you.*

He put his arms on Megan's shoulders and felt
her whole body arch toward him. No resistance
there....

*On the other hand, there are women who
want a man to take the sexual initiative. They
will say no and wait for the man to make
further overtures to which they willingly respond.*

Tom leaned into Megan, pressing her back
against the door. He felt a jolt when his hips came
into contact with hers, his body hardening in in-
stantaneous response to her heat. When she
voiced no protest to his touch, he bent his head,
searching for her mouth. He nibbled at her lips,
tasting the soft skin with his tongue and teeth.

Megan began to panic. She could feel what little resistance she had to Tom eroding as he began his gentle assault on her mouth, his hips pressing intimately into hers. She had to find a way to distract him.

"Would you like a cup of coffee?" she asked.

Tom lifted his head only slightly. "Would you?"

"Uh... I guess I'd like something cold."

"Something hot and something cold. Sounds good to me," he murmured in her ear.

Megan shivered with desire as she groped for the doorknob. "Let's go inside, shall we?"

It was dark inside. Megan reached for a light switch, but Tom's hand was there to stop her.

"We don't need the light."

"But your coffee—"

"Did you really invite me in here to have a cup of coffee, Megan?"

His mouth was on her throat, his tongue bathing the racing pulse over which she had no control.

Tom shut the door behind them with his foot, leaving them with only the light from the moon streaming in the front picture window.

"Where's your bedroom, Megan?"

"Tom, it's too soon to—"

"Too soon for this?" His hands were on her

breasts, kneading them, his thumbs skimming the tips, bringing them to hardness.

Megan moaned and Tom caught the sound with his mouth. She returned his kiss urgently, feeling caught up in a spiral of desire that had nothing to do with thinking or being sensible.

She felt Tom lifting her to bring her body in line with his need. She could feel the hard ridge pressing into her abdomen and arched her body closer.

"Ahh, Megan, I want you."

"And I want you," she breathed in reply. With the last shred of sanity she had left she tried once more to stop their heedless rush toward ecstasy. "It's too soon, Tom. There's so much we don't know about each other—"

"I know everything I need to know."

Somehow the zipper on her costume was down again and Megan felt the heat and wetness of Tom's mouth and tongue on her breast. He was sucking, drawing the nipple into his mouth to play with it.

"Oh, my God," she moaned. "Tom, we can't...."

But it was only her mind saying no; her body was screaming *yes!* at the top of its lungs.

His hand reached down inside the zipper to

stroke the soft skin of her belly and then he reached farther to touch the core of her.

Megan jerked as he reached the sensitive nub, and her hand automatically grasped at his wrist to stop him.

"Too rough?" he questioned, his voice harsh with need. "I'll be more careful."

He touched again, his callused fingertips gently abrading, teasing, taunting, dipping inside her to touch the wetness and then returning to caress the heat and heart of her, building the tension, driving her wild. She could feel her body tautening, feel the urgent pull inside her, and recognized it for what it was. And she wanted it. She wanted what he could give her. So, though she knew she should stop him, she grasped his shoulders with her hands to keep from falling and used her mouth to give him back what pleasure she could. She kissed his neck, his ears, his chin, biting and nipping and sucking, loving the taste of him.

She heard herself groan with pleasure, and needing something to hang onto, she clamped down with her teeth on Tom's shoulder. She cried out again in fulfillment as the tension erupted throughout her body in waves of unbearable ecstasy. The sound was stolen by Tom's mouth, his tongue miming the action of his fingers inside her as she experienced a release so powerful it left her totally enervated.

The next thing Megan was aware of was Tom lifting her into his arms, her head lolling against his strong shoulder as he carried her into her bedroom. She barely had time to register the fact that he'd fortuitously ended up in her room, which was on the left side of the hall, rather than Sarah's, which was on the right, before she felt his welcome weight on her body.

"Megan, Megan, I knew it would be like this with us. Let me love you, sweetheart. Here, let me help you out of this outfit."

She was naked to his gaze in moments, and it wasn't until then that she realized Tom was still fully dressed. At that same moment she became aware of the phone ringing.

"Let it ring," he said, his eyes reverently appraising her body.

For a moment Megan had no thoughts of answering it. Then she remembered her children weren't safe at home. What if something had happened to Christopher or Sarah? She would never forgive herself. And so, knowing that it was probably Stephanie, or her mother, or one of a dozen other friends, she picked up the phone.

"Hello? He what?" Megan sat up so abruptly

that she bumped Tom's chin with her forehead. "Ow! It's nothing. Go on."

Megan was oblivious to Tom's injury, and rubbed her own forehead absently as she listened and talked. "When did it happen? So you took him to the hospital? Where is that? How long ago? Did you call the doctor? What did he say? I'll be right there."

Megan dropped the phone back on the hook and turned on the lamp beside the bed at the same time. The light illuminated *YOU DON'T HAVE TO STAY SINGLE*, which was on her bedside table. She had the presence of mind to turn the book over to hide the title as she climbed off the bed and crossed to her dresser drawers to pull out a pair of jeans and a sweatshirt.

"Do you mind telling me what the hell's going on?" Tom asked, still rubbing his bruised chin.

Megan took one look at him and knew she was dealing with a frustrated, sexually aroused male. "There's been an emergency. I have to go."

Tom was feeling particularly uncharitable at the moment, but what made it worse was his certainty that it was the elusive "other man" in Megan's life that she was rushing off to comfort. "Who got hurt? Who are you leaving this bed to take care of?"

Megan was mortified by Tom's insinuation, but

she had a feeling the only explanation that was going to be sufficient right now was the truth— and she shuddered to think how he would react to that. His gaze was hot on hers, watching her as she dressed. It was all very well to touch in the dark, but the lamp was revealing every stretch mark she had. She angled her body away and yanked up her jeans.

"I haven't got time to talk now," she said. "I have to go to the hospital."

"I'll drive."

"There's no need."

"I'll drive."

Knowing he was angry enough to insist, Megan didn't argue. She let him open the right-hand door of his car for her and sat down stiffly inside.

Once he was seated with the engine running he asked, "Where are we going?"

"Jackson Memorial Hospital. Head south on I-95. I'll give you more directions when we get closer." Megan's face was white with fear and her hands were trembling. She clasped them together and closed her eyes, unaware that she'd been murmuring a prayer.

"Who's hurt?" Tom demanded.

"Christopher."

"Who's Christo—"

"My son."

Tom was stunned into silence.

Now that she'd told him that much, Megan couldn't seem to stop talking. Everything came blurting out. "Chris was spending the night with his friend, Jeff. They were playing touch football and Chris tripped and fell. He hit his head on one of the metal water sprinklers in the yard. The doctor thinks he just has a concussion, but they're still doing tests. He hasn't regained consciousness since it happened."

"When was that?"

"Several hours ago."

Tom didn't know what to say. He remembered what he'd been through when his own son had been so ill. But Todd had just been a newborn baby and he and Sally hadn't yet formed the kind of bond that apparently existed between Megan and her son.

"How old is he?"

"He's only eight." The words came out as a moan of anguish.

Tom followed Megan's directions and they soon arrived at the emergency entrance to Jackson Memorial.

"I'll let you out here and go park. I'll join you as soon as—"

Megan didn't wait to hear the rest of what Tom said. She was already on her way inside. She was

appalled at what she found. It was easy to ignore
the fact that Miami was a big city until you came
face to face with the traumatic results of urban
life. Knifings, shootings, drug overdoses, wife
beatings, heart attacks, car accidents, broken
bones—the cacophony of those in pain and those
treating their pain was terrifying.

Tom found Megan standing frozen just inside
the door and put his arm around her waist, moving
her toward the admissions desk.

"We're here to see Christopher Padget," he
told the woman in receiving. "Can you tell us
where we can find him?"

She typed Christopher's name into a computer
and said, "They're running some tests upstairs.
You can wait there."

Tom followed the nurse's directions and escorted Megan upstairs to the appropriate nurse's
station. As soon as Megan identified herself the
nurse said, "It won't be long now. The doctor
will be with you as soon as he's finished the tests.
You can wait over there."

Christopher's friend, Jeff, and Jeff's mother,
Lizabeth Simpson, were sitting in the waiting
room.

"I'm so glad you're here," Lizabeth said, rising and rushing forward to hug Megan. "I got
worried when I couldn't get you on the phone.

It's the waiting that's so terrible. The nurse says we should know something soon.''

Jeff was crying and saying it was all his fault, that even though it was getting dark he'd insisted they keep playing. Megan put a hand on his shoulder to comfort him. "I'm sure it was an accident, Jeff. These things happen.''

Lizabeth saw the clerical collar Tom wore and said, "A priest, Megan? It's not that serious!''

Megan would have laughed except her sense of humor failed her at the moment. "This is Tom Steele. You remember I told you Tom and I were going to a costume party tonight? He's still wearing his costume.''

"Oh, I see,'' Lizabeth said, only Megan could tell she didn't, really.

"I couldn't reach Sarah to tell her what happened,'' Lizabeth added. "Do you want to try calling her yourself?''

"Sarah?'' Tom asked.

"My daughter.'' Megan was too worried about Chris to respond to the bemused look on Tom's face other than by saying, "She's spending the night with friends tonight, too.''

"How old is Sarah?'' His voice was so soft she wouldn't have heard him except that he was speaking into her ear.

"She's fourteen. Almost fifteen.''

"Maybe it would be better to wait and call her when you know something definite," Tom suggested.

Megan sighed and wilted onto one of the vinyl-covered couches in the waiting room. "You're right. She'd only worry and there's nothing she can do right now."

Tom sat down beside Megan, wondering why she hadn't said anything to him about her children. Two of them! A boy and a girl—and the girl was fourteen—almost fifteen! But then, he hadn't been forthright about Todd, either.

Fortunately they didn't have long to wait for news about Chris. The doctor joined them within fifteen minutes of their arrival. "Are you Mrs. Padget?"

Megan jumped up. "Yes, I am."

"And this is Mr. Padget?" he asked, turning and extending his hand to Tom.

"I'm Tom Steele, a friend of the family."

The doctor turned back to Megan. "I must say, Mrs. Padget, that your son is a very lucky little boy."

"Then he's going to be all right?"

"Yes, he is. He regained consciousness half an hour ago. He's got a concussion, and he'll have quite a headache, but our tests didn't show any other problems. He'll have to stay in bed for a while, and then take it easy a little longer, but he should recover fully.''

"Thank God," Megan murmured. Without being aware she did so, she leaned back against Tom, whose arms came around to support her. "Can I see him?"

"Certainly."

Tom didn't ask if he could go along, he simply stayed with Megan as the nurse directed her to her son's room. He kept his arm around her as he followed her inside to where a small, towheaded boy lay covered in white sheets except for his head and shoulders.

"Hi, Mom," Chris said in a frail voice.

"Hi, honey. Guess the sprinkler won that one, huh?''

"Yeah. I'm sorry I spoiled your date."

"You didn't spoil anything." Megan felt her face flushing bright red.

"Hi," Chris said, his dark brown eyes locked on Tom. "I'm Chris. Are you going to marry my mom?''

Megan gasped, her face flushing an even brighter red, if that was possible. "Tom and I have only just met—"

"I like your mom a lot," Tom interrupted.

"Yeah. But do you like football?" Chris asked.

A grin slowly widened on Tom's face. "I sure do."

"Good. I'm kinda sleepy, Mom. Will you stay with me?"

"Don't worry, honey. I'll be here."

Megan reassured Lizabeth and Jeff that Chris would be fine and urged them to go home and rest until the next day, when they could visit him. Then she checked with the nurses and found out they were willing to put a folding cot in Chris's room for her.

"It's too late now to call Sarah," Megan said, turning to Tom, "but I don't want her to come home to an empty house tomorrow, either. Would you mind staying at my house—and waiting for her?"

"Won't she be upset to find a stranger there?"

"She knows what you look like."

At Tom's questioning look Megan explained. "She saw you that first day we met, when I was shopping."

"All right. I'll be glad to stay. Do you want me to bring her here?"

"Please. And ask her to bring me some clean things to wear, if you would."

"Sure."

They stood staring awkwardly at one another

for a moment before Tom said, ''Well, I'd better let you get some rest.''

''I'll see you in the morning.''

''Right.''

Megan watched Tom turn and walk away, wondering what he was thinking. Damn, damn, damn! If only she'd told him the truth when she'd had the chance. When she thought about it she realized he'd taken things quite calmly, considering the fact that she'd lied to him—admittedly by omission—and then left him sexually high and dry. She'd find a way to make it all up to him. Because after tonight there was no hiding from the truth. Tom Steele was a very special man, very possibly the right one for her. And she was going to give them both every chance to find that out for sure.

Seven

His Book: "What Do Her Criticisms Mean?"

"Are you sure you're feeling up to this, Chris?" Megan asked, brushing a hank of shaggy blond hair back from her son's brow.

"Jeez, Mom, it's been a month. I'm fine."

"He's the same old bonehead," Sarah gibed.

"Sarah, don't talk about your brother that way."

"All I meant was that he's back to normal."

Megan rolled her eyes at Sarah's not-too-subtle insult.

"I'm really looking forward to this football game, too," Sarah said.

"Is it the game you're looking forward to? Or spending more time with Tom?" Megan questioned.

"Both. He's a really nice guy, Mom. And he knows a lot about a lot of things."

"Yeah," Chris agreed. "And he sure can throw a football better than you, Mom."

Megan acknowledged the spurt of irritation she experienced at her children's open admiration of Tom Steele, and immediately felt petty and foolish. After all, it was a blessing that Tom had found a way to explain the new math concepts to Sarah that hadn't left her confused. And Chris had basked in the approval that only a man could give to a little boy who was seeking a role model. But she could see it was going to be harder to share her children with Tom than she'd thought. She'd become possessive of their attentions over the past five years when they'd only had a mother to turn to.

When Tom had shown up with Sarah at the hospital on the morning after Chris's accident, Megan had discovered that he wasn't annoyed by the fact that she had two children; he was positively overjoyed.

"I love kids," he'd explained when they'd had

time alone to talk. "I'd have had a houseful of them if it had been up to me. Have you thought about having any more?"

"Not lately," Megan had answered evasively. "Besides, I'm getting a little old to be having babies."

"Really? You don't look old." He'd reached up and playfully traced the small wrinkles around her eyes with his thumbs.

"Character lines," they'd said almost in unison.

They'd laughed, and she'd felt warm inside with the sound of Tom's rich, booming laughter. But she hadn't admitted to him that her age had nothing to do with the fact that she wouldn't be having any more children.

"How old are you?" she'd asked. "I see a strand or two of gray in here." She'd run her fingers through his hair, marveling at its soft texture.

"I'll be thirty-six next August," he'd replied with a relaxed smile. "Is that old enough for you?"

I'm four years older than you are! "My birthday's in August, too," she'd volunteered. "Isn't that a coincidence?" but she didn't volunteer her age. And she noticed he didn't ask.

She'd thought a lot in the past month about

whether it was fair to deceive Tom the way she had—to suggest that she had a choice about whether or not to have any more babies. He apparently wanted more children—a son in his image, he'd said. She could tell by the way he acted with Sarah and Chris that he'd make a wonderful father. In fact that was the source of a great deal of her current aggravation. Her children seemed to forget she existed whenever Tom was around.

She was still feeling annoyed when the source of her irritation arrived at the door.

"Hi, Tom!" Chris shouted, racing to let him in.

"Hello, Tom!" Sarah followed her younger brother to the door with equal excitement.

Megan watched as Tom stepped inside, lifted Chris clear off the ground and gave him a quick hug before settling the boy in the crook of one arm. Chris's arms looped easily around Tom's neck. Meanwhile, Tom slipped his other arm around Sarah's waist and pulled her snugly to his side. Megan noticed how Sarah's whole body leaned into Tom, evidencing her trust in him. In little more than an instant three persons had joined ranks...and become connected. She knew it was ridiculous, but she felt excluded.

"So how are the two of you today?" Tom's

cheeks dimpled as he grinned. "Ready to watch the Dolphins dump the Colts?"

"You bet!" Chris replied.

Megan saw the pleasure in her children's faces mirrored in Tom's gaze as he looked back at them. Then he lifted his eyes and met hers. She knew the distress he was seeing on her face confused him, and she quickly turned away to get her feelings under control. The next thing she knew Tom's arms were around her waist and she felt his broad, muscular chest against her back. He was strong and capable...capable of taking control of her children and her life.

"Hello, Megan," he whispered in her ear. "I missed you."

Megan blushed, since it had only been a matter of a few hours since she'd sent him out the front door. They'd spent the better part of the previous night and early-morning hours necking on her living-room couch.

"Tom...the children—"

"Have a pretty good idea how I feel about you," he said, nuzzling her neck and sending involuntary shivers down her spine.

Megan was feeling crotchety and contrary. She pulled away from him and said, her voice sharp, "You've made sure of that, haven't you?"

When Megan turned to face Tom she saw the

shock and hurt in his eyes. What was wrong with her? She hadn't meant to say such a mean thing. But instead of the apology she knew she should make she said, "We're going to be late if we don't leave right now. Sarah, Chris, go on out to the car. We'll be with you in a minute."

Megan's throat closed in pain as she met the accusing looks on her children's faces before they turned to leave.

"I'll get the cooler," Tom said.

"I can carry it," Megan countered.

"But why should you have to when I'm here?"

Megan watched the muscles in Tom's arms bulge beneath his short-sleeved cotton knit shirt as he lifted the cooler. She watched a frown form when he realized how heavy it was. "What's in this thing?"

"I packed some extra sodas."

"For us and what army?" he said, laughing.

"It's a warm day. I thought we might get thirsty," Megan replied, more than a hint of asperity in her voice.

"It's all right, Megan. I think I can handle the extra weight."

But Megan refused to be soothed by his attempt at conciliation. "Give it to me." She stepped in front of Tom and reached for the handholds.

Tom stopped and looked down at her as though

she'd lost her mind. "What the hell's going on, Megan? You've done nothing but snipe at me since I walked in the door. Is it that time of the month?"

"How dare you make such a remark!"

"Give me another explanation for the way you're behaving," he challenged.

"I don't have to explain anything to you."

"Maybe not. But I'm not moving another step until you do."

"Maybe I don't like the way you take over and do things before you're asked!" she retorted.

His voice was so soft she had to listen hard to hear his reply. "Is that what you really think? That I'm trying to take over?"

"Aren't you?"

Tom set the cooler down on the dining-room table and grasped Megan by the arms. "Let's get something straight right now. I care a great deal about you, Megan. And I think the world of Sarah and Chris. But the last thing I want to do is *impose* myself on this family. Any time you want me out of here all you have to do is say the word. Is that understood?"

Megan stared at the tuft of hair that showed at the opening of Tom's shirt, too ashamed to look him in the eye. But he wasn't about to let her get away with that kind of cowardice. His forefinger

levered its way under her chin and tilted her face
upward. Still she kept her gaze down, seeing only
his tightly compressed lips and jutting chin
through her lowered lashes.

"All right, Megan. What's it to be?"

She cleared her throat. "I may have exaggerated the situation...a bit."

"And?"

"And I hope you'll spend the day with us even
though I've been acting like a total idiot."

Tom chuckled. "*Is* it that time of the month?"

Megan snorted and jerked her chin away from
his touch. "For heaven's sake! So what if it is?
What does that have to do with anything?"

Tom's chuckle became a full-throated laugh.
"Nothing. Let's get out of here. I promised the
kids we could throw a football around the parking
lot before the game."

Megan watched as Tom hefted the cooler again
and headed out the door ahead of her. Why
couldn't she have been more honest with Tom
about her fears? Why couldn't she have admitted
that it was going to take her some time to adjust
to the children's growing reliance on him? Why
couldn't she have just said that she was crazy in
love with him and it scared her to death to think
he might not be just as much in love with her?

Tom spent the first half of the game watching

Megan carefully when she wasn't looking. What he saw confused and worried him. She was enjoying the contest on the field, all right. But her eyes lacked sparkle, and the lilt was missing from her laugh. And he couldn't think of a single reason that should be so. They'd spent some part of every day together for the past month since Chris's accident. He hadn't pressed her to make love simply because they hadn't had the privacy they both desired. However, they'd pleasured one another in different ways. He didn't doubt her attraction to him, nor his to her. So what was wrong?

At that moment one of the several men who'd been drinking beer at the far end of the aisle stood up and carelessly began making his way toward the stadium stairs. In the process he stepped on toes and spilled beer on those he passed. Tom was watching him in disgust when the man stepped on Megan's toe. As she yelped and jerked her foot out of his way he lost his balance and spilled part of his tall cup of beer on Sarah. He turned on Megan snarling, "Sonofa—"

The man never got a chance to finish. Tom wasn't even aware of moving. He simply found himself with two handfuls of the man's shirt in his fists. He lifted the drunken man off the ground and rasped in a deadly voice, "Apologize to both of them. Now."

"'Scuse me," the man slurred, his eyes wide with fright, both hands scrunching the top of his paper cup.

"Now I suggest you find somewhere else to watch the rest of the game."

Tom lifted the drunk and set him down beyond Chris, watching with steely eyes until he was gone. Then he sat down with a calm that was dangerous for its quiet. "Are you both all right?"

"I'm a little wet," Sarah said, her nose wrinkled with distaste as she brushed off her shorts. "But I'll dry."

"And you, Megan?"

"I could have taken care of the situation if you'd given me the chance. He was drunk. Do you really think it was necessary to manhandle him like that?"

"Nobody hurts my fam—" Tom bit his tongue to catch himself. But from the look in Megan's eyes he was too late.

"We're missing the game." She abruptly turned away from him to stare at the field.

Megan hadn't mentioned the incident again, but she'd been distant, silent. And when he'd tried to kiss her good night, she'd stiffened. He was hurt, but afraid to ask her what was wrong, afraid she didn't care for him as much as he cared for her.

That evening, after he'd dropped Megan and her kids off, he didn't go straight home. The house he'd rented was too empty, and he was too frustrated by the day's events. He'd proved to himself that with the right motivation, he could be violent. He found himself heading for Randy and Irene's place.

"Well, well. Look what the cat dragged in, Irene."

"Tom! What a nice surprise. You look like you got a little sun today. Did you go to the game?"

"Yeah."

"But not alone," Randy surmised.

"Naw."

"Megan Padget?"

"Yeah."

"I've seen happier faces on cadavers," Randy said. "Pull up a chair and tell big brother all about it."

"Would a beer help?" Irene asked.

Tom grimaced. "Yeah."

Randy turned to his wife and said, "Loquacious, isn't he?" He sat down in a comfortable chair across from the couch where Tom had sprawled. "The only words in your vocabulary tonight seem to be *yeah* and *naw*. Want to talk about what's wrong?''

"Yeah."

"Did she throw you out?"

"Naw."

"Well, that's something at least."

Irene handed Tom an ice-cold bottle of beer. "Would a woman's perspective help?"

Tom took several swallows of the drink. "Yeah."

Irene sat on the arm of Randy's chair and leaned back. "So, what do you want to know?"

"Why would Megan suddenly start to criticize everything I do?"

"Give me an example," Irene said.

Tom thought of the incident with the drunk, but realized it was too revealing of his own feelings. There were enough other examples that would serve his purpose. "Today when we were at the game, I offered to buy Sarah some peanuts. Megan said that was a dumb idea, because it would just make a mess. Later, Chris spilled his drink and I said I'd buy him another one. Megan said since Chris had spilled it he could get his own soda."

"Both incidents occurred when you made suggestions to her children," Irene noted.

"I guess they did. So what?"

"You haven't read all of *HOW TO MARRY THE WOMAN OF YOUR DREAMS*, have you?" Randy asked.

"Why do you say that?"

"Because there's a whole chapter entitled, 'What Her Criticisms Mean.'"

"I assume you've read it," Tom said. "So why don't you condense it for me?"

Randy quoted:

A woman doesn't criticize a man without reason. Unfortunately, what she says and what she really means aren't always the same thing.

"Would you mind translating that into English?" Tom said irritably.

Irene leaned forward and put a hand on Tom's shoulder. "It means that something could be bothering Megan about your relationship with her children."

"But I love her kids!"

"More than you love Megan?" Irene asked.

"Of course not!"

"Have you told Megan that?"

"I would have if I'd thought it was necessary. She knows how I feel about her."

"Are you sure?"

Tom was silent for a moment. "It couldn't be anything as simple as that."

Irene shrugged. "I'm not saying it is. But it might be. How long has Megan had the children to herself?"

"She was divorced five years ago. Her ex-husband died two years ago."

"She's had a lot of time to establish a close relationship with her children. Maybe you're threatening that relationship."

"I don't want to take away from Megan's closeness to the kids. I only want to be a part of..." Tom remembered Megan's reaction to his slip in referring to her and her children as his family. "She doesn't want me to be a part of their family?" Tom's brow furrowed in thought. "Do you think that's it?"

"Only Megan knows for sure, Tom. My suggestion is that you talk to her," Randy said. "And read that chapter on a woman's criticisms. Maybe it'll give you some ideas about how to handle the situation."

"I guess it's worth a try anyway." Tom leaned forward to finish his beer. "I'd better get home. It's late."

Randy and Irene both rose to see Tom to the door.

"If you feel like talking some more, you know where we are," Randy said.

"Thanks." Tom gently cuffed Randy on the chin with his fist. "It's a comfort to know that. I mean it."

When Tom got home, he pulled his birthday book from under a pile of papers that had accumulated on top of it and turned to the chapter entitled, "What Her Criticisms Mean."

Don't ignore what a woman says in pique or anger. Often that is when she's being most honest.

In a day and age where communication between the sexes is clouded with confusion, you can't afford to bury your head in the sand and refuse to hear words that may hurt.

Was that what he'd done? Refused to hear what he didn't find to his liking? What had Megan said when he'd picked up the cooler this morning? Something about taking control of things when he hadn't been asked. What *exactly* had she said? Tom thought for a moment and heard Megan speaking again.

Maybe I don't like the way you take over and do things before you're asked.

Take over. Take control. He couldn't be mak-

ing the same mistakes now that he'd made so long
ago with Sally. He no longer needed to be the one
in charge. He'd learned from his past mistakes.
He'd changed. Or so he'd thought. What had Megan said after the incident with the drunk?

*I could have handled the situation if you'd
given me the chance.*

It was hard to accept the fact that Megan didn't
want his help. Not with lifting and carrying. Not
with her children. Not even with handling a
drunk. What *did* she want from him?

He turned back to his book, looking for more
answers.

*When in doubt as to what a woman is thinking,
ask her.*

It wasn't that simple, Tom thought. He'd already asked Megan a couple of times today what
was wrong and she hadn't given him a straight
answer. He read the next few lines with a grim
look on his face.

*If you can't get her to tell you what she's
thinking, tell her what you're thinking and
see if you're both on the same wavelength.*

Tom picked up the phone and dialed Megan's

number, even though it was late and even though he knew she was probably already in bed. He felt an undeniable sense of urgency. This couldn't wait. He had to repair whatever damage he'd caused today, and he wanted to do it now.

"Who's calling?"

It wasn't until Tom heard Megan's voice, husky with sleep, that he actually looked at the clock and saw it was long past midnight. Hell, maybe her defenses were down and he'd get the answers he sought.

"I couldn't sleep," he said.

"I'll let you come over and make breakfast tomorrow at six a.m. Then maybe you'll get tired at a decent hour," she mumbled.

"I've been thinking, Megan."

"That's nice."

"Are you awake?"

"I guess so."

"I've been thinking...."

"Hmm?"

"Maybe I've been sticking my nose in where it doesn't belong with regard to Sarah and Chris, interfering in things that were better left alone."

Tom waited, but Megan didn't say anything. At last he heard, "Hmm."

Tom's chest hurt. She wasn't contradicting him. He forced himself to go on. "So maybe it would be better if I stayed away from you and the kids for a while.''

Silence again.

Tom's stomach felt queasy. ''Did you hear what I said?''

''Hmm.''

''Am I right?''

''You know best, Tom.''

Tom's head felt as if burly blacksmiths with heavy hammers were pounding away inside. ''I won't be seeing you for a while then.''

''If you say so.''

''Good night, Megan.''

''Good night, Tom.''

''I love you,'' he whispered.

''Hmm.''

Tom hung up the phone in a state of shock. He looked down at the book in his lap.

Be willing to accept the answers you get, even if they weren't the ones you expected. Not every woman is right for every man.

Tom grabbed the book and threw it across the room with all his might. It slammed against the wall with a resounding *thwack* and fell in a ruffled heap on the hardwood floor.

Eight

Her Book: "Meeting His Mother"

The next morning Megan could vaguely recollect getting a phone call from Tom the night before, but couldn't remember much of the conversation. She'd been so keyed up after the day they'd spent together that she'd taken a sleeping pill to help her get some rest. She'd only wakened long enough to answer the phone and then put it back on the hook when she heard the irritating bleep that told her Tom had long since hung up at the other end.

She'd tried calling him all day, but his answering machine was on. She caught up with Stephanie at lunch and asked, "Have you seen Tom around on campus today?"

"Haven't you heard? He's gone to Panama."

"Panama?"

"Seems the U.S. ambassador needed some advice."

Megan stared at the gently swaying fronds of the palm trees lining the campus quadrangle and tried to think calm thoughts. "He didn't even call me to say he was going."

Or was that what he'd called to say last night? Megan just couldn't remember.

"When is he supposed to be back?" she asked Stephanie.

"Why are you asking me these questions? He's your boyfriend."

Megan glared at Stephanie who quickly said, "I heard from the dean's secretary that he's only supposed to be gone for a couple of days."

But a couple of days turned into two weeks. In fact, Tom still hadn't contacted Megan by the time Thanksgiving vacation arrived. As much as she'd objected to Tom involving himself in her children's lives, his absence was deeply felt at a table set for three.

"This is a time for thanksgiving. Why the long

faces?'' she demanded as she served up plates heaped with honey-glazed ham, twice-baked sweet potatoes, asparagus, blueberry muffins and warm port-wine-and-cranberry sauce.

"I wish Tom were here," Chris said.

Sarah mashed her fork into her sweet potatoes, making designs. "I miss him. Mom, do you think there's a chance that you and he...I mean, he really seemed to like you. Why hasn't he come to see us?"

"I told you he went to Panama," Megan answered.

"But he didn't even call to say goodbye," Chris said. "I thought he liked me."

"He does like you," Megan reassured her son.

"Then why hasn't he called?"

"I suspect because he's been very busy. He's doing an important job. He probably doesn't have—" Megan cut herself off as she realized what she'd been about to say—that he hadn't had time. Surely Tom could have found a few moments in the past two weeks to call and let them know he was thinking of them. If he was.

If only she could remember that telephone call!

As they were eating their pumpkin pie the phone rang.

"I'll get it," Chris shouted as he jumped up from the table. "I'll bet it's Tom."

But it wasn't Tom. It was Irene Steele.

"Tom called Randy to say he'll be back on Monday. He was invited to spend Thanksgiving with the ambassador's family and decided to stay. Anyway, what I wanted to ask was whether you and your children could come to a barbecue Randy and I are giving next Saturday. Please say yes."

Megan's brain was still trying to cope with the fact that Tom had found time to call his brother but not her and her children. It was hard not to take out her growing anger with Tom on Irene. If the fact that Tom had ignored them meant he planned to do a replay of his former disappearing act, this invitation from Irene might be the only chance she'd have to confront him about his insensitivity to her children's feelings—not to mention her own.

"We'd love to come," she heard herself say. "What time do you want us there?"

Megan had expected to have trouble finding the street where Irene and Randy Steele lived because Coral Gables was a maze of banyon-shaded boulevards that curved and wound without any rhyme or reason. The task was living up to her worst expectations. To add to her worries, Chris was bouncing around in the car like a parakeet gone wild in a glass cage. Megan knew he was just excited—and a little worried—about seeing Tom again. That explained his behavior, but it didn't make it any less nerve-racking.

Chris threw his upper body halfway over the front seat to complain loudly about his sister. "Mom, Sarah pinched me."

"Only after he pulled my hair!"

"Sit down, Chris! If I have to stop suddenly you'll go right through the windshield."

"When are we going to get there, Mom? I'm hungry," he complained.

"I don't see how you could be. You had two granola bars and a container of yogurt before we left home."

"That was over an hour ago," Sarah pointed out. She leaned over the seat beside Chris. "Where are we, Mom? Are we lost?"

Megan looked down at the directions Irene had given her over the phone, then back up again, searching for the concrete corner stones used for street signs in Coral Gables. "I'm sure it's not far now, Sarah. If you'll both sit down and sit still for a few more minutes, we'll be there."

But it was half an hour later that Megan finally backtracked and found the large Spanish-style house she was looking for.

Megan gave Irene a quick hug before turning

to shake Randy's hand. Randy had about the same build as Tom, but he was slightly shorter, and his features weren't nearly as distinctive. It was like comparing a cougar and a leopard. They were both dangerous cats, but the beauty of the leopard took your breath away.

"Where's Tom?" Chris asked as soon as he realized the man he'd come to see wasn't there.

"He should be here soon," Irene answered. "How would you like to play in the backyard with Charlie until he arrives?"

"Who's Charlie?"

"Come and see," Irene said mysteriously as she led Chris out the back door.

Sarah's curiosity got the better of her. "I think I'll go, too."

Megan was left alone with Randy.

"Charlie is our Afghan hound," he explained. "She just had a litter of six pups."

"Sarah and Chris will love seeing them." Megan wasn't sure what to say next, because the obvious topic of discussion was Tom—who hadn't called her once the entire week he'd been back. Nor had she picked up the phone. She'd waited until today to talk with him, knowing that what she had to discuss was better said face-to-face.

"I'm glad we have a chance to talk before Tom gets here," Randy said.

Megan had been so totally lost in her thoughts that she hadn't realized Randy had closed the distance between them. He was now standing directly across from her, his feet planted far apart, his white-knuckled hands in fists on his hips. She recognized again the threat of danger she'd felt upon meeting him. She could see he was angry, but she had no idea why. He didn't leave her in suspense for long.

"I want to know why you let my brother fall in love with you and your kids if you weren't serious about a permanent relationship with him."

"Not serious? He's the one who stopped seeing me!"

"That's not what I heard."

"Then you heard wrong. The last time I saw or spoke with Tom was three weeks ago. My children were devastated when he left for Panama without a word, and he hasn't contacted any of us since. You tell me how your brother could let two impressionable children fall in love with him and then turn his back on them!"

"Why don't you ask me yourself."

Megan whirled to find Tom standing in the doorway. She felt a fierce rush of pleasure at seeing him and quickly tamped it down. This was a golden opportunity to confront Tom about her grievances and she didn't intend to let it pass her by. "Do you deny that you left for Panama without a word to me or the children?"

"No."

"Do you deny that you haven't bothered to pick up the phone and call for three weeks?"

"No."

"Do you deny that you've been avoiding me for the past week since you've been back?"

"No."

Megan turned back to confront Randy, her hands on her hips. "Do you still think I'm responsible for ending my relationship with your brother?"

"Wait a minute," Tom said, putting his hand on Megan's shoulder and turning her back around to face him. "Do you deny that you told me—on several occasions—during the last day we spent together that I was sticking my nose in where it didn't belong?"

Megan flushed. "I may have—"

"Do you deny that when I suggested it might be better if I stayed away from you and the kids for a while that you agreed it would be for the best?"

"What? I most certainly do deny it! Whatever gave you such an idea?"

"You did," Tom said between gritted teeth.

"When? I never said any such thing."

"You're conveniently forgetting my phone call the night before I left for Panama. I know what I heard, Megan."

There was a moment of charged silence while Megan assimilated the fact that she must have said something to Tom while she'd been half asleep. "I know you called...that is I remember answering the phone and hanging it up again. But Tom, I don't remember anything else you said that night. And I certainly don't remember asking you to stay away! I'd taken a sleeping pill and—"

Tom nearly crushed Megan as his arms folded around her. "God, all the time we've wasted because of a stupid misunderstanding!"

Megan gripped him tightly around the waist as she hid her face in the curve of his shoulder, breathing deeply of his male scent. She stood on tiptoe to press her cheek against his throat. "Oh, Tom, I would never, never suggest you stay away. Don't you know I need you? Sarah and Chris need you."

His mouth slanted onto hers, his tongue probing. She willingly opened to him, her arms sliding up and around his neck, her fingertips tunneling into the shaggy hair at his nape. It was several minutes before they came up for air.

"The children—"

Tom looked up long enough to see that Randy

was gone. "My brother'll keep them in the backyard for a while longer. Oh, Megan, I've been
slowly dying the past three weeks without you. I
missed you. I missed the kids. What have you all
been doing?"

"I think first I'd like an explanation for how
you could think I didn't want to see you anymore."

Tom wasn't about to explain to Megan that
he'd been following the advice in a book designed
to help him find a wife. It was too humiliating.
"I guess I got my wires crossed. You made it
pretty clear you could do things by yourself, that
you didn't need my help."

Megan took Tom's hand and pulled him over
to the couch so they could sit down together.
"I've been on my own a long time, Tom. It's hard
to share the kids, and myself, with you. But I'm
trying—"

Tom cut her off with a quick, hard kiss. "I
promise not to go off half-cocked next time. Now,
if we don't catch up with the rest of the gang I'm
going to end up hauling you off to one of Randy's
bedrooms."

Megan automatically linked her arm around
Tom's waist as they rose and headed outside together.

Sarah's and Chris's welcome was so enthusiastic Tom was literally bowled over onto the grass. Tears burned at the back of Megan's eyes as she watched Tom hug her daughter and tickle her son until all three were laughing so hard they were gasping for air.

Irene walked over to stand beside Megan and watch her brother-in-law's antics. "He'll make a wonderful father for those two kids. It's a shame Sally doesn't let him spend more time with Todd. He's about the same age as Chris if I recall correctly."

"Todd?"

Irene's eyes widened in alarm and her hand came up to cover her mouth. "I've stuck my foot in it, haven't I? Tom hasn't told you about his son?"

Megan shook her head no.

Irene put a hand on the arms Megan had crossed protectively in front of her. "Ask him. He'll tell you what you want to know."

Megan kept telling herself all afternoon that it wasn't such a bad thing that Tom hadn't mentioned Todd. After all, she was keeping an equally important secret from him, so what right did she have to be hurt? She cried inside because she'd wanted to be the one to give him that son and couldn't. It was too late for that. Much, much too late.

It wasn't until Sarah and Chris were in bed later that evening that Megan finally asked Tom about Todd. They were lying on the couch together, their bodies aligned with one another.

Tom's hands cupped Megan's breast possessively, and he dipped his head down to kiss the pulse at her throat. "God, I've missed you," he said with a groan.

Megan felt a frisson of desire skitter down her spine and knew that if she didn't speak now, in a few moments neither of them would be doing any talking.

"Is it true that you have a son?"

Tom slowly sat up, rearranging Megan sideways in his lap with his arm supporting her back. He turned her so he could see her face. "How did you find out?"

"Irene. Why didn't you tell me yourself?"

"I try not to think about Todd too much. He was very sick as a child and spent a lot of time in the hospital. I hardly had a chance to get to know him before Sally and I divorced. Sally took him and moved all the way to California, so I can't be with him as often as I'd like. I've only seen him a few times—for a couple of weeks total, maybe—since he was born."

"How old is he?"

"Eight."

Megan looked up into Tom's eyes. "Is that why you spend so much time with Chris? Because he's a substitute for your own son?"

Megan saw the pain in Tom's expression and knew she'd misjudged him. "I'm sorry." She ran a hand through her hair in agitation. "You said you wanted children. I thought it was because you didn't have any of your own."

"I would like more children." His voice was soft, dreamy almost. "I'd like to make Sarah and Chris mine."

"Oh, Tom, I—" Megan's voice broke in a sob of mixed pain and pleasure as she leaned against the hard wall of Tom's chest. How could she marry him without telling him the truth? But would he want her when he knew she couldn't give him any more children?

"I'm hoping now that Todd is a little older Sally will let him visit me in the summer. Do you think Todd and Chris will get along?"

"They'll probably fight like cats and dogs, but that's normal."

"Megan, there's something else I wanted to ask before...before we had our misunderstanding." He tipped Megan's chin up so he could see her eyes. "I'd like for you and the kids to meet my mother and stepfather."

Megan felt her face flushing. She couldn't help

remembering what *YOU DON'T HAVE TO STAY SINGLE* had to say about this all-important step.

When a man introduces you to his family it means he's thinking about marriage.

"When would we meet them?" she asked. "Didn't you say your mother lives in San Antonio?"

"I'd like to fly you and the kids out there with me over Christmas."

"Oh, Tom, we can't."

Megan had been watching his face so she saw the disappointment flash in his eyes before he was able to hide it.

"It's not that I don't want to," Megan explained. "It's just that it's so close to Christmas and I've already made plans with Gary's parents—the children's grandparents—to come here for Christmas. Then Sarah and Chris are going to spend New Year's with my folks. I'm sorry."

Megan was as disappointed as Tom was. "I wish there were some way—"

"What about leaving Sarah and Chris with your parents and joining me in San Antonio by yourself?"

"I couldn't do that!"

"Why not?"

"I haven't left the kids alone with anyone for any length of time for—"

"For too long, I'm sure," Tom interrupted. "Come to San Antonio for New Year's," he coaxed. "I want my mother to meet you."

And what if she didn't go? Would it make a difference to their relationship? Megan thought not, but she wanted to please Tom...and she relished the thought of some time alone with him.

"All right, I'll come."

Tom flashed a wicked grin. "I missed Thanksgiving without you. Shall we celebrate now?"

Megan settled back in his arms and traced the line of his jaw with her forefinger. She left her thumb test the fullness of his mouth, then lifted her head up to nip at his lower lip and worry it gently with her teeth. Before he could catch her mouth with his she drew back teasingly. Her hands cupped his face and she could feel the roughness of the day's growth of beard under her fingertips. She brought his face down to hers and kissed his cheeks, his eyelids, his nose and his chin. Finally she reached for his mouth.

At that point, Tom's patience gave up the ghost. His lips descended, capturing Megan's with a fire that caused her blood to race. His hands sought out the pleasure points on her body, touching with need, with hope, with love. Their clothes were a barrier, and soon buttons had been undone and cloth shoved out of the way so that flesh met willing flesh.

The sound of Chris's voice jarred them both. Tom sat up abruptly, nearly dumping Megan on the floor. She grasped his arm to help her stand, and began frantically rebuttoning her blouse and pulling up her shorts as Tom zipped up his jeans and rearranged his disheveled shirt.

"I'm coming, darling. I'll be right there," Megan shouted. Thank goodness Chris hadn't come looking for her.

"Is Tom still here?" Chris called from the bedroom.

Tom cleared his throat, in an effort to rid his voice of the last vestiges of passion. "I'm here, Chris."

"Will you come in and talk to me?"

Tom looked to Megan for concurrence, and when he got it said, "I'll be right there."

Megan followed after Tom, helping him tuck his shirt back into his jeans.

Tom sat down on the bed beside Chris. "What did you want to talk about, Tiger?"

"You're not going to go away and leave us again, are you?"

"I'll be going to see my mom and stepfather for Christmas, but I won't go without saying goodbye, and you'll know when I'm coming back."

"Will you give me a hug good-night?"

Megan watched as the two men in her life exchanged a masculine embrace.

"Good night, Tiger."

"Good night, Tom."

Megan took her turn hugging Chris and tucked him in snugly before she left the room with Tom.

Once they were back in the living room Tom said, "I'd better go." His mouth came down hard, his tongue searching, but he forced himself to pull back. "I'm looking forward to having some time alone with you in San Antonio."

"Me, too."

Megan could still taste him on her lips after he'd left. She ached. It was terrible to feel like this. But it was wonderful to know that soon she'd be able to slake her hunger for Tom.

That night she lay in bed with a silly grin on her face. her world was right again. She felt a bit of trepidation about meeting Tom's mother and consoled herself by picking up *YOU DON'T HAVE TO STAY SINGLE* and turning to the chapter called, "Meeting His Mother."

Certain rules of etiquette and decorum apply when you meet a man's mother for the first time. Expect her values to be different and be ready to adjust accordingly. Follow her lead.

One last warning: Watch your step! Your relationship with his mother is laced with pitfalls.

Megan fell asleep imagining herself curtsying to a plump little woman dressed in a pillbox hat, conservative suit, white gloves and pumps.

Three weeks later Megan was sitting at the San Antonio airport waiting for Tom to arrive, wearing an outfit designed to make her look as sexless as possible. She knew it was ridiculous, but the more she'd read, the more she'd been sure it was important to dress, act and speak conservatively around Tom's mother.

Tom had missed Megan more than he'd thought possible, and he was impatient to hold her in his arms, to catch the sweet gardenia scent of her hair as he tasted her mouth with his. When he finally spied her he realized why he hadn't noticed her sooner. She was wearing a shapeless gray-green dress that made her fade into the airport wall. Her face was pale and drawn, and she didn't seem to be wearing any makeup. Her beautiful golden-brown hair was pulled back severely and hidden in a knot behind her head. He wasn't conscious of the frown on his face as he approached her.

Megan caught sight of Tom just before he reached her. He didn't look the least bit pleased to see her. Had he changed his mind about her in the three weeks they'd been separated?

"Megan? Is something wrong? Are the kids okay?"

"No, everyone's fine. What makes you ask?" He didn't even take her in his arms, and she felt too uncertain to walk forward the few steps necessary to put herself there. This wasn't the romantic reunion she'd imagined, where she flew into Tom's arms and he slanted his lips onto hers.

Tom shook his head, still frowning at her. "I just thought…" He couldn't tell her she looked like death warmed over. But he wasn't about to lie and say she looked great, either. He settled for the one thing he could say with complete honesty. "I'm glad you're here."

Then he stepped forward and folded her into his arms—and everything was wonderful.

"I missed you." He groaned with pleasure as his lips came down to devour hers.

Megan was still reeling from the potent kiss when Tom began hurrying her toward the baggage-claim area.

"I promised Mom we'd be back in time for

supper. Your plane was late so we'll have to hurry to make it."

They were in the car and headed away from the airport before Megan worked up the courage to say, "What's your mother like?"

Tom grinned. "It's a little late to be asking that, isn't it? You'll be seeing for yourself in a few minutes."

Megan smiled bleakly. "I suppose you're right. Is there anything I should know before I meet her?"

"Like what?"

She shrugged. "I don't know. I guess I thought…if there was a subject I shouldn't talk about or anything."

"Just be yourself, Megan, and she'll love you."

Megan's heart was pounding with fear when she stepped inside the foyer of the huge old two-story Victorian home in Alamo Heights.

They were greeted by a small, perfectly coifed woman wearing three-inch heels and an elegant hot-pink silk pantsuit with a deep décolletage. There was a welcoming smile on her face and a twinkle in her deep-set blue eyes.

No pillbox hat, no white gloves, no pumps. Megan wondered what other false preconceptions she harbored about this woman. *How I wish I'd worn something with buttons down the front for Tom!*

"I'm so glad you were able to get here in time," Tom's mother said in a rumbling contralto. "You know how the General is, Tom. Cocktails at 7:30, dinner promptly at 8:00, come hail or high water. I'm so glad to meet you, my dear. Tom has told me so much about you and your two wonderful children. I hope you had a good Christmas. We had a perfectly marvelous one here, except I do miss the snow. Tom, take Megan's suitcase to the downstairs bedroom while I get her something to drink before dinner. What can I get you, dear?"

Megan found herself bereft of Tom, ensconced in a cushioned wicker settee on a glassed-in porch, holding an icy margarita in her hand, and wondering why she had been so worried about meeting this perfectly charming woman.

"Please call me Isabel," Tom's mother said. She slipped off her high heels and tucked her bare toes under her on the couch. "I was surprised when Tom asked if he could invite a woman to come visit. I thought he'd decided never to marry again."

Megan choked on a sip of margarita. "Uh. Tom and I haven't spoken about marriage."

She felt Isabel's intense gaze examining her.

She decided to follow Isabel's lead, and slipped off her shoes, tucking her legs under her. Then she self-consciously straightened the ugly gray-green dress, which had bunched around her waist.

"Are you pregnant, my dear?"

Megan sat up with a start, her eyes wide, and managed to spill a good portion of her margarita on her lap. "Of course not!"

Without batting an eyelash, Isabel began dabbing Megan's dress with a handful of napkins from the coffee table. "I apologize for my frankness. It's just that your dress has so very much extra material in it that I thought...oh, well, in due time. I did so hope for more grandchildren."

Megan heard the wistful tone in Isabel's voice and could have cried. Would Tom's mother be so pleasant if she knew Megan's marriage to Tom would deprive her of any more grandchildren?

"I must say you're not exactly what I expected from Tom's description of you," Isabel said, filling the silence.

"Oh?"

"I thought you'd be taller. And Tom said your hair was honey brown, but I think it's more golden. Yes, definitely golden. But he was right about your eyes. They are the most marvelous color."

Megan felt herself turning red.

"What has Mother said to have you blushing already?" Tom asked as he entered the room.

Isabel turned her cheek for Tom's kiss. "I've been telling her how lovely she is. And that I expect you'll be proposing soon."

Megan saw Tom's scowl and cringed inwardly. So, Isabel was wrong and he wasn't thinking about marriage. Megan watched as he forcibly rearranged his features into a neutral expression. Then he crossed and sat down beside her on the settee, so close that she could feel the heat of him down her entire side.

He casually slipped an arm around her. "Enjoying your drink?" Then, without any warning, his lips dropped to nuzzle her neck.

Megan struggled to keep from spilling what little margarita was left in the glass. "Uh...my drink is fine. Salty." She sat up abruptly, moving away from Tom's nuzzling mouth, and grabbed several napkins from the coffee table to keep her hands busy. She felt a prickling sensation and looked up, meeting Isabel's perceptive gaze.

She knows I'm in love with her son.

Nine

Her Book: "Getting Him to Pop the Question"
His Book: "Avoiding Cold Feet When It's Time
to Commit"

Once Isabel had voiced the possibility of Megan marrying Tom, Megan couldn't get it off her mind. She'd avoided Tom's eyes the rest of the evening, sure that if she looked at him he'd guess what she was thinking. She was remembering what she'd read in *YOU DON'T HAVE TO STAY SINGLE* about how to get a man to propose.

Go places where people will treat you as though you're already a married couple; go

*shopping for the kind of items that will fur-
nish a home; talk to him in terms of the future; and last, but not least, let him know you
love him and want to spend the rest of your
life with him.*

His mother was doing a fine job of treating
them as though they were already married, and
between them they surely had enough furniture
for two houses. That left only speaking to Tom
of the future and admitting that she loved him.
But before she could do that she had a confession
to make.

After supper that evening, Isabel and the General, whom Megan had found not at all stiff and
general-like, both excused themselves and headed
upstairs to bed, leaving Megan and Tom alone on
the couch in front of the cheery fireplace in the
living room.

Megan smiled at Tom and he smiled back. Suddenly she was afraid of what he'd say when she
confessed the secret she'd kept from him.
Couldn't the truth wait a little bit longer?
Couldn't she hold on to what she had and forget
about the future? She leaned her head against his
shoulder and felt his arm encircle her warmly. It
felt so right to be with him.

Tom tightened his hold on Megan and thought how good it felt to have her here—as if they were meant to be together. It shouldn't have surprised him that his mother expected him to propose. But it had. If his mother had known how viciously Maryanne had rejected him she would understand his hesitation. He wasn't sure he'd ever trust another woman enough to open himself to a repeat of that agony.

He recalled the sober advice in *HOW TO MARRY THE WOMAN OF YOUR DREAMS*:

> *When you feel yourself falling in love with a woman you may be tempted to draw back from the relationship. This fear of commitment is natural because when you admit you're in love it leaves you vulnerable to the pain of rejection. However, if you succumb to the fear of commitment, you'll be robbing yourself of the happiness that comes from marriage to the woman of your dreams.*

Loving Megan meant taking risks. If only he had a better idea what she was thinking. Megan hadn't done or said anything to commit herself, either. And he wouldn't be so foolish as to offer his heart again to a woman who didn't want it.

He brought Megan a little closer to his side and

pressed a kiss to her temple. More than that and he wouldn't be able to leave her in a few minutes when it was time to go their separate ways to bed. His hand caressed its way up her sleeve, accidentally grazing her breast. He felt her tremble and responded by flicking his thumb gently against the nipple. He felt himself catch fire as her breast tautened beneath his touch. He turned and lay down on the couch, pulling her on top of him, and felt her arch into his swollen manhood. "God, how I've missed you! It seemed more like three months than three weeks."

"I missed you, too." She tensed as one of his hands slipped down between her thighs.

He had to find something to talk about, something to keep his mind off how much he wanted her naked under him. "How was Christmas?"

"The kids loved their presents." She ripped the buttons free on his shirt, and searched out his nipples in the mat of hair on his chest, teasing them with her tongue.

Tom moaned. "You can stop that in about a hundred years."

Megan realized Tom's lips had discovered one of the solitaire diamond earrings she was wearing in her ears. "I love my Christmas present. I was surprised when I opened it." *I hoped you might be thinking of diamonds in another kind of setting.*

She shoved his shirt off his shoulders and admired his skin, which glowed bronze in the light from the fire. "You are so beautiful."

"You're the one who's beautiful." He unzipped her gray-green dress down the back and bared her to his gaze. He reached out and took one nipple into his mouth, feeling it come to life under the lace bra.

Megan's breasts felt full and achy as Tom sucked first one and then the other. She pressed her belly against his arousal, wanting more, needing more, but knowing this was not the time or the place.

"Tom, please... Your parents—"

"My parents never come downstairs once they've gone to bed."

"But they might—"

"The General is a creature of habit. They won't bother us. I want you, Megan. I need you."

There was no talk of love from Tom, only *want* and *need*. But she hadn't spoken the words either. She wanted to tell him she loved him, but couldn't. Soon there was no more time to think, as her senses took control. Her fingers entwined in the crisp black hair on Tom's chest, then slipped around to his back and down to his taut buttocks. She arched her body into the male need she could feel hardening against her.

The soft whimpering sound in Megan's throat drove Tom wild. In moments he'd slipped them off the couch onto the carpet and divested them of the rest of their clothes. He craved the delicious feel of his skin against hers. At last they both lay naked before a crackling fire that was nothing compared to the heat burning within them.

He poised himself above her, his thighs pressed against hers, his weight resting on his hands. It would take only a single thrust to bring them together. Yet he paused.

"Megan?"

Megan could see the fierce need in Tom's eyes, and the control that held him rigidly in place. She reached up with her hands and cupped his face, bringing it down for her to kiss. "I want you, Tom. I need you. I love—"

He joined their bodies in one powerful thrust, cutting off her sweet words of love. He tilted her hips with his hands for even deeper penetration. Megan felt the fullness of him and a satisfying oneness, as he began moving in an age-old rhythm. She lifted her legs and bound him to her, releasing him only so that he could thrust again.

His breathing was harsh in her ear and she sought out his lips, his cheeks and chin, and finally his mouth. His tongue mimed the rhythm of lovemaking and Megan sucked on it in an attempt to capture the sensation in the same way she might have captured him inside her if she could. She could feel the spiraling tension, feel her muscles tensing, tightening, feel her heart pounding. She could sense the rising crest of desire in both of them and reached out to meet it. She rode with it, caught on a never-ending wave of ecstasy that tumbled her into a well of dark, deep passion.

Tom's mouth absorbed Megan's cries. She was so intensely giving, so loving, he found himself soaring to heights he'd never reached with another woman. It had taken long minutes before he'd recovered enough to say anything, only to discover that Megan was asleep. He felt a smile form on his face as he looked down at the woman in his arms. He wondered how he'd ever thought he could live without her. Somehow he would have to find the courage to admit his love, and to convince her that they belonged together.

The next morning Megan woke to find herself in bed in the guest room. She was wearing a flimsy nightgown that she had no recollection of donning. She could hardly believe she and Tom had made love in the middle of the living-room floor in his mother's house. She grinned. It had been a crazy thing to do, but was indicative of how crazy she felt about Tom. She wondered if he realized how much she loved him.

"Good morning, sleepyhead."

She automatically pulled the covers up to hide the sheer bodice of her negligee. Two splotches of color grew on her cheeks as she replied, "Good morning."

Tom sat down beside her on the bed and set the breakfast tray he'd brought with him on the end table. When he spoke his voice was husky. "You don't know how hard it was to leave you here alone last night. I wanted to wake up with you in my arms this morning."

"That sounds wonderful. I'd like to see your head on the pillow beside mine."

"Megan, I think we have to talk."

Megan cleared her throat. "About what?"

"Last night you said you loved me."

He tipped her chin up with his hand so her eyes met his. "Did you mean it, or were those just words of passion?"

Megan searched his face, looking for the love she wanted to find. But his expression was carefully blank. She felt vulnerable. She would simply have to trust that his feelings were as strong as her own. "I do love you, Tom. I think I have for a long time. I've just been afraid to say the words."

He exhaled a breath he hadn't known he'd been

holding. He took her hands and gently ran his thumb over her knuckles. "I love you, too."

Megan felt her eyes filling with tears and was helpless to stop them when they trickled over.

Tom leaned over and his tongue sipped up the salty drops on her cheeks. "I hope these are tears of happiness."

"Oh, they are! They are!" Megan flung herself into his arms.

His arms circled her, hugging her tight. "Darling, darling Megan, I never thought I'd feel like this again. I want to marry you. I want to be Sarah's and Chris's father. I want us to have children of our own. I—"

Megan jerked herself out of Tom's embrace and scuttled back to the head of the bed, pulling her knees up to her chest and hugging them with her hands.

"Megan? What's wrong? What did I say?"

When Tom started to move toward her, Megan put up a hand to keep him away. "I think you'd better listen to me before you get carried away talking about marriage and children."

Megan watched Tom's features go hard, all the love disappearing as though she'd erased a chalkboard.

His voice was devoid of emotion as he announced, "I'm listening."

"I haven't been totally honest with you."

"Oh?"

Megan tried to meet Tom's gaze, but ended up looking at her toes. "How old do you think I am?"

"What the hell difference does it make?"

Megan looked up at him. "I'm thirty-nine."

"Is that supposed to mean something to me?"

"It means I'm awfully old to be having children, Tom." She took a deep breath. "Before you try and convince yourself or me that I could still have children you have a right to know...I can't."

Tom was quiet for so long she thought he must not have heard her. "I said I can't have any more children."

"I heard you," he said curtly.

It hurt to hear the pain in his voice. "I had problems when Chris was born and I had an operation. So if you want to marry a woman who can give you more children, you shouldn't marry me."

"Why did you wait until now to tell me this? Were you hoping that I'd demand fertility as a requirement for my wife, so you could claim you didn't qualify?"

Megan was stunned at the fury in Tom's voice. "No! I—"

"Don't worry, Megan. I haven't proposed yet,

if that's what's got you so scared. You don't need an excuse to—''

"It isn't an excuse!" she cried, scrambling over to confront him on her knees at the foot of the bed. "How many times did you tell me you wanted a son like you? Or ask me whether I wanted more babies? I can't marry you if children is one of the things you want from me. Because I can't give them to you!"

Megan was off the bed, past Tom and out of the room in an instant. It wasn't until she reached the hall that she realized she had no place to go. She could hear Isabel and the General in the kitchen and she couldn't very well leave the house in her nightgown. She turned around and immediately slammed into Tom's chest. He captured her by her wrists, and moved with her back into the bedroom, closing the door behind them.

"Dammit, Megan, we have to talk!"

"Let me go!"

"I will when you hear me out."

Megan could tell from the tone of Tom's voice that he wasn't about to change his mind, so she stopped pulling against his strength. The instant she did, he released her wrists and she slumped down onto the bed.

"All right. I'm listening," she said dully.

Tom stood before her, unsure where to start. He said the hardest words first.

"I love you, Megan, but—"

"But that's not enough, is it?" Megan snapped.

Megan found herself yanked up into Tom's embrace, her mouth punished by his. She stiffened against his sensual assault, a sob growing in her throat. She shoved uselessly against his chest with the heels of her hands. She moaned, a helpless, hopeless sound, and felt his mouth immediately soften. He used his lips to plead with her to accept him, not to turn him away. Because she loved him, Megan found herself reaching out to him, returning his love a hundredfold.

They were bound in each other's arms when Tom's mother opened the door.

"Oh, my. Excuse me. I knocked, but—"

Tom felt his face flush as he abruptly released Megan and stepped back. He was shocked by the puffiness of her lips. It had happened again. That total loss of control where Megan was concerned. It frightened and infuriated him at the same time. He loved her. He wanted her. But what would happen if he married her?

His voice was harsher than he meant it to be when he spoke to Megan. "I'll talk to you later." Then he turned on his heel and left the room.

Megan stared after him, confused by what had

just transpired. "Uh...we were just..." She was sure it had been quite clear to Tom's mother what they'd been doing.

"Has he proposed yet?"

Megan's distraught cry brought Isabel across the room to fold the younger woman in her arms. "There, there. It can't be that bad."

"It's awful," Megan said through the tears that fell freely. "I can't marry Tom."

"But whyever not? Surely you know he loves you."

"He says he does. But—"

"No buts. There's nothing to keep you apart."

"Except that I can't have any more children," Megan said bitterly.

Isabel sighed. "So that's what this is all about. How thoughtless of me to have made the remarks I did. If I'd only known...."

"You see why I can't marry Tom."

"I don't see anything of the kind. If I know my son, the fact that you can't have children isn't what has him upset. It's something else. Something that goes back a long way. Something that I blame myself for."

By now Megan's tear-streaked eyes were wide with curiosity.

"Let's sit down a minute, shall we?"

Megan sat down cross-legged on the bed, and

to her surprise Isabel shed her shoes and joined her.

"Has Tom told you anything about his childhood?"

"A little."

"Did he tell you about his father?"

"Yes," Megan admitted.

"Then you know how he beat me when he was drunk. He wasn't a bad man, only a weak one. Tom watched his father and vowed that he'd never act like that with a woman. For Tom that meant never letting a woman get too close.

"I was surprised when he married Sally, and sorry when it didn't work out. He told me later that he hadn't been able to let her share his life, that he'd shut her out. He never gave himself permission to let his senses rule, and not his head. After a while, she couldn't take it anymore and left him.

"You're the first woman Tom has brought here to meet me since Sally divorced him. I've been watching you two together. For whatever reason—and reason probably has very little to do with it—Tom has let down his barriers with you. I suspect he loves you more than he's willing to admit, even to himself."

Megan's brow furrowed. "I hadn't realized. If

you're right, I've just hurt him very badly. I've got to find him and make things right."

"There'll be time enough for that." Isabel picked up the tray of food that Tom had brought. "This must be ice cold. Why not finish dressing and join me for breakfast?"

Megan managed to meet Isabel's encouraging smile with one of her own. "All right."

Tom wasn't at breakfast. He'd left a message with the General that he had some errands to run. Megan smiled brightly and made conversation at the table even though she was dying inside. Maybe Isabel was wrong. Tom might have let down his barriers for a while, but they were certainly up again, as high and impenetrable as ever.

It was dark by the time Tom returned to his mother's home. He'd spent most of the day at the Alamo. It was dark and cool inside the stone building and with the strong sense of reverence he always felt when he walked inside, he found it a perfect place to think. When he was finished thinking he'd had one more stop to make before returning home. Now he needed to find Megan and share the knowledge he'd acquired.

But Megan was nowhere to be found. He located his mother on the glassed-in porch and demanded, "Where is she?"

"She's gone."

He gave a cry of pain like a wounded animal. "How long ago did she leave?"

"She couldn't get a flight until late. You may still be able to catch her, if that's what you want to do."

Tom turned on his heel to leave but was drawn up short by Isabel's, "Wait!"

"What is it, Mother? I have a plane to catch."

"I'll expect you to bring my new grandchildren to meet me this summer."

Tom grinned. "Count on it!" And then he was gone.

Ten

His Book: "Putting the Ring on Her Finger"

Tom had proposed twice in his lifetime. The first time the woman had said yes, but the marriage had ended in failure. The second time he'd been refused in words so cruel, words that had left such deep scars, that he'd remained single rather than face that kind of pain again. Now he was on his way to ask another woman to become his wife. And he was scared.

He thought Megan loved him enough that she would say yes. But he wasn't positive. The fact that she'd run from him was evidence that they still had problems that needed to be resolved. To calm his doubts he fell back on the safety valve that had gotten him this far. During the entire cab ride to the airport he reviewed the advice on proposing that he'd found in the last chapter of *HOW TO MARRY THE WOMAN OF YOUR DREAMS*.

A proposal should be as romantic as you can make it, for this is a moment both of you will remember for the rest of your lives. Tell her you love her, and ask her in simple, honest words to marry you.

Acknowledge her objections to marriage if she voices them, but don't let them deter you from your goal: getting her to say yes to your proposal.

When Tom first saw Megan at the airport he heaved a sigh of relief. He'd been worried that she'd somehow be able to catch an earlier flight. But the instant their eyes met, he knew she was as scared as he was, and that if he didn't act quickly and decisively, they were in danger of losing everything they'd found with one another.

Megan knew running away had never solved anything, but it had seemed the only choice she had. She sincerely believed that until Tom could come to terms with the confession she'd made, it would be far better if they were apart. So when she saw him striding purposefully toward her at the airport, her first inclination was to flee again.

"Don't you dare run from me, Megan Padget!"

Tom's voice wasn't loud, but it was enough to stop Megan in her tracks. She turned and waited for him, her heart in her throat, afraid to hope, but unable to stop herself.

Tom would have liked to wait to propose in an intimate restaurant with champagne and caviar and a candlelit table, but that simply wasn't possible. The middle of a busy airport would have to do. But when he captured Megan's hands and looked deeply into her eyes their surroundings suddenly faded, leaving the two of them alone in the crowd.

"I love you, Megan. I want to spend the rest of my life loving you. Will you marry me?"

"I can't give you any more children," Megan felt compelled to say.

"I know that. Will you marry me?"

"I'll be a demanding wife. I'll want you to share yourself fully with me."

"I know that, too. Will you marry me?"

"I love you, Tom."

"I thought you might, but it's nice to hear you say it. Will you marry me, Megan?"

An irrepressible grin broke out on Megan's face. "Yes, yes, yes, yes! I'll marry you!"

Tom lifted her into his arms and swung her around in a circle, a burst of euphoric laughter breaking the awful tension that had built within him. "God, woman, you've run me a merry chase! But I've caught you now and I'm not about to let you go. Do you still want to go home to Miami?"

"We could be totally alone there," Megan said breathlessly. "The kids will be gone for a few more days. Would you mind?"

"That sounds great to me. We can plan what we're going to say to Sarah and Chris."

They didn't need an airplane, they were both flying so high on happiness, but they had luggage to think of, so they waited for the next plane together. They were delayed by a layover in Atlanta, so when they turned on the lamp in Megan's bedroom it was well past midnight. A feeling of contentment, laced with anticipation, arced between them.

Megan felt unaccountably shy undressing for bed, knowing that Tom was doing the same across the room from her. "This feels strange."

"How so?"

"I don't know. Kind of natural, but new, if you know what I mean."

A wicked grin flashed on Tom's face. "Natural but new. Sounds like something I'd like." He drew on a pair of cotton pajama bottoms that hung low on his hips.

Meanwhile Megan donned the silky nightgown that had been Stephanie's birthday gift to her. It reminded her of the other gift she'd received that day, the one that had brought her to this place, with this man. She felt a rush of love for her children, who in their youthful innocence had wanted her to find this happiness, never realizing the mountains that would have to be climbed in the process.

Megan crossed the room and stepped into Tom's embrace. "If you'd told me on my last birthday that I'd find the right man and be engaged to him before the new year, I'd have laughed in your face," Megan admitted, her lips twisting wryly. "Yet here I am, and here you are, and...we are engaged, aren't we?"

Tom chuckled. "It seems in all the excitement I've been a bit remiss. Hold on." He left her and went to rummage in the pocket of his jeans. He came back a moment later and took her left hand in his. "I bought this for you today."

Megan gasped as Tom slid a beautiful sapphire and diamond engagement ring on her finger. She threw her arms around him and gave him a crushing hug. "It's beautiful! You're wonderful! I love you so much!"

After that, although they were both exhausted, they were also too excited to sleep. They opened the bottle of champagne Megan kept in the bottom of the refrigerator in case of a special occasion, and took it with them back into the bedroom. What followed was a night of holding one another, of tender touching and of talking sweet and low. They shared their hopes and dreams, and finally, when it was nearly dawn, they shared their fears.

"I have a question for you," Tom said. "Would you and the kids like to move to Washington?"

Megan had avoided thinking about the issue of where they would live, because she felt sure it was a potential powder keg. But this had been a night for honesty, so she said, "Is there any way you could stay here? I mean, could you still be a political consultant in Miami?"

"Is there a particular reason why you don't want to move?"

"My mom and dad live close by. I love my job. And the children have put down roots. I'm sure we could all adjust if we had to, but to be frank, I'd rather stay here."

Tom's brow furrowed in thought. "It would

mean .a lot more traveling for me if I lived in Miami. I'd have to be gone from you and the kids at times to do it. But there would be the compensation of being closer to my South American connections.

"Also, I haven't told you because I wasn't sure I wanted to do anything about it, but St. Mark's has offered me a permanent position as chairman of the political science department. I don't see any reason why we can't give living here a try. If things get too difficult we can reassess and see whether it makes sense to move later on."

"I feel like I'm doing all the taking and you're doing all the giving," Megan said.

"Don't kid yourself. We'll both have to make compromises. That's what marriage is all about— two people who love each other learning to bend so that the needs of both are met."

"Are you sure you don't feel cheated when you have to make concessions?" Megan asked. "For instance, will you be sorry later that you married a woman who can't give you more children?"

Megan appreciated the fact that Tom didn't rush to reassure her, that he took the time to formulate what he wanted to say. Because what he said allayed her fears for all time.

"Yes, I'm sorry we won't be able to make a baby together. That would have meant a lot to me.

But it would only have been one more blessing added to what we already have. I love Sarah and Chris. I'd like to adopt them, if you—and they—want me to. And I have a son, Todd, that I hardly know. Maybe it's time I did. That's three children, Megan, more than enough for any man. I'm not so foolish as to yearn for grapes to make wine, when my cup is already full to overflowing.''

Two idyllic days followed during which Tom and Megan got out of bed only long enough to eat and regain their energy for another loving free-for-all. It was hard for Megan to kiss Tom goodbye when he finally left the morning her children were supposed to return home. They'd agreed that she should break the news of their engagement to Sarah and Chris, and that he would join them for dinner that evening.

Megan was unbelievably nervous, but told herself it was ridiculous to be worried about how her children would receive the news of her engagement to Tom. After all, they were the ones who'd bought her *YOU DON'T HAVE TO SAY SINGLE.* And they both loved Tom.

She waited until her parents had left before she said, ''Can the two of you come into the living room for a minute? I'd like to talk to you.''

''What's up, Mom? Is something wrong? It's Tom, isn't it?'' Sarah said.

"Nothing's wrong, and Tom will be here for supper." *If the next few minutes go all right.*

Chris sprawled on the sofa. "So why do you want to talk to us?"

"I have an announcement to make." Megan took a deep breath before saying, "Tom and I have decided to get married."

Both Sarah and Chris started talking at once.

"Wait till my friends hear about this! Did he give you a ring? Can I get a new dress for the wedding?"

"Is he going to be our dad now? When are you getting married? Is he going to live here with us?"

"I'll answer all your questions," Megan said, "but first let me make sure that what I'm hearing is that you're both happy about this news."

"Of course I am!" Sarah shouted.

"Yeah! This is great!" Chris echoed.

"So when are you getting married?" Sarah asked.

"We thought we'd have the wedding over spring break and take a short honeymoon then."

Sarah grinned. "That's neat, Mom. I knew that book would do the job. I told Chris so when I saw it in the store."

"I agreed with you, didn't I?" Chris said.

They were still arguing over who was most re-

sponsible for her upcoming marriage when Tom
arrived for supper that evening. Megan watched
Tom's eyes light up when he saw her. When his
glance shifted to Sarah and Chris, Megan knew
they were experiencing the same warm glow of
love.

"I wish you were marrying Mom sooner,"
Chris told Tom as they were clearing the table
after supper.

"Why is that?"

"'Cause if you were my dad maybe you'd take
me to the Superbowl."

Tom laughed and ruffled Chris's hair.
"There'll be other years. Let's wait until the Dolphins make it and we'll all go. How does that
sound?"

"Wow! Mom, did you hear what Tom said?"

Megan smiled at Chris's enthusiasm. It was
amazing how a child could condense the parental
role so tidily. It wouldn't all be honey and roses,
but she felt certain that their love would help them
over the rough spots. She realized she was looking forward now to the time when Tom would
share the responsibilities and pleasures of being a
parent.

As it turned out, the few months until spring
break was barely enough time to organize a wedding. Megan felt indebted to her mother and father, to Stephanie and to Irene, for taking much

of the burden off her shoulders. Despite their help, or perhaps because of it, she and Tom never had a moment alone. To make matters more complicated, Sarah brought her girlfriends over to gawk at Tom, and Chris brought his friends over so Tom could play football with them. Her time with him was reduced to stolen kisses and snatched embraces. She ached with wanting Tom, and knew it was the same for him.

By the time their wedding day arrived they had both reached a peak of sexual anticipation. It wouldn't have taken much for Megan to step into the nearest empty room with Tom and give free rein to her desires. Fortunately—or unfortunately—she never found Tom and a free room in the house at the same time.

They held the wedding in the backyard, where the bougainvillea draped the arbor that covered the outdoor patio. The gardenia bushes Megan had planted when she'd first moved into the house were full of blossoms, the aroma of which permeated the whole backyard. There were only a few of Megan's and Tom's closest friends present, along with both sets of parents, Megan's children and Irene and Randy. Still, Megan was very much aware of being in the limelight. When the minister asked, "Do you take this man to be your lawfully wedded husband?" she had to swallow over a lump in her throat before she could say, "I do."

She heard Tom's solemn response, but the rest of the wedding was a blur, as was the reception. Nor was she much aware of the flight to Key West where they had made reservations to stay at a quaint guest house. In fact, it wasn't until Tom closed the door of their room and they were utterly, completely alone that the fog lifted and Megan realized where she was and what she'd done.

"We're married."

"That's the usual result of a wedding," Tom replied, his lips quirking. "Are you all right, Megan? You seem a little—"

"Spaced out?" Megan offered with a rueful smile. "That's because I can't believe all this is real. I feel like I've been in limbo the past few months. It's hard to believe we're finally alone together...."

It was as though speaking that truth crystallized the need that had grown between them over the past months. Tom took a step closer, then stopped. His glance slid to the bed, to the comfortable, overstuffed chair in the corner, to the lushly carpeted floor and then back to Megan.

"Where would you like to make love for the first time as man and wife?"

She looked up at him from under lowered

lashes. "In the shower." She blushed as his brows rose in surprise. "It's always been a fantasy of mine, if you want to know the truth."

When she started to pull off the cotton shirt she'd traveled in, he reached out a hand and stopped her. Slowly, sensually, he unfastened the line of buttons at her throat until he'd revealed the shadow between her breasts. He nudged the shirt open with his fingers, then leaned over to press a line of kisses along her shoulder and down across her breastbone. When he could no longer stand the torment of touching without seeing, his hands gripped the bottom of the shirt and easily drew it over her head, leaving Megan temptingly dressed in the laciest bra she owned.

She waited for him to remove his own shirt, but instead he took her hands and brought them to his chest. "Would you mind returning the favor?"

"My pleasure," she said, a shy smile curving her lips. Megan indulged herself by taking her time releasing his buttons, then threading her fingers through the crisp hair on his chest, finding his nipples and playing with them until he gasped. She laid her cheek against his chest and listened to the thundering beating of his heart. When she finally slipped the shirt off his shoulders she could feel him trembling with need.

He reached over to undo the front clasp on her bra and removed it. Then he drew her close. She sighed with pleasure at the feel of her breasts nestled against the wiry hair on his chest.

"God, Megan, you feel so good! I want my skin against yours everywhere." His hands fumbled with the catch on her skirt and Megan helped him undo it. The next few moments were frenzied as they divested themselves of their clothes. When they finally stood naked before one another, Megan took Tom's hand and led him into the sea green-and-peach-tiled bathroom.

She started to step into the tub, but Tom's hand delayed her. "Let me adjust the water for us first. How would you like it? Hot? Lukewarm?"

"How about a little on the cool side?" Megan suggested.

Tom grinned at her. "I'm afraid that's not going to do much to dampen my ardor."

Megan's glance skipped down and she could see what he meant. "I just thought…we'll get so warm…."

Tom laughed. "You're absolutely right, of course. Come on, step in. I think the temperature's right now."

He took her elbow to support her as she stepped into the tub. He followed behind her and stood facing her, his body shimmering as the water sluiced off him. He unwrapped a bar of soap and began making a rich lather in his hands. "Any places you'd like me to pay special attention to?"

Megan felt flushed with excitement. It was difficult to speak frankly, but she was determined to do so. "My throat. My breasts. My stomach. The small of my back. And...anything else that catches your fancy."

Tom's eyes were hooded, his body tense as he gently wrapped his arms around her and placed his thumbs on the dimples just above her buttocks. "Here?"

Megan's arms went around Tom's neck. She closed her eyes and swayed toward him. "Uh huh."

While the shower pulsed down on them, he massaged the small of her back with his thumbs, working out the knots that had formed during the long day.

Megan felt deliciously languorous by the time Tom gripped her around the waist with one of his hands and brought the other up to caress her neck. His thumb found the rapidly beating pulse in her throat and he leaned down to whisper in her ear, "You're so beautiful, Megan. I love the feel of your body under my hands. Sleek and soft. Warm and wet and willing. I want you."

Megan trembled from the sheer eroticism of his

words. When his hand slipped down to her breast, she arched her back, and felt her nipple hardening in the palm of his hand.

"Please," she murmured.

"What do you want, sweetheart? Tell me. I only want to please you."

"Would you...touch me with your mouth?"

She felt his body shudder as he gathered her to him, cupping her breast and pressing it upward with his hand at the same time his mouth came down to possess her. He bit down on the nipple, causing a pleasurable pain that he immediately soothed with his tongue. Then he sucked her breast into his mouth, causing a spasm of desire to shudder through her.

Megan's fingernails dug into Tom's shoulders, and her mouth found the lobe of his ear, biting and licking in the same way he was caressing her breast.

His hand slid down her belly, across to her hipbones and beyond to the curls sheltering her femininity. When he found her bud of desire with his thumb, she flowered for him.

She wanted to give, but she was caught in a vortex of taking. She clung to Tom, mindlessly seeking out whatever part of him she could touch with her mouth and hands. His shoulders, his chest, his hips, his buttocks, at last caressing that part of him that was stiff and ready for her.

Breathlessly she pleaded with him. "Tom… Tom…please…I want you."

His mouth found hers in a kiss that sent both of them reeling. He turned their bodies so he was leaning against the tile wall for a moment, long enough to warm it for her, and then he turned them again so that she was pressed against the smooth surface. She felt the muscles in his back and shoulders bunch as he lifted her easily. A moment later he was deep inside her and her legs were wrapped around his hips. He pressed her hard against the wall, moving himself deeper, tilting her hips, needing more, taking more…and giving more.

Megan responded in an ecstatic frenzy, arching, holding him when he sought to leave her, demanding that he take from her, that he give to her, that they slake the need born of their love for one another.

"My God, Megan. You feel so good. I don't think I can wait—"

"Tom…I can't either.…"

In the moment of extremity they both cried out, harsh, painful sounds that had nothing to do with pain, but everything to do with the wonder of the heaven they'd created on earth.

Megan was panting hard, sucking air to relieve her tortured lungs, and so was Tom. He slowly eased her legs down and held her until he was sure she could stand on her own. Even then he was reluctant to free her from his embrace. He took her with him as he stepped back into the strongest part of the shower spray.

They let the water pour over them, cooling the steamy heat that rose from their feverish bodies.

Tom finally reached over and shut off the water. He wrapped Megan in a fluffy towel and found another one for himself. Then he lifted her up and carried her into the bedroom. He pulled the covers down and laid her on the clean, white sheets before joining her there. He held her close in his arms, not wanting to sleep, but feeling an inevitable drowsiness.

"Megan," he murmured, already half asleep.

"What, Tom?"

"Do you think if we practice that we can get it perfect?"

Megan smiled to herself. "I'm willing to give it a try if you are."

"It's going to be wonderful, Megan. I promise you that."

"We'll be one of those couples who lives happily ever after. You just wait and see if we aren't," Megan concurred, as her eyes drooped closed.

They drifted off to sleep, certain of their love for one another and of their willingness to make their marriage work. They were blissfully unaware that each of them had received a wedding gift designed to make their pronouncements come true.

For in Tom's suitcase was his present from Randy and Irene—a book called *HOW TO MAKE YOUR MARRIAGE LAST*.

And in Megan's suitcase was her present from Sarah and Chris—a book called *ONE HUNDRED WAYS TO KEEP THE ROMANCE IN YOUR MARRIAGE*.

* * * * *

SPECIAL EDITION

Stories of love and life, these powerful
novels are tales that you can identify with—
romances with "something special" added in!

Fall in love with the stories of authors such
as **Nora Roberts, Diana Palmer, Ginna Gray**
and many more of your special favorites—as
well as wonderful new voices!

Special Edition brings you
entertainment for the heart!

SSE-GEN

SILHOUETTE®
Desire®

Do you want...

Dangerously handsome heroes

Evocative, everlasting love stories

Sizzling and tantalizing sensuality

Incredibly sexy miniseries like **MAN OF THE MONTH**

Red-hot romance

Enticing entertainment that can't be beat!

You'll find all of this, and much *more* each and every month in **SILHOUETTE DESIRE**. Don't miss these unforgettable love stories by some of romance's hottest authors. Silhouette Desire—where your fantasies will always come true....

DES-GEN

WAYS TO *UNEXPECTEDLY* MEET MR. RIGHT:

♡ Go out with the sexy-sounding stranger
   your daughter secretly set you up with
   through a personal ad.

♡ RSVP yes to a wedding invitation—soon
   it might be your turn to say "I do!"

♡ Receive a marriage proposal by mail—
   from a man you've never met.....

These are just a few of the unexpected
ways that written communication
leads to love in Silhouette Yours Truly.

Each month, look for two fast-paced, fun and
flirtatious Yours Truly novels
(with entertaining treats and sneak previews
in the back pages) by some of your favorite
authors—and some who are sure to
become favorites.

YOURS TRULY™:
Love—when you least expect it!

FIVE UNIQUE SERIES
FOR EVERY WOMAN YOU ARE...

From classic love stories to romantic comedies to emotional heart tuggers, Silhouette Romance is sometimes sweet, sometimes sassy—and always enjoyable! Romance—the way you always knew it could be.

SILHOUETTE® *Desire*®

Red-hot is what we've got! Sparkling, scintillating, *sensuous* love stories. Once you pick up one you won't be able to put it down...only in Silhouette Desire.

Silhouette®SPECIAL EDITION®

Stories of love and life, these powerful novels are tales that you can identify with—romances with "something special" added in! Silhouette Special Edition is entertainment for the heart.

SILHOUETTE·INTIMATE·MOMENTS®

Enter a world where passions run hot and excitement is always high. Dramatic, larger than life and always compelling—Silhouette Intimate Moments provides captivating romance to cherish forever.

▼ SILHOUETTE YOURS TRULY™

A personal ad, a "Dear John" letter, a wedding invitation... Just a few of the ways that written communication unexpectedly leads Miss Unmarried to Mr. "I Do" in Yours Truly novels...in the most fun, fast-paced and flirtatious style!

▼ *Silhouette* ROMANCE™

What's a single dad to do when he needs a wife by next Thursday?

Who's a confirmed bachelor to call when he finds a baby on his doorstep?

How does a plain Jane in love with her gorgeous boss get him to notice her?

From classic love stories to romantic comedies to emotional heart tuggers, **Silhouette Romance** offers six irresistible novels every month by some of your favorite authors! Such as…beloved bestsellers **Diana Palmer, Annette Broadrick, Suzanne Carey, Elizabeth August** and **Marie Ferrarella,** to name just a few—and some sure to become favorites!

Fabulous Fathers…Bundles of Joy…Miniseries… Months of blushing brides and convenient weddings… Holiday celebrations… You'll find all this and much more in **Silhouette Romance**—always emotional, always enjoyable, always about love!